kare kano

his and her circumstances

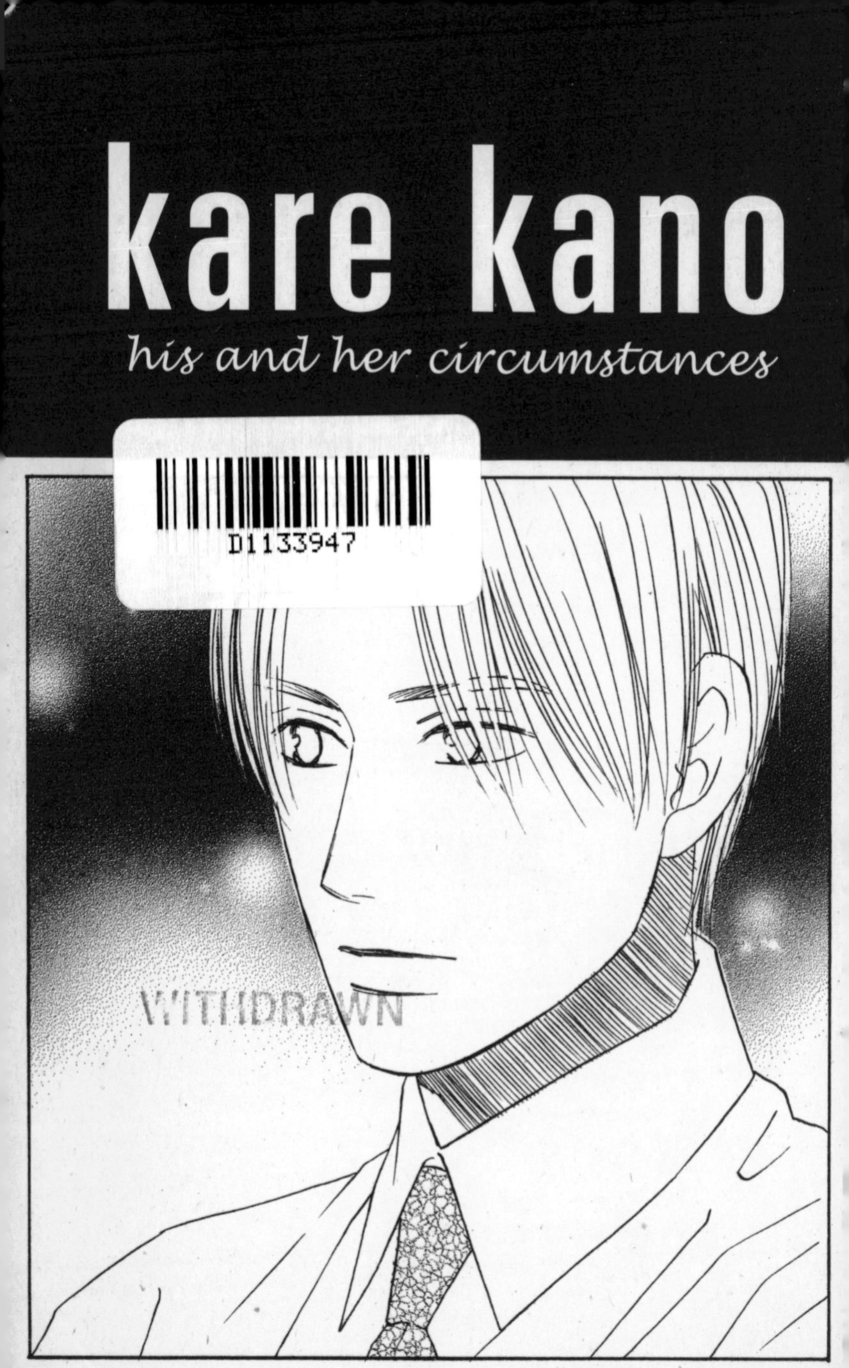

Kare Kano Vol. 19
Created by Masami Tsuda

Translation - Michelle Kobayashi
Copy Editor - Hope Donovan
Retouch and Lettering - Bowen Park
Production Artist - Erika "Skooter" Terriquez
Cover Design - Gary Shum

Editor - Carol Fox
Digital Imaging Manager - Chris Buford
Production Manager - Jennifer Miller
Managing Editor - Lindsey Johnston
VP of Production - Ron Klamert
Publisher and E.I.C. - Mike Kiley
President and C.O.O. - John Parker
C.E.O. and Chief Creative Officer - Stuart Levy

A  Manga

TOKYOPOP Inc.
5900 Wilshire Blvd. Suite 2000
Los Angeles, CA 90036

E-mail: info@TOKYOPOP.com
Come visit us online at www.TOKYOPOP.com

ISBN: 1-59816-182-2

First TOKYOPOP printing: April 2006
10 9 8 7 6 5 4 3 2
Printed in the USA

kare kano

his and her circumstances

volume nineteen

by Masami Tsuda

HAMBURG // LONDON // LOS ANGELES // TOKYO

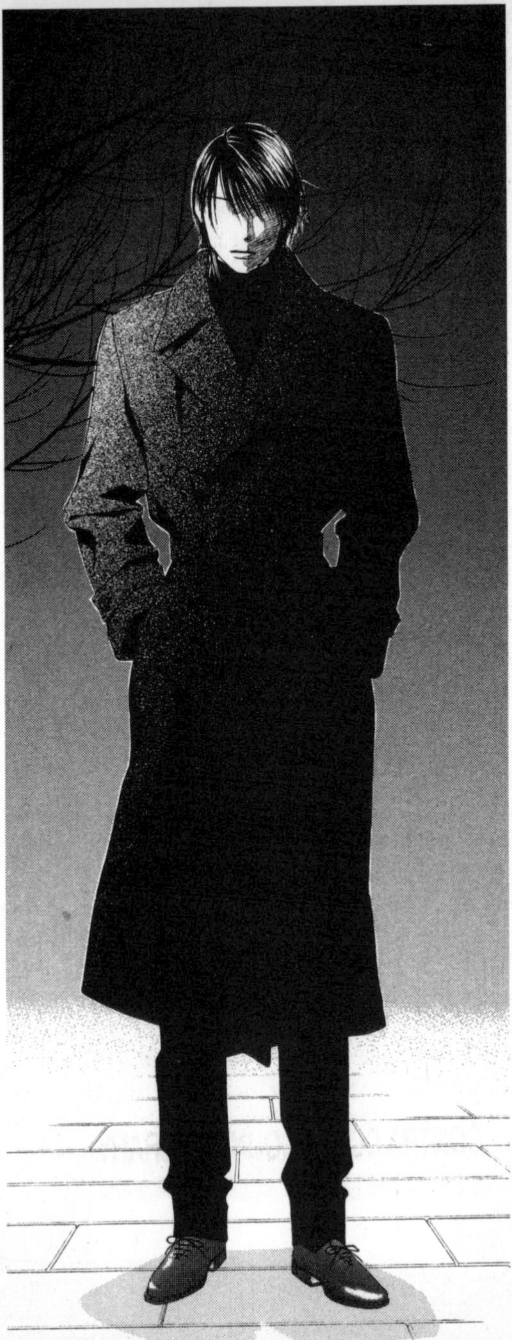

KARE KANO: THE STORY SO FAR

Yukino Miyazawa seemed like the perfect student: kind, athletic and smart. But in actuality, she was the self-professed "queen of vanity"--her only goal was to win the praise and admiration of others, and her sacred duty was to look and act perfect during school hours. Only at home would she let down her guard and let her true self show.

But when Yukino entered high school, she met her match: Soichiro Arima, a handsome, popular, ultra-intelligent guy. At first when he stole the top seat in class from her, Yukino saw him as a bitter rival. But over time, she learned that she and Soichiro had more in common than she had ever imagined. As their love blossomed, the two made a vow to finally stop pretending to be perfect and simply be true to themselves.

Still, they had plenty of obstacles. Jealous classmates tried to break them up, and so did teachers when their grades began to suffer as a result of the relationship. Yet somehow Yukino and Soichiro's love managed to persevere. But their greatest challenge was yet to come.

For although Soichiro's life seemed perfect, he'd endured a very traumatic childhood...and the ghosts were coming back to haunt him. His father left him early, and his mother was so abusive that his uncle adopted him and raised him as his own. But when Soichiro started to get nationwide attention for his high school achievements, his birth mother resurfaced, hoping to cash in. Soichiro met with her a few times to learn more about the family that abandoned him...until he realized she had nothing for him but more abuse and lies. With that (and a little help from his friends), he severed contact.

Soichiro had been keeping the family drama secret from Yukino, afraid it would destroy everything they'd worked for in their relationship. But she finally broke down his walls and made him tell her everything. Now their relationship is stronger than ever. Which is good, because Yukino thinks she might be pregnant...

And now Soichiro's delinquent dad has returned to Japan, after years of touring the world as a jazz musician. Soichiro has very mixed feelings about the man who abandoned him, but is enjoying his father's company somewhat in spite of himself. If nothing else, it's another opportunity to learn about his family's checkered past...

kare kano
volume nineteen

TABLE OF CONTENTS

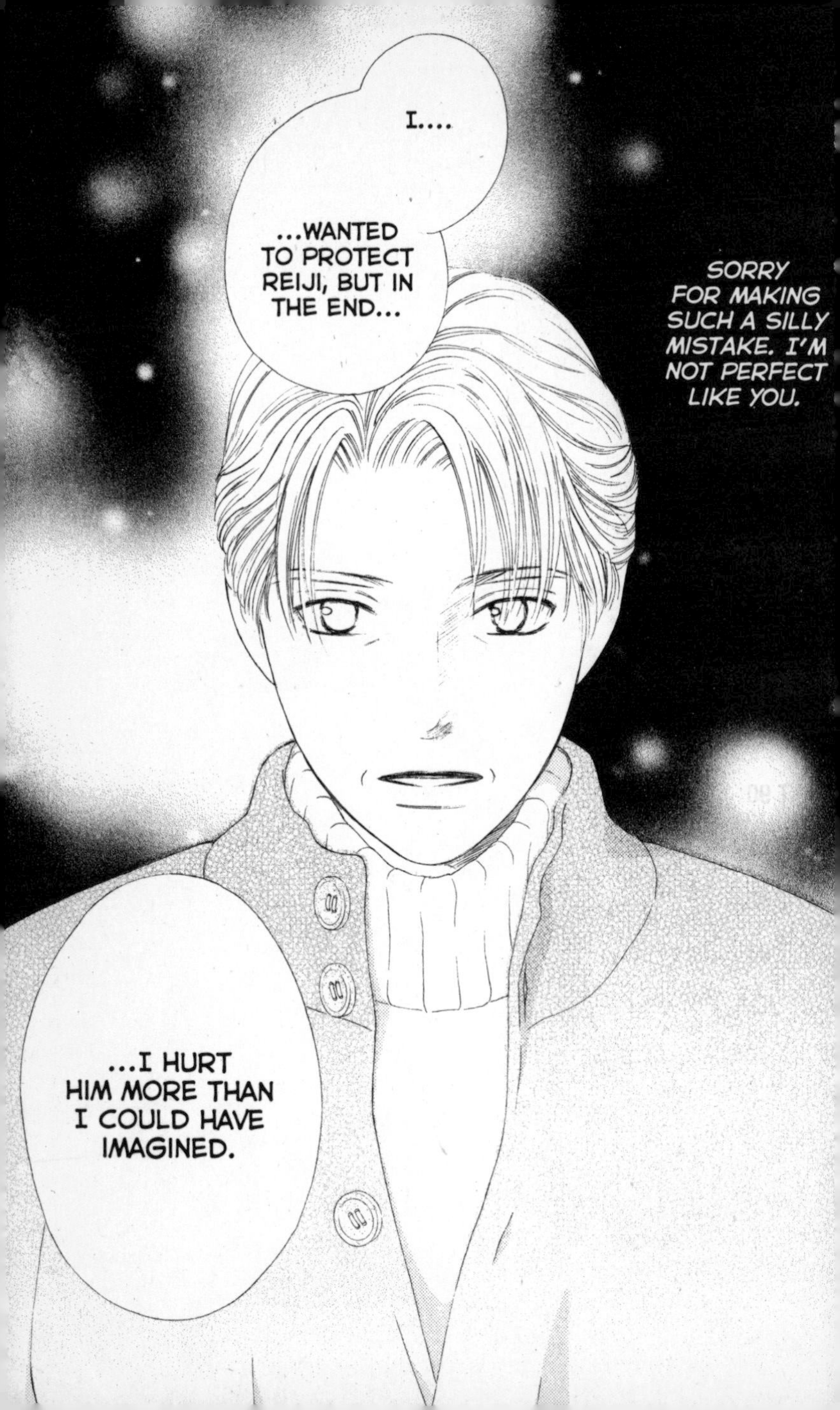
SORRY FOR MAKING SUCH A SILLY MISTAKE. I'M NOT PERFECT LIKE YOU.
I....
...WANTED TO PROTECT REIJI, BUT IN THE END...
...I HURT HIM MORE THAN I COULD HAVE IMAGINED.

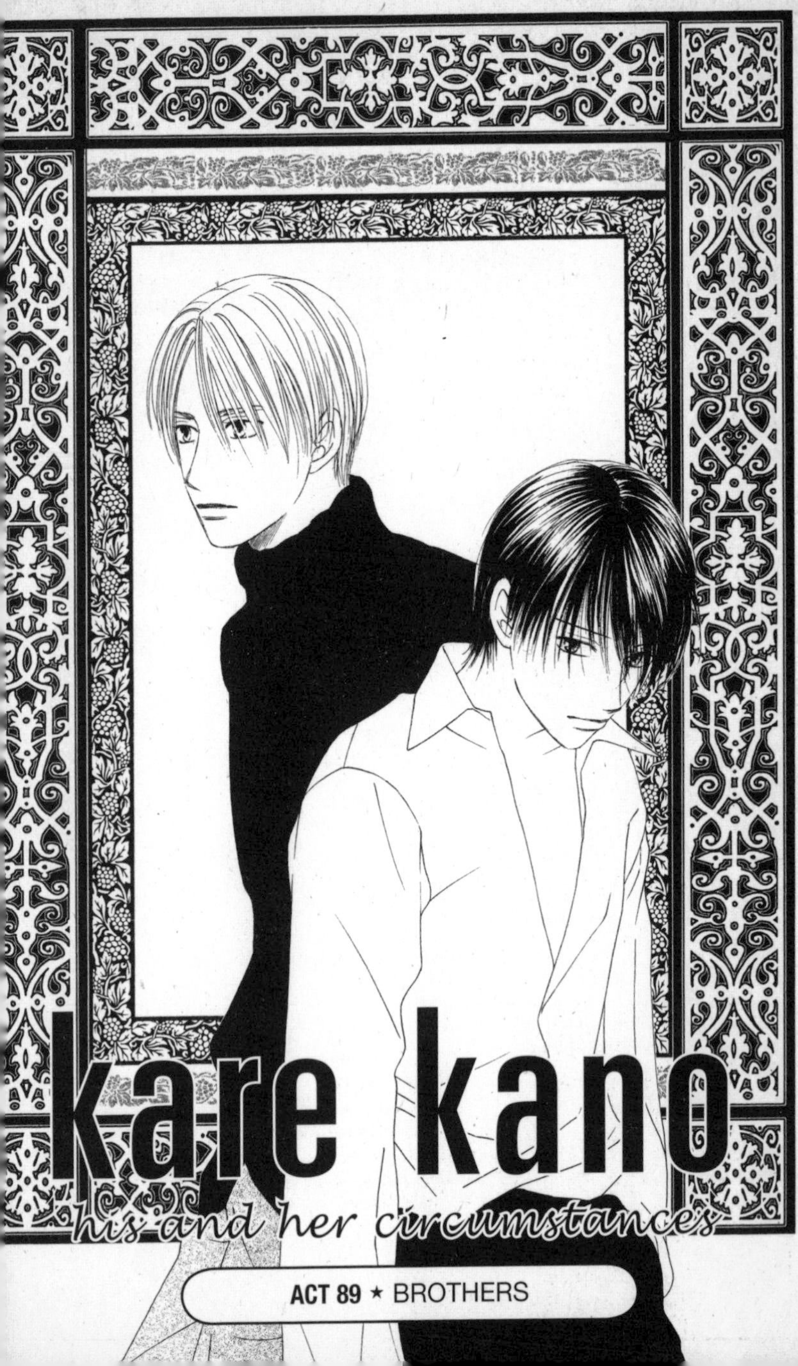
kare kano
his and her circumstances
ACT 89 ★ BROTHERS

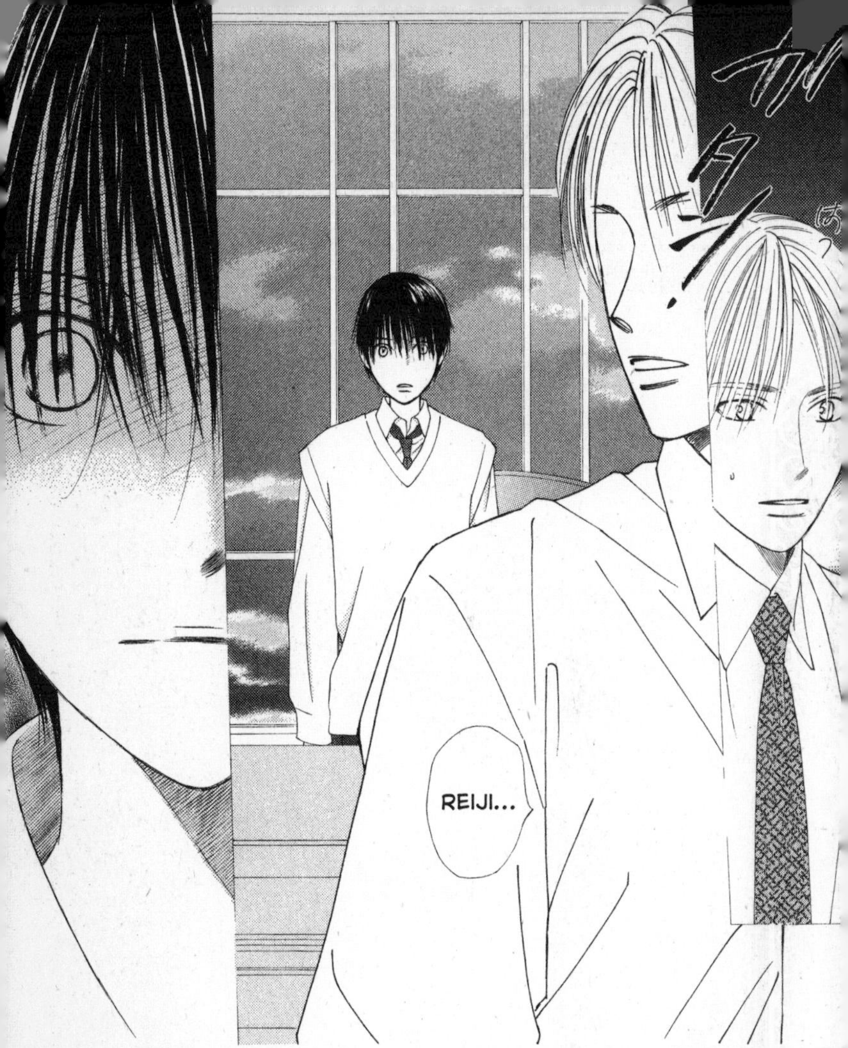
REIJI...

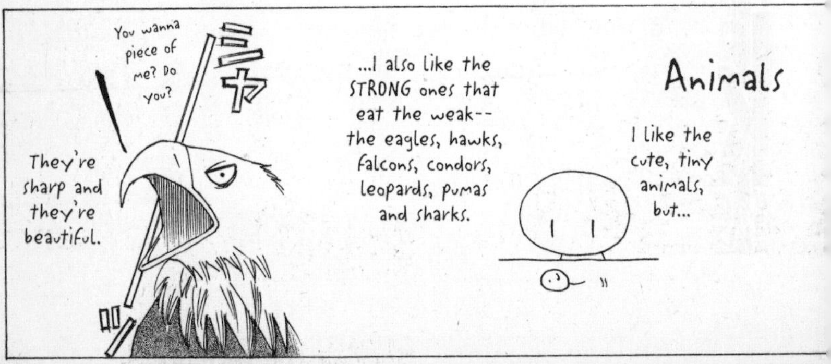
Animals
I like the cute, tiny animals, but...
...I also like the STRONG ones that eat the weak--the eagles, hawks, falcons, condors, leopards, pumas and sharks.
They're sharp and they're beautiful.
You wanna piece of me? Do you?

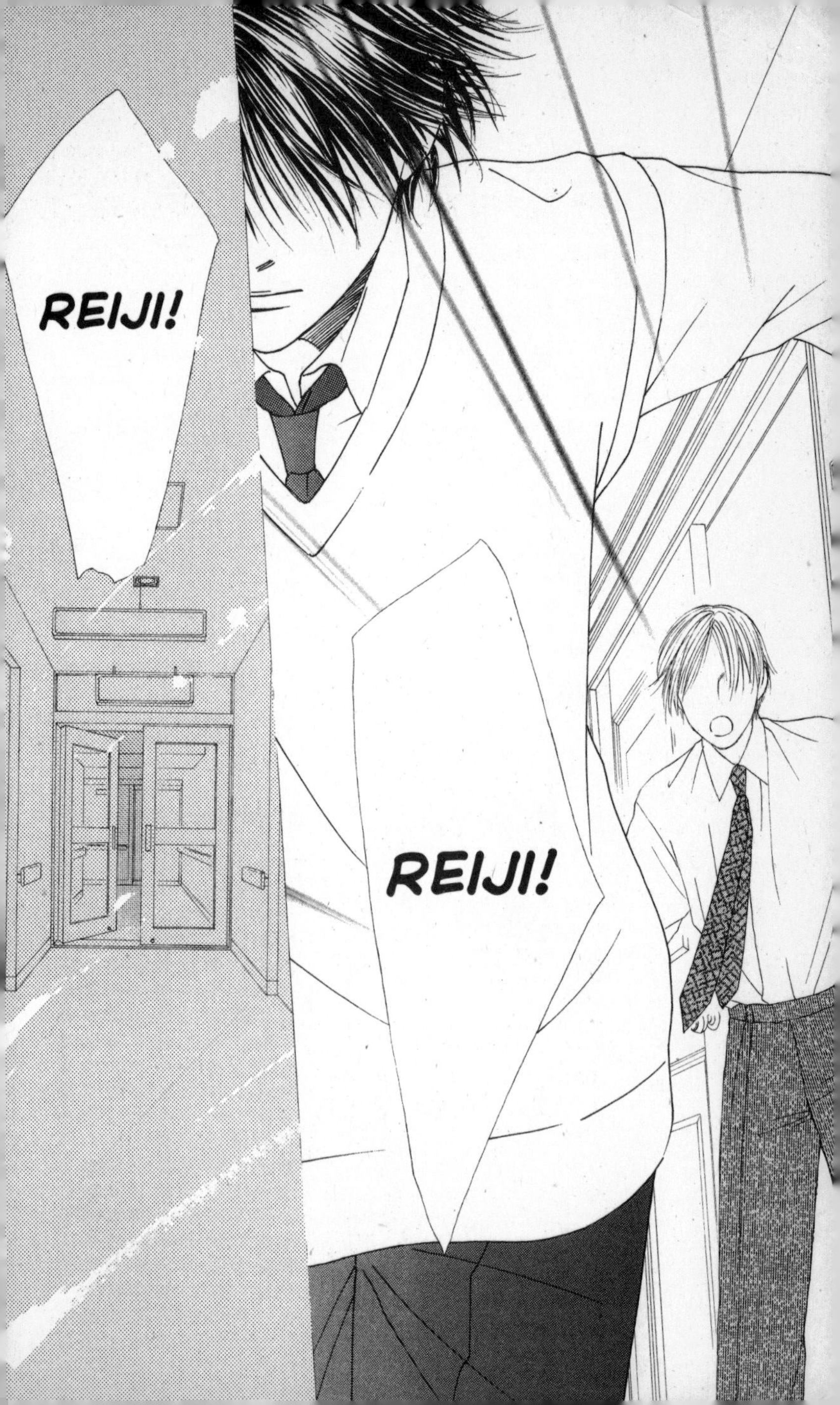
REIJI!
REIJI!

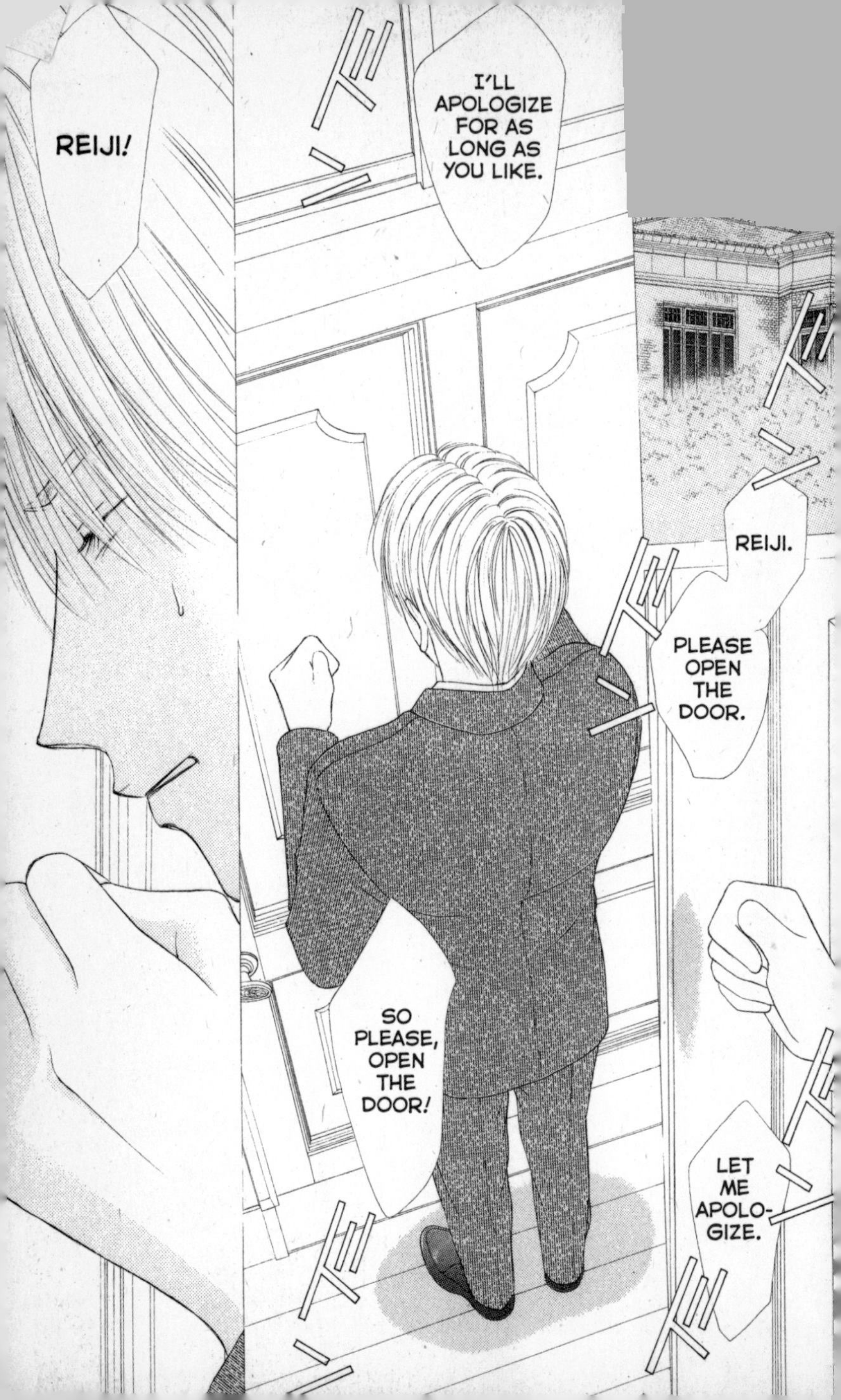
REIJI.
PLEASE OPEN THE DOOR.
LET ME APOLOGIZE.
I'LL APOLOGIZE FOR AS LONG AS YOU LIKE.
SO PLEASE, OPEN THE DOOR!
REIJI!

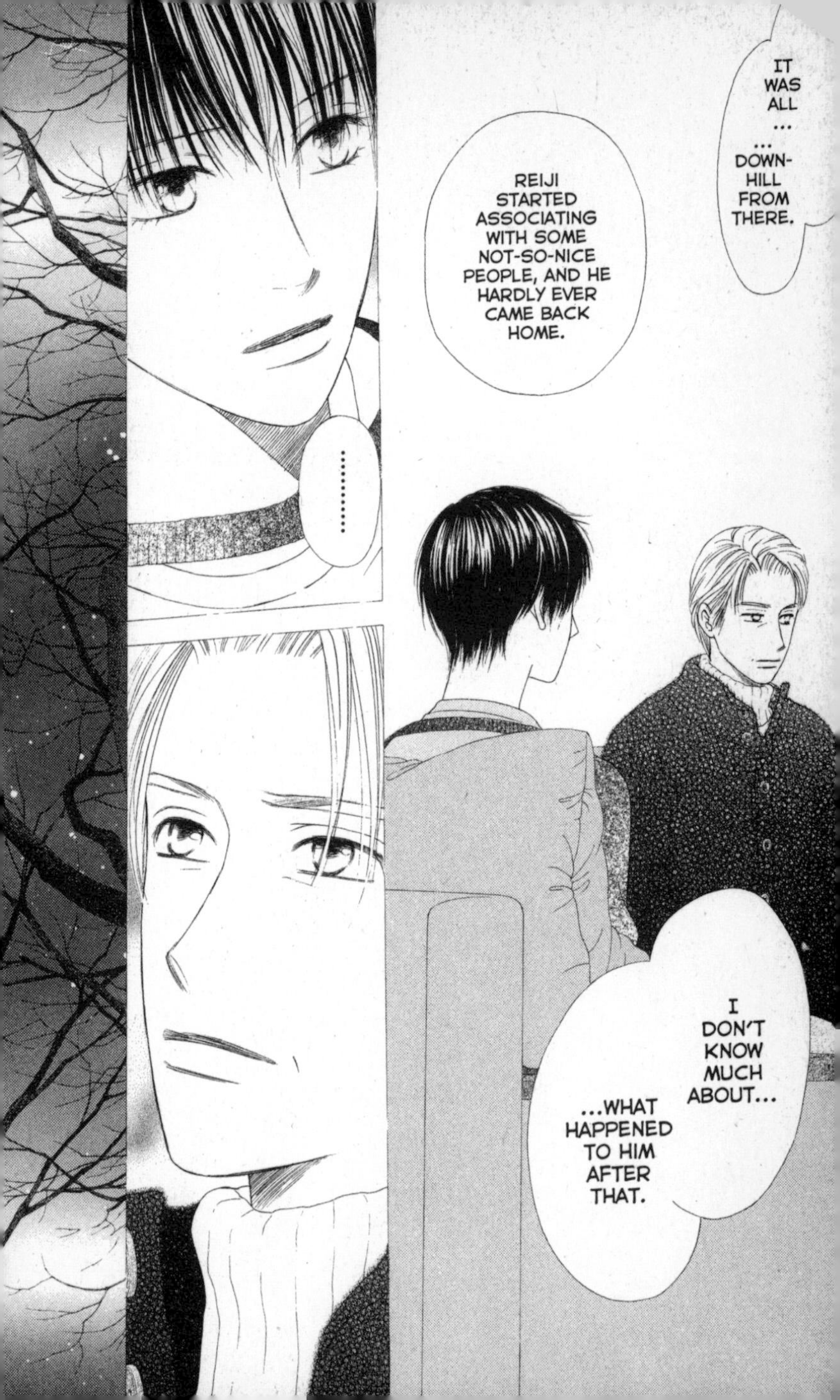
IT WAS ALL ... ... DOWN-HILL FROM THERE.
REIJI STARTED ASSOCIATING WITH SOME NOT-SO-NICE PEOPLE, AND HE HARDLY EVER CAME BACK HOME.
I DON'T KNOW MUCH ABOUT...
...WHAT HAPPENED TO HIM AFTER THAT.
....

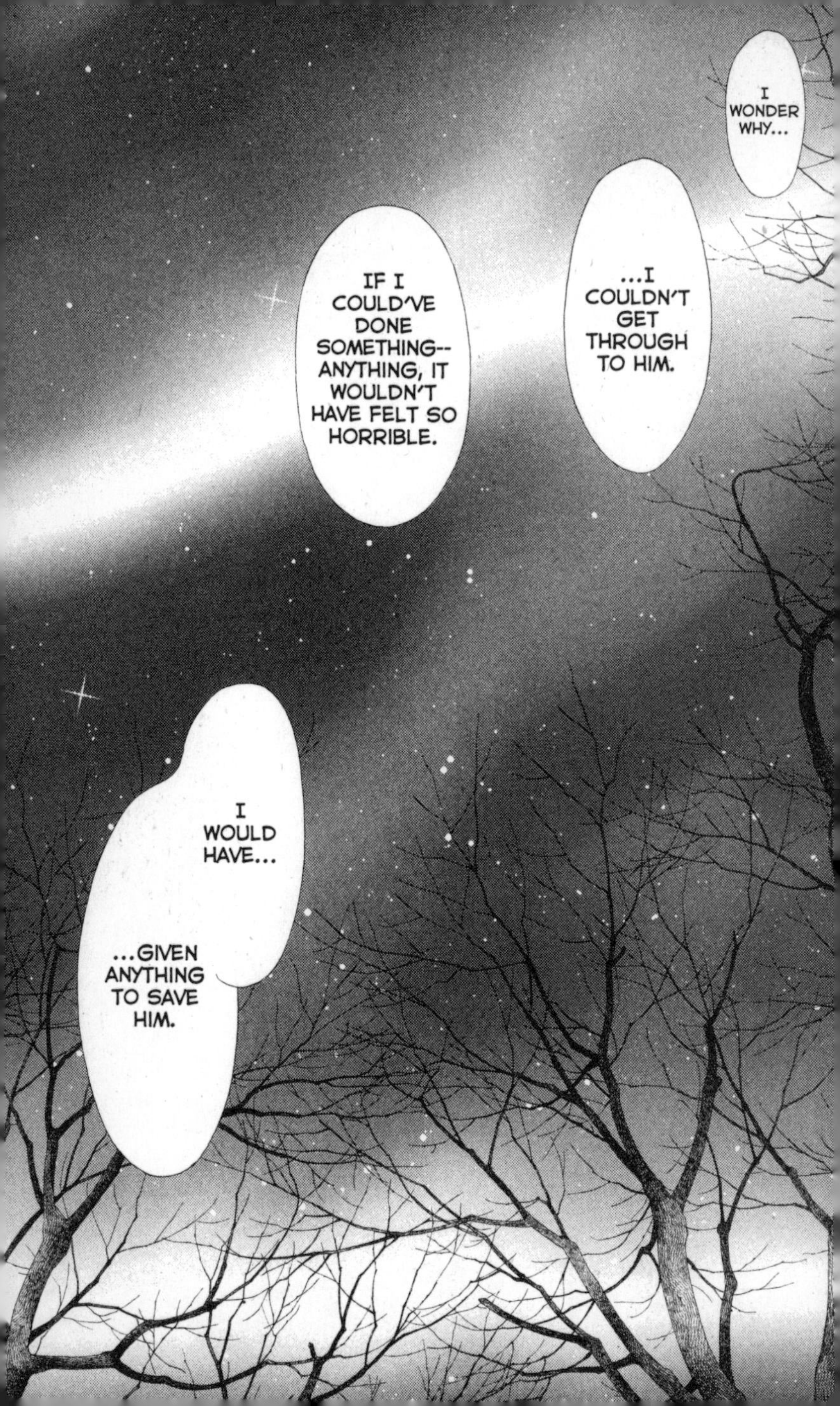
I WONDER WHY...
...I COULDN'T GET THROUGH TO HIM.
IF I COULD'VE DONE SOMETHING--ANYTHING, IT WOULDN'T HAVE FELT SO HORRIBLE.
I WOULD HAVE...
...GIVEN ANYTHING TO SAVE HIM.

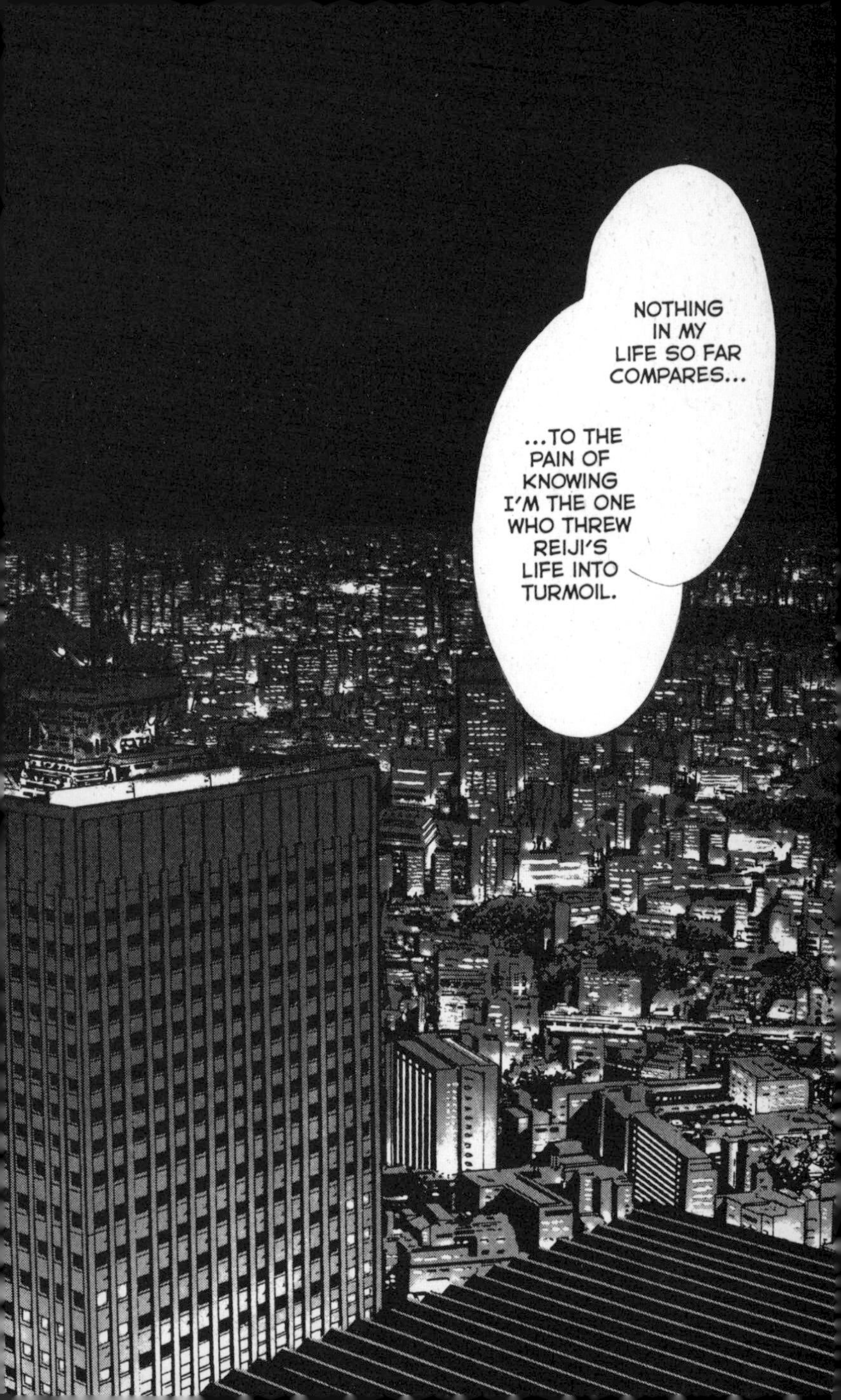
NOTHING IN MY LIFE SO FAR COMPARES...
...TO THE PAIN OF KNOWING I'M THE ONE WHO THREW REIJI'S LIFE INTO TURMOIL.

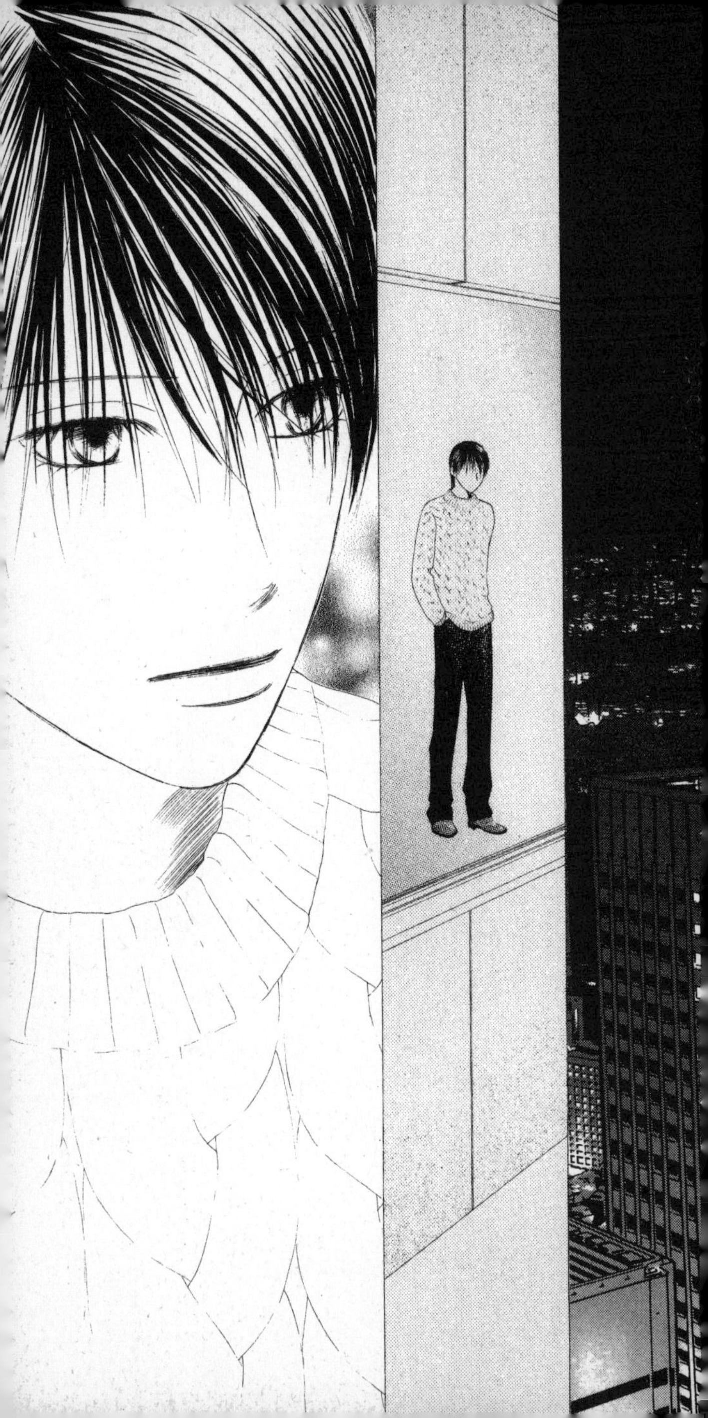

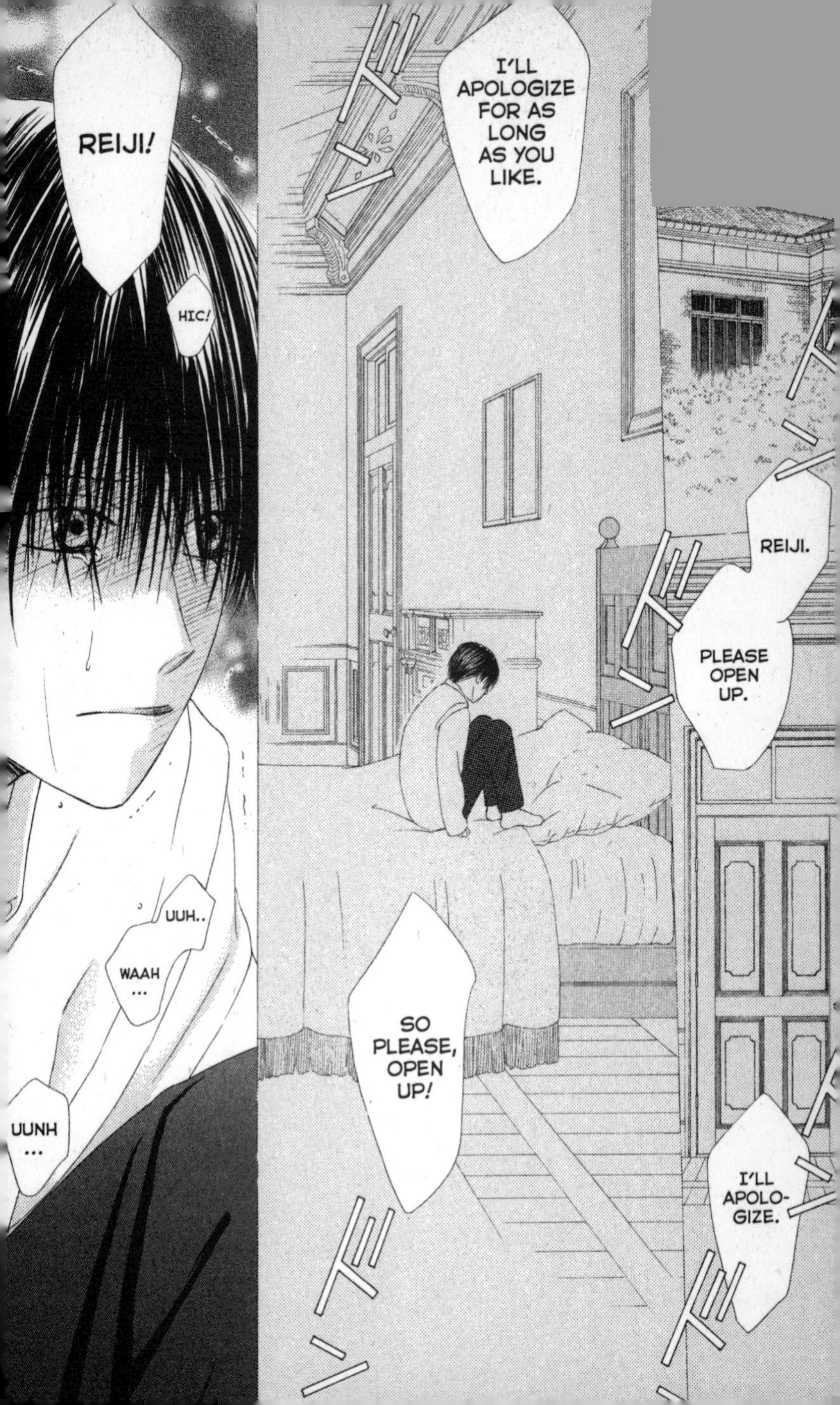
REIJI.
PLEASE OPEN UP.
I'LL APOLO-GIZE.
I'LL APOLOGIZE FOR AS LONG AS YOU LIKE.
SO PLEASE, OPEN UP!
REIJI!
HIC!
UUH..
WAAH ...
UUNH ...

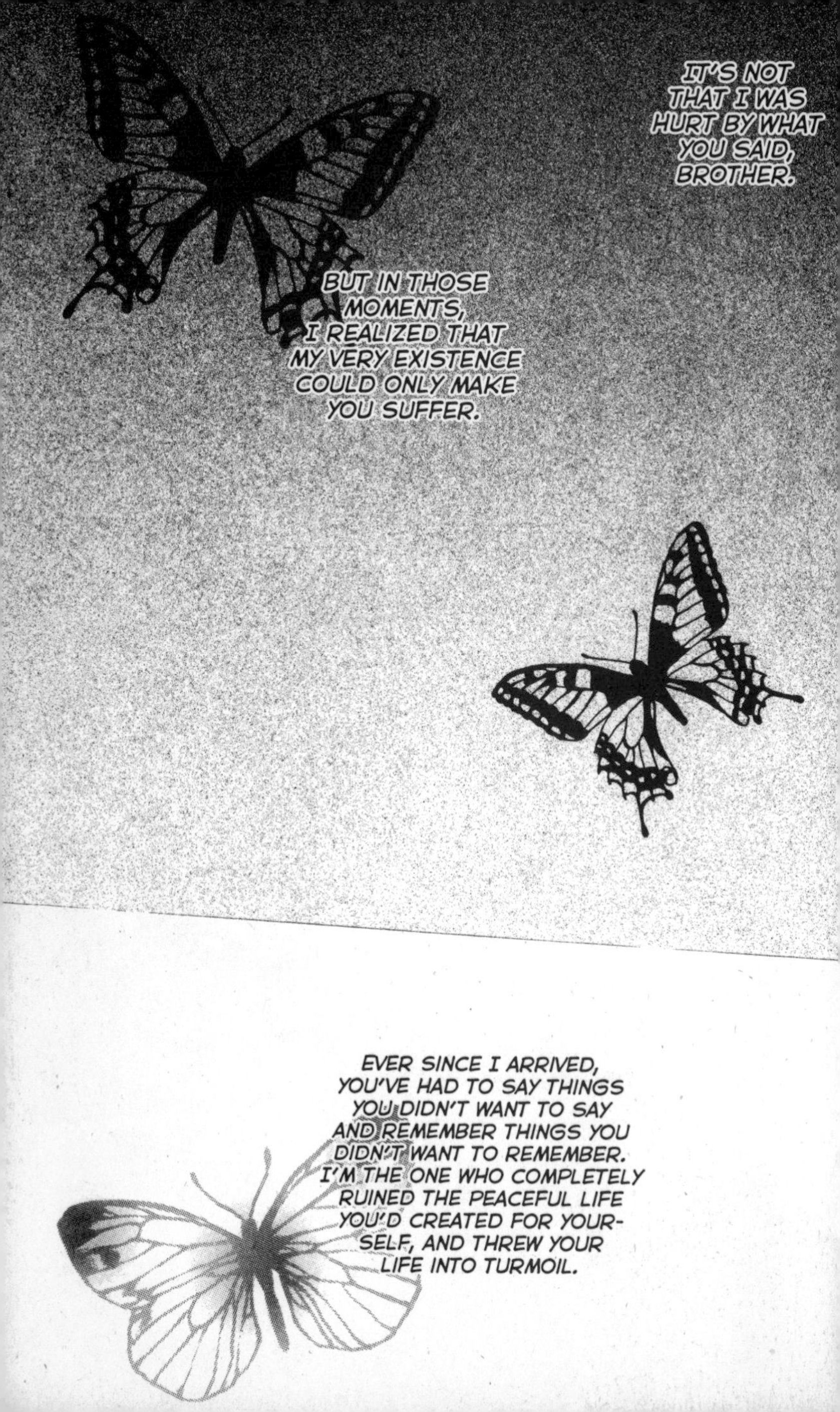
IT'S NOT THAT I WAS HURT BY WHAT YOU SAID, BROTHER.
BUT IN THOSE MOMENTS, I REALIZED THAT MY VERY EXISTENCE COULD ONLY MAKE YOU SUFFER.
EVER SINCE I ARRIVED, YOU'VE HAD TO SAY THINGS YOU DIDN'T WANT TO SAY AND REMEMBER THINGS YOU DIDN'T WANT TO REMEMBER. I'M THE ONE WHO COMPLETELY RUINED THE PEACEFUL LIFE YOU'D CREATED FOR YOURSELF, AND THREW YOUR LIFE INTO TURMOIL.

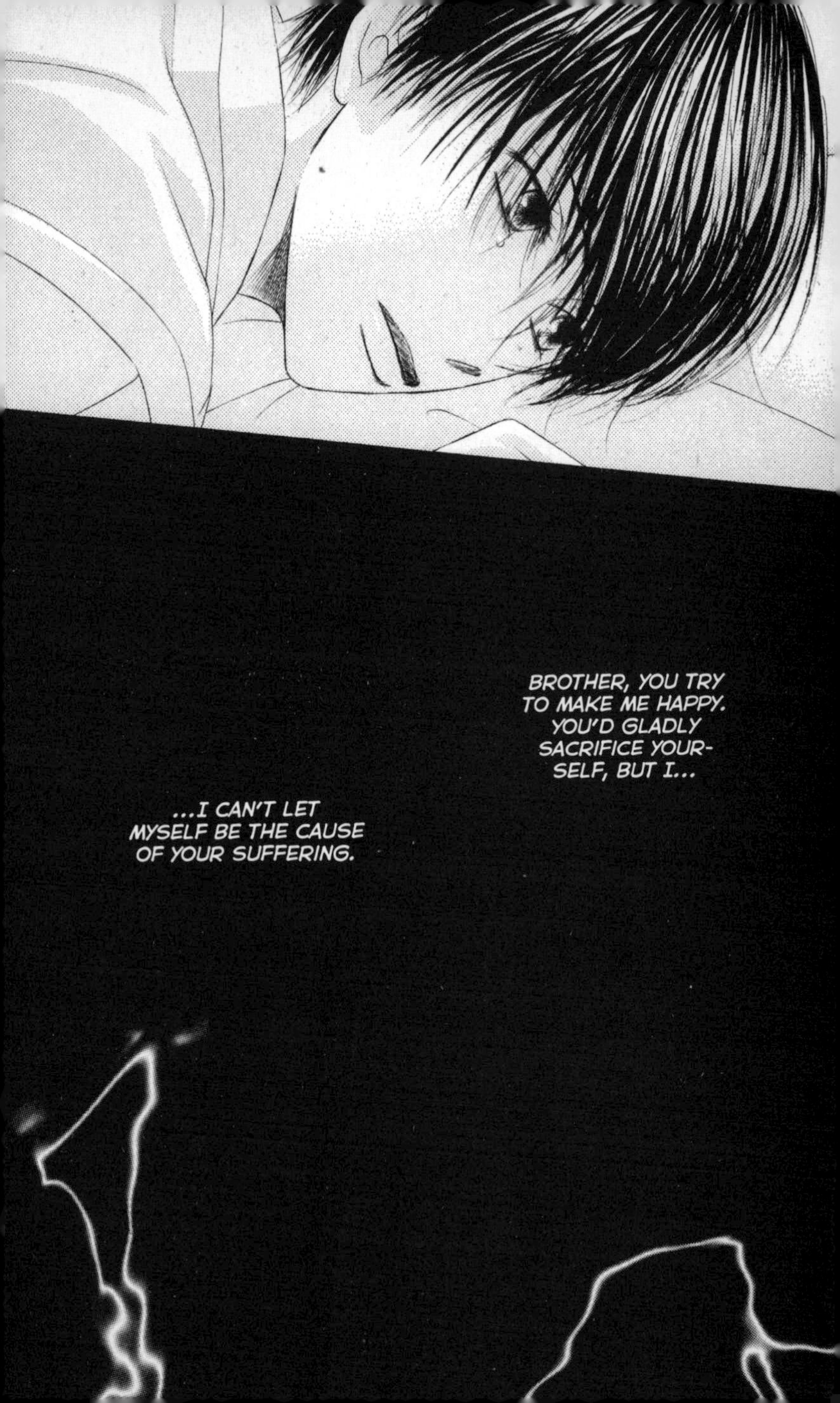
BROTHER, YOU TRY TO MAKE ME HAPPY. YOU'D GLADLY SACRIFICE YOUR-SELF, BUT I...
...I CAN'T LET MYSELF BE THE CAUSE OF YOUR SUFFERING.

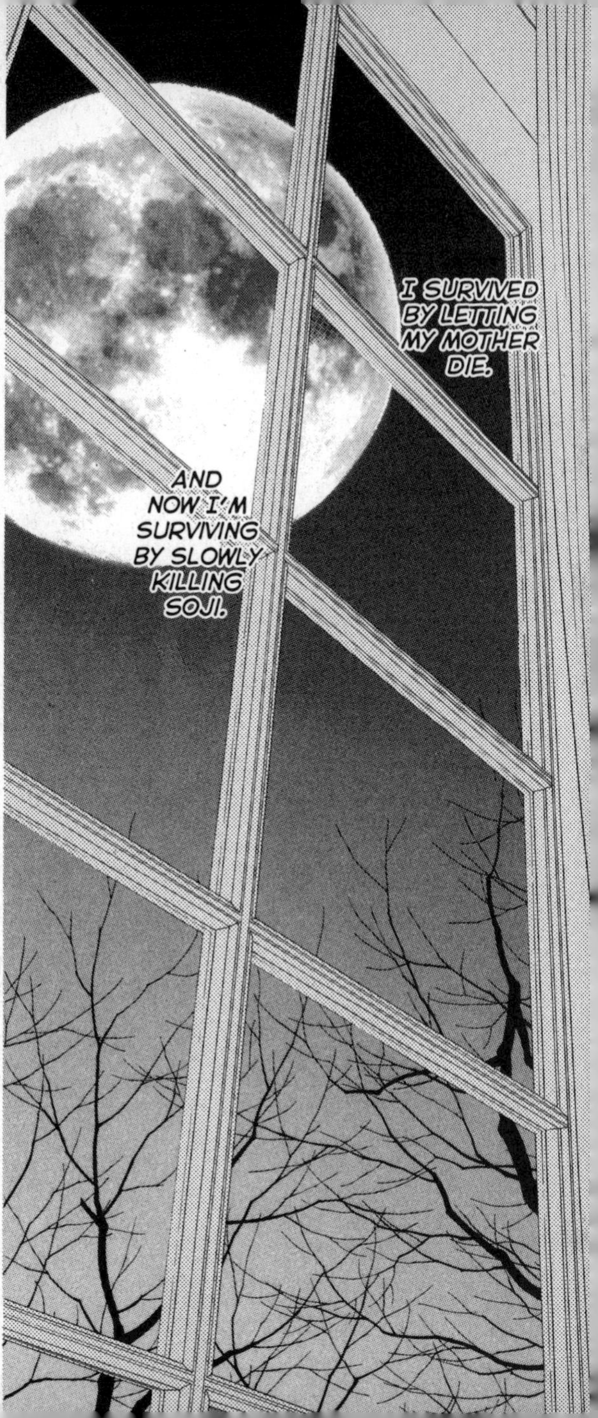
I SURVIVED BY LETTING MY MOTHER DIE.
AND NOW I'M SURVIVING BY SLOWLY KILLING SOJI.

1

Hello. This is my 23rd manga, *Kare Kano* Volume 19.

This volume has a lot of powerful stories, and I worked my butt off on them.

I wanted them to be so good I would have no regrets about the results. I wonder how many tickets I ended up giving to other people this year because I was working so hard... I should've gotten out a little more...

I wore myself out, but I managed to get through it somehow. Just a few moments ago in the bath, though, when I realized I was trying to wash my hair with facial cleansing foam, I got a little worried about my mental state.

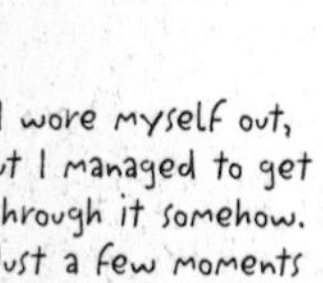

SO SAD.

I'M SO SAD.

SO SAD.

SO SAD.

SO SAD...

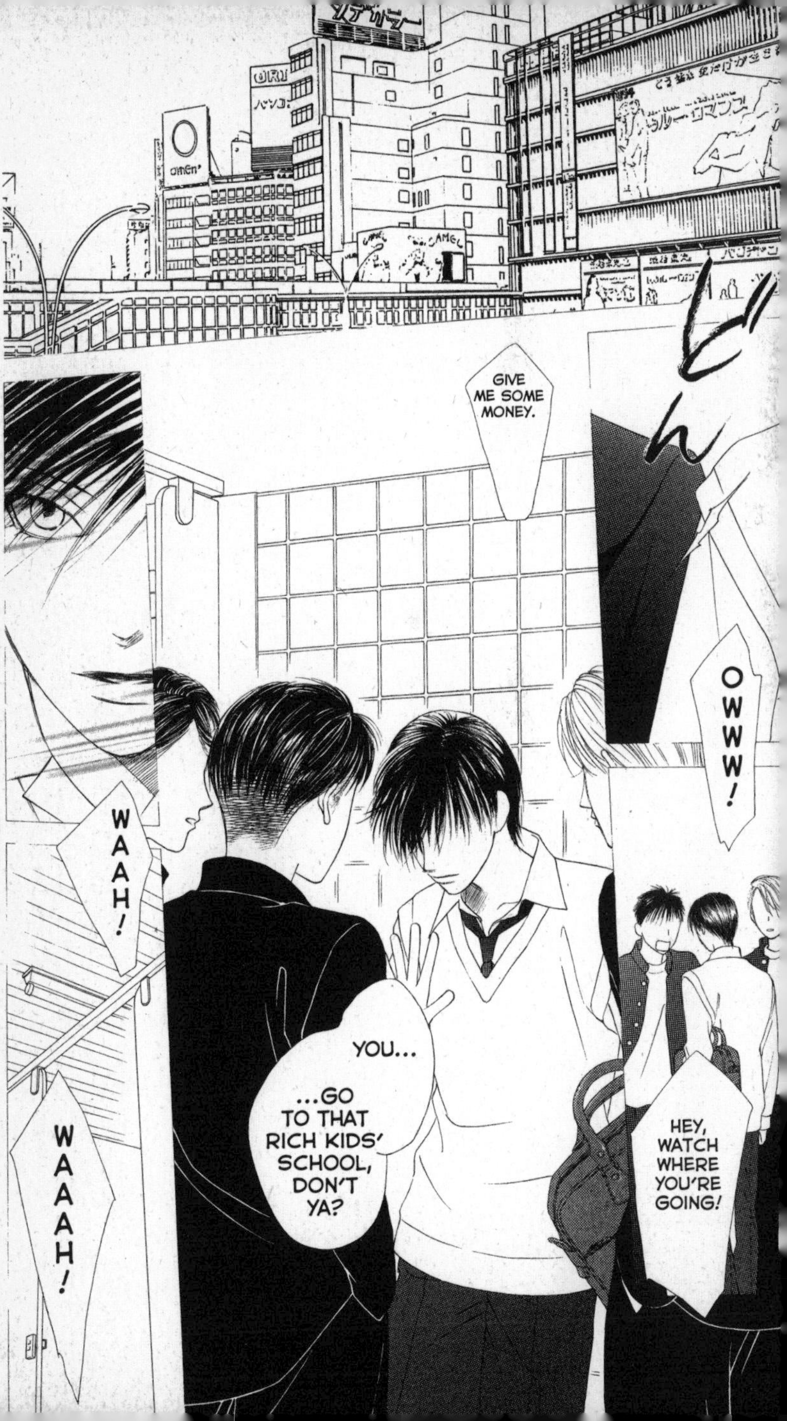
どん
OWWW!
HEY, WATCH WHERE YOU'RE GOING!
GIVE ME SOME MONEY.
YOU...
...GO TO THAT RICH KIDS' SCHOOL, DON'T YA?
WAAAH!
WAAAAH!

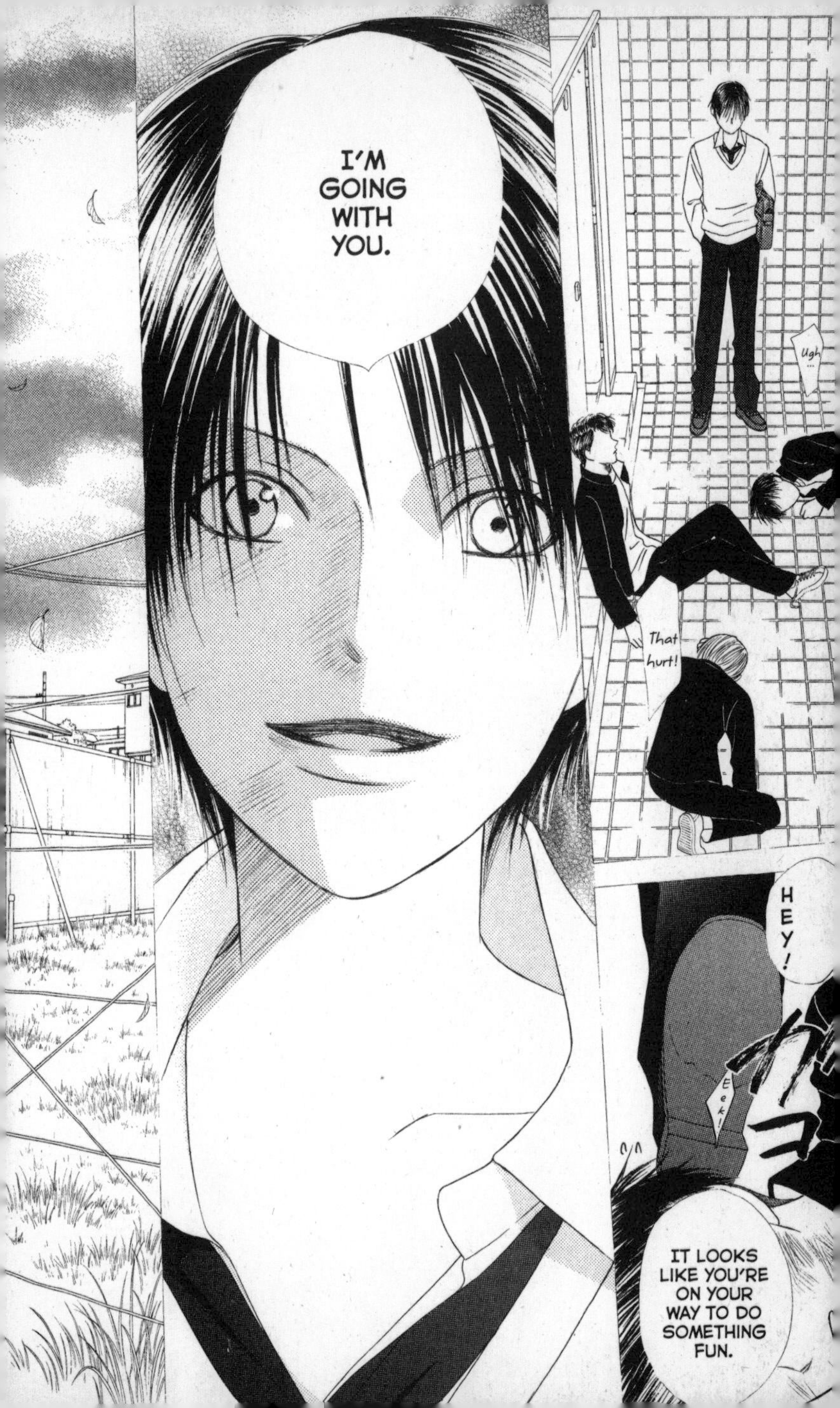
Ugh...
That hurt!
HEY!
Eek!
IT LOOKS LIKE YOU'RE ON YOUR WAY TO DO SOMETHING FUN.
I'M GOING WITH YOU.

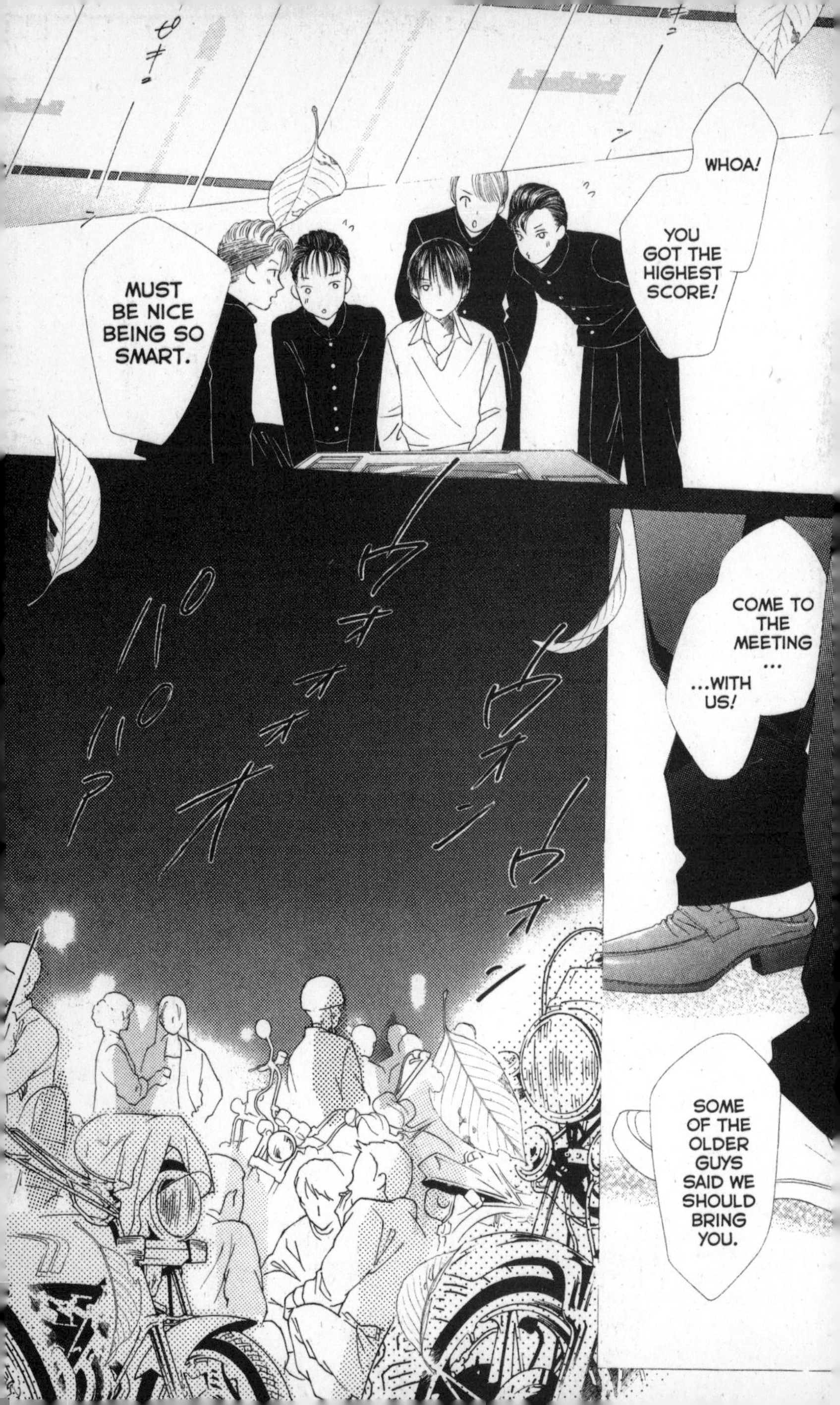
WHOA!
YOU GOT THE HIGHEST SCORE!
MUST BE NICE BEING SO SMART.
COME TO THE MEETING ...
...WITH US!
SOME OF THE OLDER GUYS SAID WE SHOULD BRING YOU.

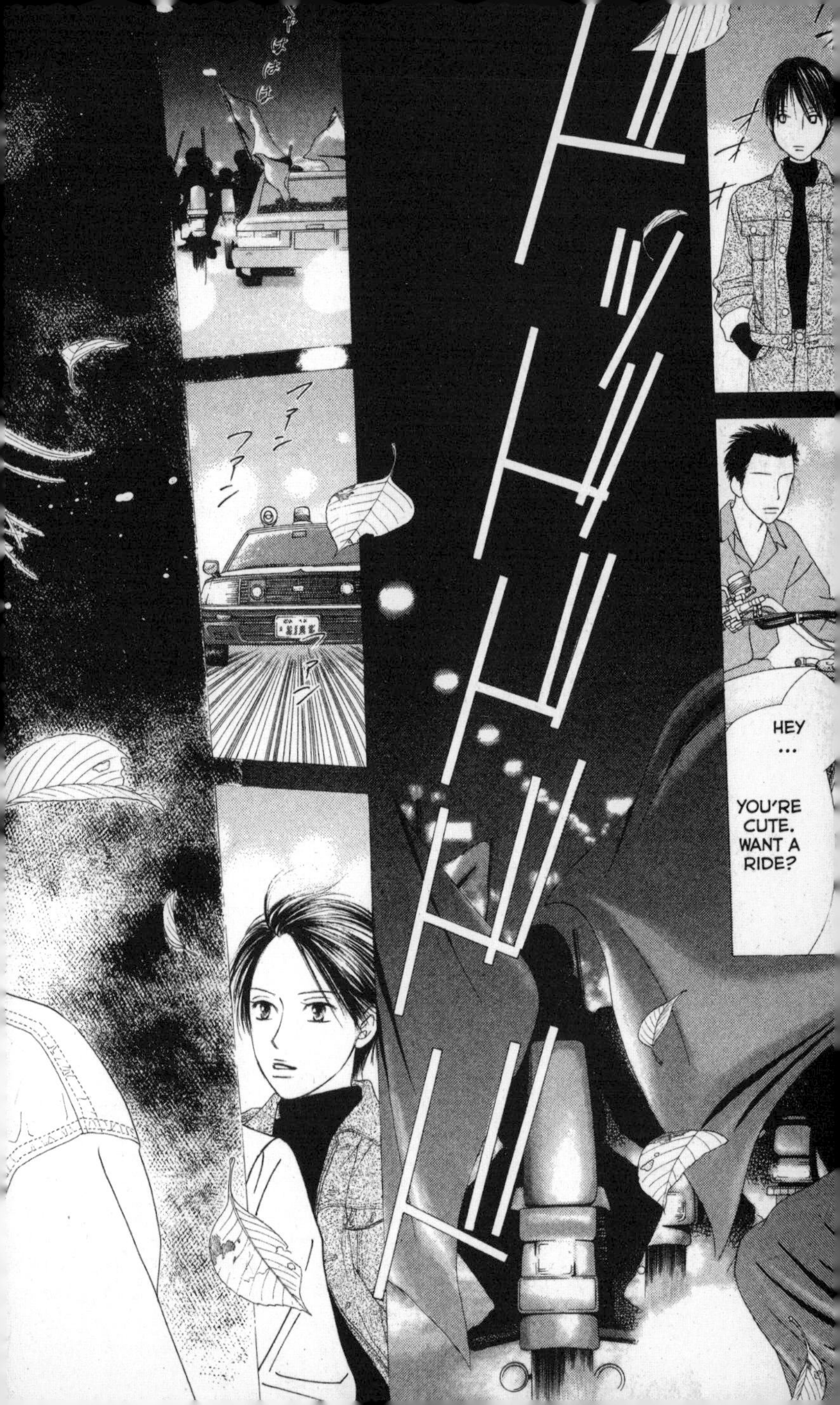
HEY ...
YOU'RE CUTE. WANT A RIDE?
ファン ファン

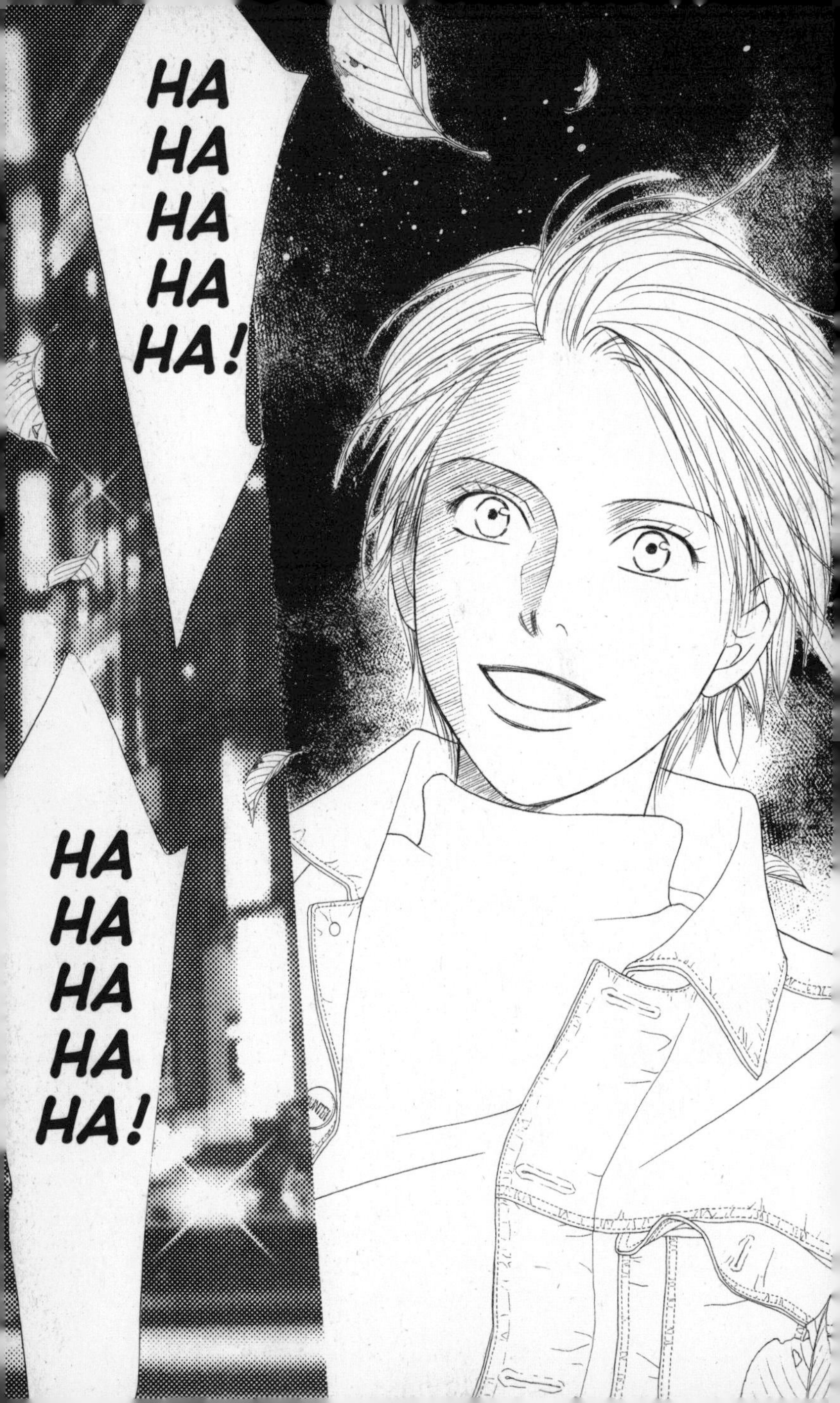
HA HA HA HA HA!
HA HA HA HA HA!

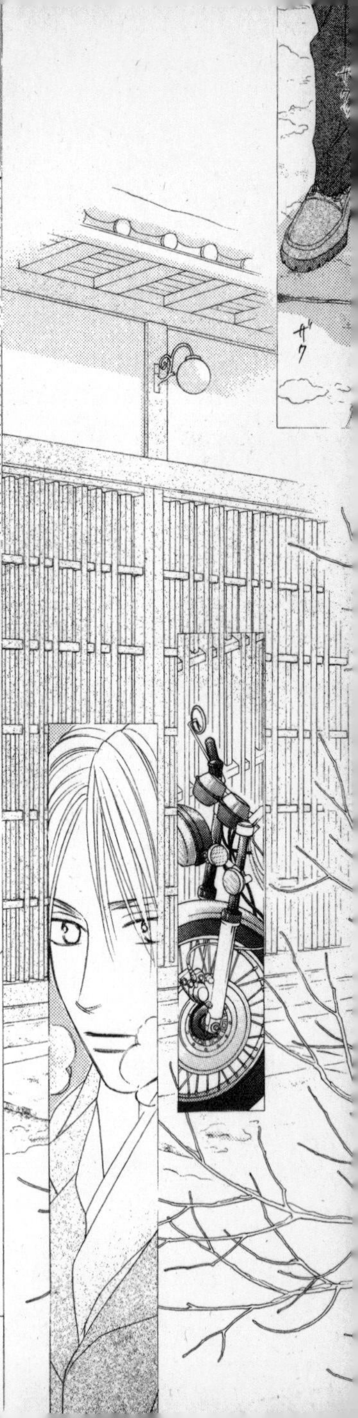
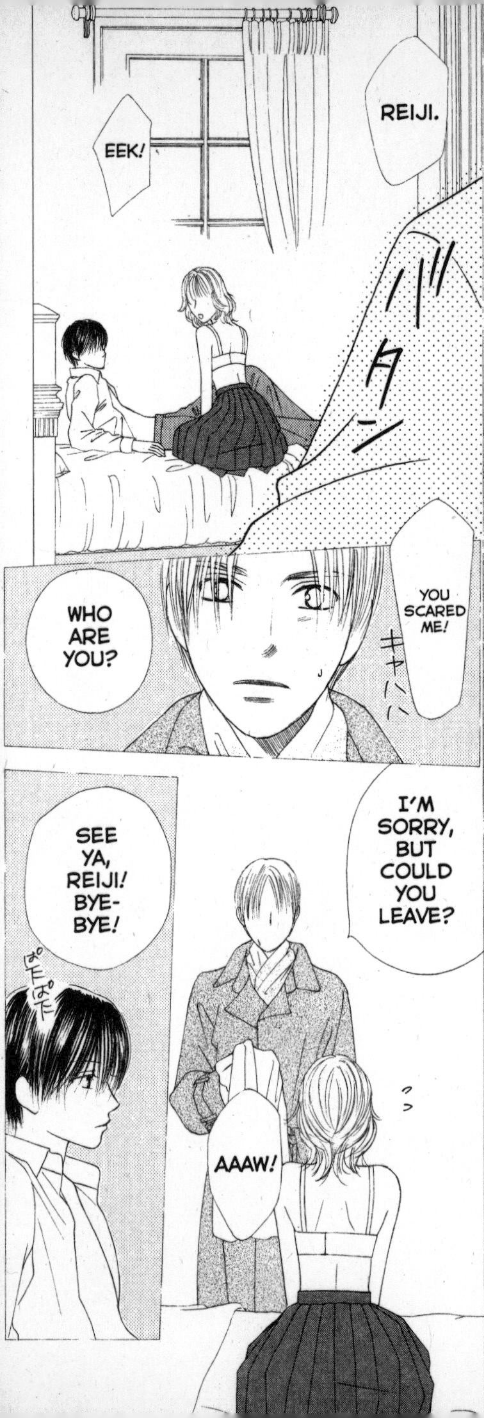
REIJI.
EEK!
バタン
YOU SCARED ME!
キャハハ
WHO ARE YOU?
I'M SORRY, BUT COULD YOU LEAVE?
AAAW!
SEE YA, REIJI! BYE-BYE!
ぱたぱた

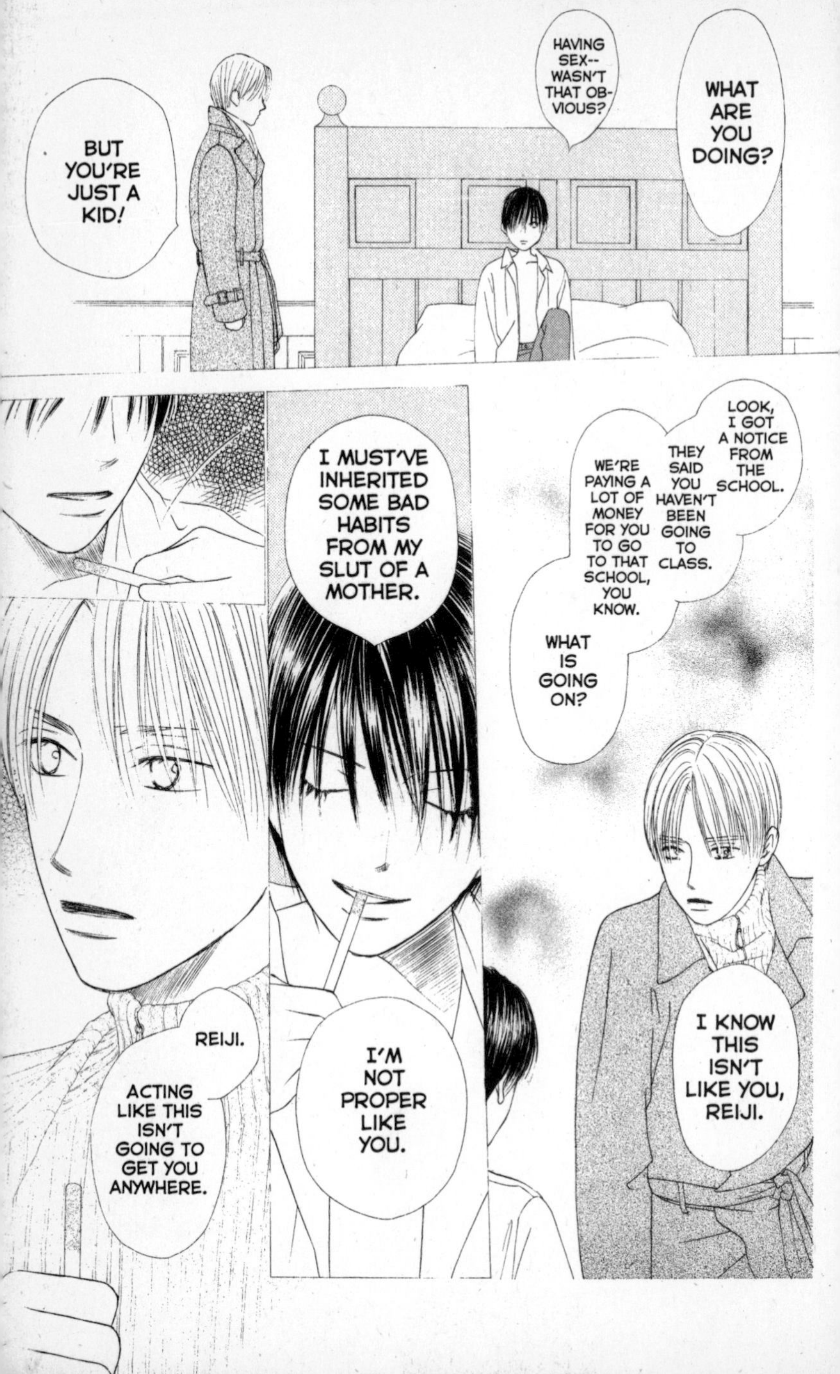
WHAT ARE YOU DOING?
HAVING SEX-- WASN'T THAT OBVIOUS?
BUT YOU'RE JUST A KID!
LOOK, I GOT A NOTICE FROM THE SCHOOL.
THEY SAID YOU HAVEN'T BEEN GOING TO CLASS.
WE'RE PAYING A LOT OF MONEY FOR YOU TO GO TO THAT SCHOOL, YOU KNOW.
WHAT IS GOING ON?
I KNOW THIS ISN'T LIKE YOU, REIJI.
I MUST'VE INHERITED SOME BAD HABITS FROM MY SLUT OF A MOTHER.
I'M NOT PROPER LIKE YOU.
REIJI.
ACTING LIKE THIS ISN'T GOING TO GET YOU ANYWHERE.

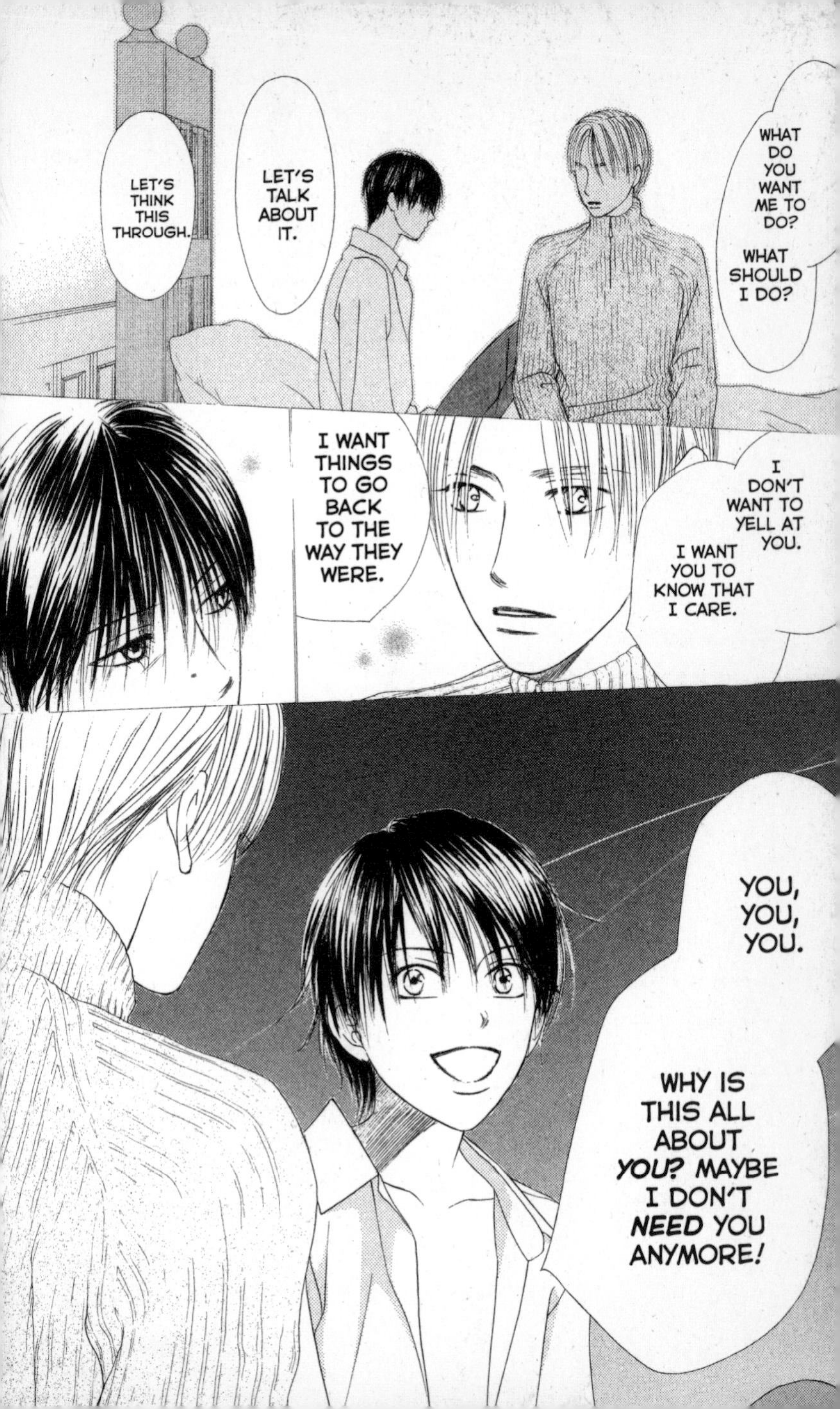

WHAT DO YOU WANT ME TO DO?
WHAT SHOULD I DO?
LET'S TALK ABOUT IT.
LET'S THINK THIS THROUGH.
I DON'T WANT TO YELL AT YOU.
I WANT YOU TO KNOW THAT I CARE.
I WANT THINGS TO GO BACK TO THE WAY THEY WERE.
YOU, YOU, YOU.
WHY IS THIS ALL ABOUT *YOU?* MAYBE I DON'T ***NEED*** YOU ANYMORE!

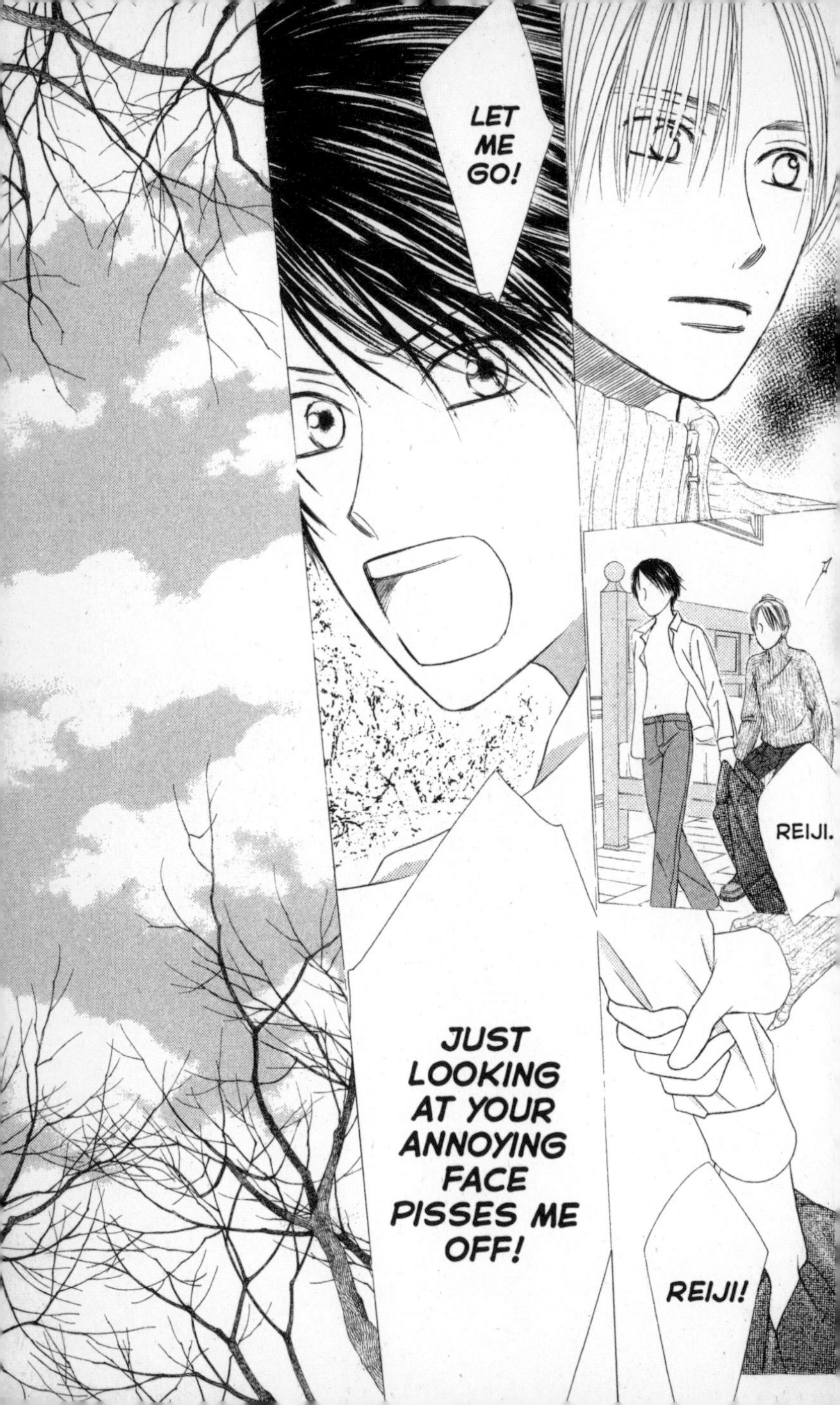
REIJI.
REIJI!
LET ME GO!
JUST LOOKING AT YOUR ANNOYING FACE PISSES ME OFF!

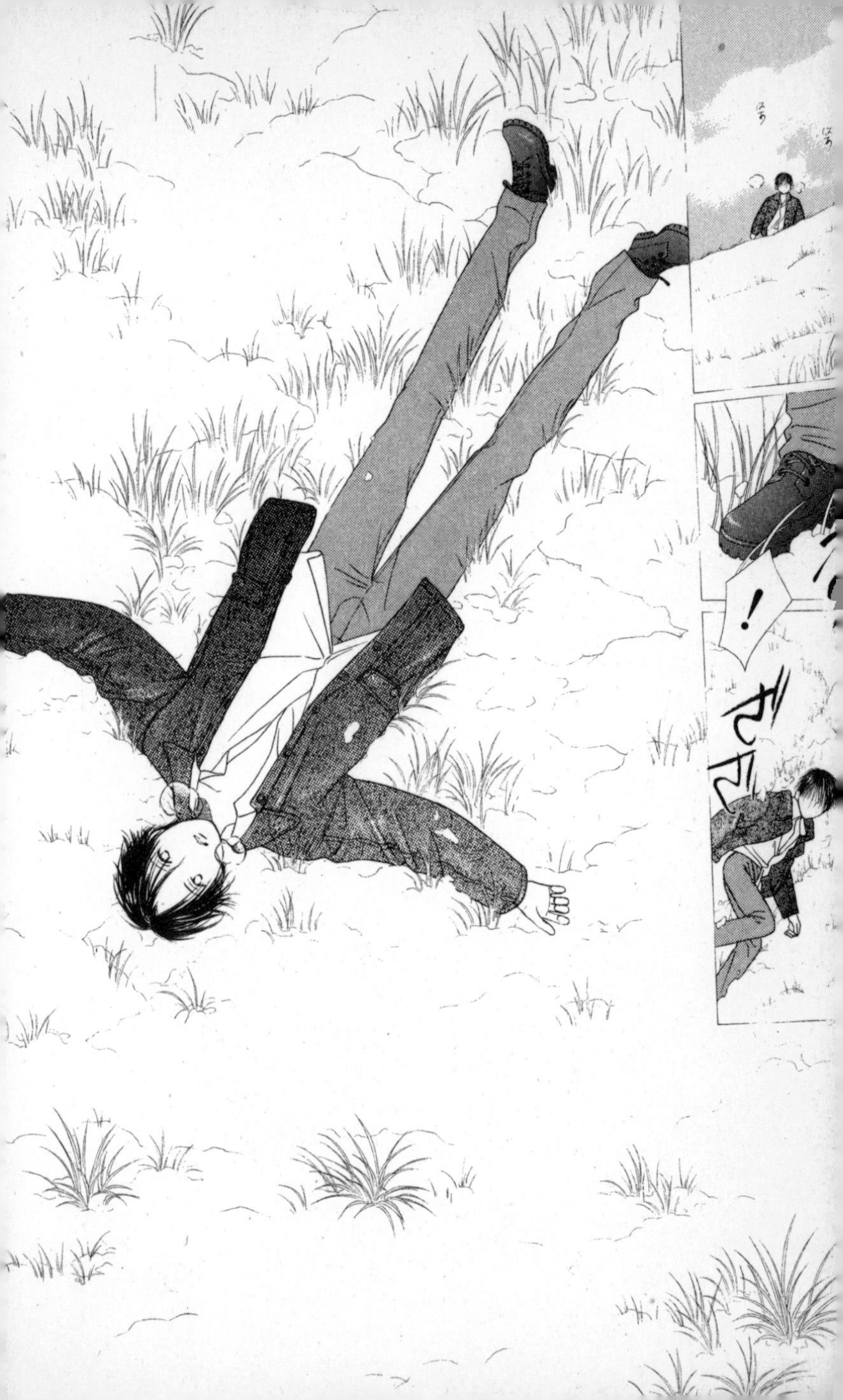
!

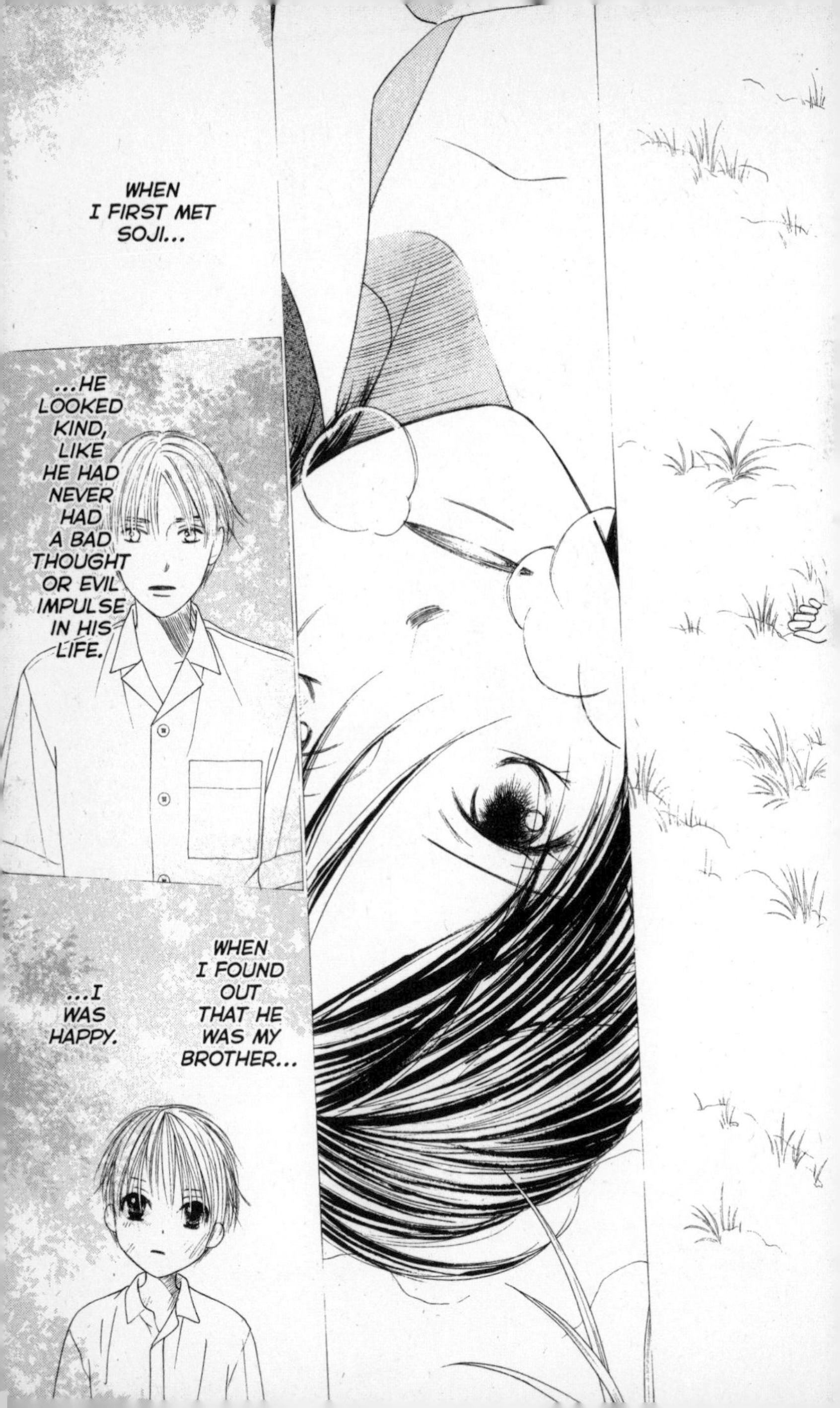
WHEN I FIRST MET SOJI...
...HE LOOKED KIND, LIKE HE HAD NEVER HAD A BAD THOUGHT OR EVIL IMPULSE IN HIS LIFE.
WHEN I FOUND OUT THAT HE WAS MY BROTHER...
...I WAS HAPPY.

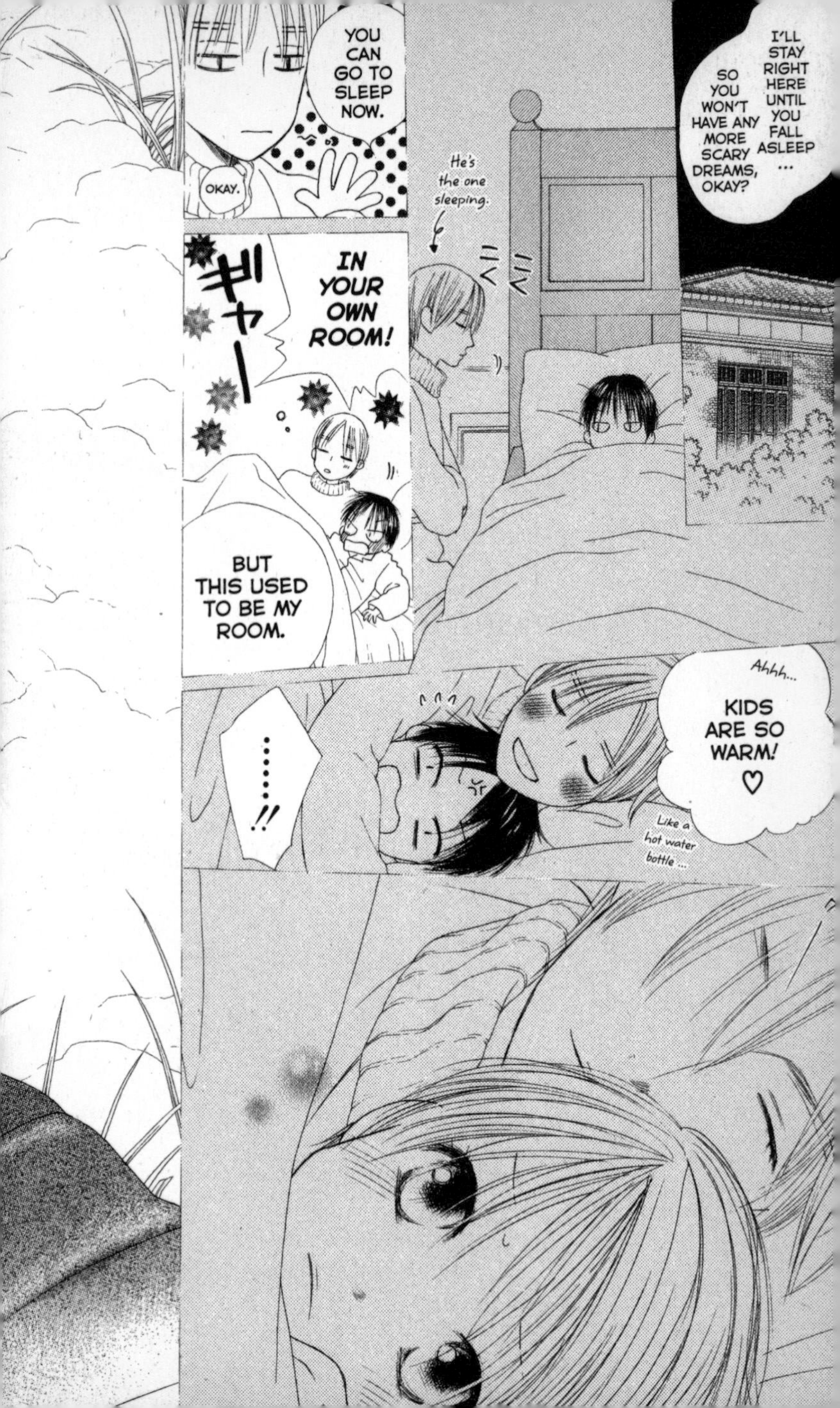

I'LL STAY RIGHT HERE UNTIL YOU FALL ASLEEP ...
SO YOU WON'T HAVE ANY MORE SCARY DREAMS, OKAY?
He's the one sleeping.
YOU CAN GO TO SLEEP NOW.
OKAY.
IN YOUR OWN ROOM!
ギャー
BUT THIS USED TO BE MY ROOM.
Ahhh...
KIDS ARE SO WARM! ♡
Like a hot water bottle...
......!!

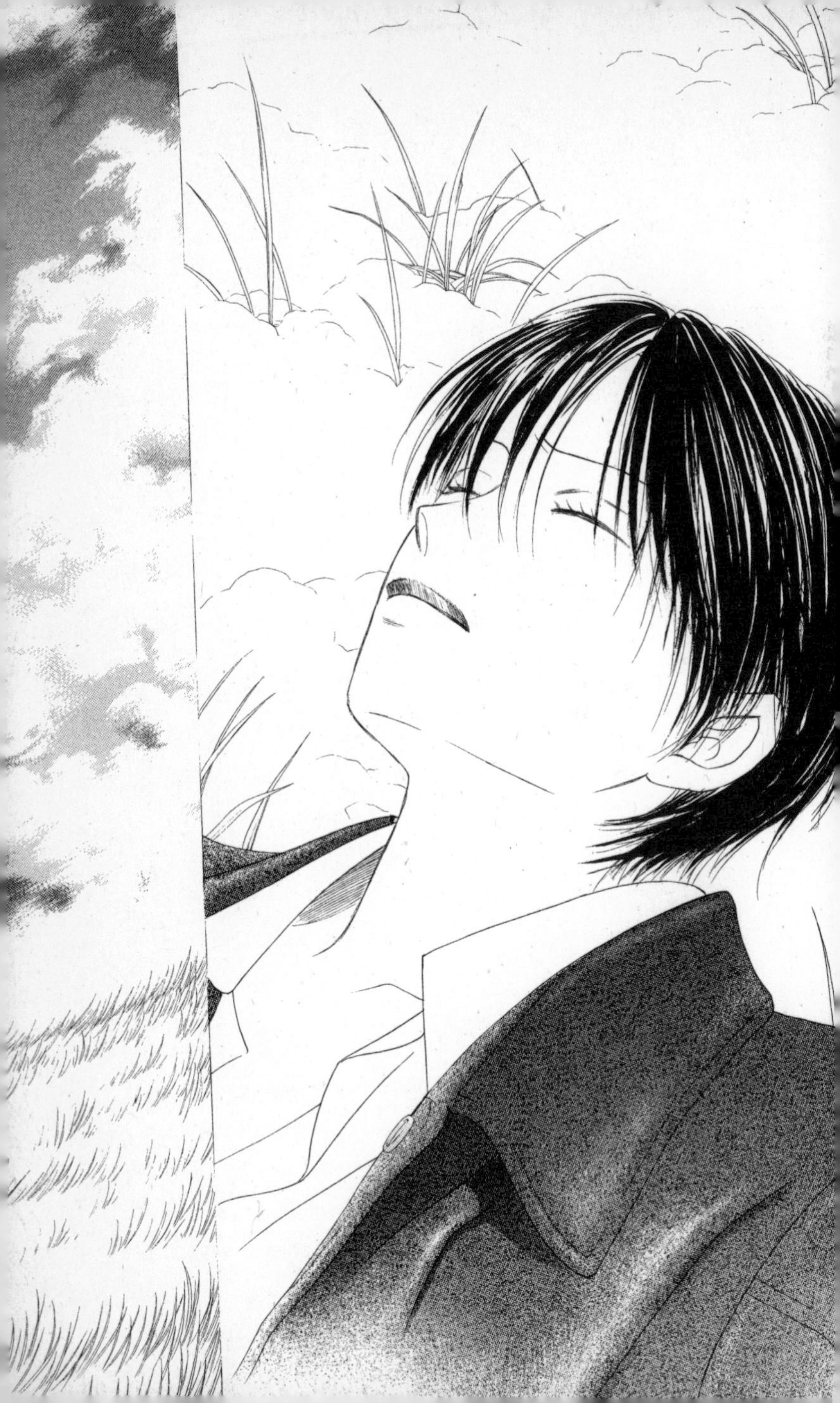

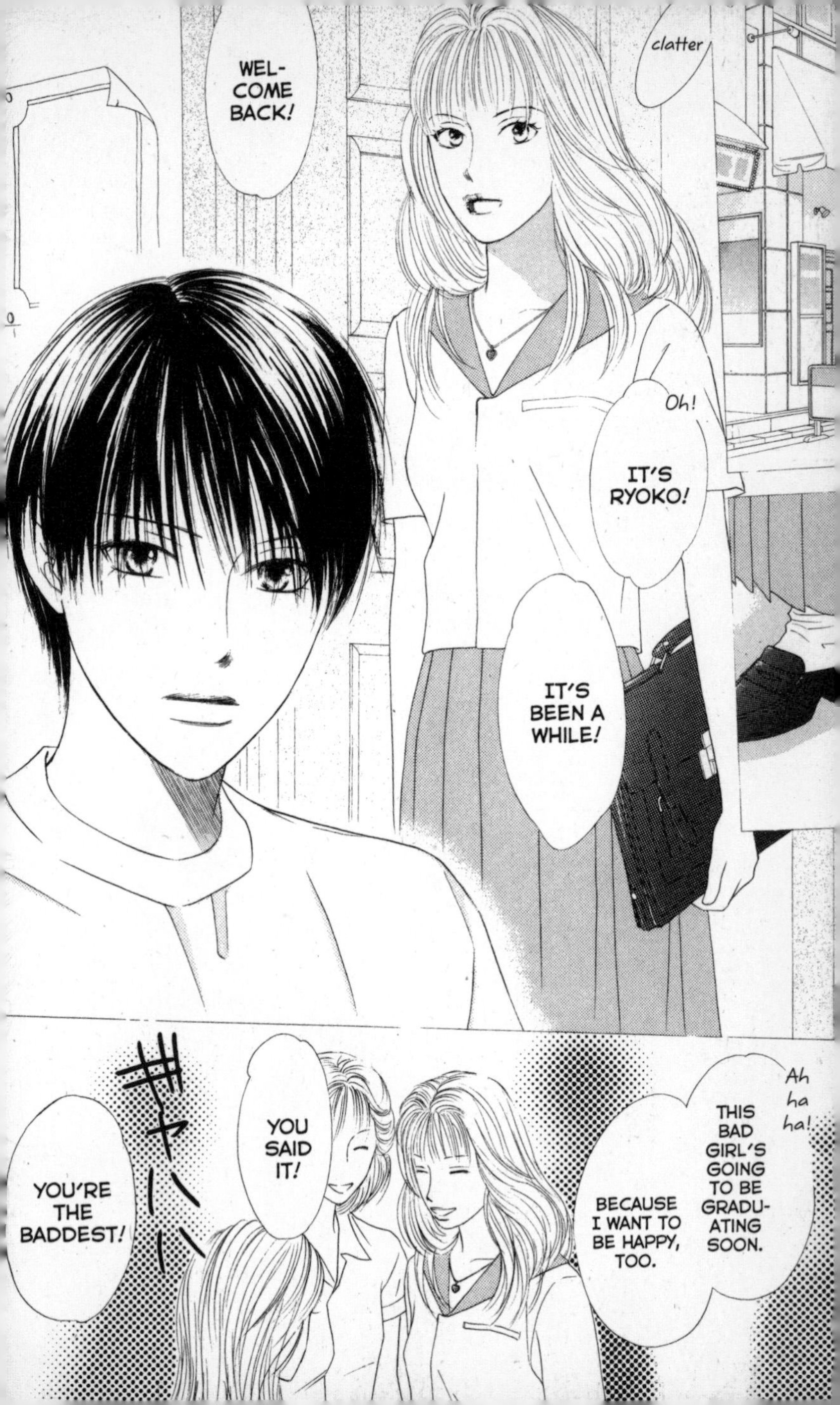
clatter
WEL-COME BACK!
Oh!
IT'S RYOKO!
IT'S BEEN A WHILE!
Ah ha ha!
THIS BAD GIRL'S GOING TO BE GRADU-ATING SOON.
BECAUSE I WANT TO BE HAPPY, TOO.
YOU SAID IT!
YOU'RE THE BADDEST!

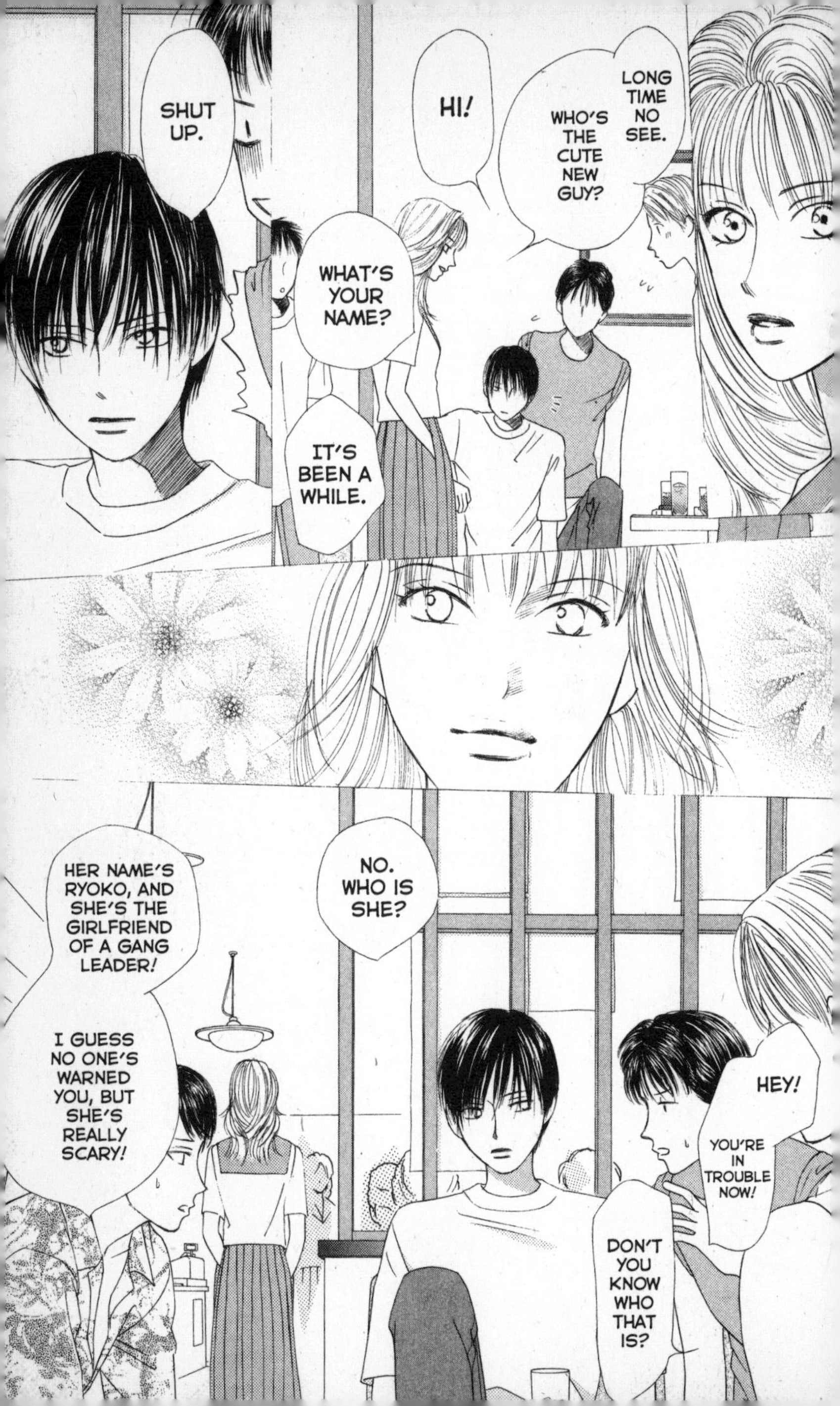

LONG TIME NO SEE.
WHO'S THE CUTE NEW GUY?
HI!
WHAT'S YOUR NAME?
IT'S BEEN A WHILE.
SHUT UP.
HEY!
YOU'RE IN TROUBLE NOW!
DON'T YOU KNOW WHO THAT IS?
NO. WHO IS SHE?
HER NAME'S RYOKO, AND SHE'S THE GIRLFRIEND OF A GANG LEADER!
I GUESS NO ONE'S WARNED YOU, BUT SHE'S REALLY SCARY!

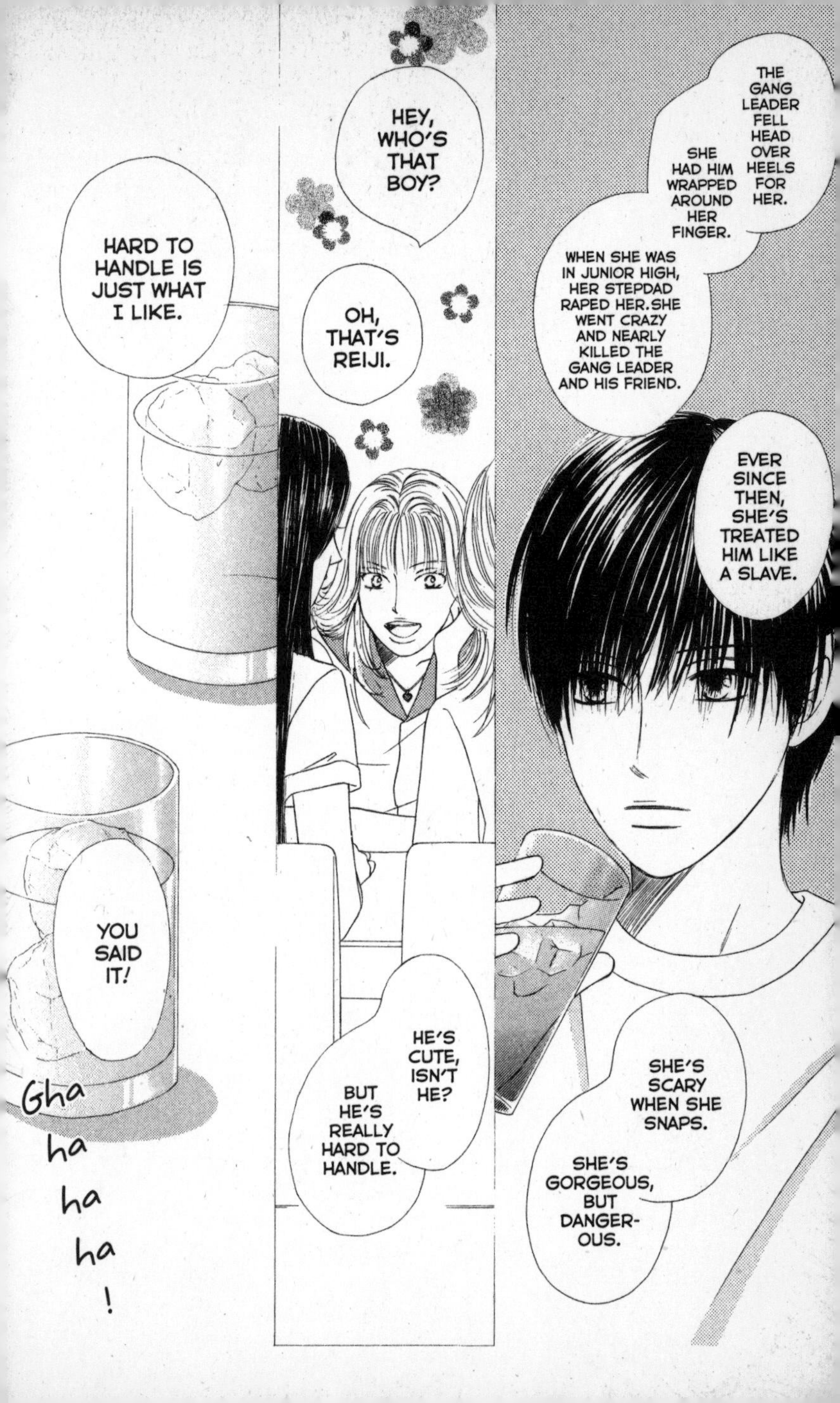

THE GANG LEADER FELL HEAD OVER HEELS FOR HER.
SHE HAD HIM WRAPPED AROUND HER FINGER.
WHEN SHE WAS IN JUNIOR HIGH, HER STEPDAD RAPED HER. SHE WENT CRAZY AND NEARLY KILLED THE GANG LEADER AND HIS FRIEND.
EVER SINCE THEN, SHE'S TREATED HIM LIKE A SLAVE.
SHE'S SCARY WHEN SHE SNAPS.
SHE'S GORGEOUS, BUT DANGER-OUS.
HEY, WHO'S THAT BOY?
OH, THAT'S REIJI.
HE'S CUTE, ISN'T HE?
BUT HE'S REALLY HARD TO HANDLE.
HARD TO HANDLE IS JUST WHAT I LIKE.
YOU SAID IT!
Gha ha ha ha!

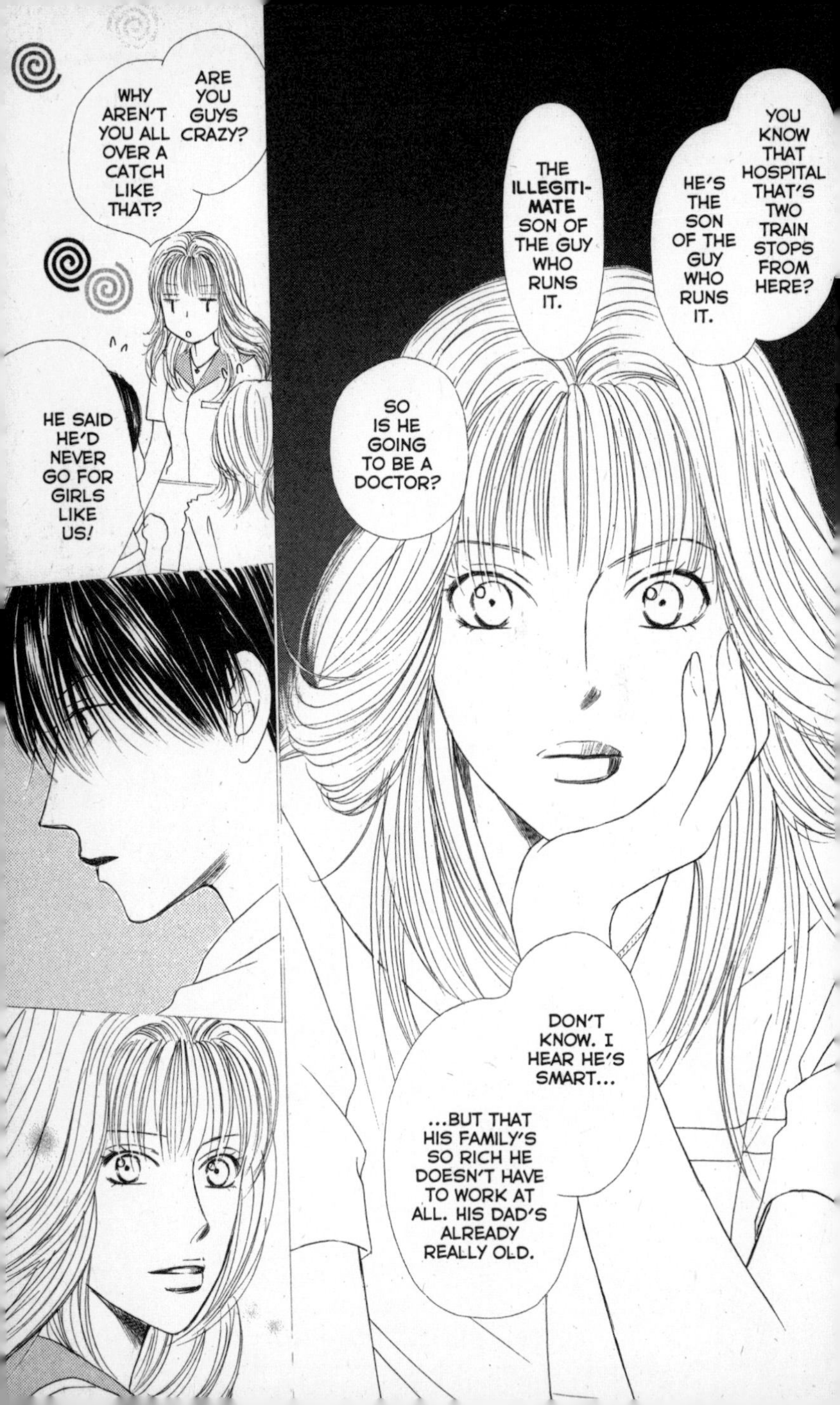
YOU KNOW THAT HOSPITAL THAT'S TWO TRAIN STOPS FROM HERE?
HE'S THE SON OF THE GUY WHO RUNS IT.
THE ILLEGITIMATE SON OF THE GUY WHO RUNS IT.
SO IS HE GOING TO BE A DOCTOR?
DON'T KNOW. I HEAR HE'S SMART...
...BUT THAT HIS FAMILY'S SO RICH HE DOESN'T HAVE TO WORK AT ALL. HIS DAD'S ALREADY REALLY OLD.
ARE YOU GUYS CRAZY?
WHY AREN'T YOU ALL OVER A CATCH LIKE THAT?
HE SAID HE'D NEVER GO FOR GIRLS LIKE US!

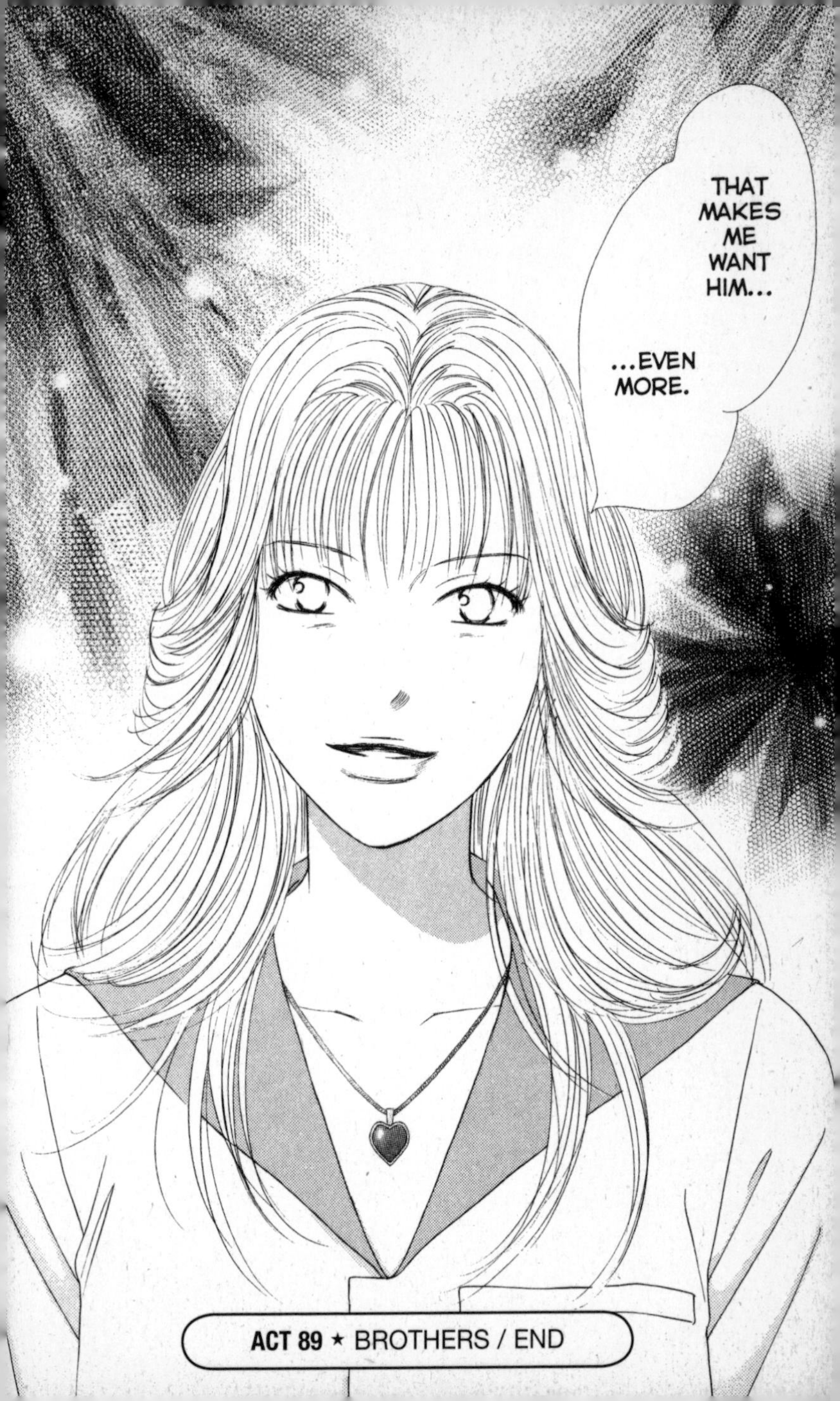
THAT MAKES ME WANT HIM...
...EVEN MORE.
ACT 89 ★ BROTHERS / END

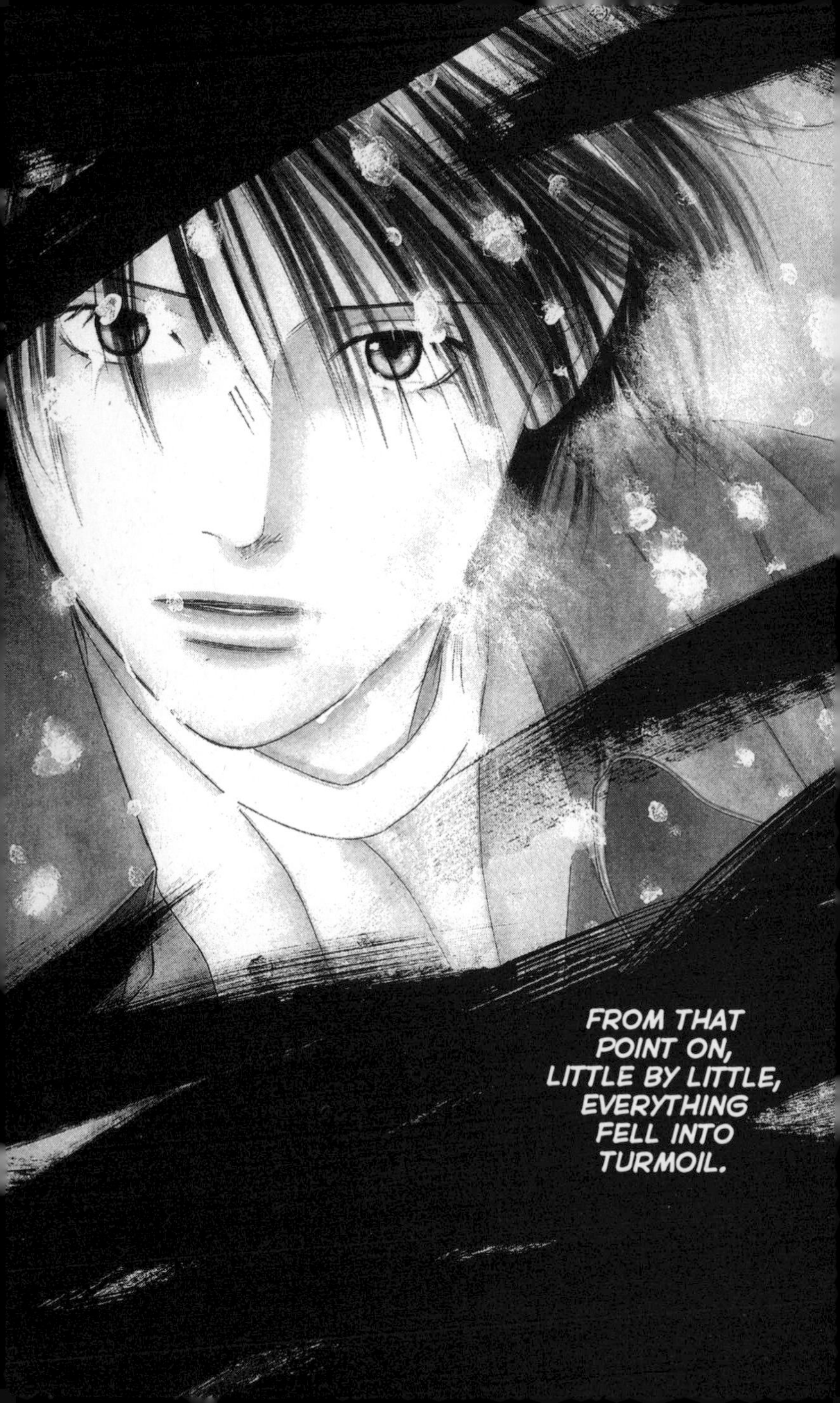
FROM THAT POINT ON, LITTLE BY LITTLE, EVERYTHING FELL INTO TURMOIL.

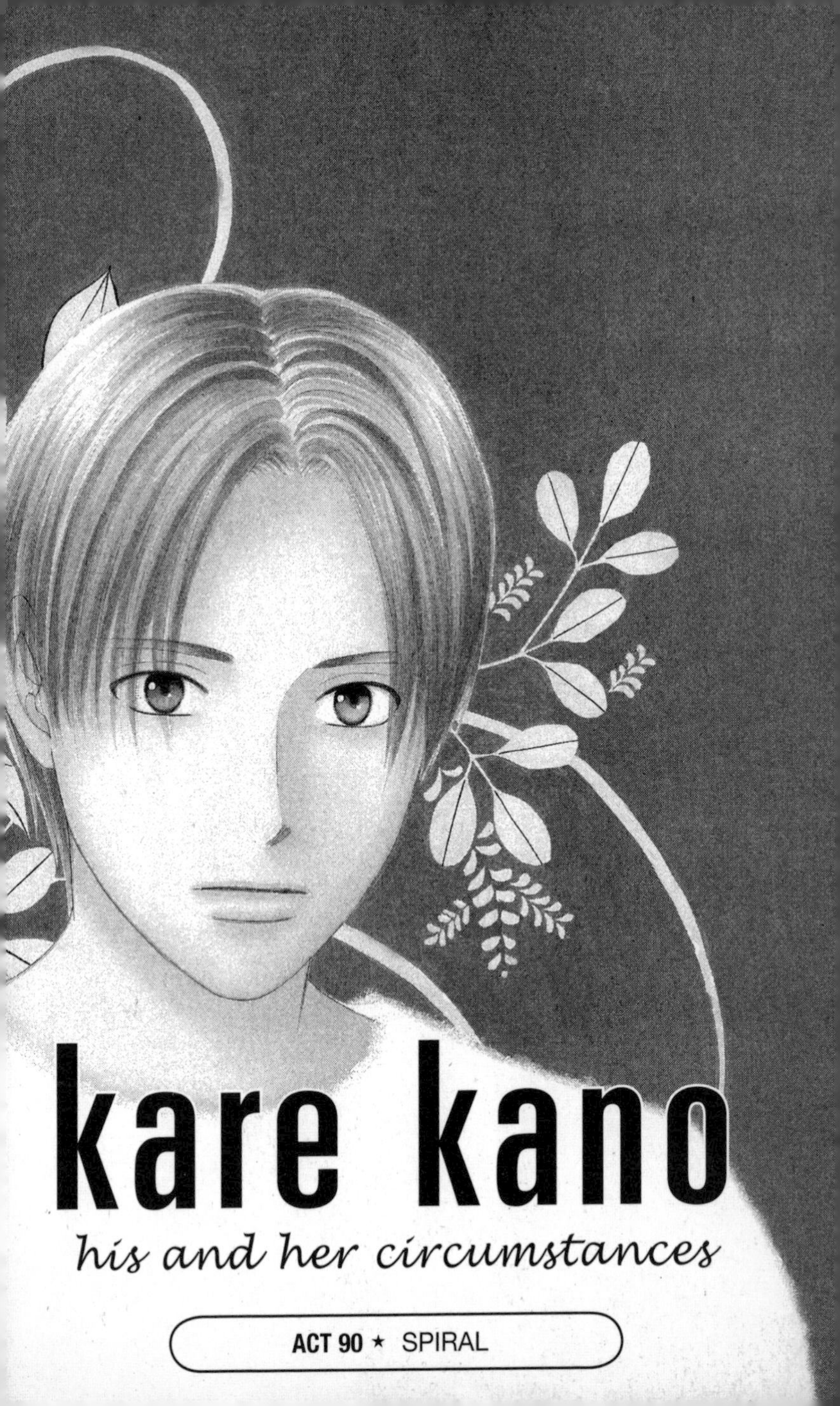

kare kano

his and her circumstances

ACT 90 ★ SPIRAL

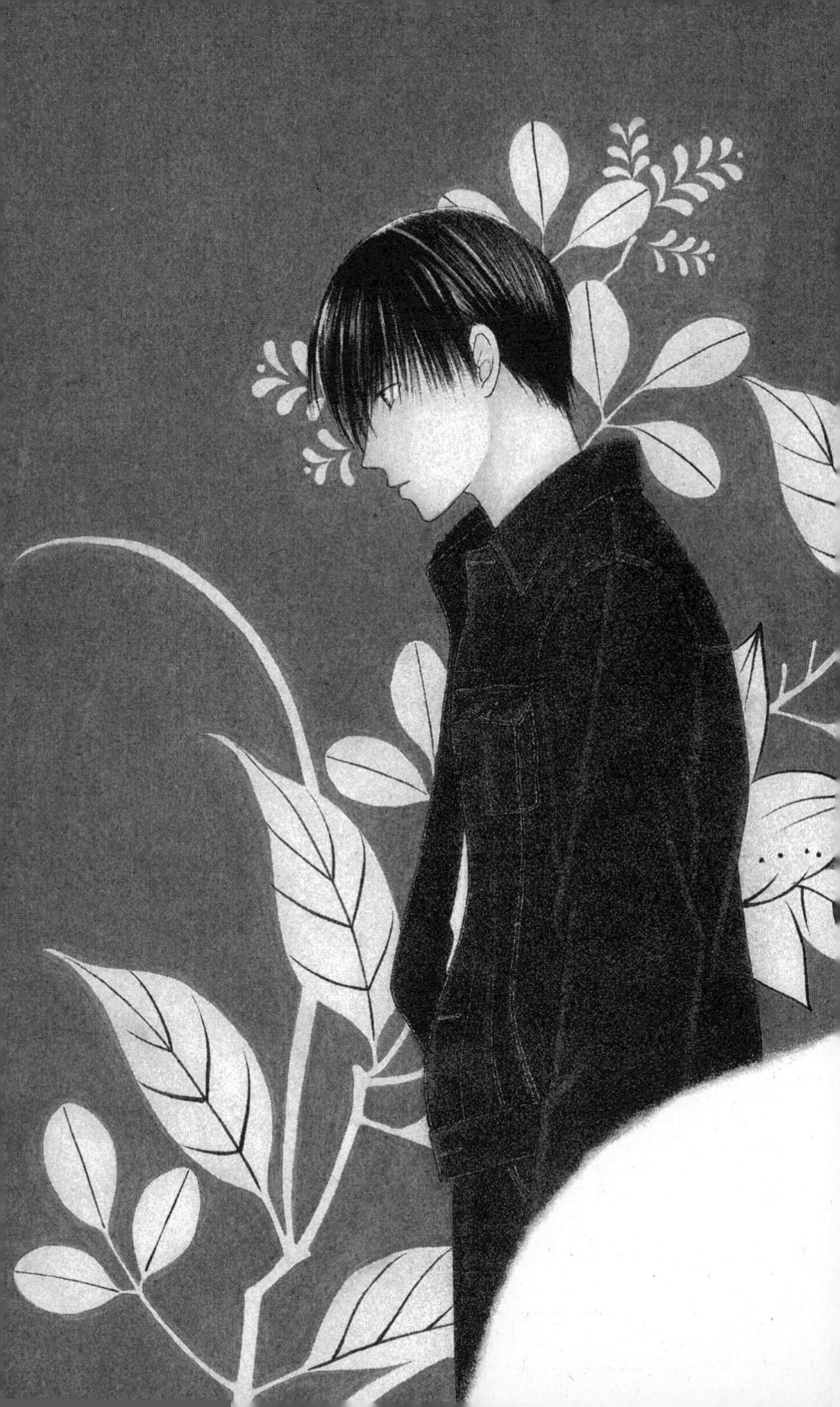

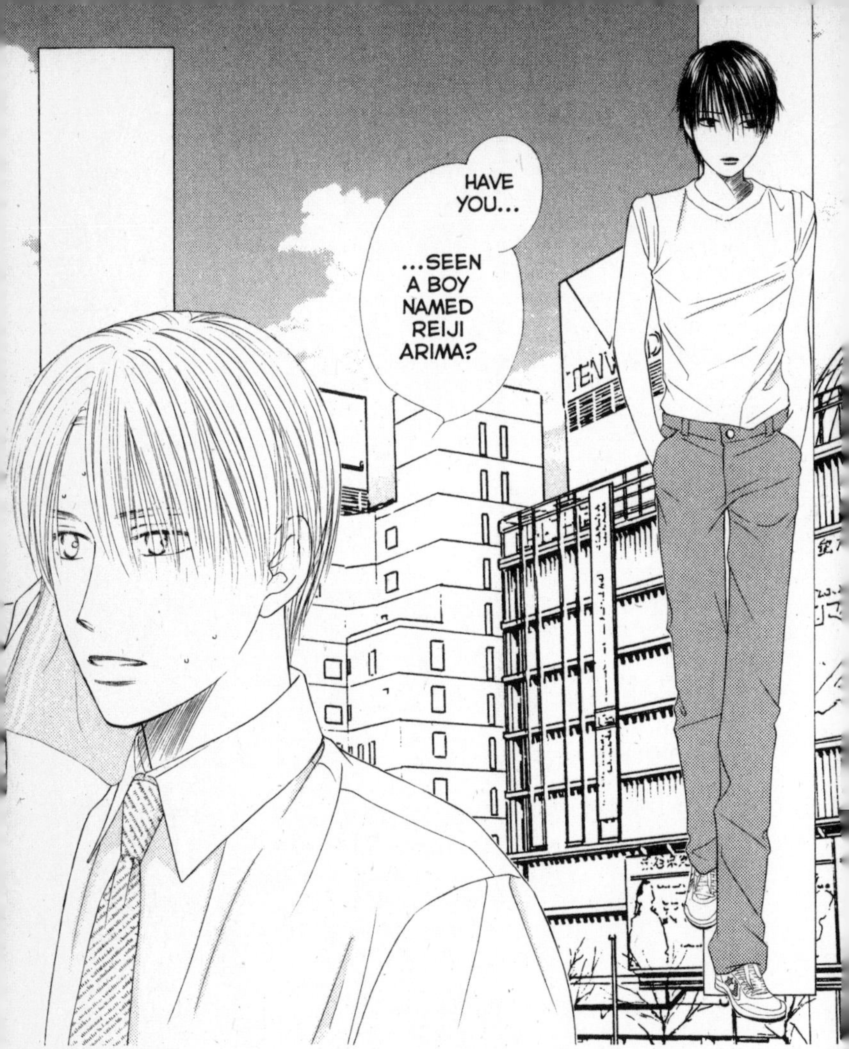
HAVE YOU...
...SEEN A BOY NAMED REIJI ARIMA?

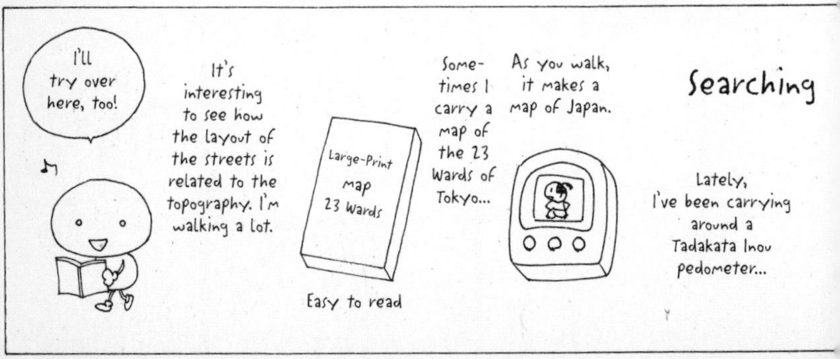
Searching
Lately, I've been carrying around a Tadakata Inou pedometer...
As you walk, it makes a map of Japan.
Sometimes I carry a map of the 23 Wards of Tokyo...
Large-Print map 23 Wards
Easy to read
It's interesting to see how the layout of the streets is related to the topography. I'm walking a lot.
I'll try over here, too!

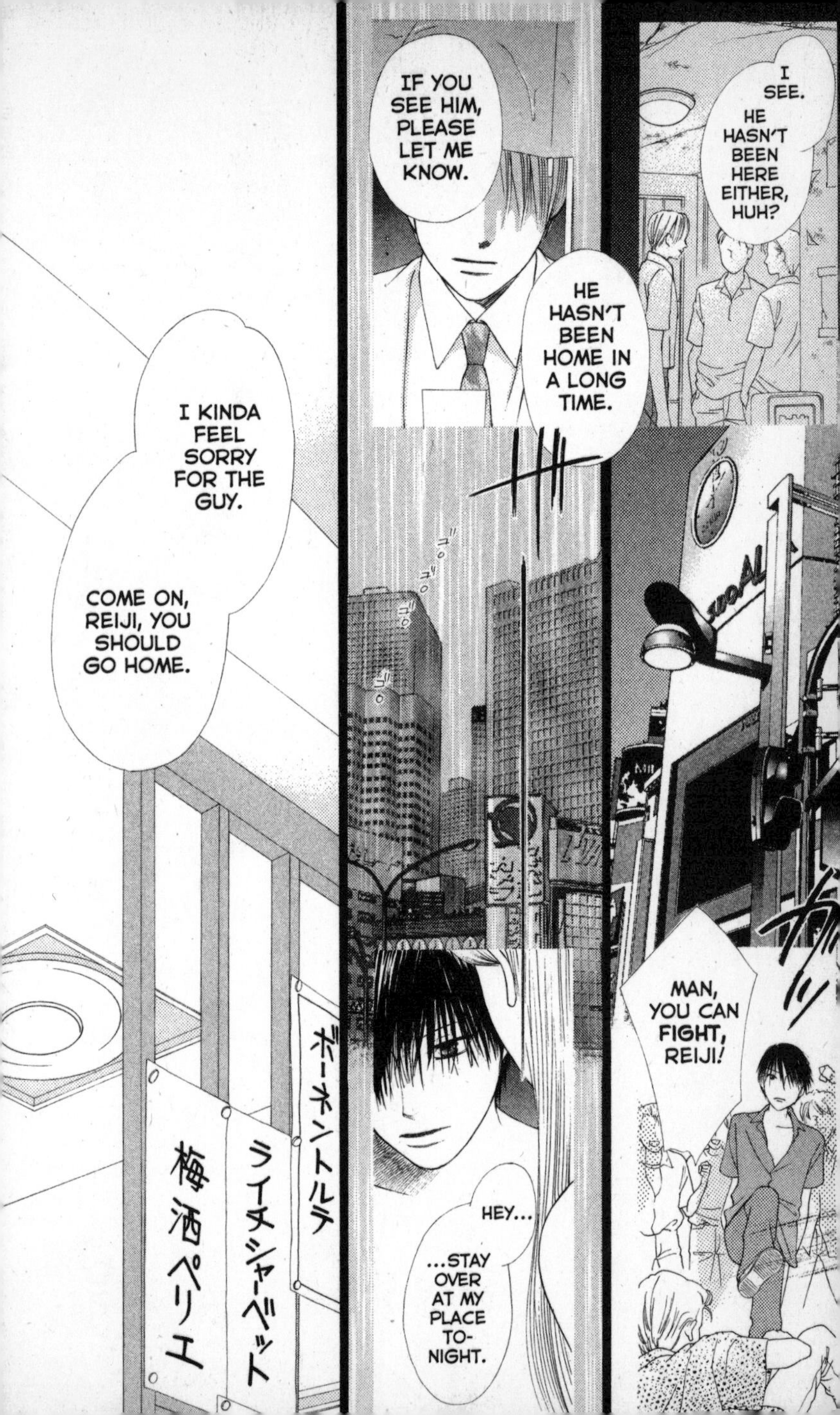
I SEE.
HE HASN'T BEEN HERE EITHER, HUH?
HE HASN'T BEEN HOME IN A LONG TIME.
IF YOU SEE HIM, PLEASE LET ME KNOW.
MAN, YOU CAN FIGHT, REIJI!
HEY...
...STAY OVER AT MY PLACE TO-NIGHT.
I KINDA FEEL SORRY FOR THE GUY.
COME ON, REIJI, YOU SHOULD GO HOME.
ボーネントルテ
ライチシャーベット
梅酒ペリエ

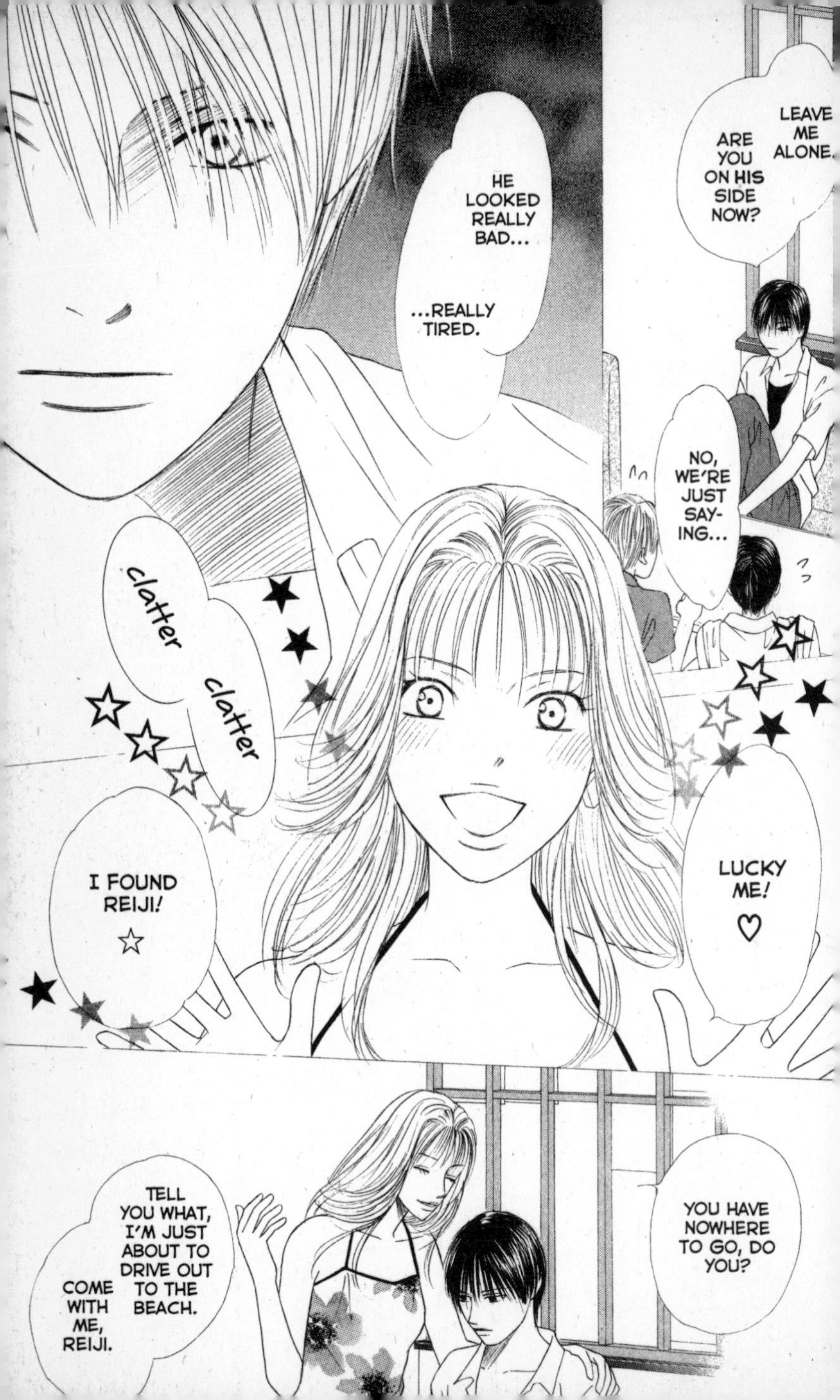
LEAVE ME ALONE.
ARE YOU ON HIS SIDE NOW?
NO, WE'RE JUST SAY-ING...
HE LOOKED REALLY BAD...
...REALLY TIRED.
clatter
clatter
LUCKY ME! ♡
I FOUND REIJI! ☆
YOU HAVE NOWHERE TO GO, DO YOU?
TELL YOU WHAT, I'M JUST ABOUT TO DRIVE OUT TO THE BEACH.
COME WITH ME, REIJI.

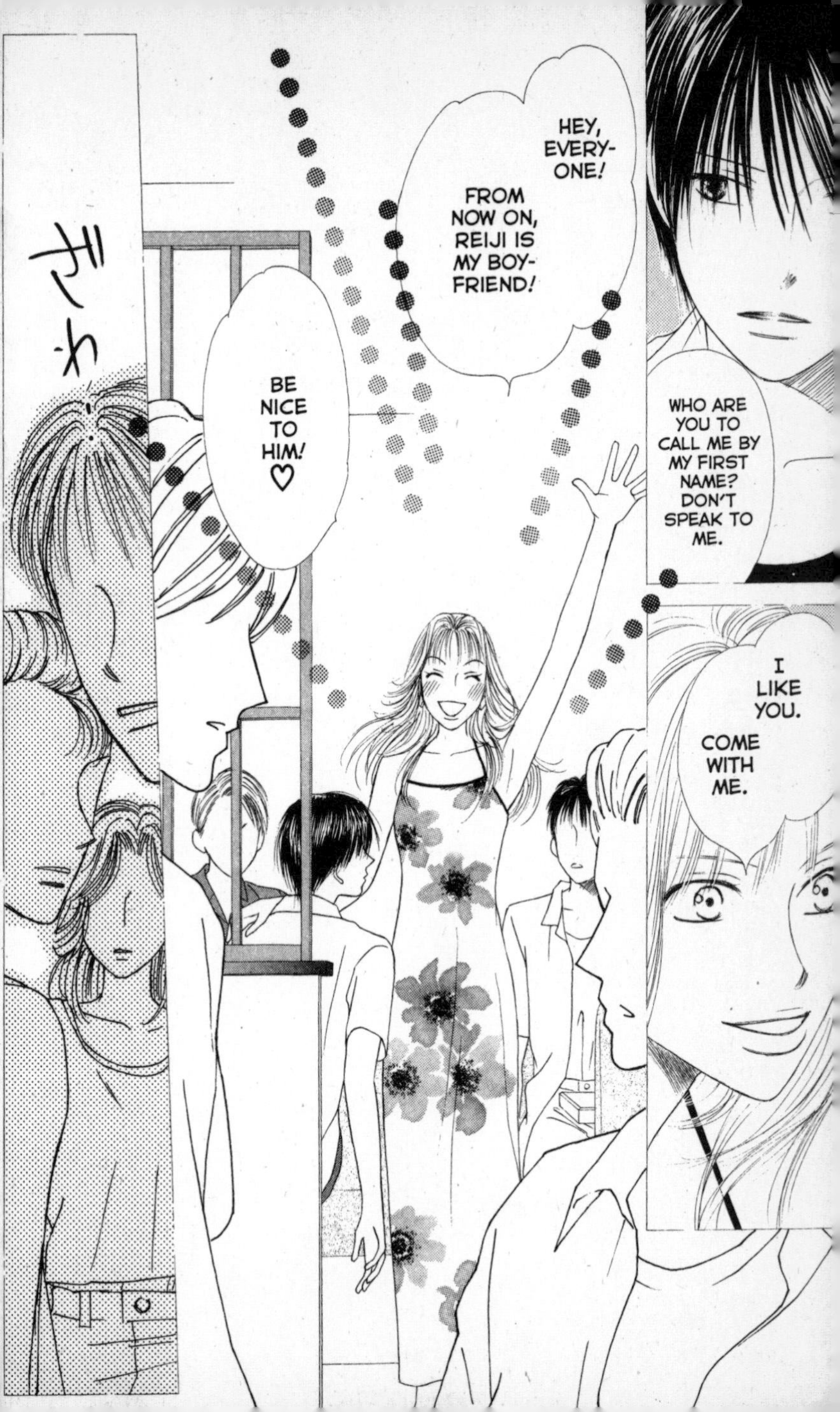

WHO ARE YOU TO CALL ME BY MY FIRST NAME? DON'T SPEAK TO ME.
I LIKE YOU.
COME WITH ME.
HEY, EVERY-ONE!
FROM NOW ON, REIJI IS MY BOY-FRIEND!
BE NICE TO HIM! ♡

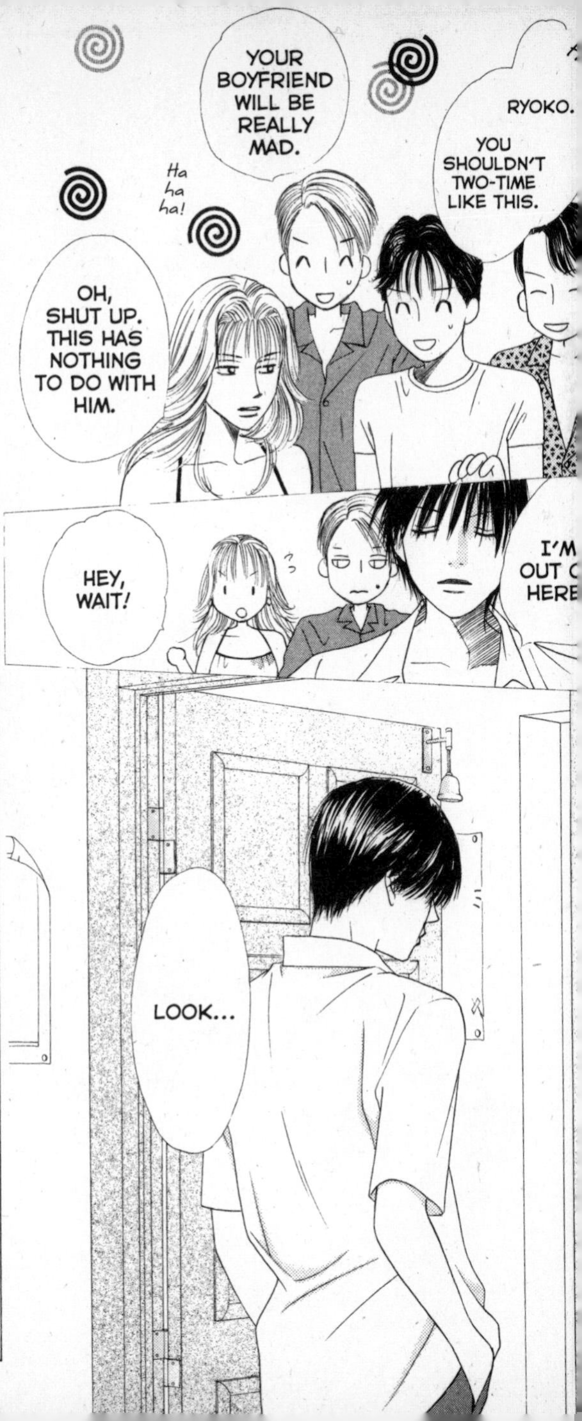
RYOKO.
YOU SHOULDN'T TWO-TIME LIKE THIS.
YOUR BOYFRIEND WILL BE REALLY MAD.
Ha ha ha!
OH, SHUT UP. THIS HAS NOTHING TO DO WITH HIM.
I'M OUT O HERE
HEY, WAIT!
LOOK...

2

My favorite gadgets! ♡

* Cell Phone
By INFOVAR. White.

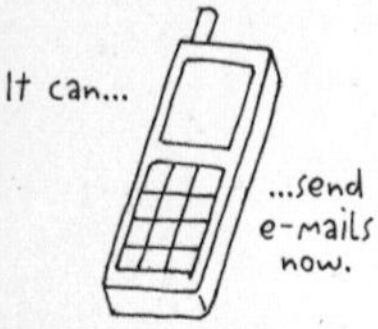
It can...
...send e-mails now.

* Tabletop TV set

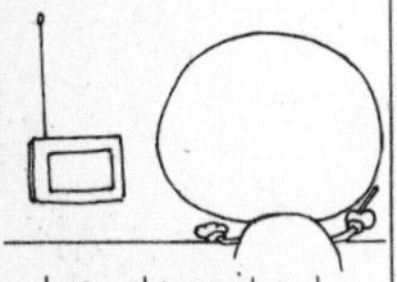

I can charge it and take it into the bathroom with me. I don't watch much TV, but this is convenient for those times when I want to watch a little. Like when I'm working.

I'm also fiddling around with a digital camera and a DVD recorder. It's kind of interesting.

I wanted a sewing machine, so I bought one of those too, but my eyes are so tired right now, it's hard to use.

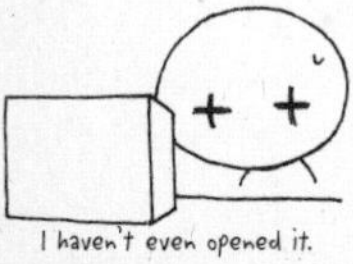

I haven't even opened it.

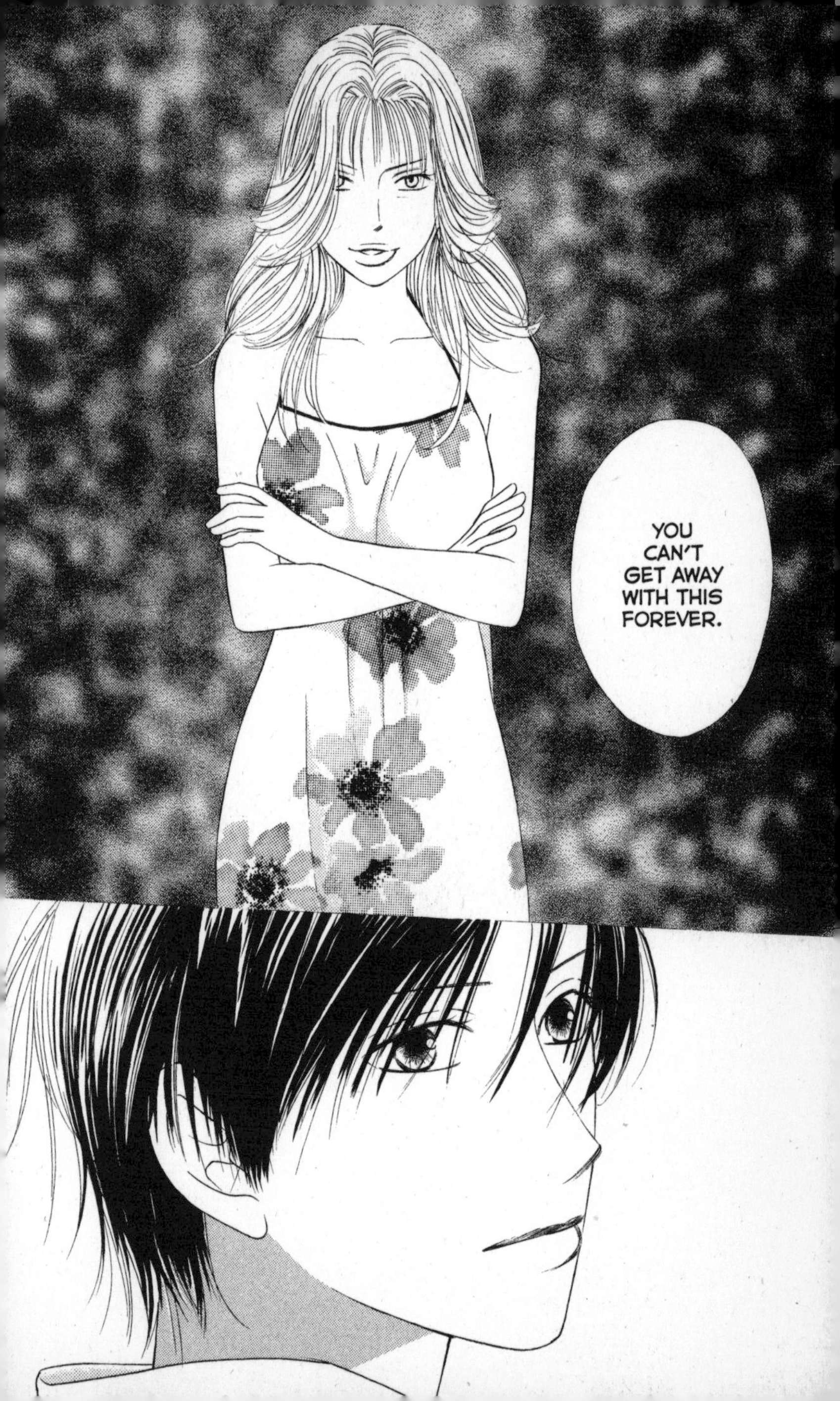
YOU CAN'T GET AWAY WITH THIS FOREVER.

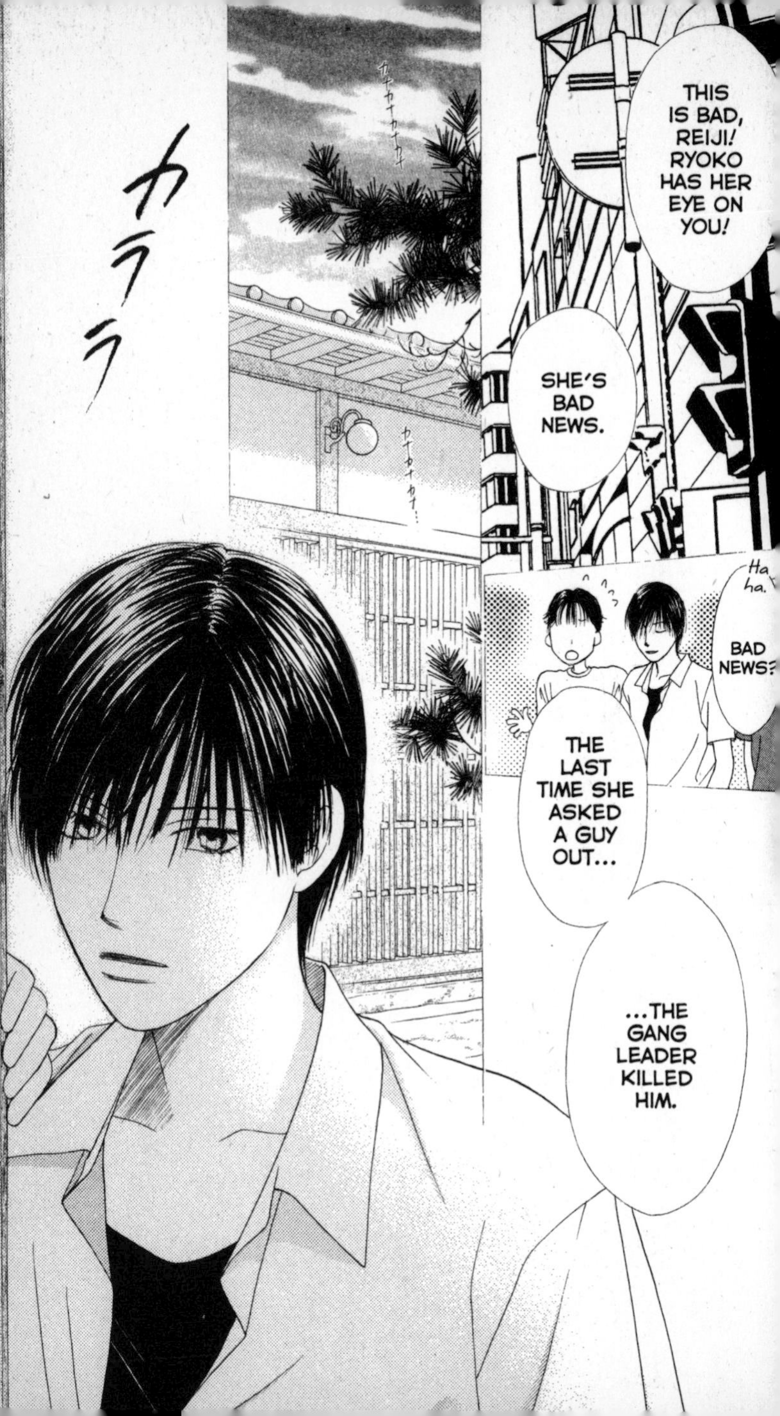
THIS IS BAD, REIJI! RYOKO HAS HER EYE ON YOU!
SHE'S BAD NEWS.
Ha ha.
BAD NEWS?
THE LAST TIME SHE ASKED A GUY OUT...
...THE GANG LEADER KILLED HIM.
カナカナカナカナ
カナカナカナ…
カララ

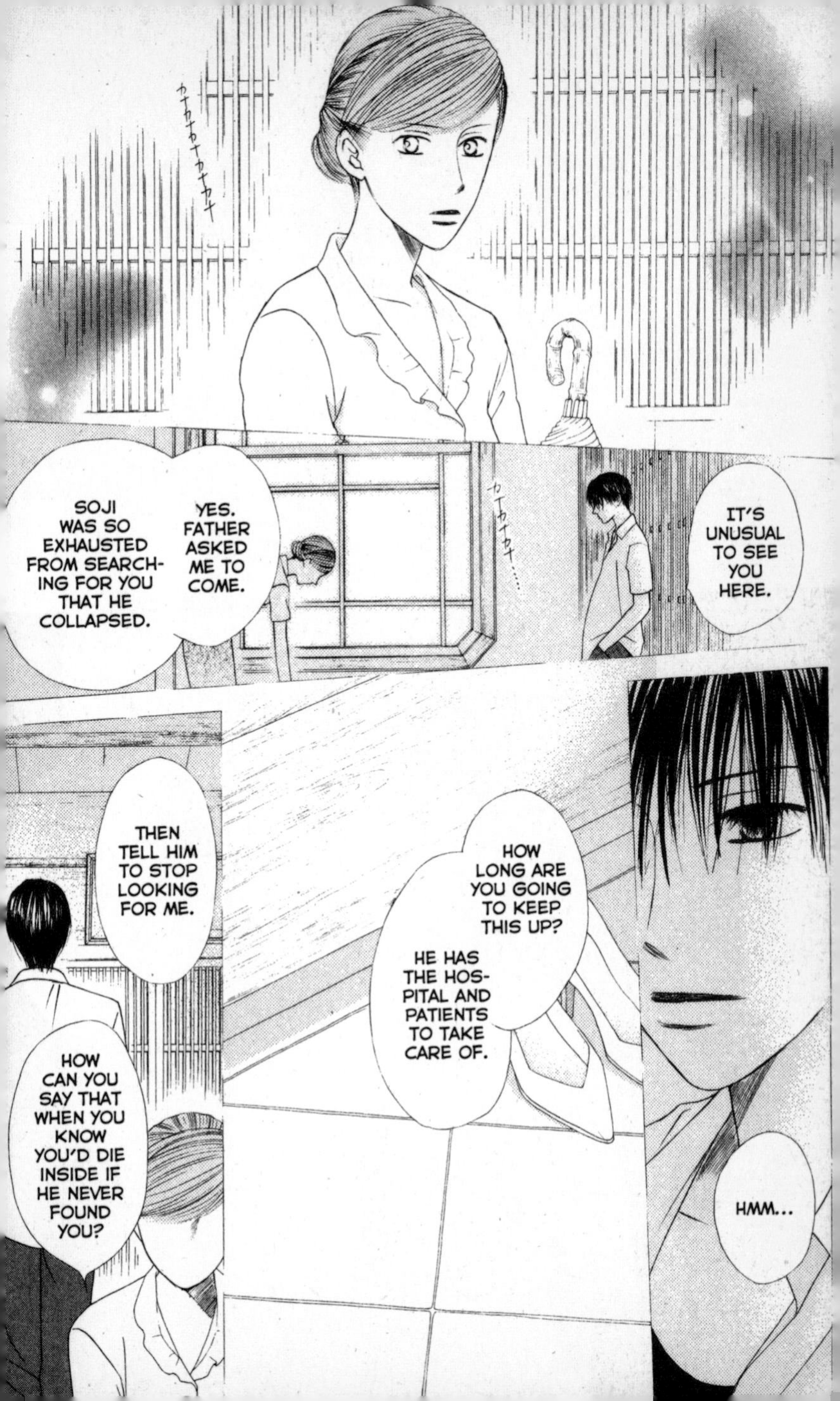

IT'S UNUSUAL TO SEE YOU HERE.
YES. FATHER ASKED ME TO COME.
SOJI WAS SO EXHAUSTED FROM SEARCH-ING FOR YOU THAT HE COLLAPSED.
HOW LONG ARE YOU GOING TO KEEP THIS UP?
HE HAS THE HOS-PITAL AND PATIENTS TO TAKE CARE OF.
HMM...
THEN TELL HIM TO STOP LOOKING FOR ME.
HOW CAN YOU SAY THAT WHEN YOU KNOW YOU'D DIE INSIDE IF HE NEVER FOUND YOU?

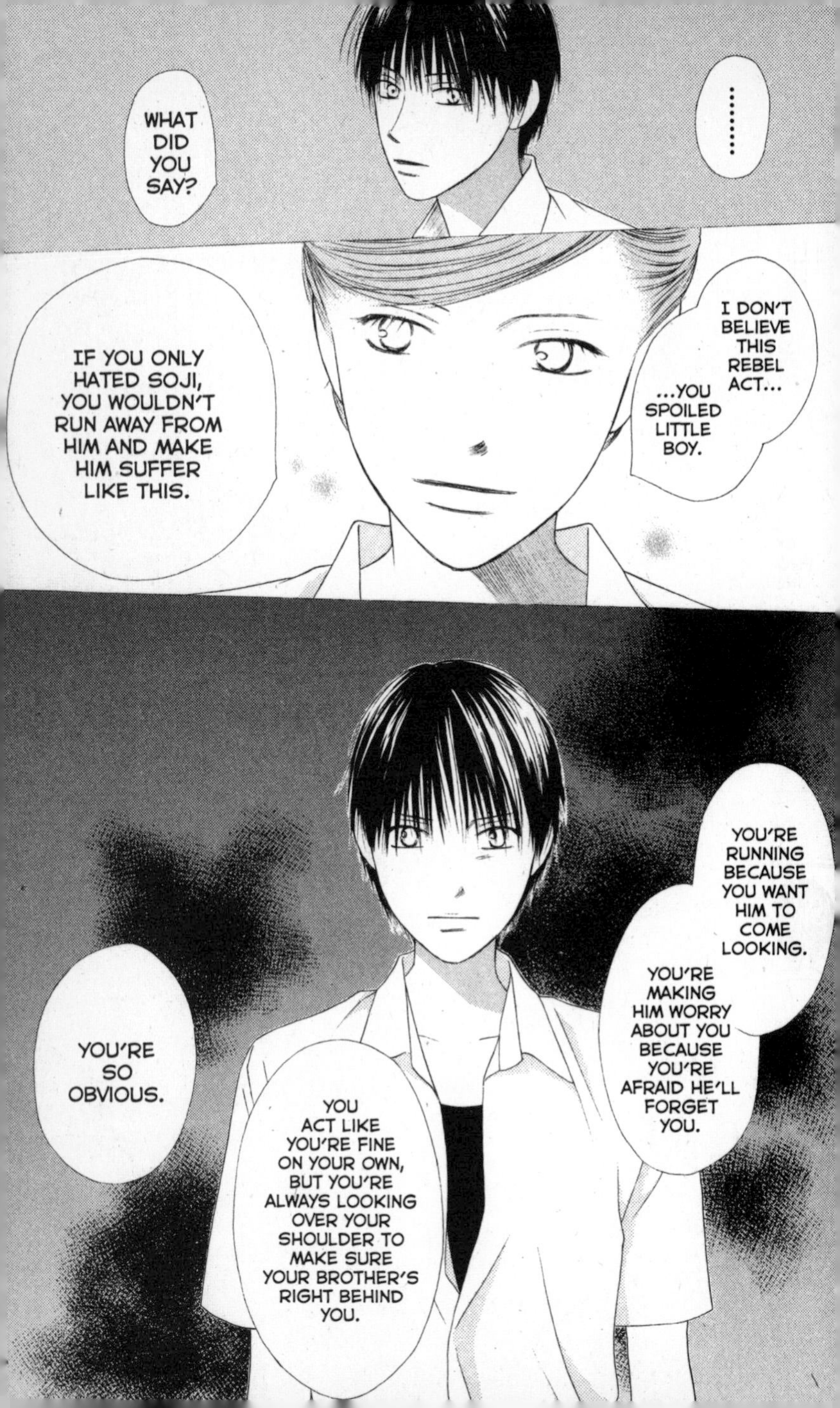
......
WHAT DID YOU SAY?
I DON'T BELIEVE THIS REBEL ACT...
...YOU SPOILED LITTLE BOY.
IF YOU ONLY HATED SOJI, YOU WOULDN'T RUN AWAY FROM HIM AND MAKE HIM SUFFER LIKE THIS.
YOU'RE RUNNING BECAUSE YOU WANT HIM TO COME LOOKING.
YOU'RE MAKING HIM WORRY ABOUT YOU BECAUSE YOU'RE AFRAID HE'LL FORGET YOU.
YOU ACT LIKE YOU'RE FINE ON YOUR OWN, BUT YOU'RE ALWAYS LOOKING OVER YOUR SHOULDER TO MAKE SURE YOUR BROTHER'S RIGHT BEHIND YOU.
YOU'RE SO OBVIOUS.

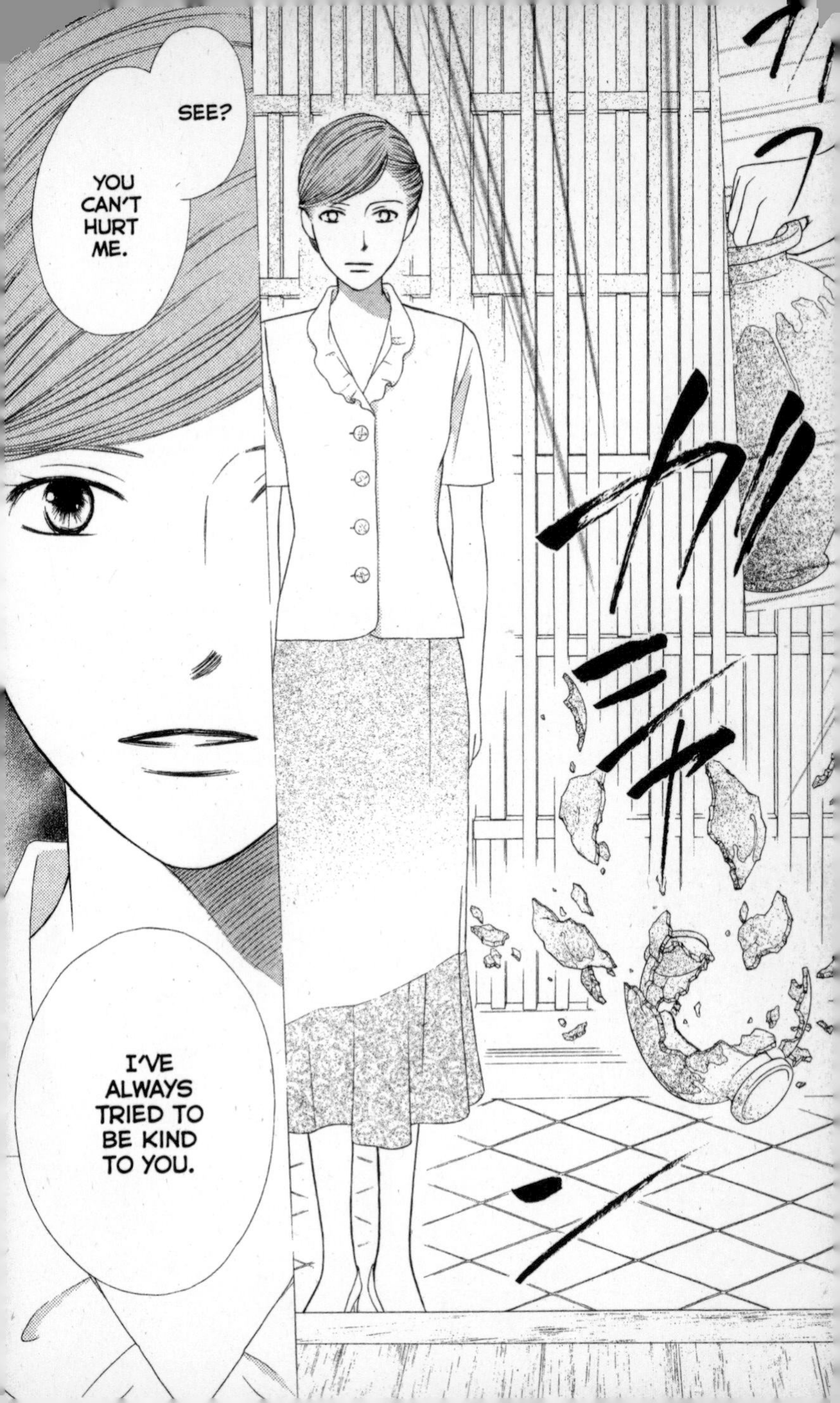
SEE?
YOU CAN'T HURT ME.
I'VE ALWAYS TRIED TO BE KIND TO YOU.

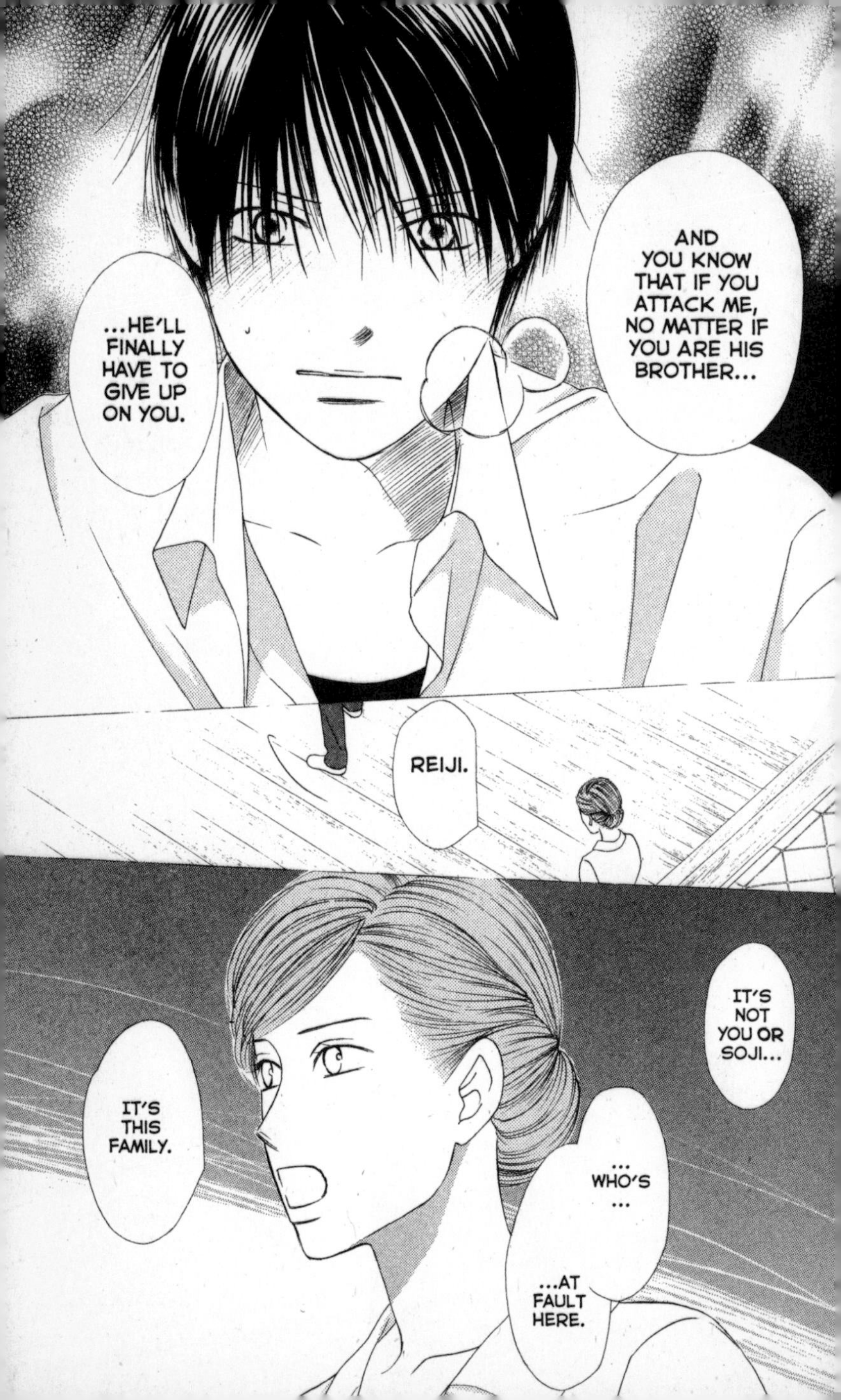
AND YOU KNOW THAT IF YOU ATTACK ME, NO MATTER IF YOU ARE HIS BROTHER...
...HE'LL FINALLY HAVE TO GIVE UP ON YOU.
REIJI.
IT'S NOT YOU OR SOJI...
... WHO'S ...
...AT FAULT HERE.
IT'S THIS FAMILY.

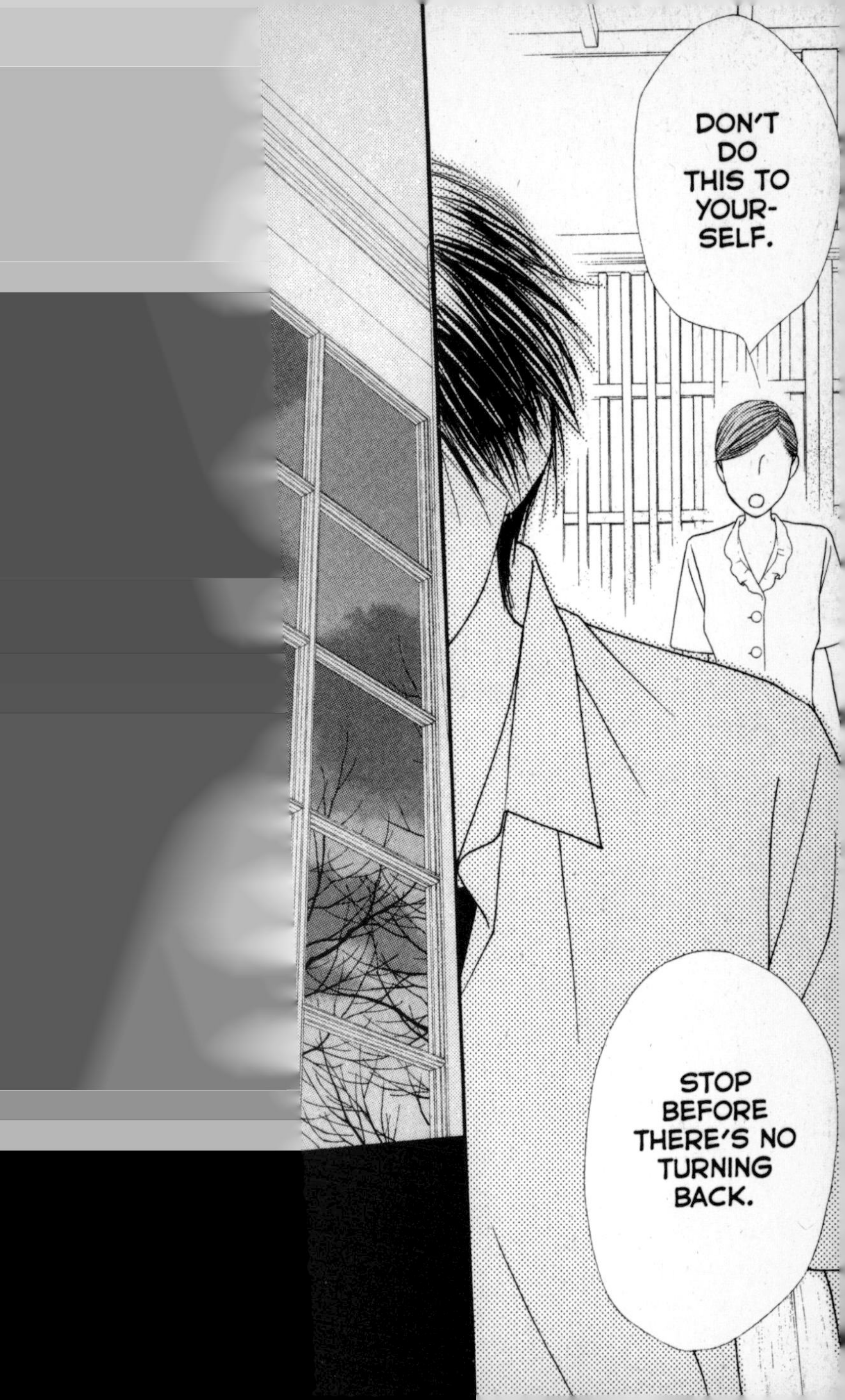
DON'T DO THIS TO YOUR-SELF.
STOP BEFORE THERE'S NO TURNING BACK.

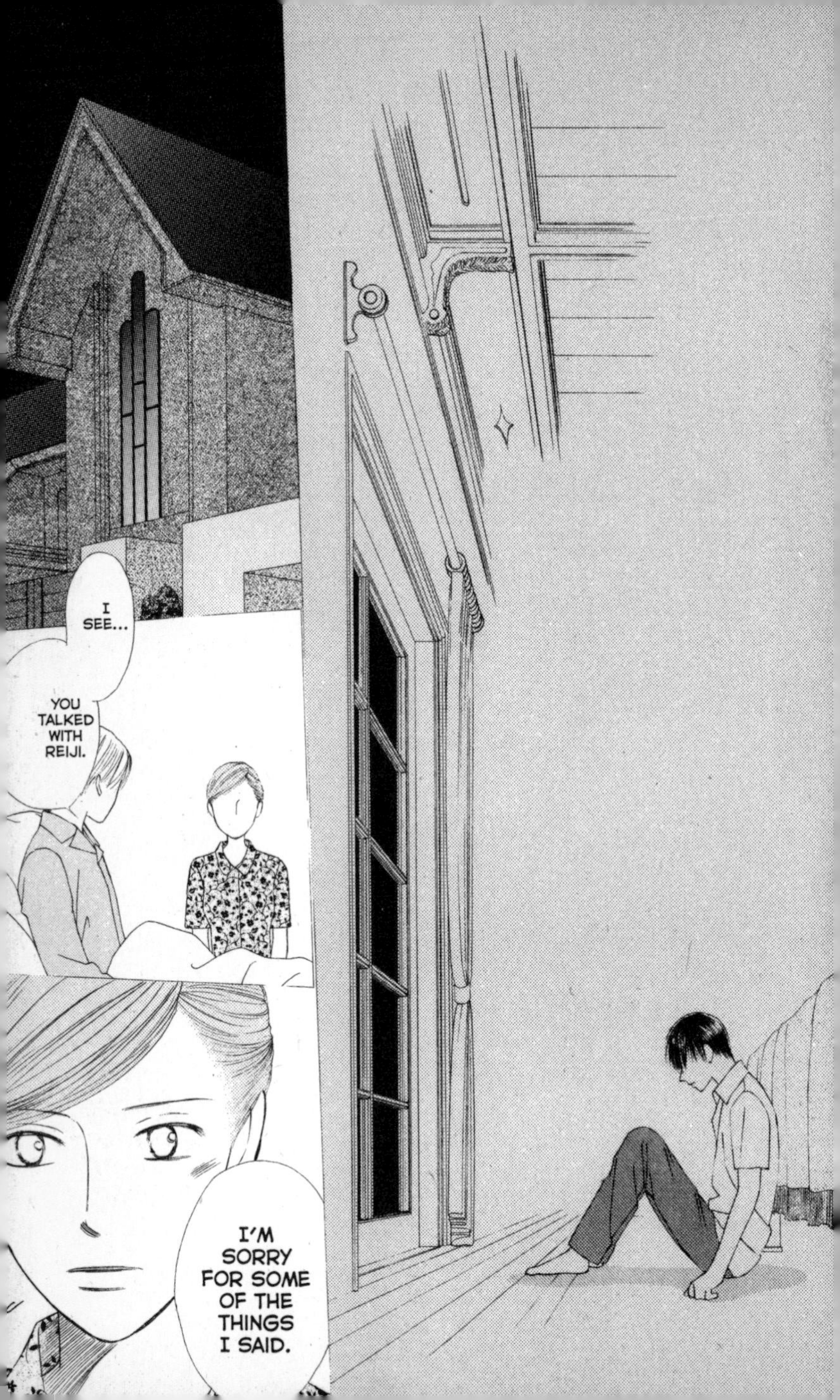
I SEE...
YOU TALKED WITH REIJI.
I'M SORRY FOR SOME OF THE THINGS I SAID.

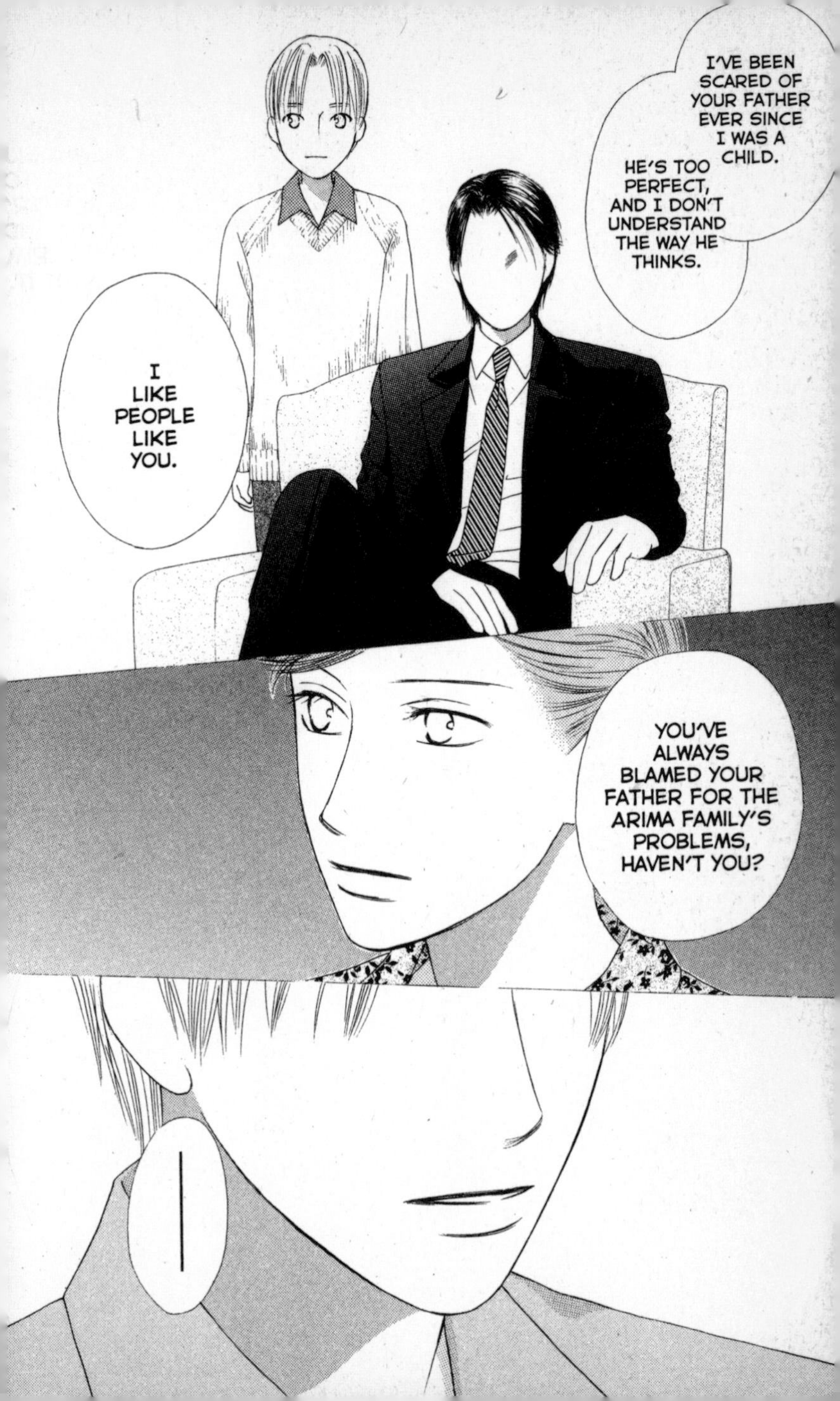
I'VE BEEN SCARED OF YOUR FATHER EVER SINCE I WAS A CHILD.
HE'S TOO PERFECT, AND I DON'T UNDERSTAND THE WAY HE THINKS.
I LIKE PEOPLE LIKE YOU.
YOU'VE ALWAYS BLAMED YOUR FATHER FOR THE ARIMA FAMILY'S PROBLEMS, HAVEN'T YOU?
—

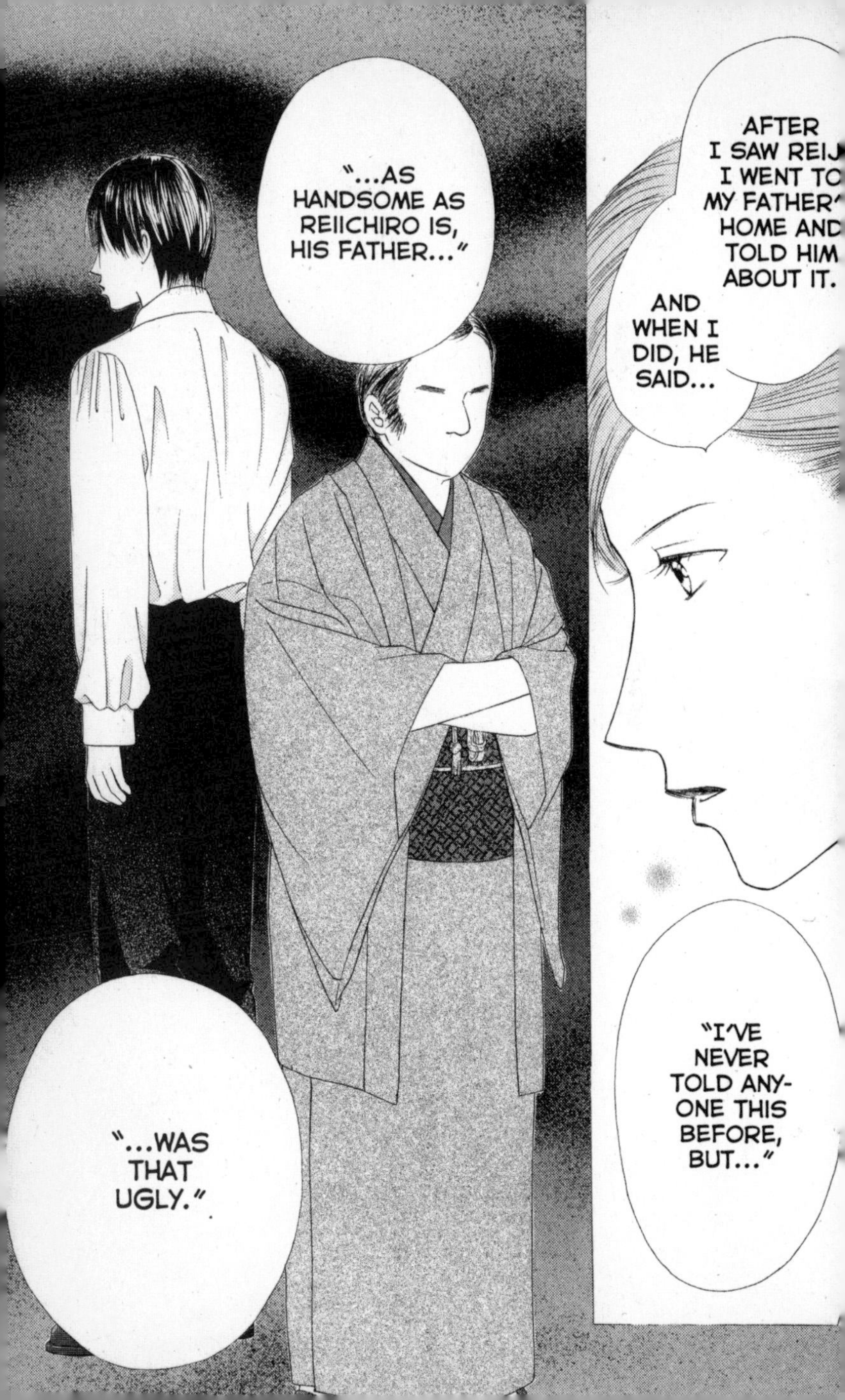
AFTER I SAW REIJ I WENT TO MY FATHER' HOME AND TOLD HIM ABOUT IT.
AND WHEN I DID, HE SAID...
“I'VE NEVER TOLD ANY-ONE THIS BEFORE, BUT...”
“...AS HANDSOME AS REIICHIRO IS, HIS FATHER...”
“...WAS THAT UGLY.”

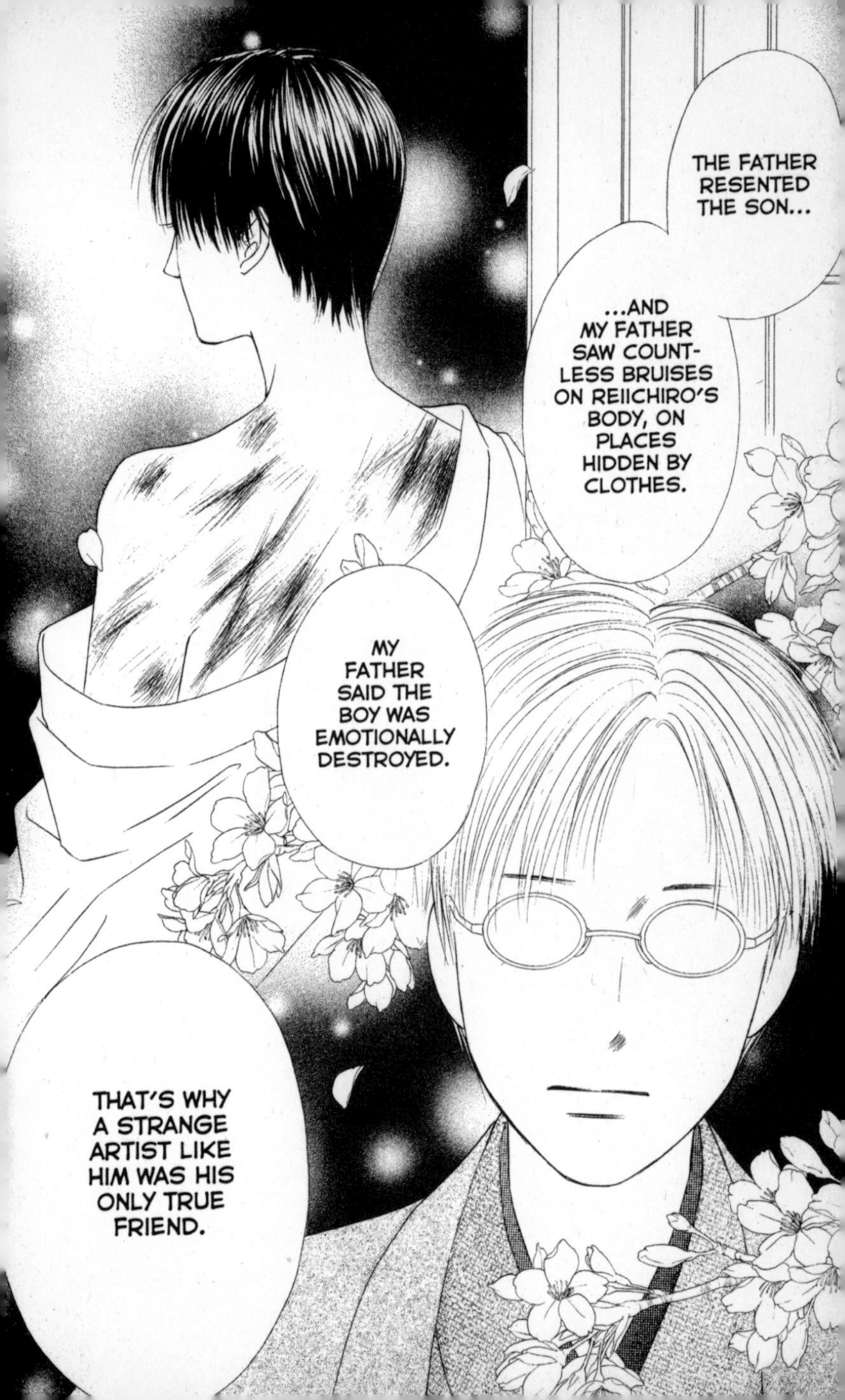
THE FATHER RESENTED THE SON...
...AND MY FATHER SAW COUNT-LESS BRUISES ON REIICHIRO'S BODY, ON PLACES HIDDEN BY CLOTHES.
MY FATHER SAID THE BOY WAS EMOTIONALLY DESTROYED.
THAT'S WHY A STRANGE ARTIST LIKE HIM WAS HIS ONLY TRUE FRIEND.

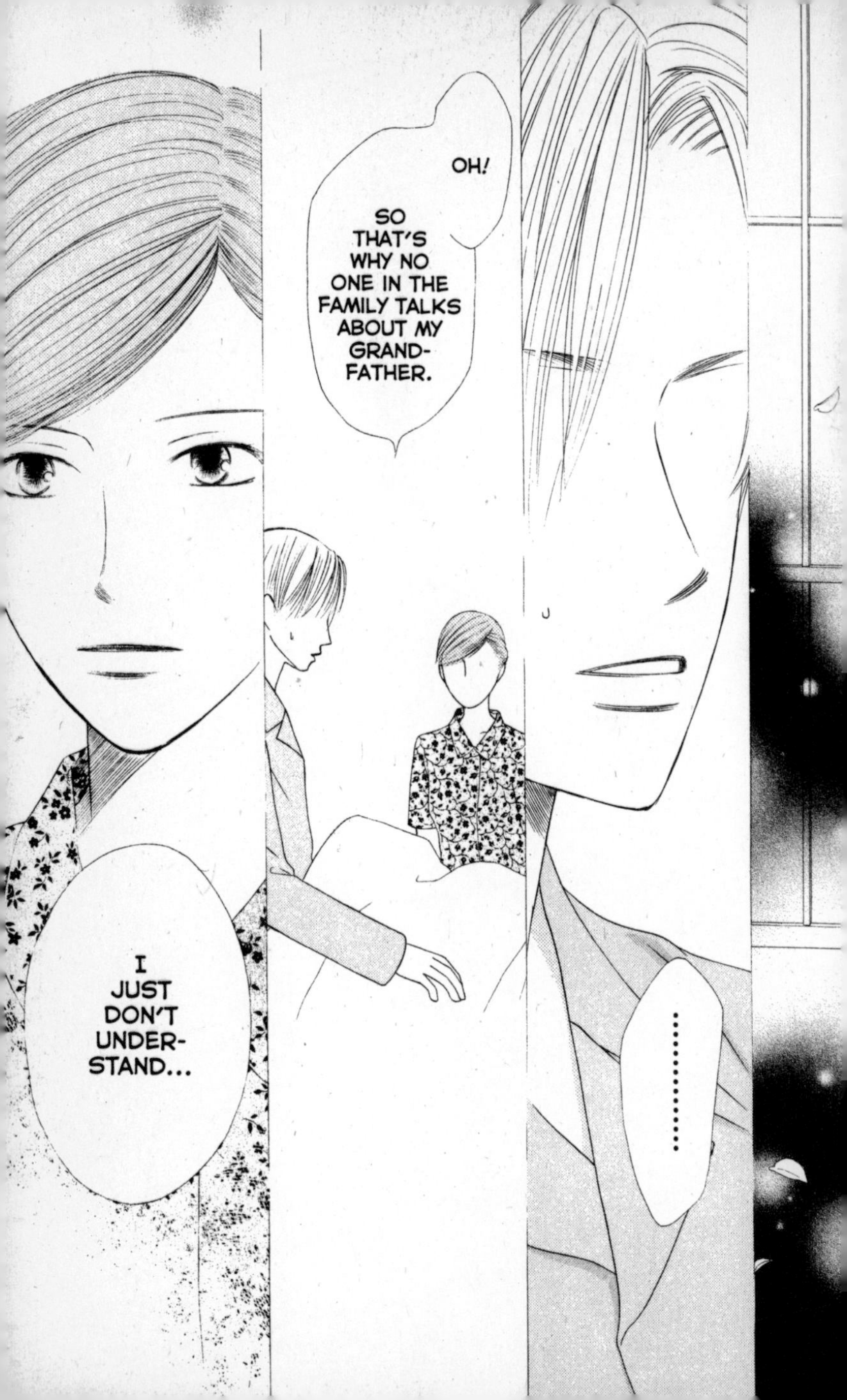
....
OH!
SO THAT'S WHY NO ONE IN THE FAMILY TALKS ABOUT MY GRAND-FATHER.
I JUST DON'T UNDER-STAND...

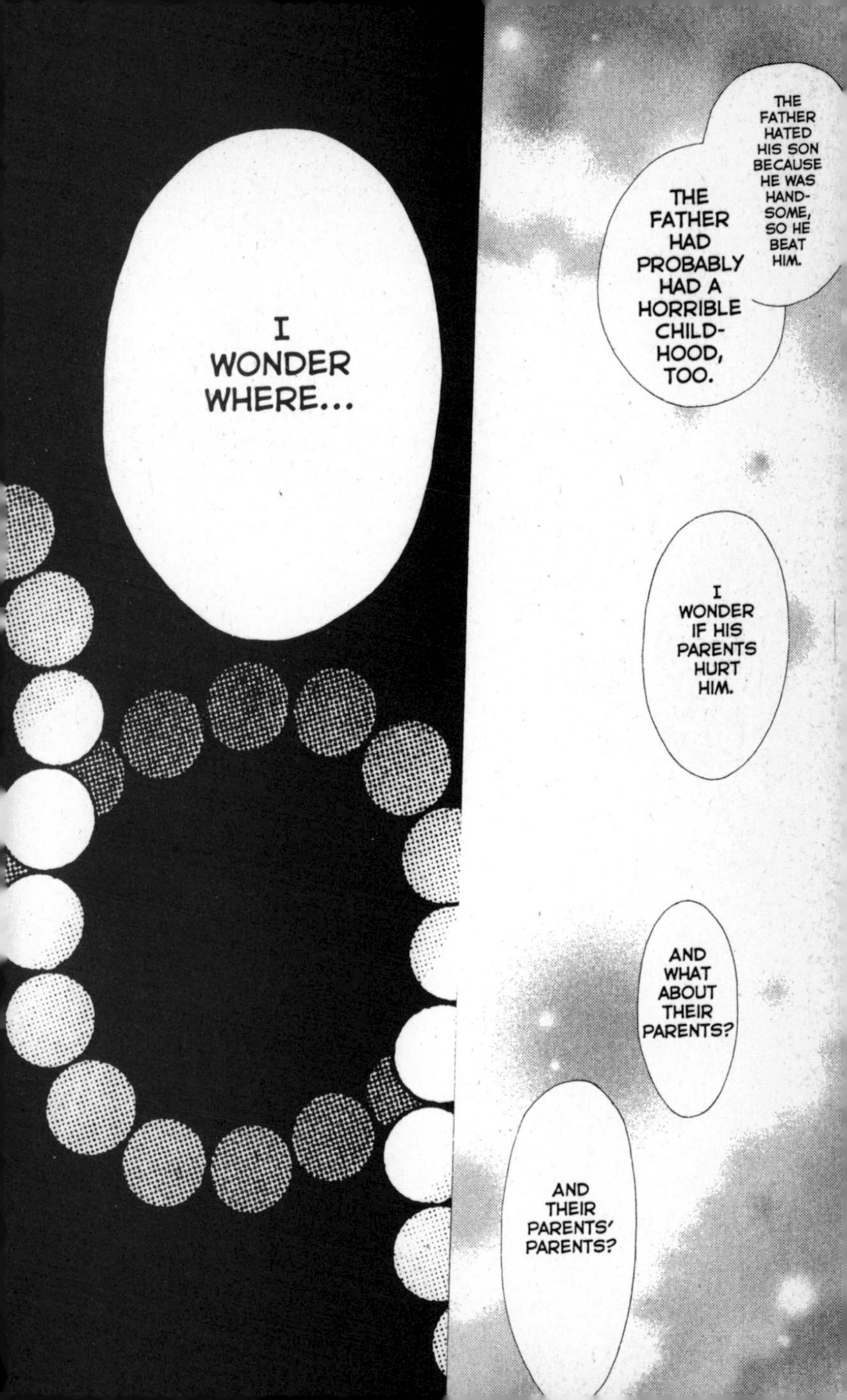
THE FATHER HATED HIS SON BECAUSE HE WAS HANDSOME, SO HE BEAT HIM.
THE FATHER HAD PROBABLY HAD A HORRIBLE CHILDHOOD, TOO.
I WONDER IF HIS PARENTS HURT HIM.
AND WHAT ABOUT THEIR PARENTS?
AND THEIR PARENTS' PARENTS?
I WONDER WHERE...

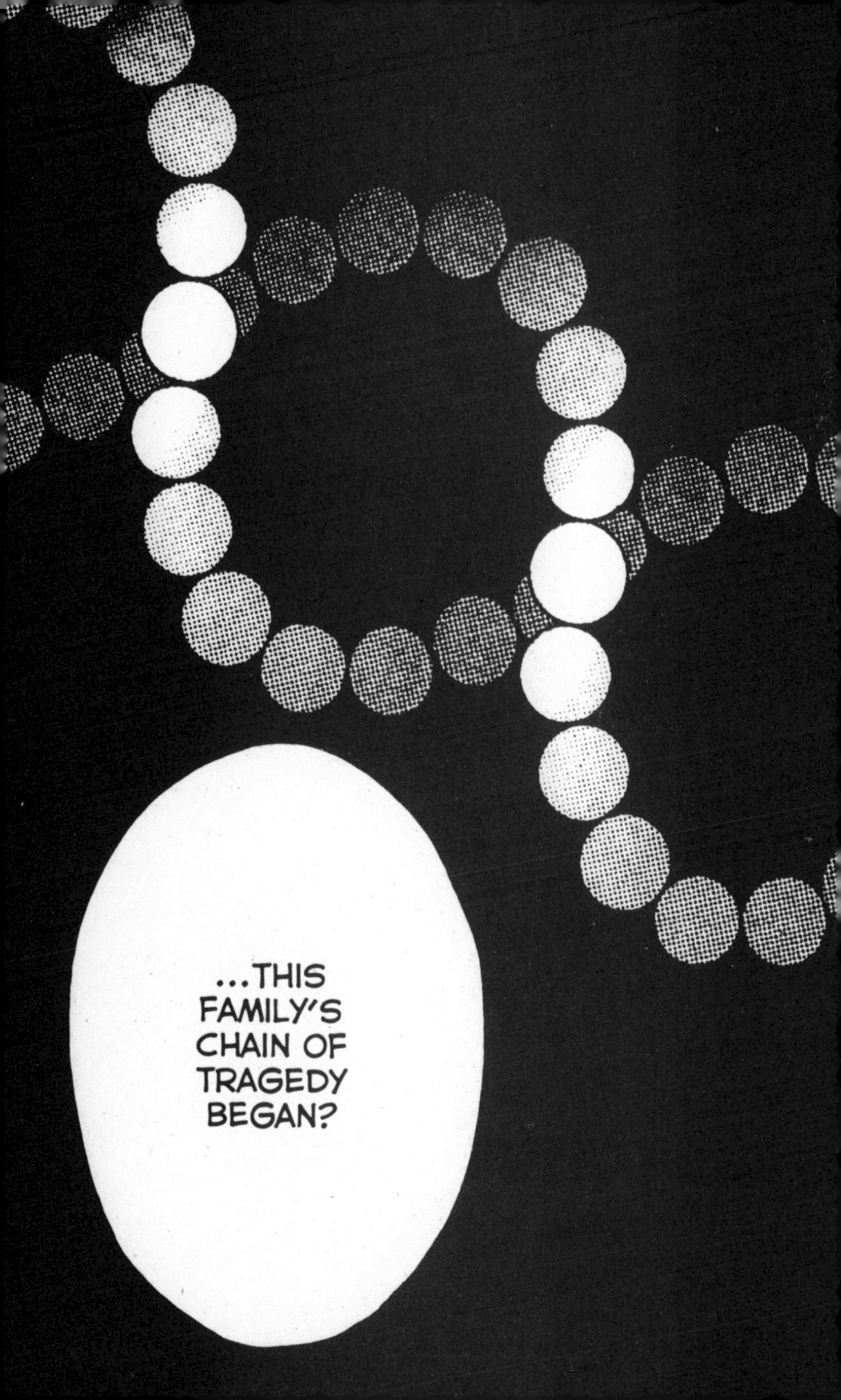
...THIS FAMILY'S CHAIN OF TRAGEDY BEGAN?

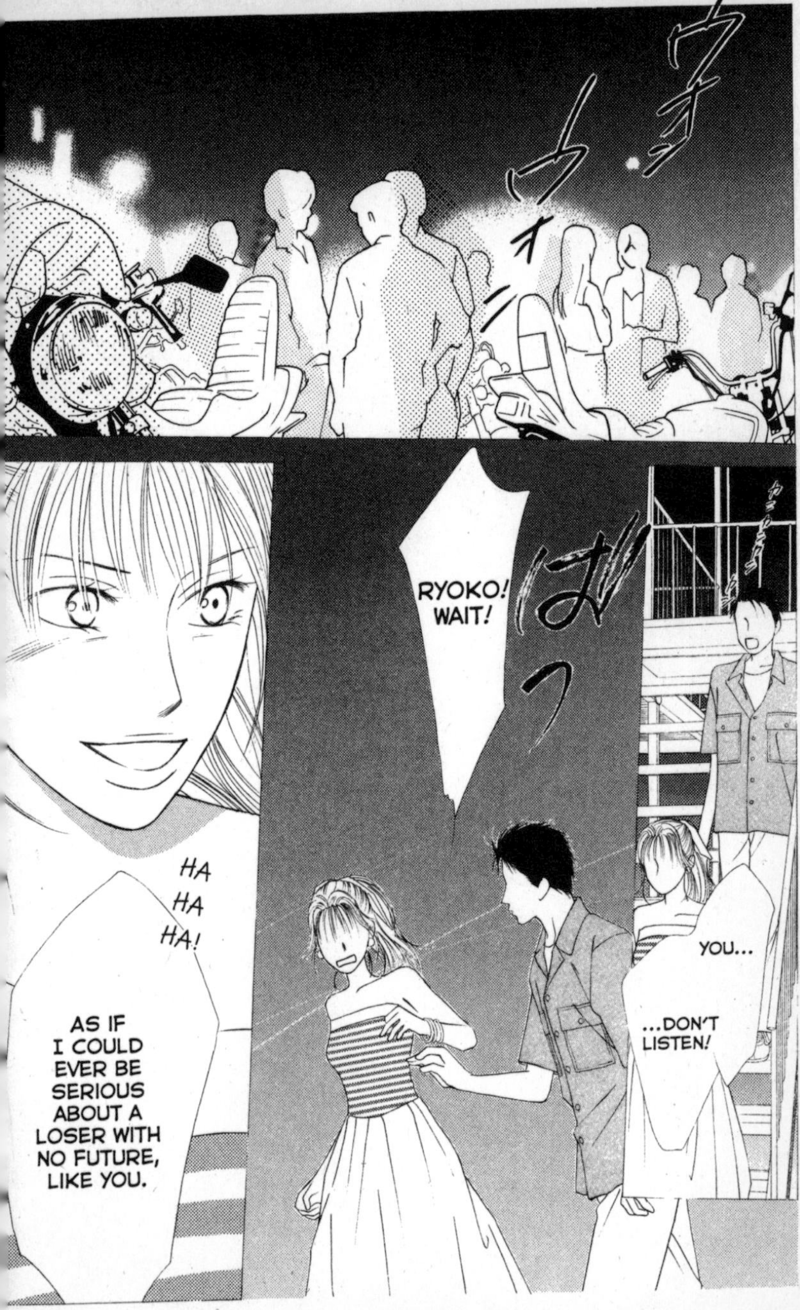
YOU...
...DON'T LISTEN!
RYOKO! WAIT!
HA HA HA!
AS IF I COULD EVER BE SERIOUS ABOUT A LOSER WITH NO FUTURE, LIKE YOU.

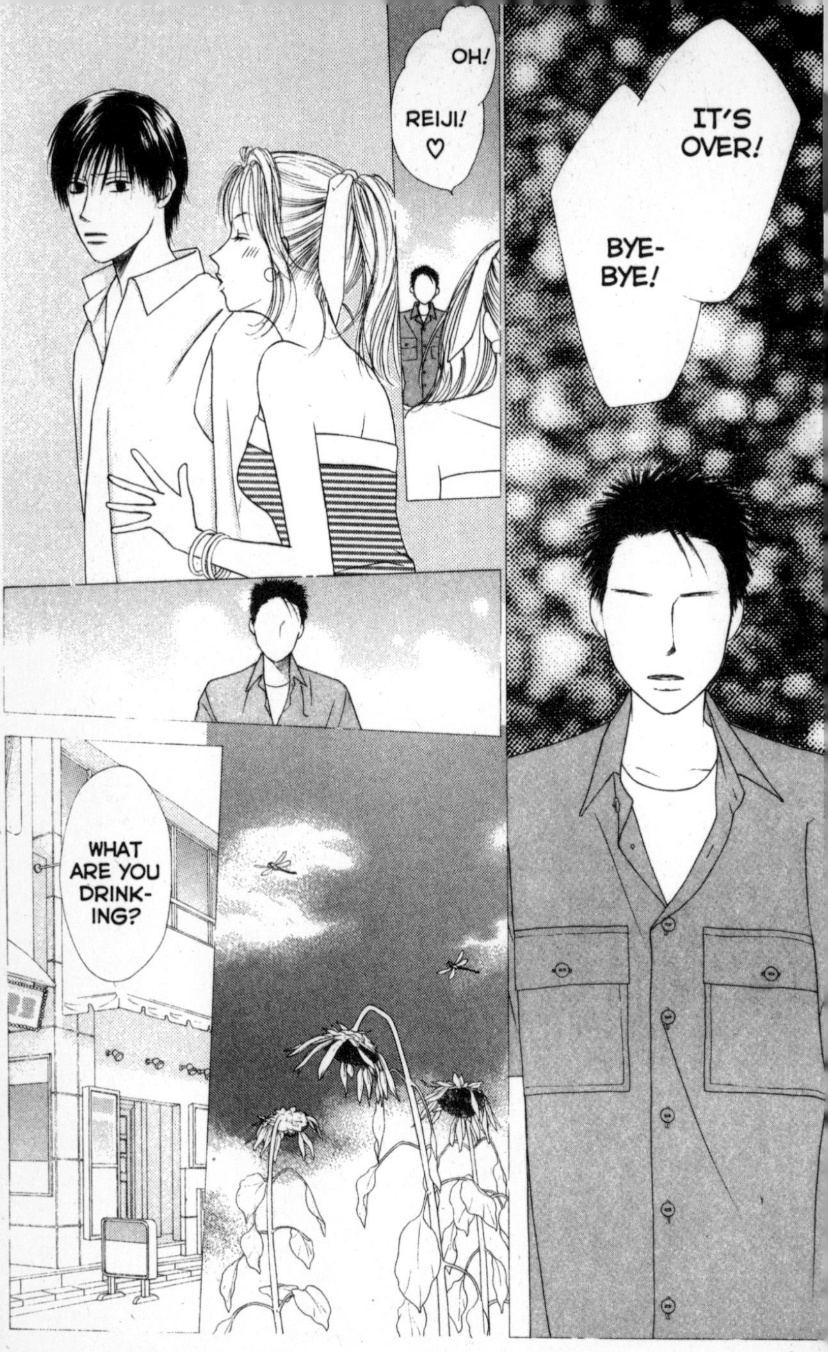
IT'S OVER!
BYE-BYE!
OH!
REIJI! ♡
WHAT ARE YOU DRINK-ING?

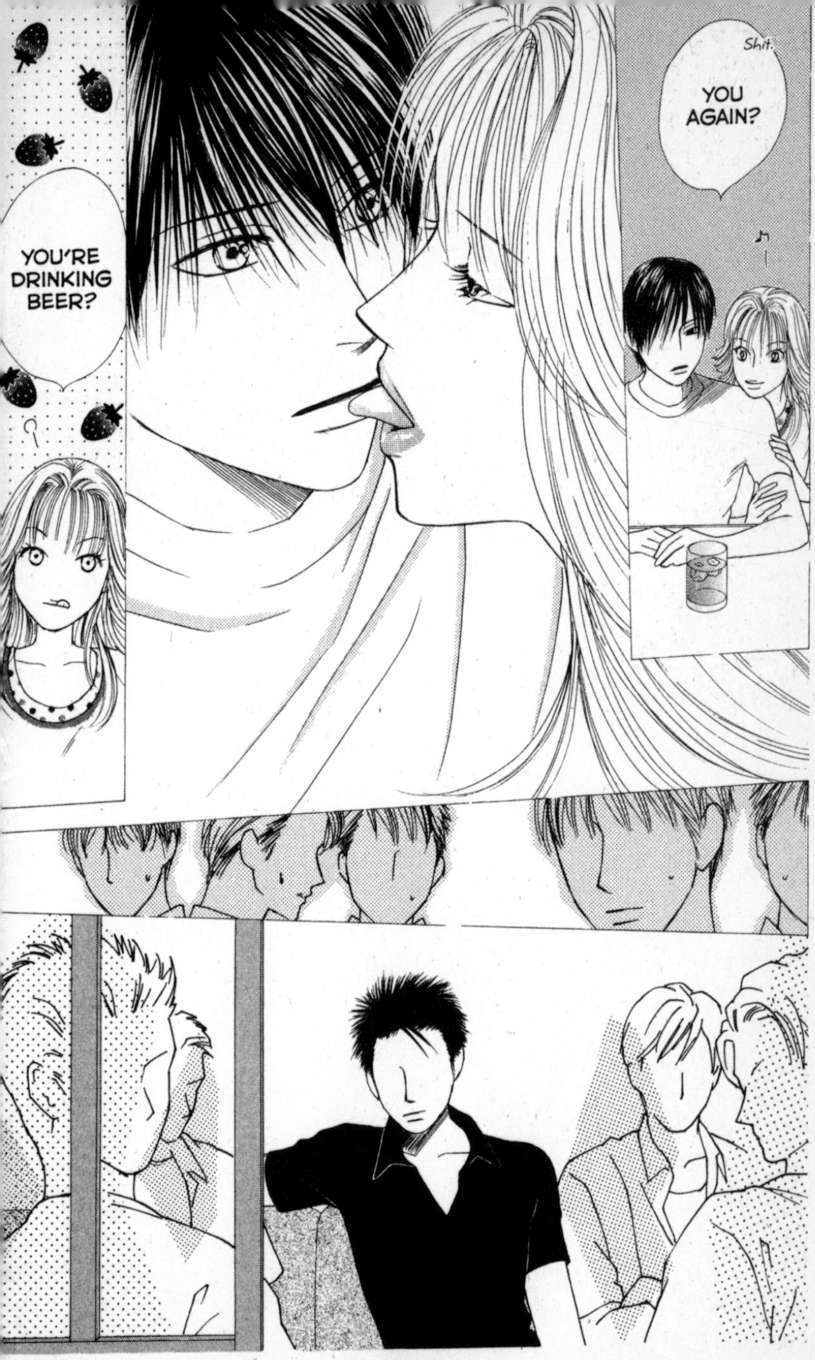
Shit.
YOU AGAIN?
YOU'RE DRINKING BEER?

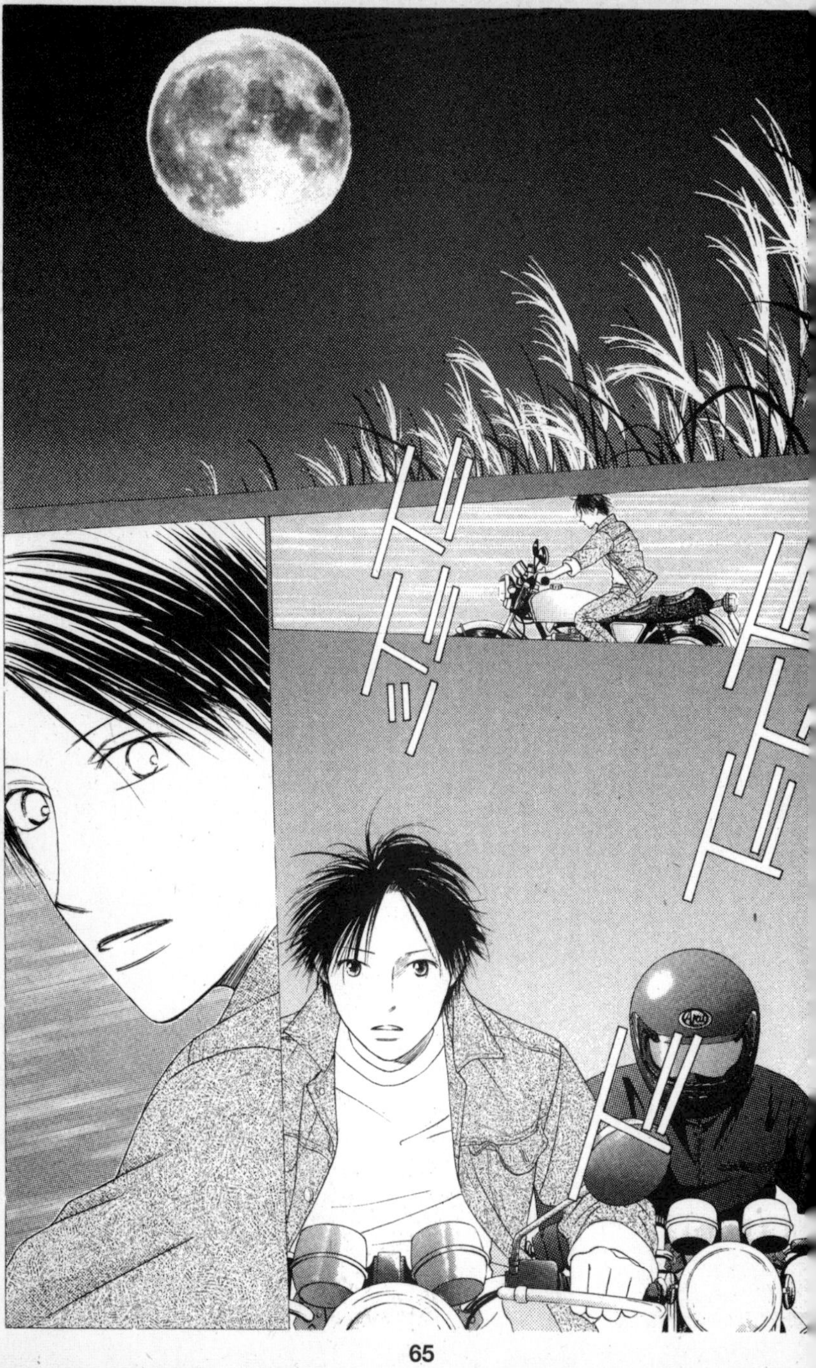
ドドド
ドドッ
ド

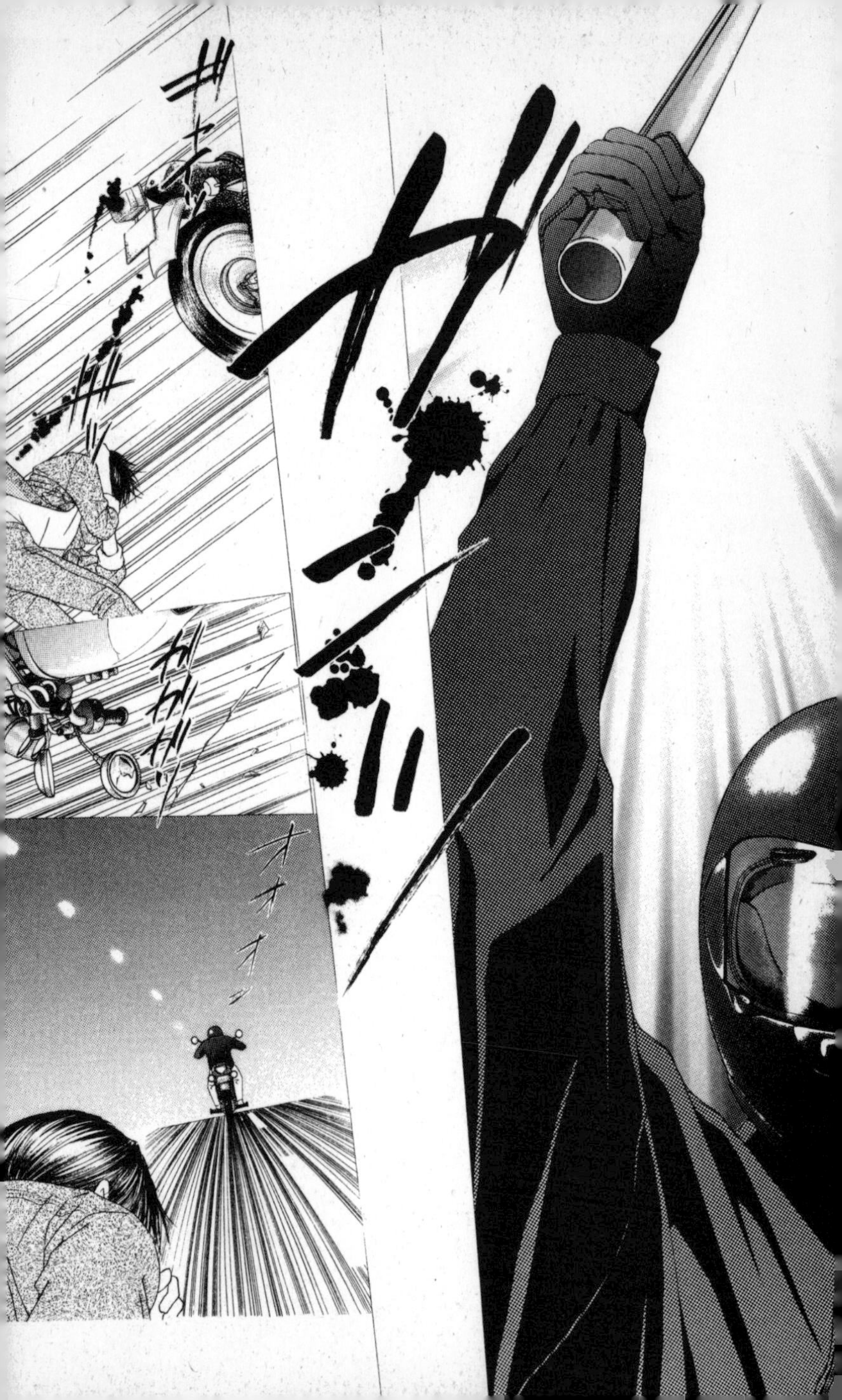
ガガガッ
オオオ

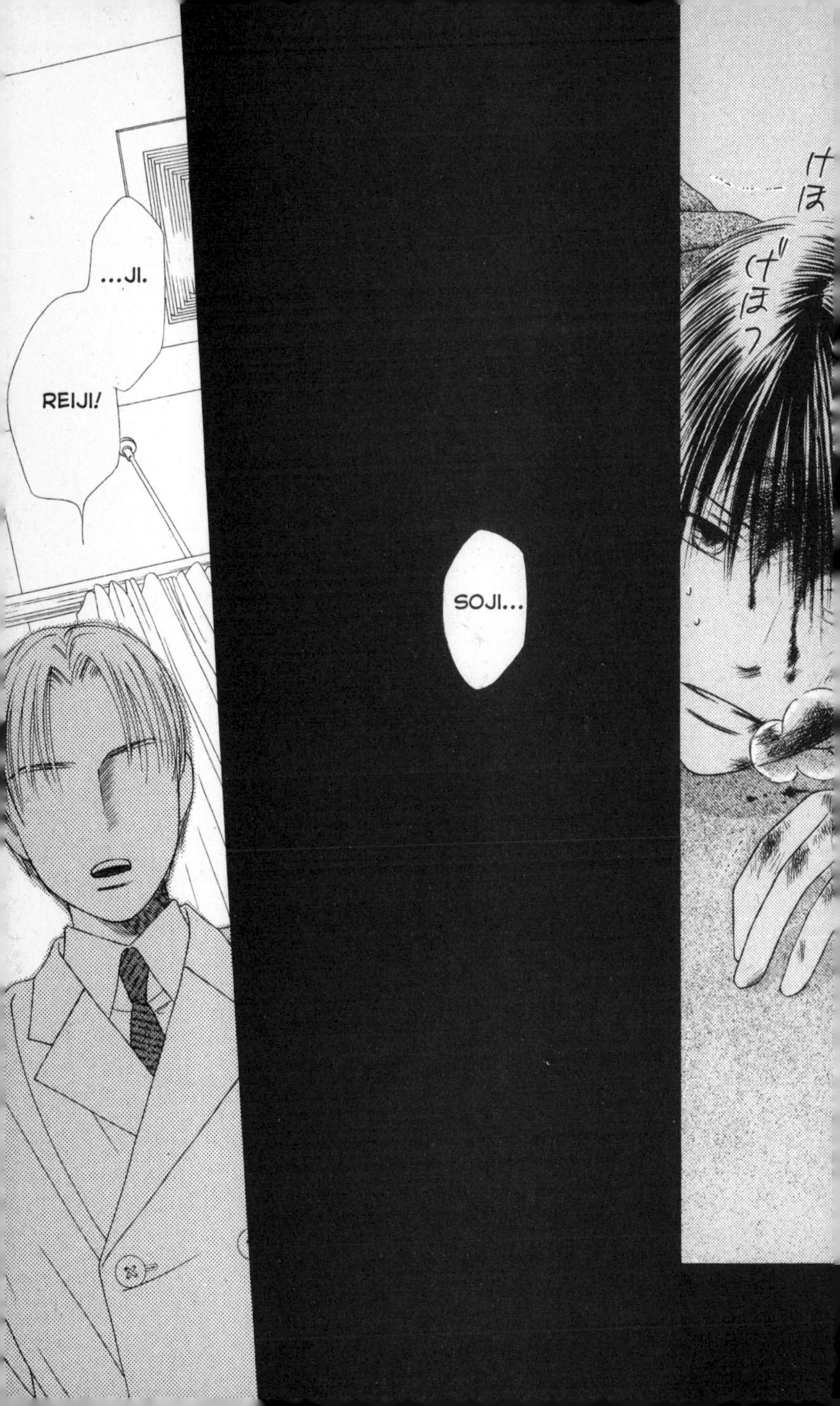
けほ
げほっ
SOJI...
...JI.
REIJI!

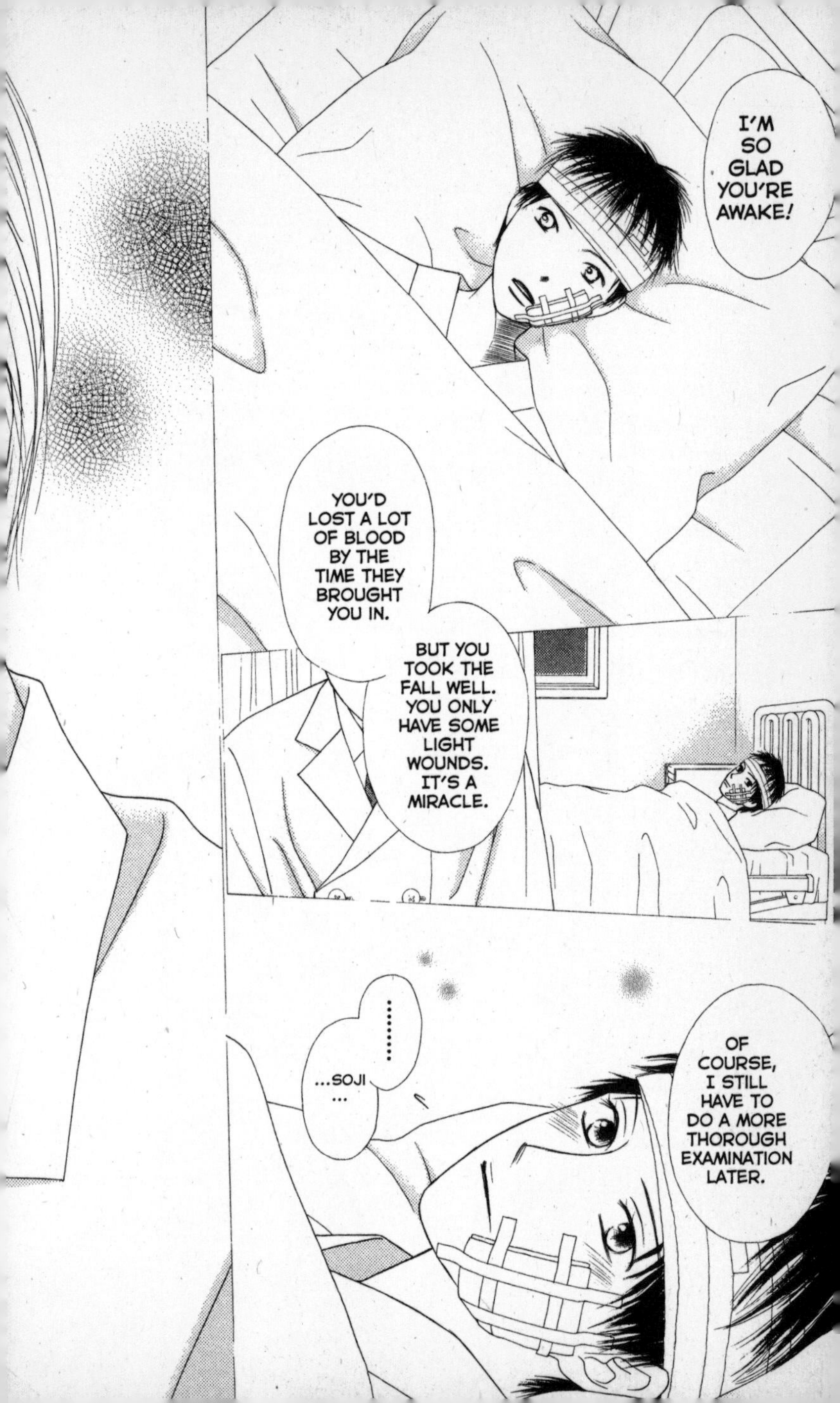
I'M SO GLAD YOU'RE AWAKE!
YOU'D LOST A LOT OF BLOOD BY THE TIME THEY BROUGHT YOU IN.
BUT YOU TOOK THE FALL WELL. YOU ONLY HAVE SOME LIGHT WOUNDS. IT'S A MIRACLE.
OF COURSE, I STILL HAVE TO DO A MORE THOROUGH EXAMINATION LATER.
....
...SOJI...

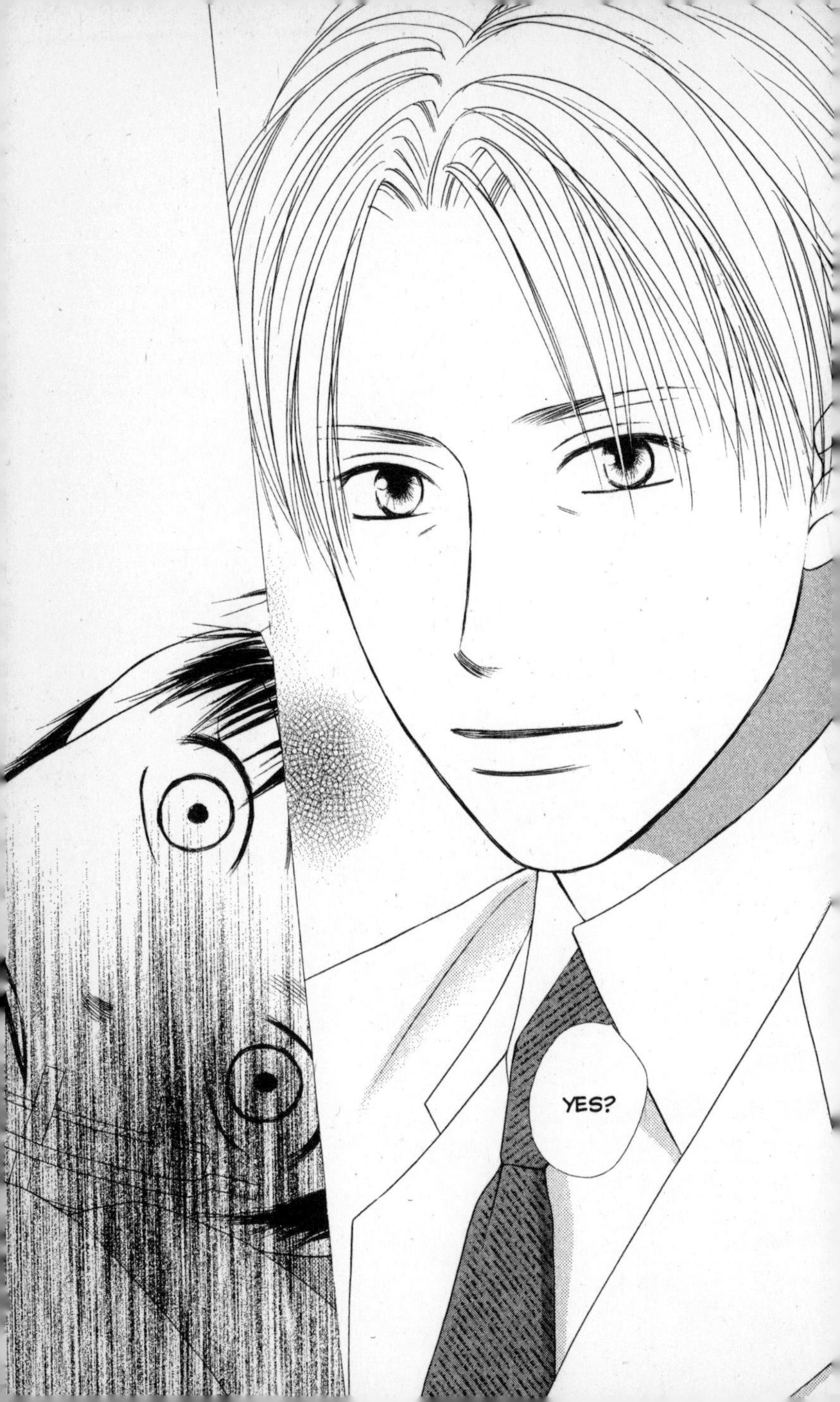
YES?

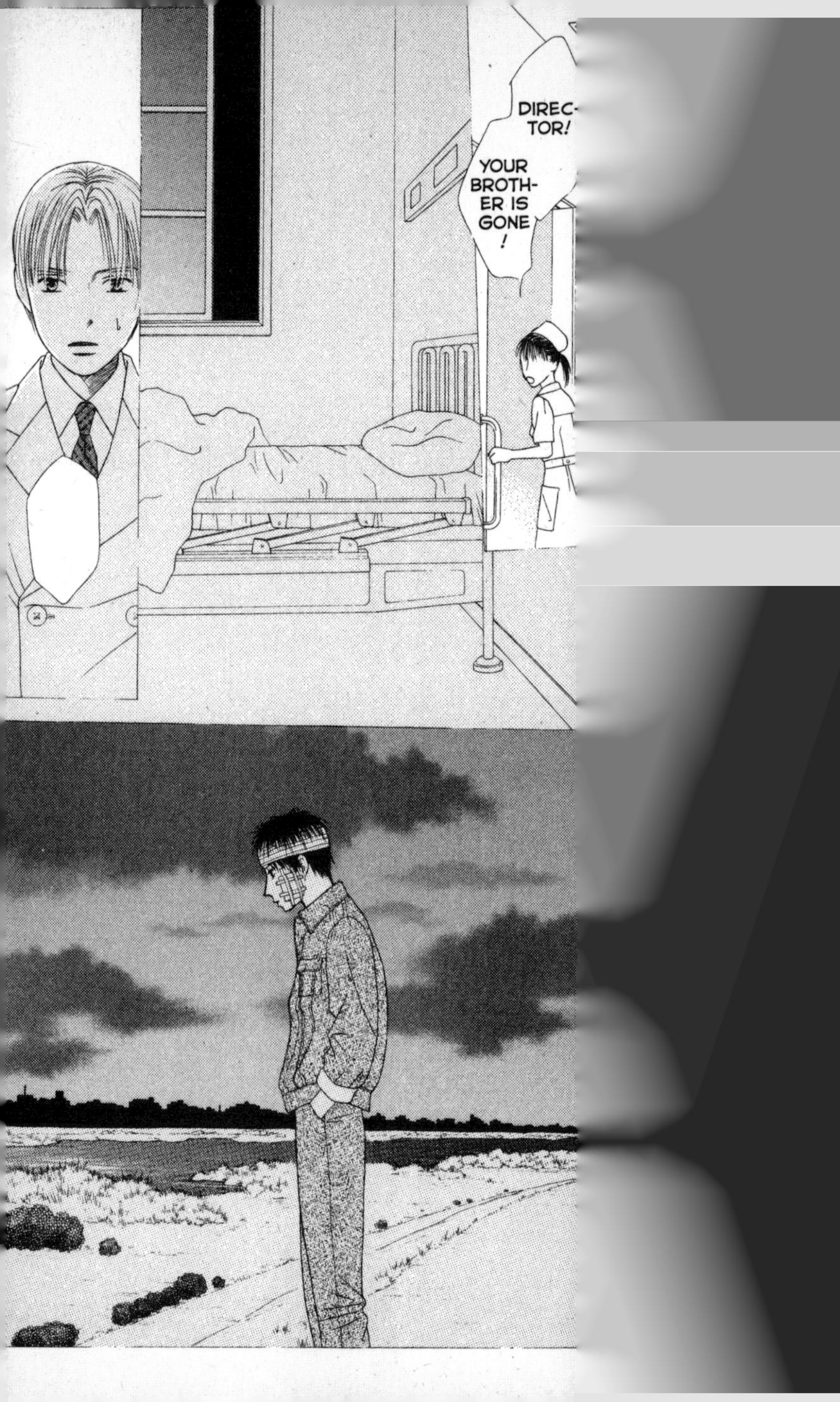
DIRECTOR!
YOUR BROTHER IS GONE!

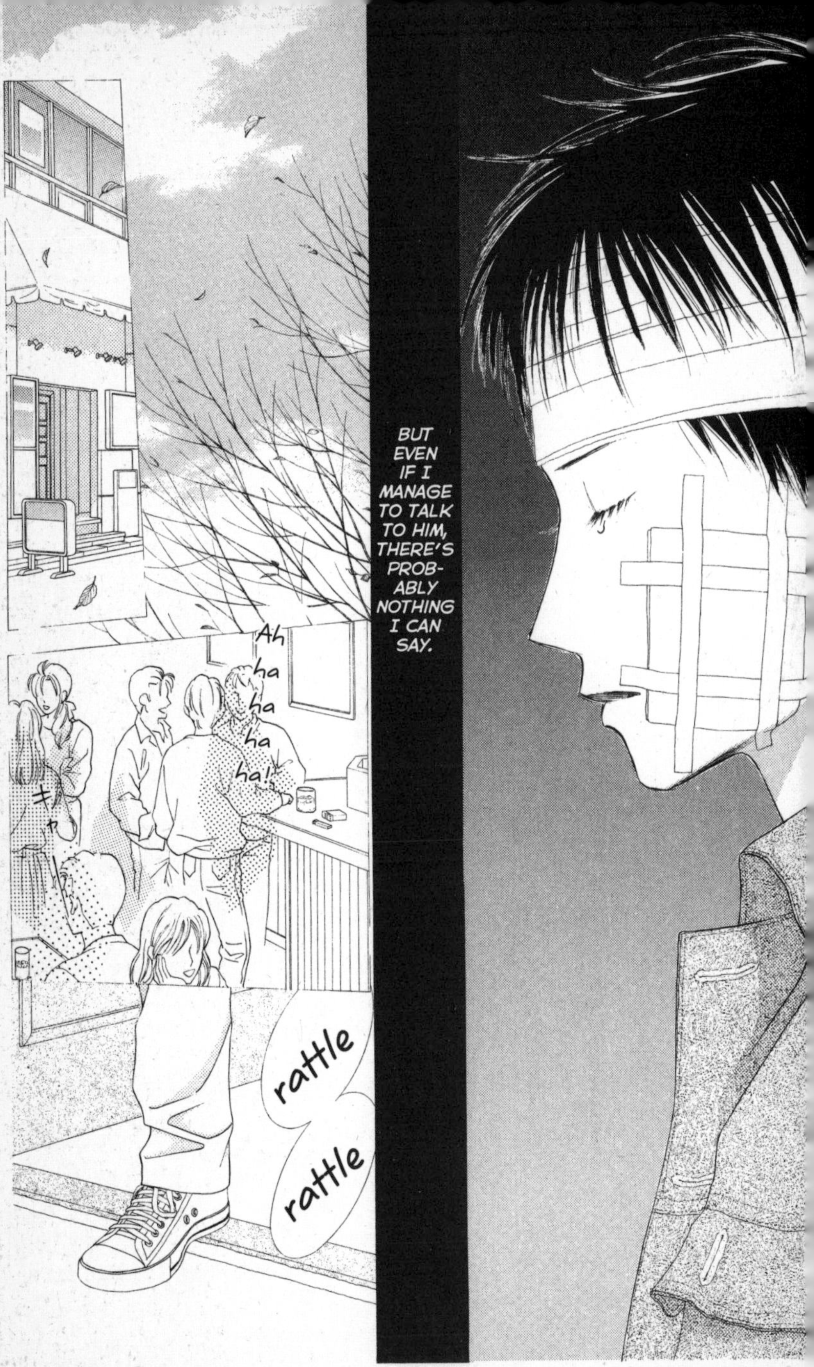
BUT EVEN IF I MANAGE TO TALK TO HIM, THERE'S PROBABLY NOTHING I CAN SAY.
Ah ha ha ha ha!
キャー
rattle
rattle

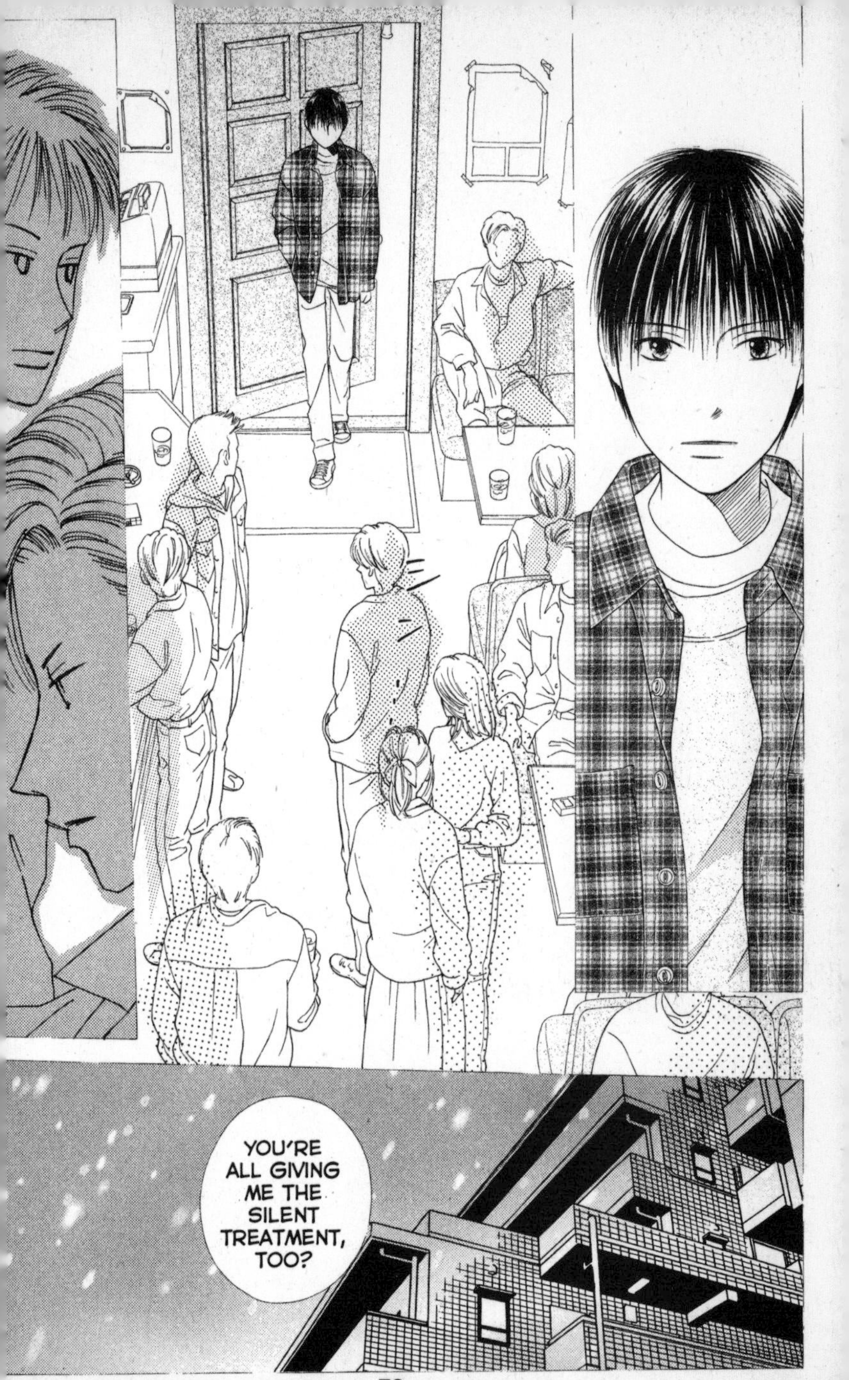
YOU'RE ALL GIVING ME THE SILENT TREATMENT, TOO?

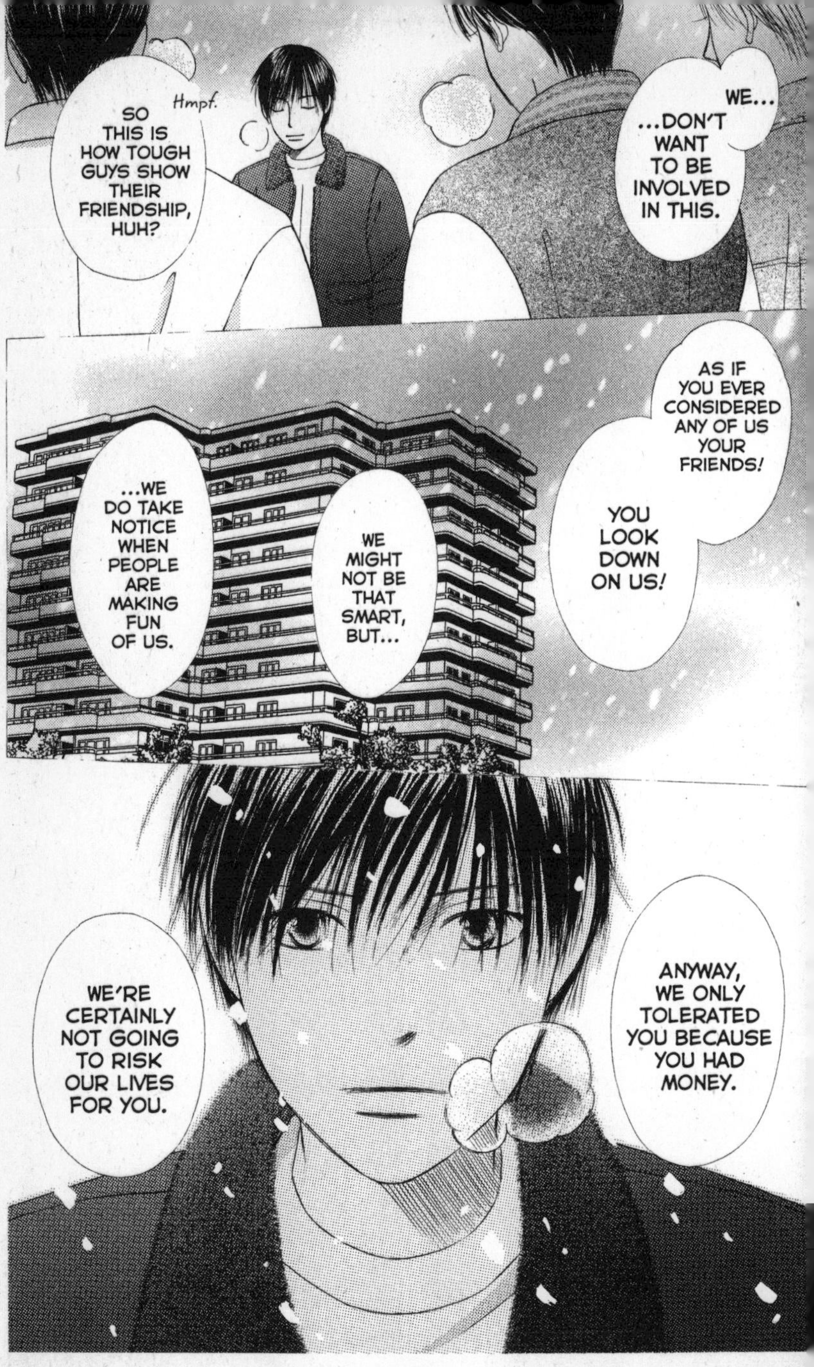
WE...
...DON'T WANT TO BE INVOLVED IN THIS.
Hmpf.
SO THIS IS HOW TOUGH GUYS SHOW THEIR FRIENDSHIP, HUH?
AS IF YOU EVER CONSIDERED ANY OF US YOUR FRIENDS!
YOU LOOK DOWN ON US!
WE MIGHT NOT BE THAT SMART, BUT...
...WE DO TAKE NOTICE WHEN PEOPLE ARE MAKING FUN OF US.
ANYWAY, WE ONLY TOLERATED YOU BECAUSE YOU HAD MONEY.
WE'RE CERTAINLY NOT GOING TO RISK OUR LIVES FOR YOU.

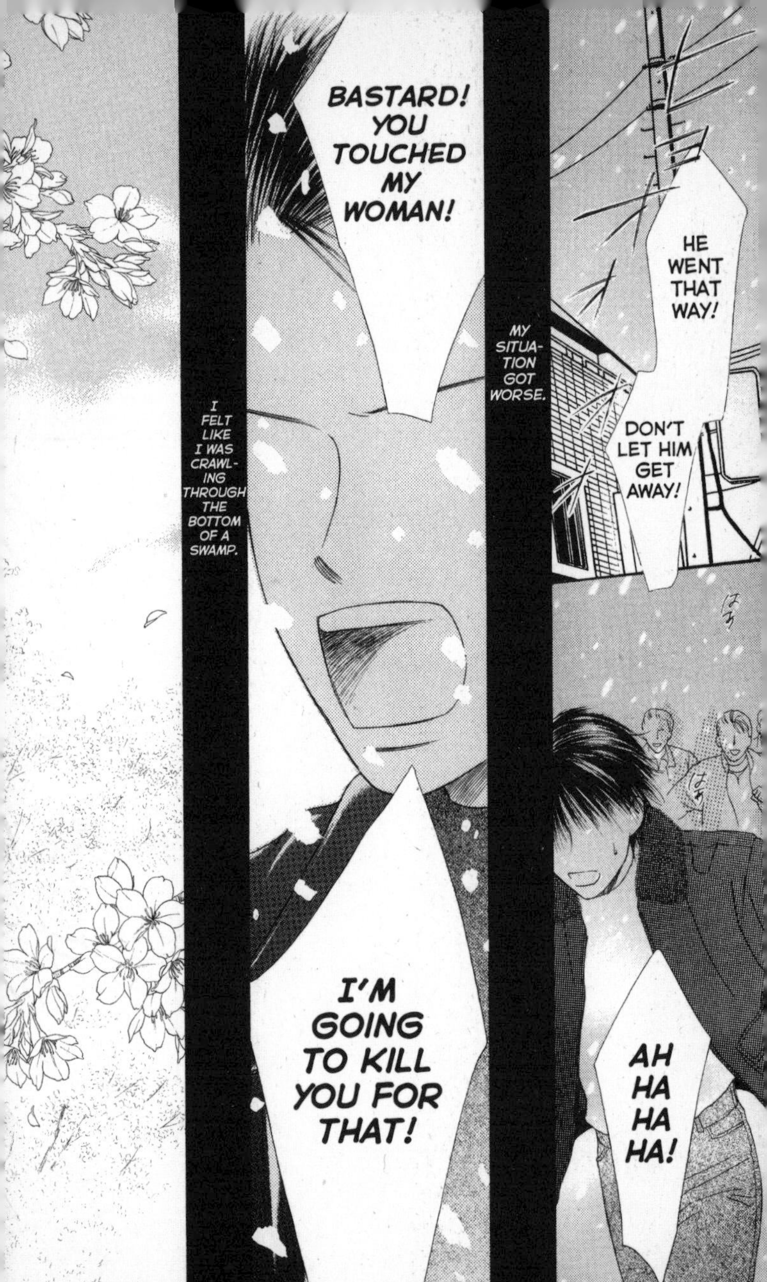
HE WENT THAT WAY!
DON'T LET HIM GET AWAY!
AH HA HA HA!
MY SITUATION GOT WORSE.
BASTARD! YOU TOUCHED MY WOMAN!
I'M GOING TO KILL YOU FOR THAT!
I FELT LIKE I WAS CRAWLING THROUGH THE BOTTOM OF A SWAMP.

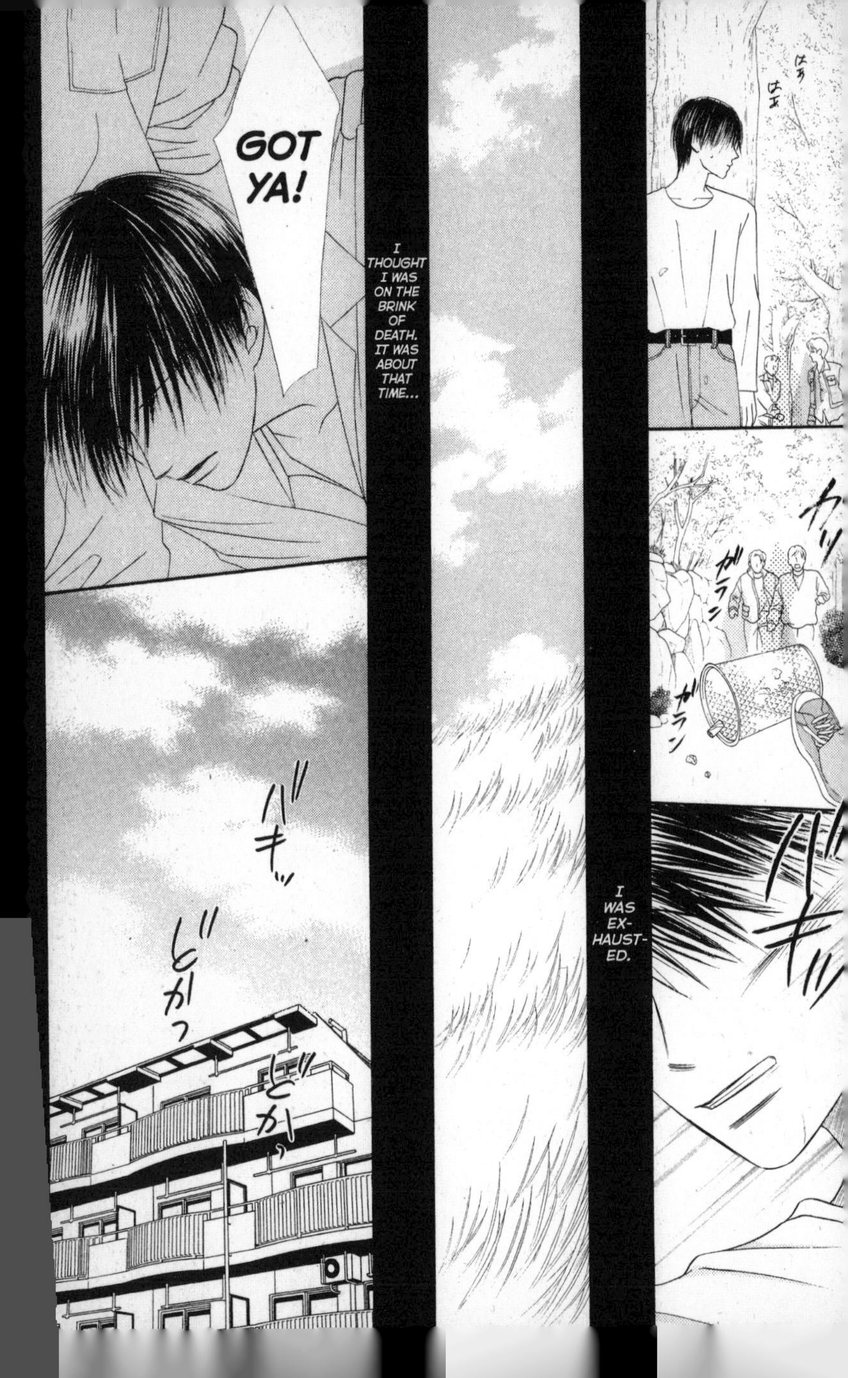
はぁ
はぁ
カッ
ガラン
ガラン
バキッ
I WAS EX-HAUST-ED.
I THOUGHT I WAS ON THE BRINK OF DEATH. IT WAS ABOUT THAT TIME...
GOT YA!
バキッ
どかっ
どかっ

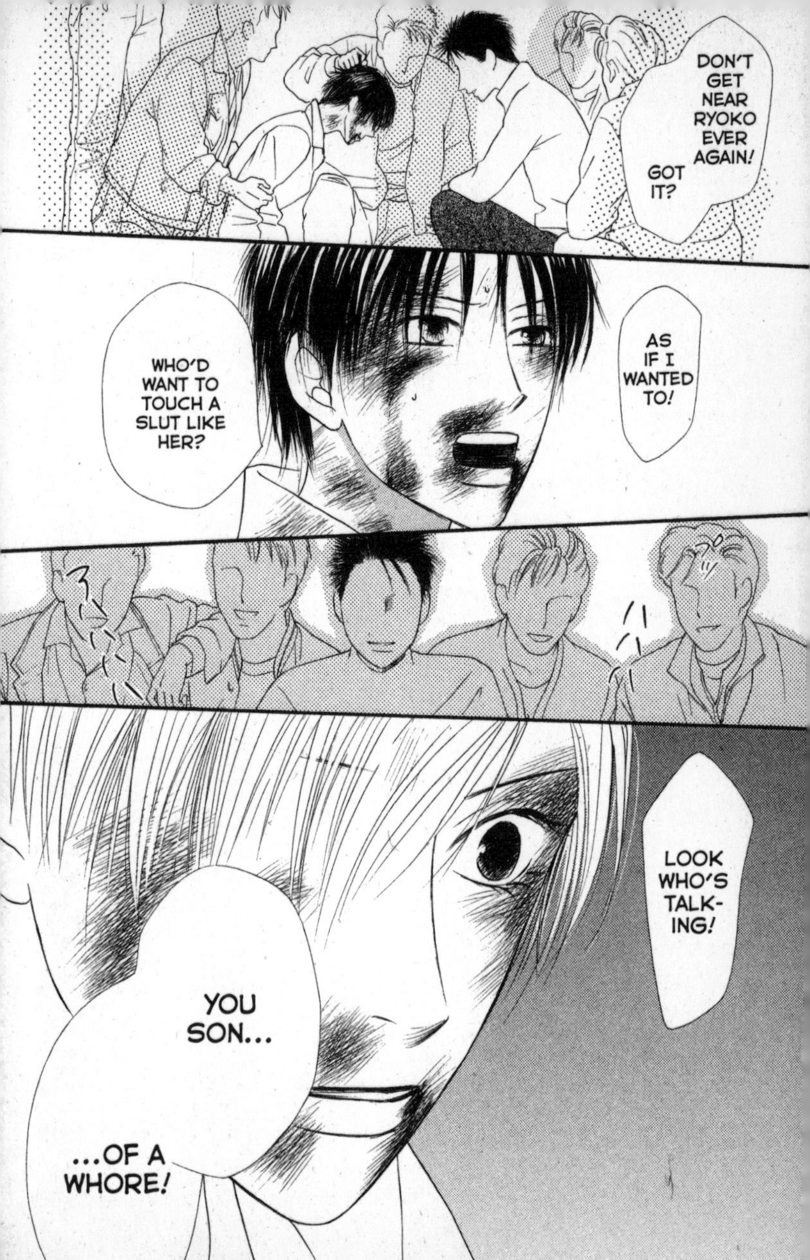
DON'T GET NEAR RYOKO EVER AGAIN!
GOT IT?
AS IF I WANTED TO!
WHO'D WANT TO TOUCH A SLUT LIKE HER?
LOOK WHO'S TALK-ING!
YOU SON...
...OF A WHORE!

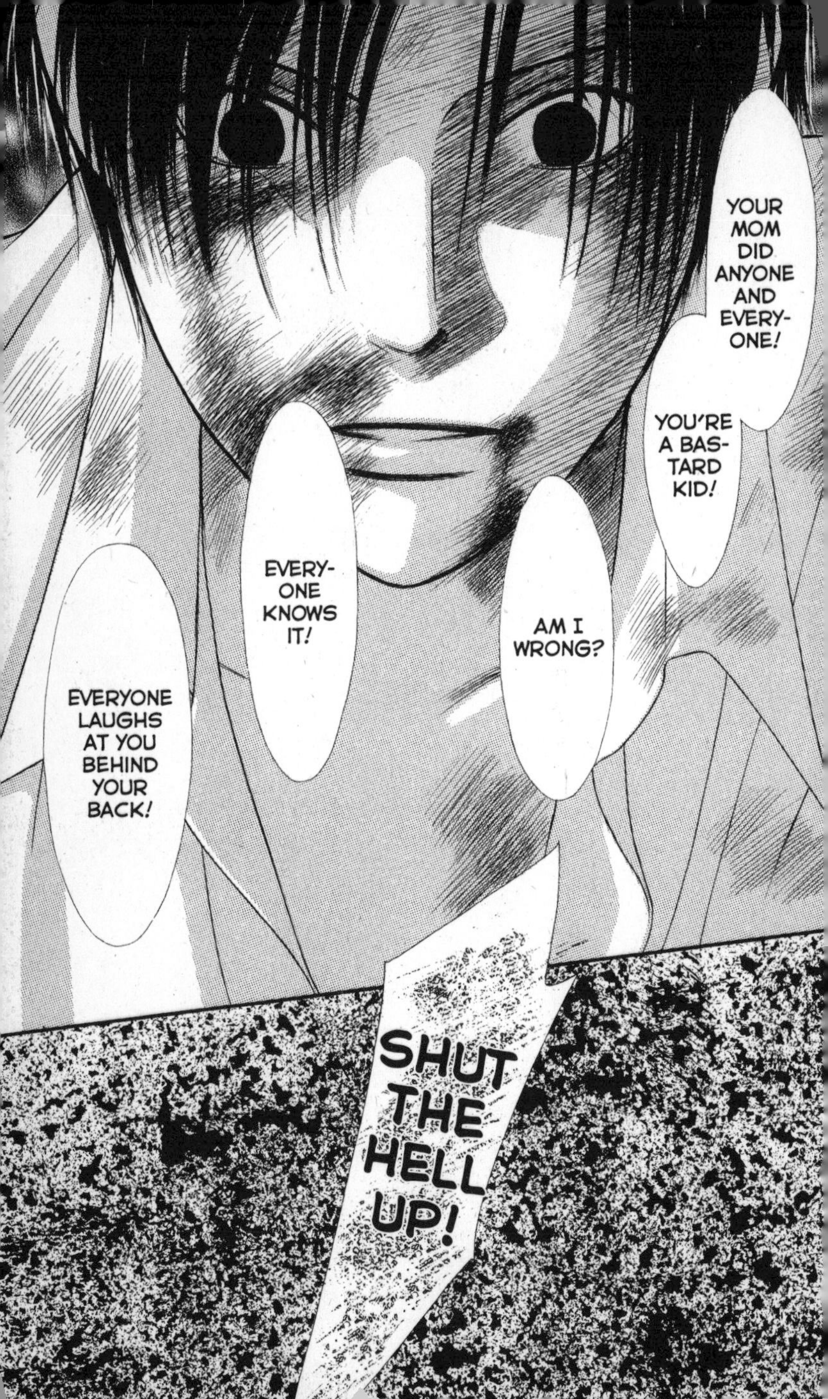
YOUR MOM DID ANYONE AND EVERY-ONE!
YOU'RE A BAS-TARD KID!
AM I WRONG?
EVERY-ONE KNOWS IT!
EVERYONE LAUGHS AT YOU BEHIND YOUR BACK!
SHUT THE HELL UP!

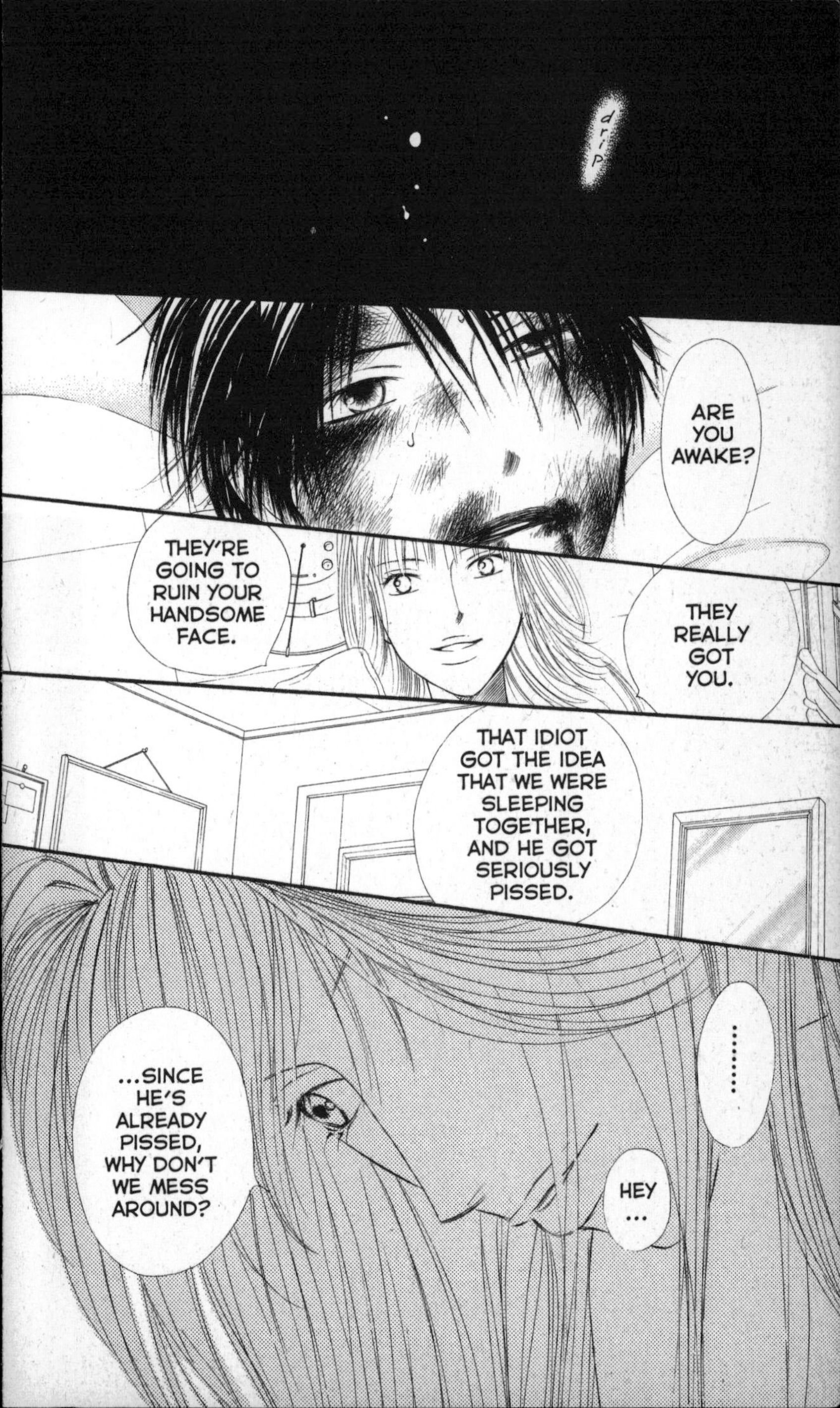
drip
ARE YOU AWAKE?
THEY REALLY GOT YOU.
THEY'RE GOING TO RUIN YOUR HANDSOME FACE.
THAT IDIOT GOT THE IDEA THAT WE WERE SLEEPING TOGETHER, AND HE GOT SERIOUSLY PISSED.
....
HEY ...
...SINCE HE'S ALREADY PISSED, WHY DON'T WE MESS AROUND?

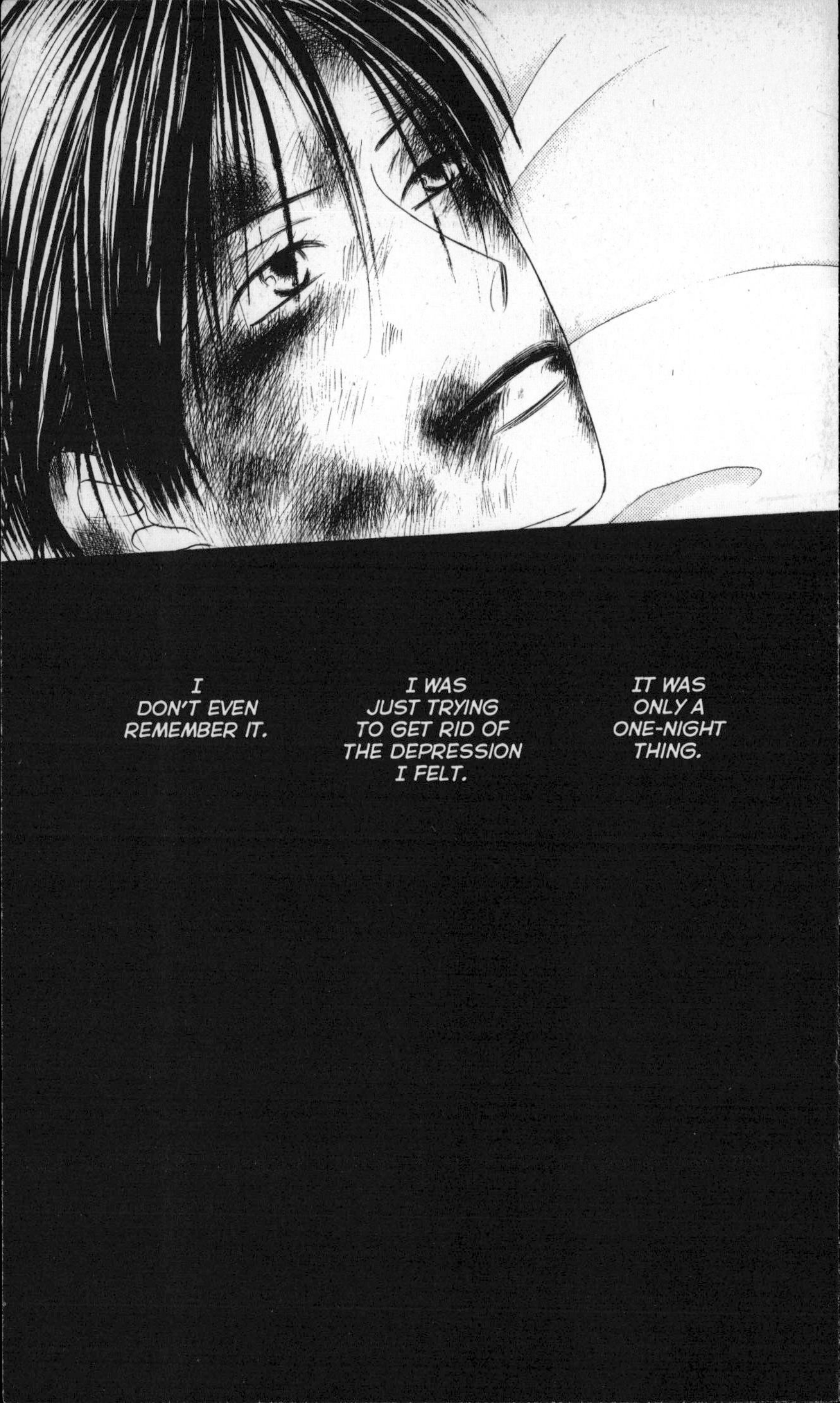
IT WAS ONLY A ONE-NIGHT THING.
I WAS JUST TRYING TO GET RID OF THE DEPRESSION I FELT.
I DON'T EVEN REMEMBER IT.

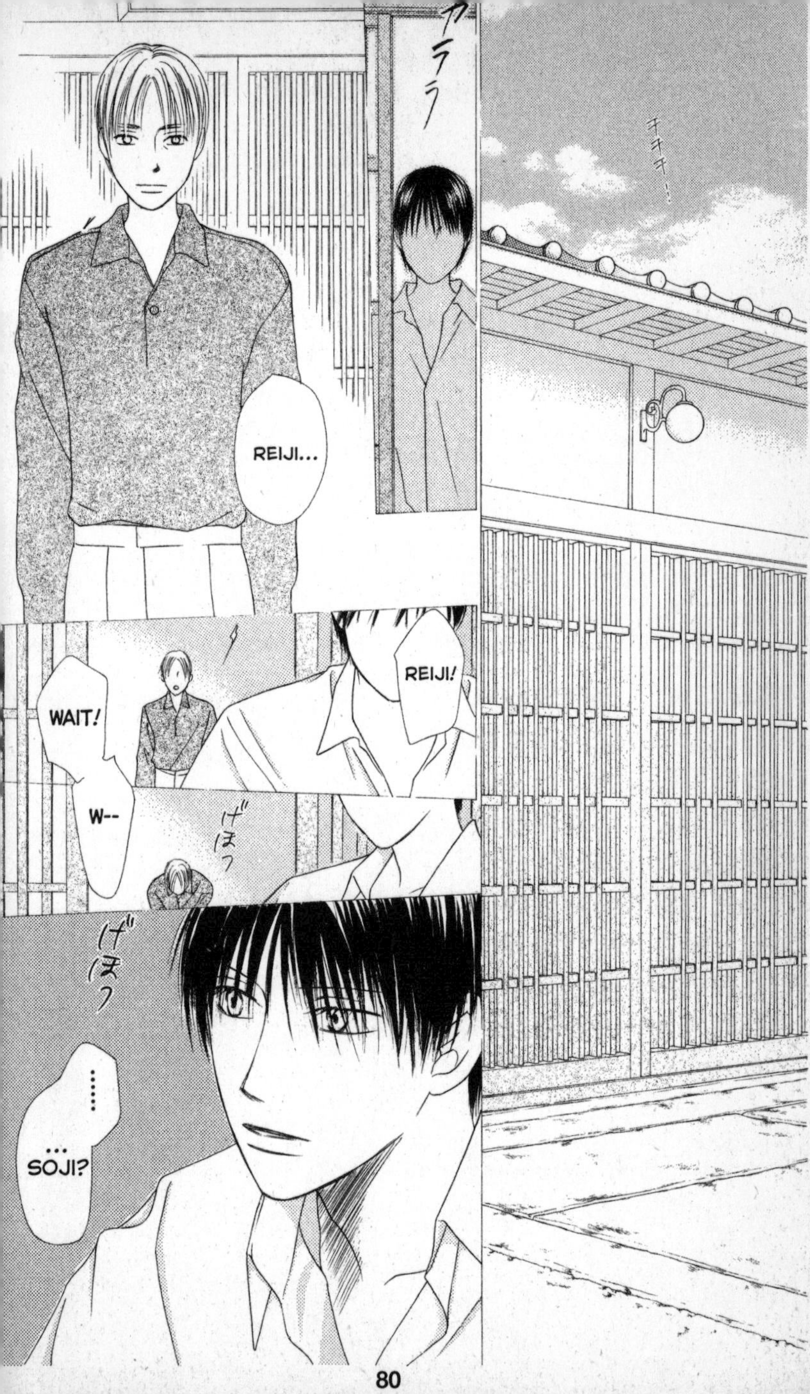
チチチ…
カララ
REIJI...
REIJI!
WAIT!
W--
げほっ
げほっ
......
...SOJI?

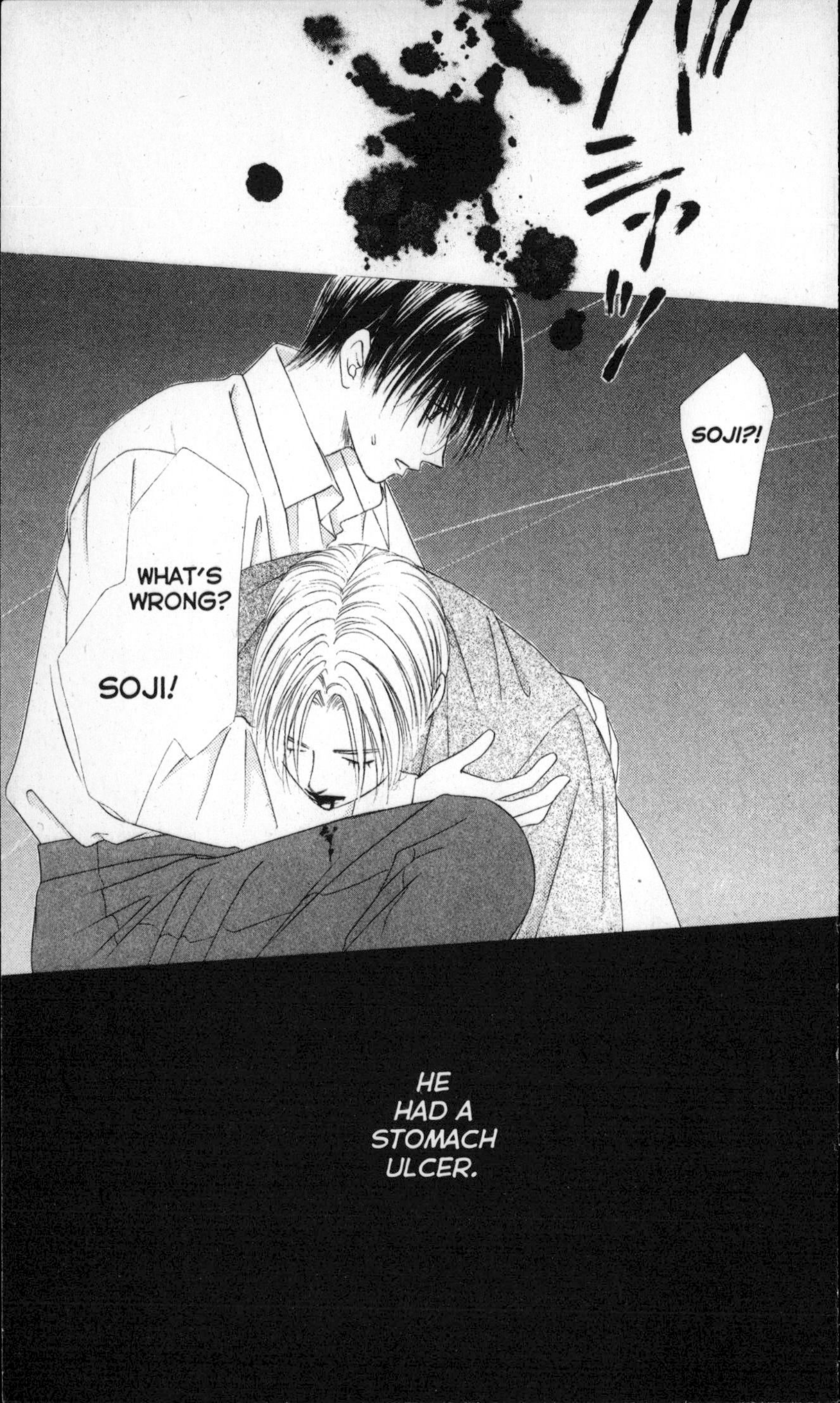
SOJI?!
WHAT'S WRONG?
SOJI!
HE HAD A STOMACH ULCER.

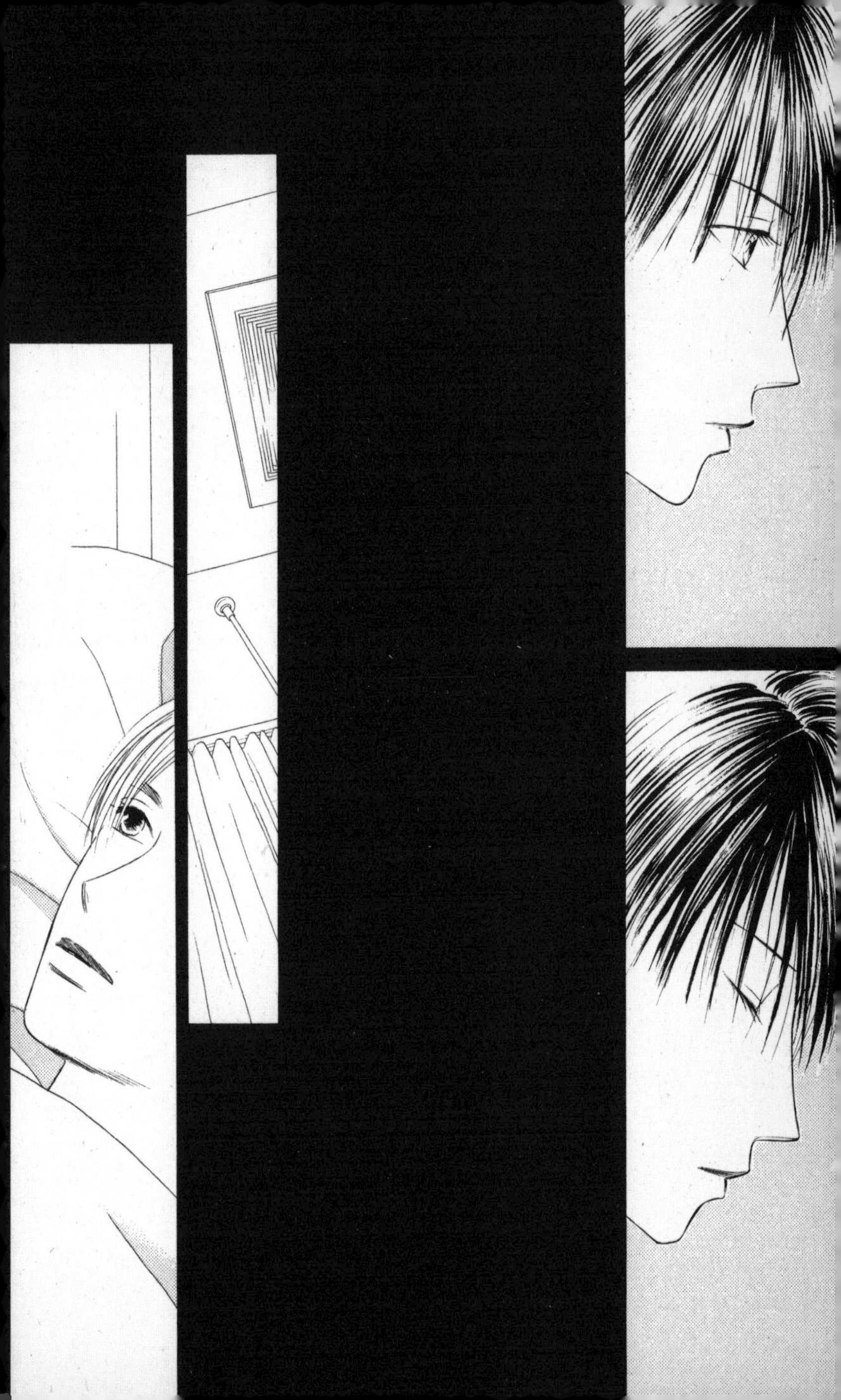

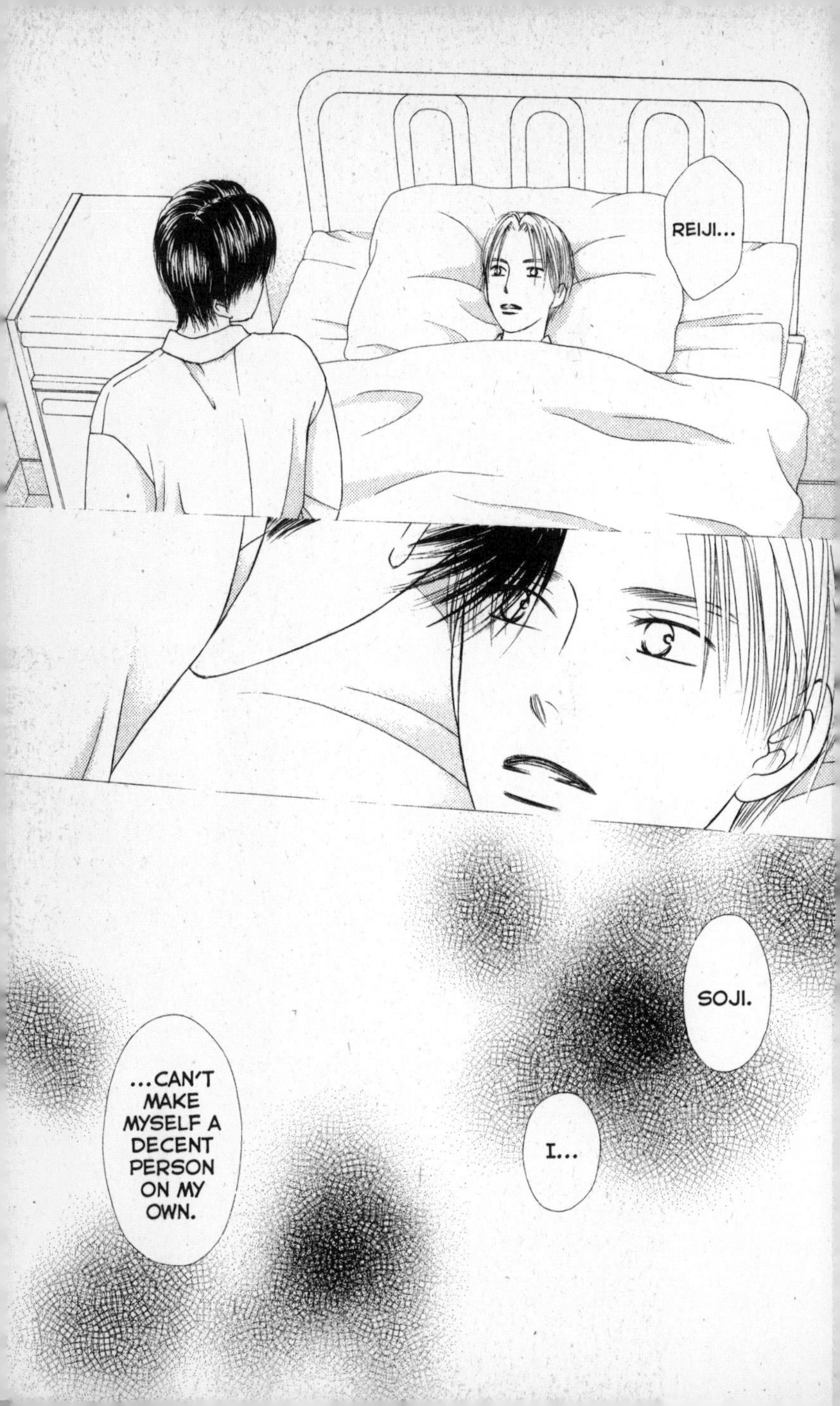
REIJI...
SOJI.
I...
...CAN'T MAKE MYSELF A DECENT PERSON ON MY OWN.

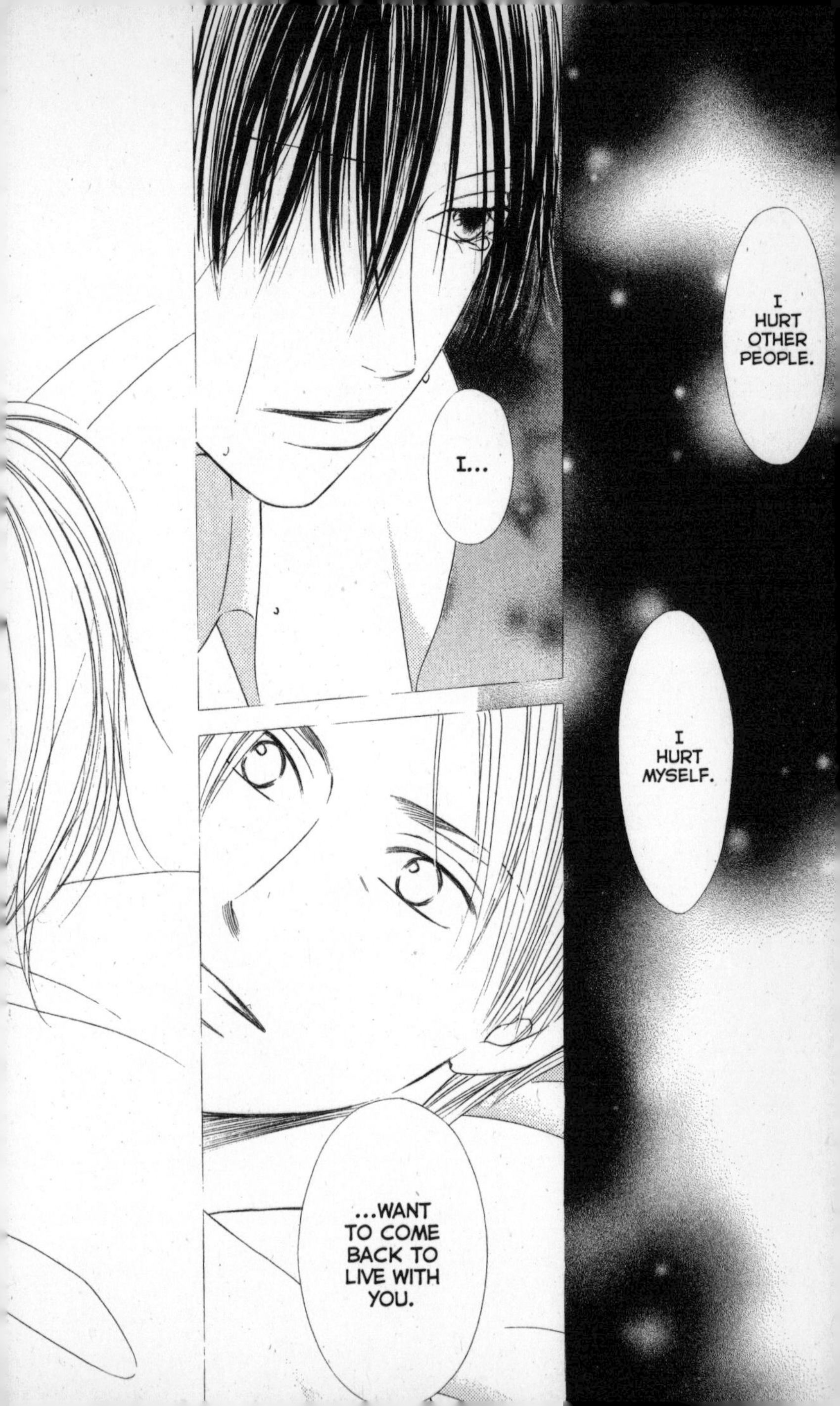
I HURT OTHER PEOPLE.
I HURT MYSELF.
I...
...WANT TO COME BACK TO LIVE WITH YOU.

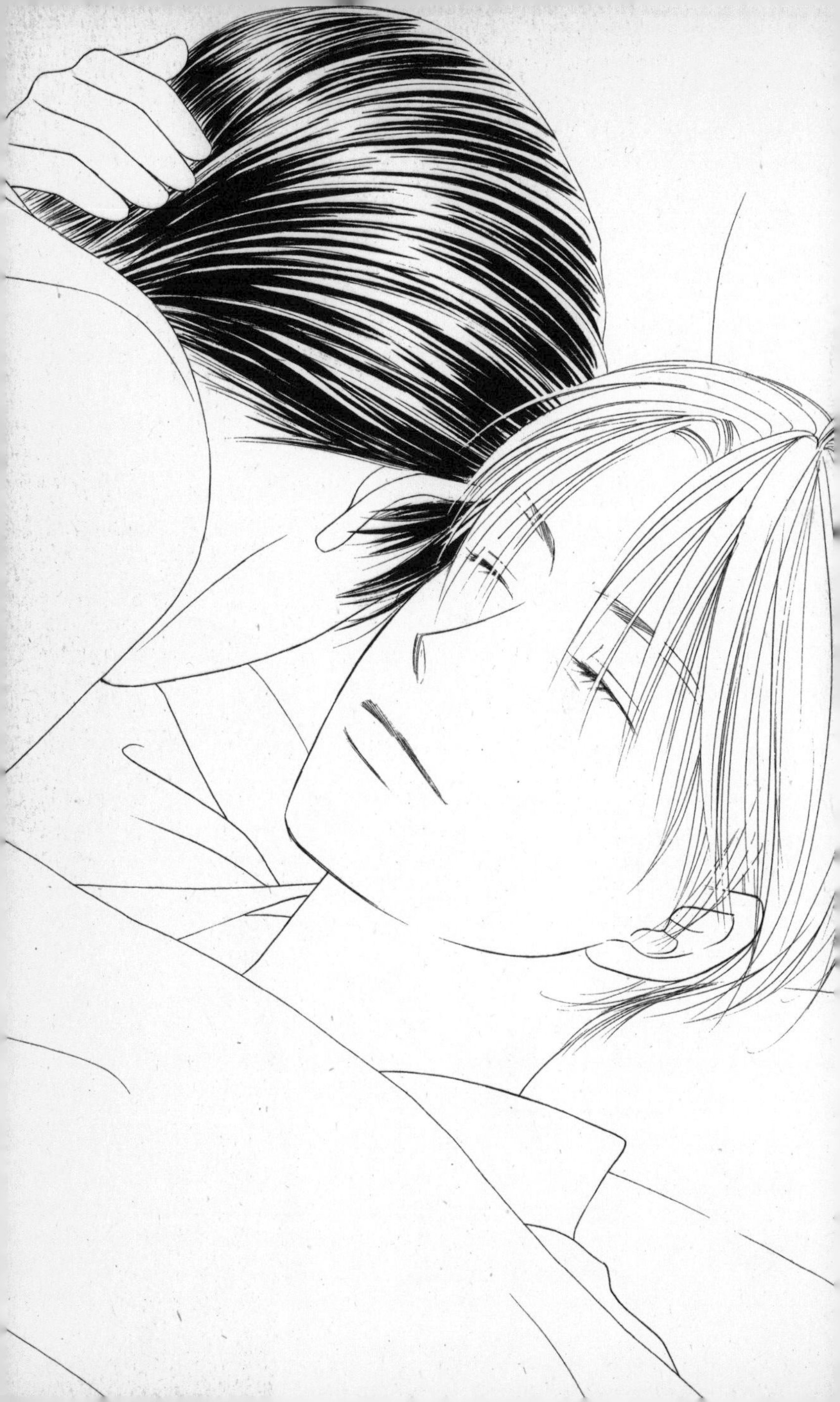

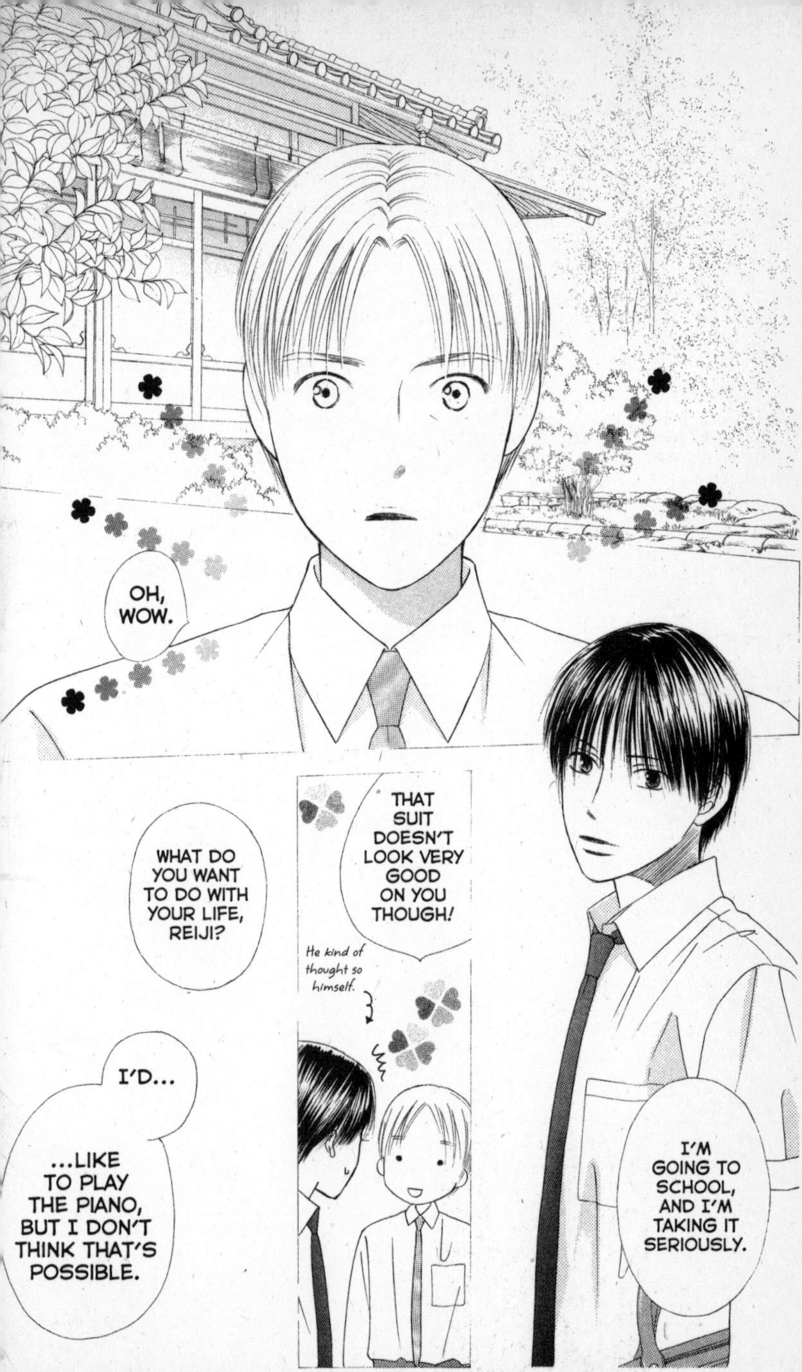
OH, WOW.
I'M GOING TO SCHOOL, AND I'M TAKING IT SERIOUSLY.
THAT SUIT DOESN'T LOOK VERY GOOD ON YOU THOUGH!
He kind of thought so himself.
WHAT DO YOU WANT TO DO WITH YOUR LIFE, REIJI?
I'D...
...LIKE TO PLAY THE PIANO, BUT I DON'T THINK THAT'S POSSIBLE.

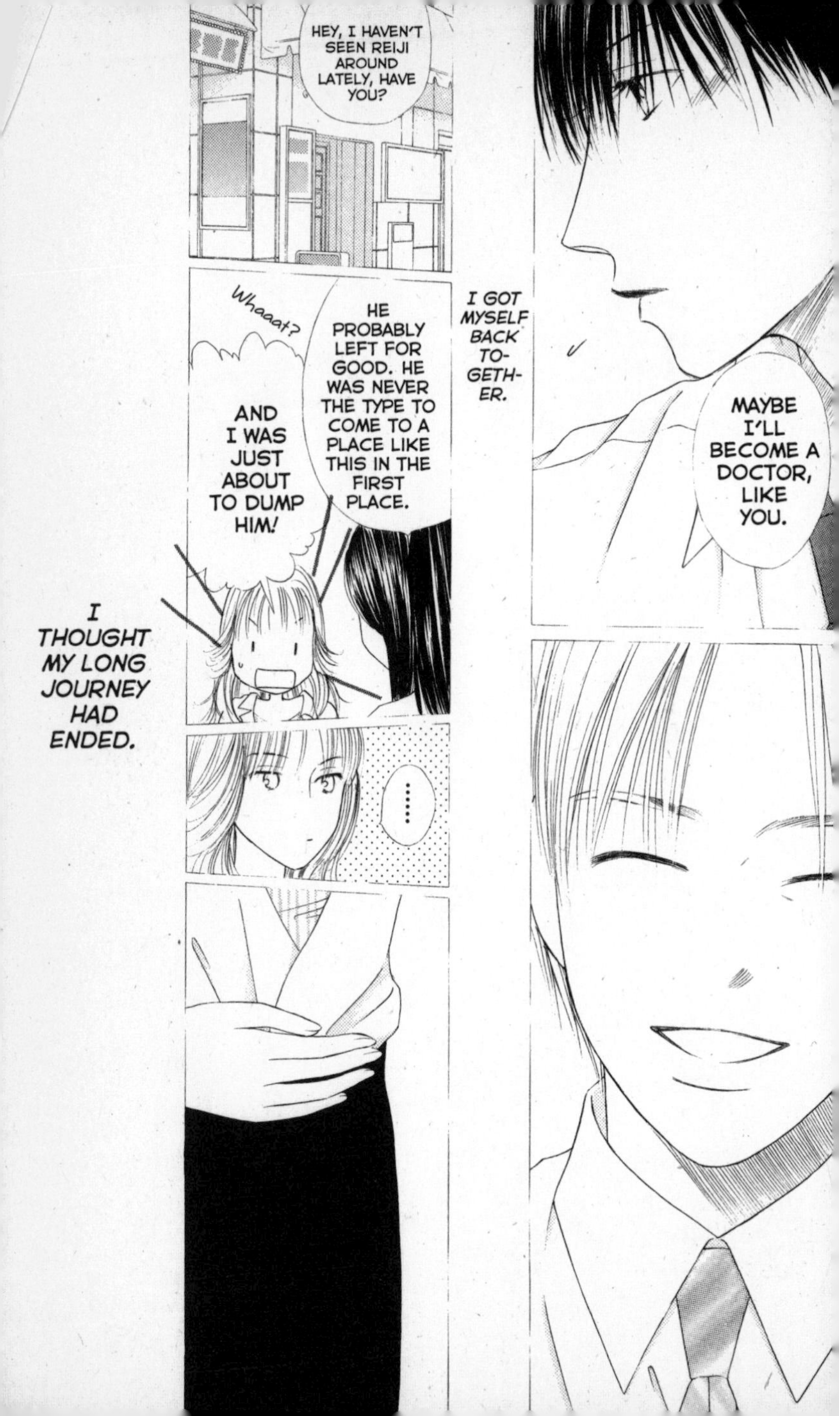
MAYBE I'LL BECOME A DOCTOR, LIKE YOU.
I GOT MYSELF BACK TO-GETH-ER.
HEY, I HAVEN'T SEEN REIJI AROUND LATELY, HAVE YOU?
HE PROBABLY LEFT FOR GOOD. HE WAS NEVER THE TYPE TO COME TO A PLACE LIKE THIS IN THE FIRST PLACE.
Whaaat?
AND I WAS JUST ABOUT TO DUMP HIM!
......
I THOUGHT MY LONG JOURNEY HAD ENDED.

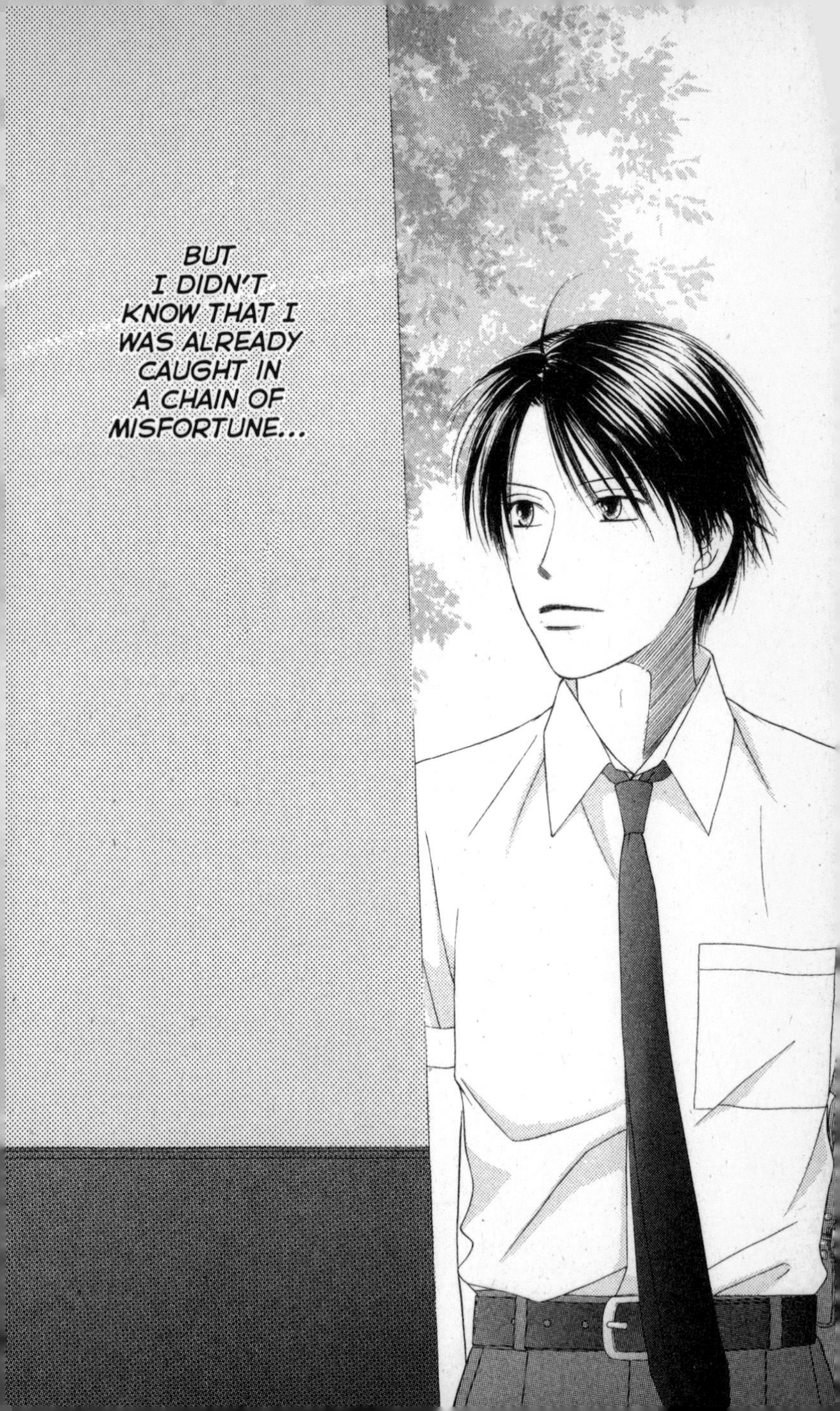
BUT I DIDN'T KNOW THAT I WAS ALREADY CAUGHT IN A CHAIN OF MISFORTUNE...

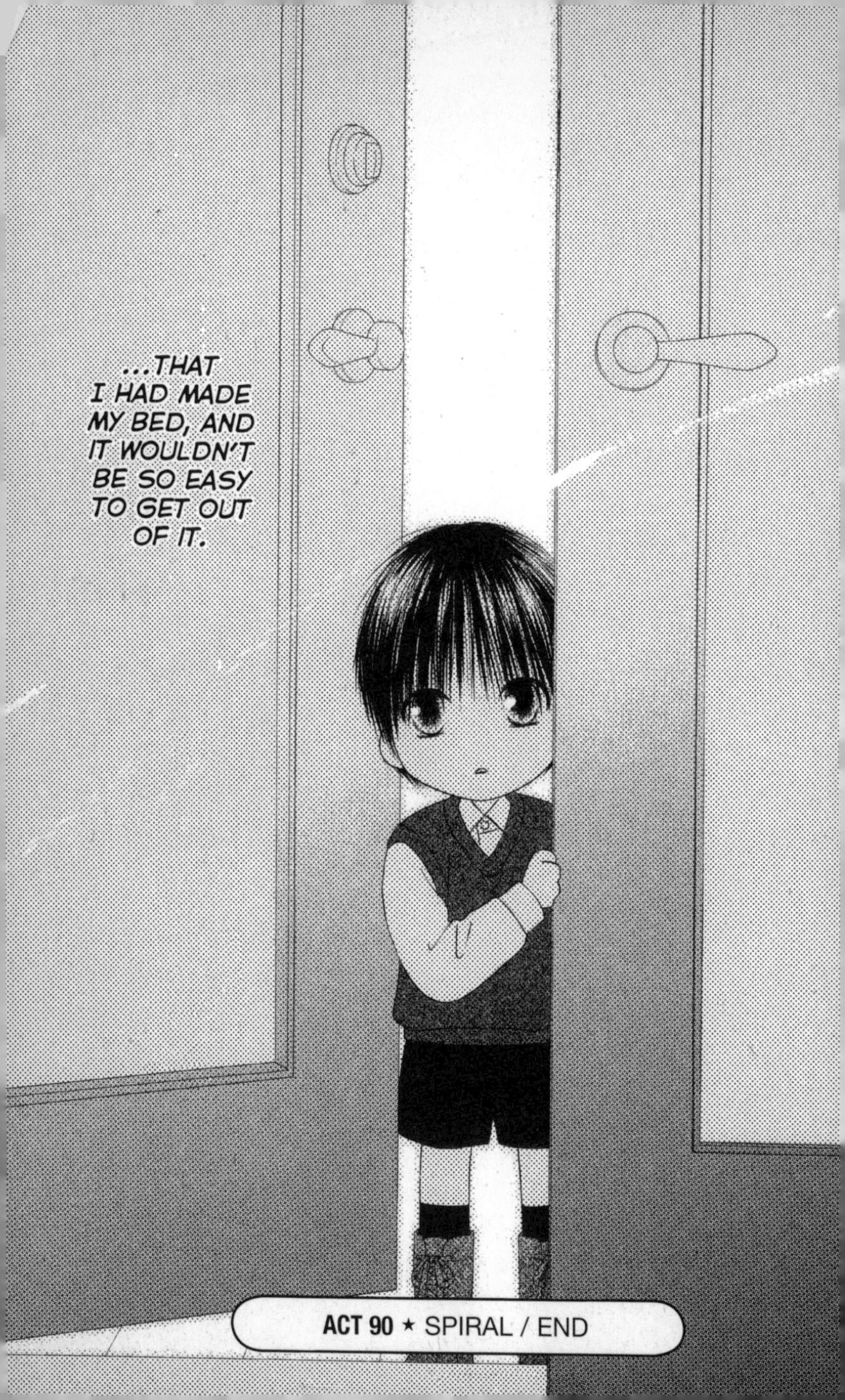
...THAT I HAD MADE MY BED, AND IT WOULDN'T BE SO EASY TO GET OUT OF IT.
ACT 90 ★ SPIRAL / END

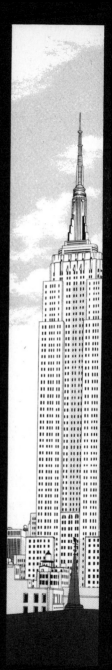

SINCE THEN,
I'VE ACHIEVED
FAME AND FORTUNE.
BUT THOSE ARE
MEANINGLESS,
MATERIAL THINGS.
YOU CAN'T
TAKE THEM
WITH YOU
WHEN YOU DIE.
ALL I HAVE IS
MY SOUL,
AND IN IT IS
A LONELINESS
I CANNOT BURY.
I WALK THE
STREETS OF
NEW YORK
SHADOWED BY
THAT ACHING
LONELINESS.

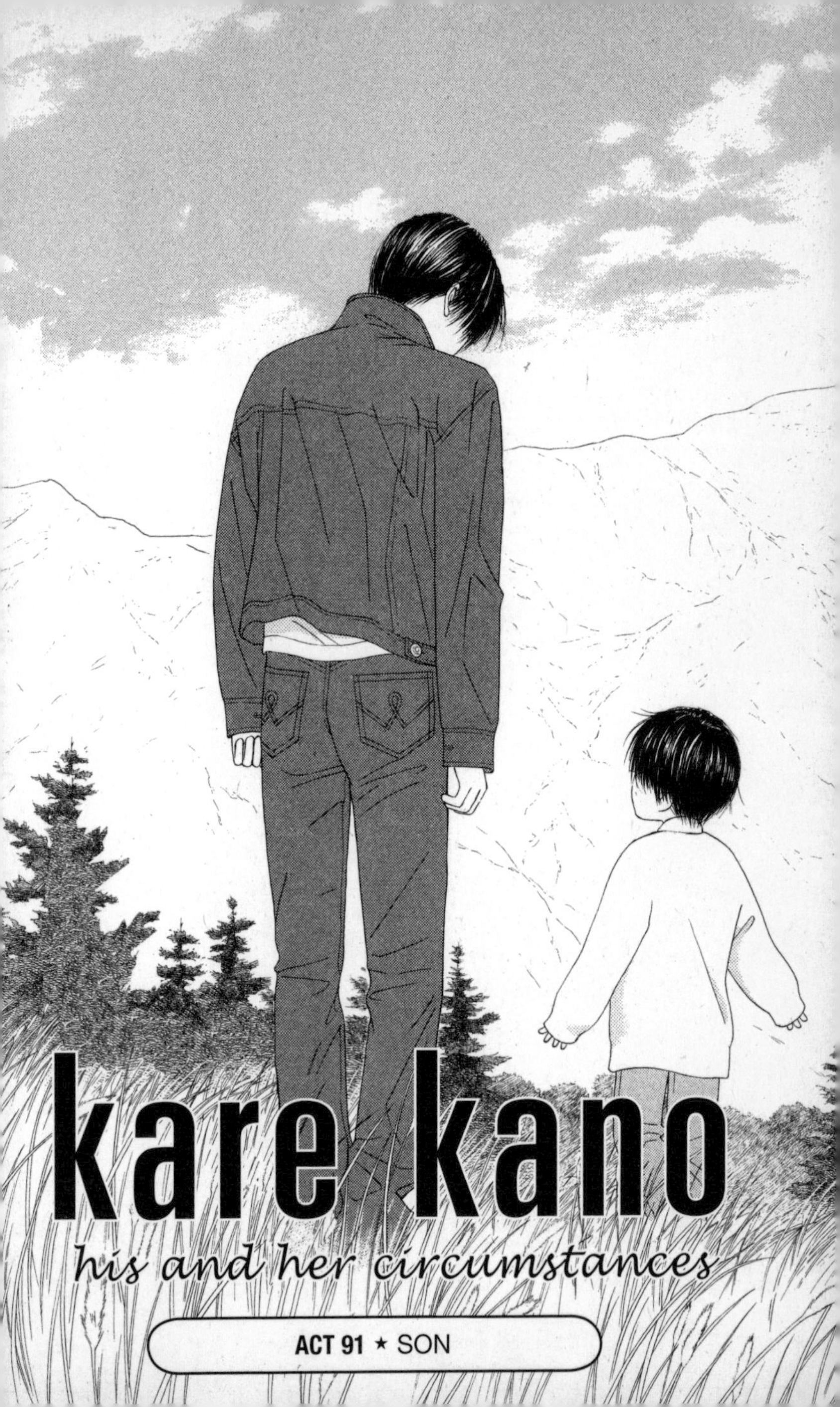
kare kano
his and her circumstances
ACT 91 ★ SON

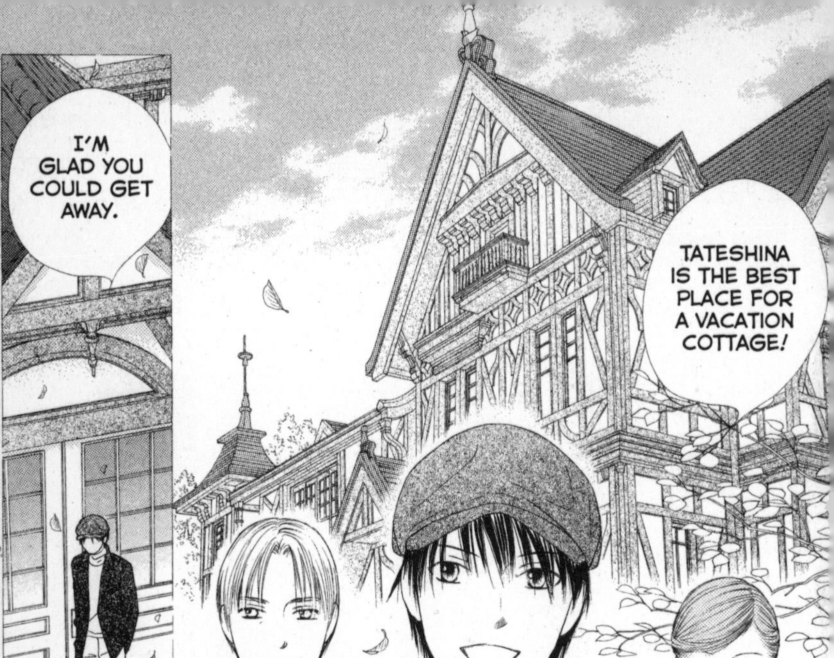
TATESHINA IS THE BEST PLACE FOR A VACATION COTTAGE!
I'M GLAD YOU COULD GET AWAY.
YEAH.

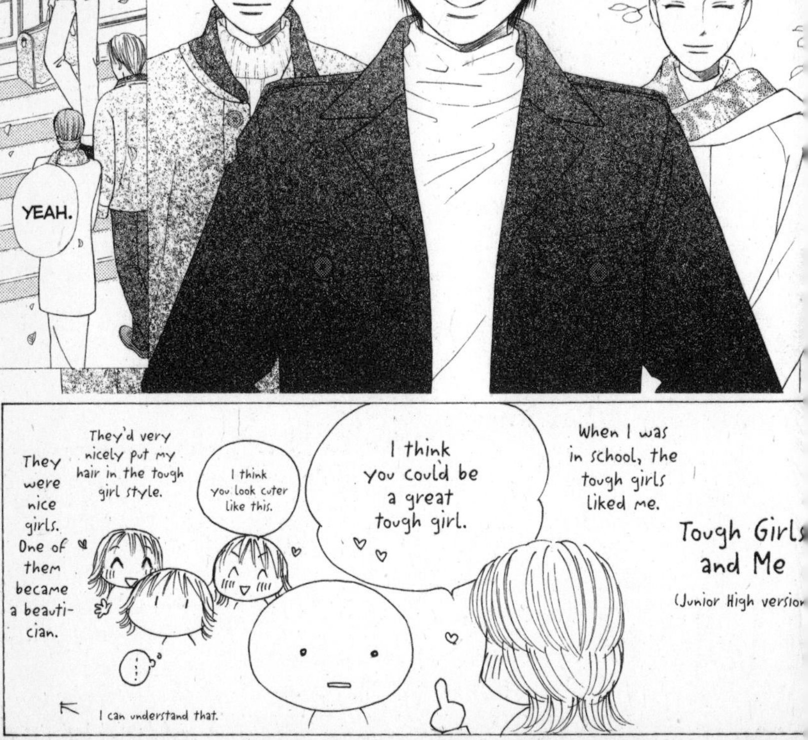
Tough Girls and Me
(Junior High version)
When I was in school, the tough girls liked me.
I think you could be a great tough girl.
I think you look cuter like this.
They'd very nicely put my hair in the tough girl style.
They were nice girls. One of them became a beautician.
...
I can understand that.

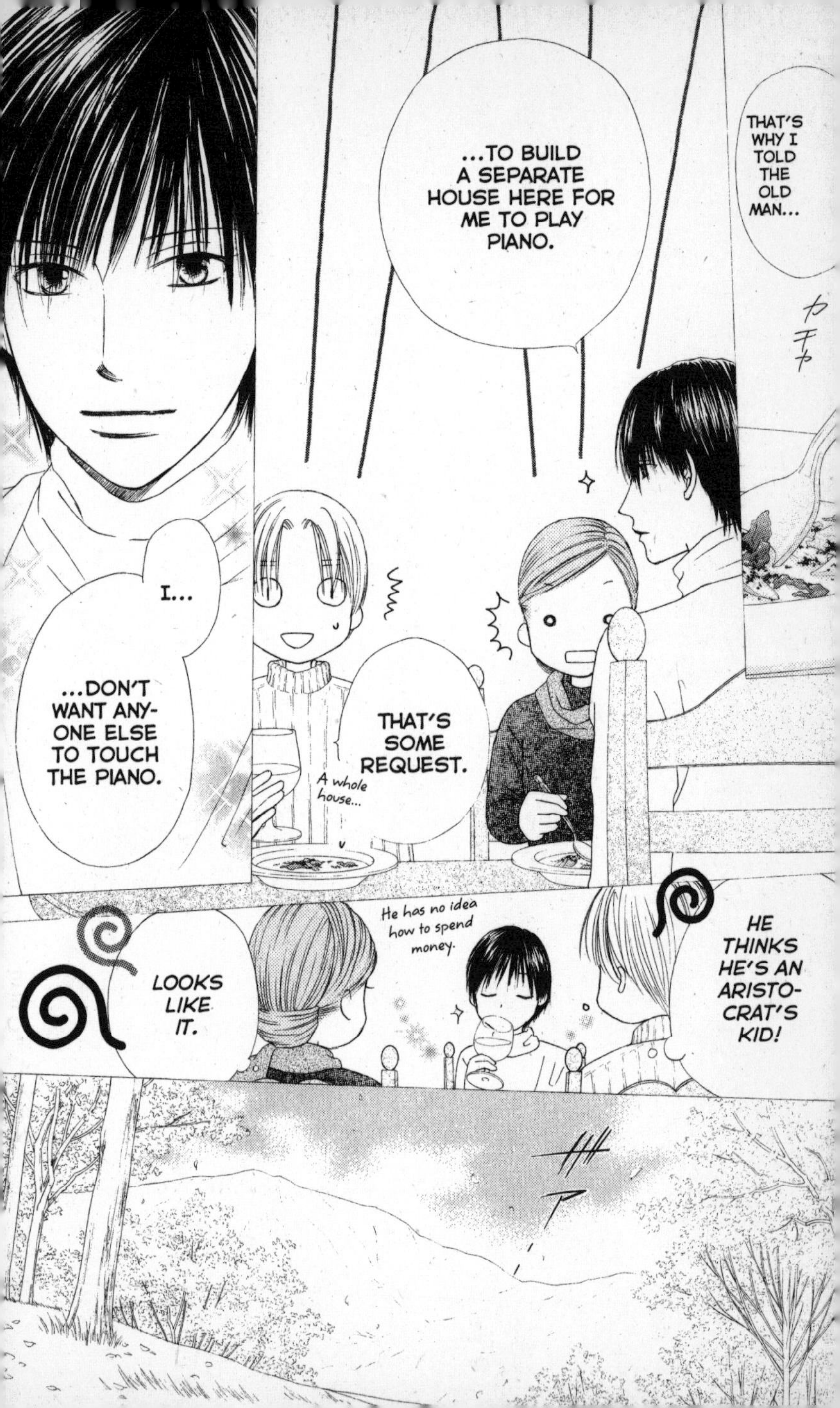
THAT'S WHY I TOLD THE OLD MAN...
カチャ
...TO BUILD A SEPARATE HOUSE HERE FOR ME TO PLAY PIANO.
THAT'S SOME REQUEST.
A whole house...
I...
...DON'T WANT ANY-ONE ELSE TO TOUCH THE PIANO.
HE THINKS HE'S AN ARISTO-CRAT'S KID!
He has no idea how to spend money.
LOOKS LIKE IT.

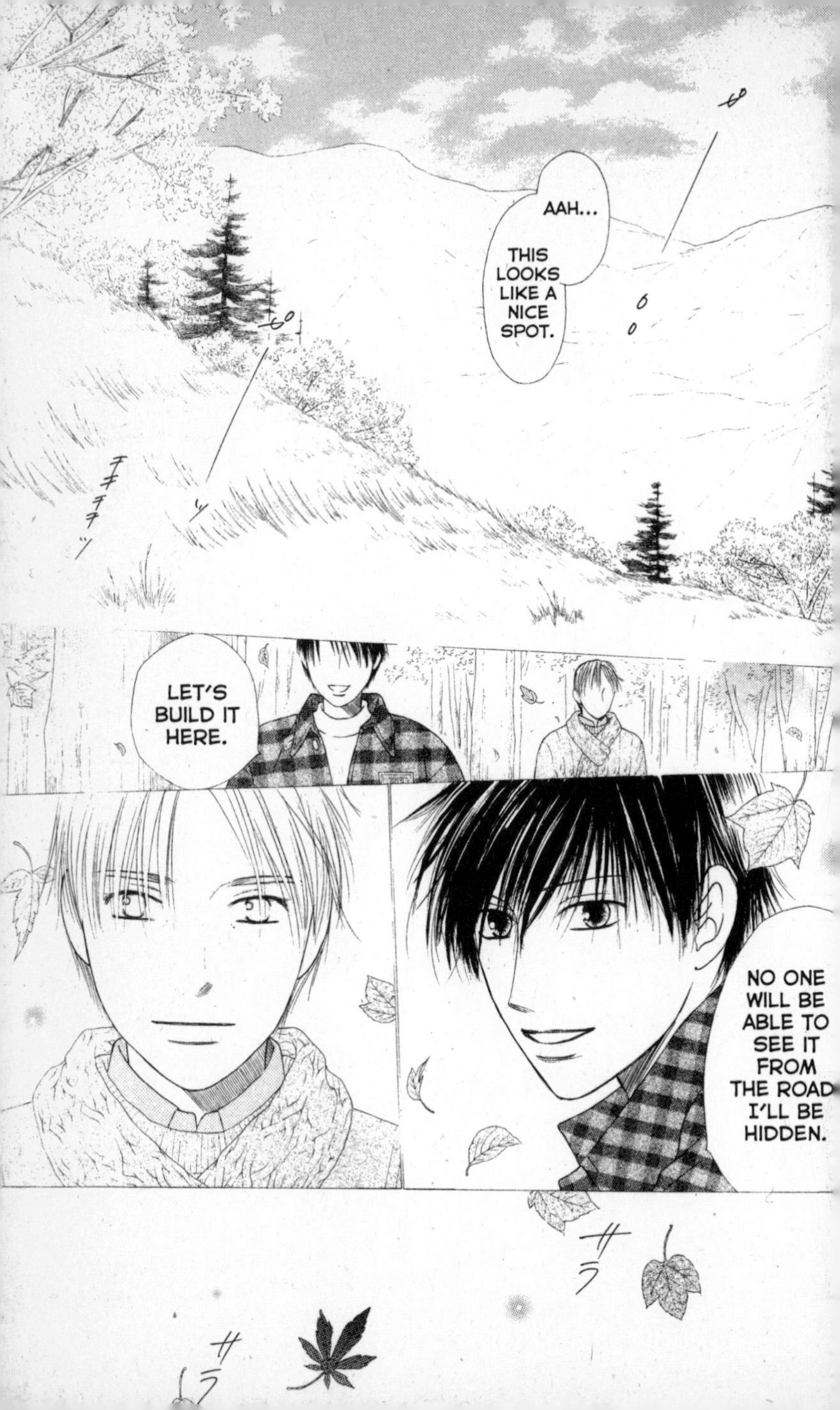
AAH...
THIS LOOKS LIKE A NICE SPOT.
LET'S BUILD IT HERE.
NO ONE WILL BE ABLE TO SEE IT FROM THE ROAD I'LL BE HIDDEN.

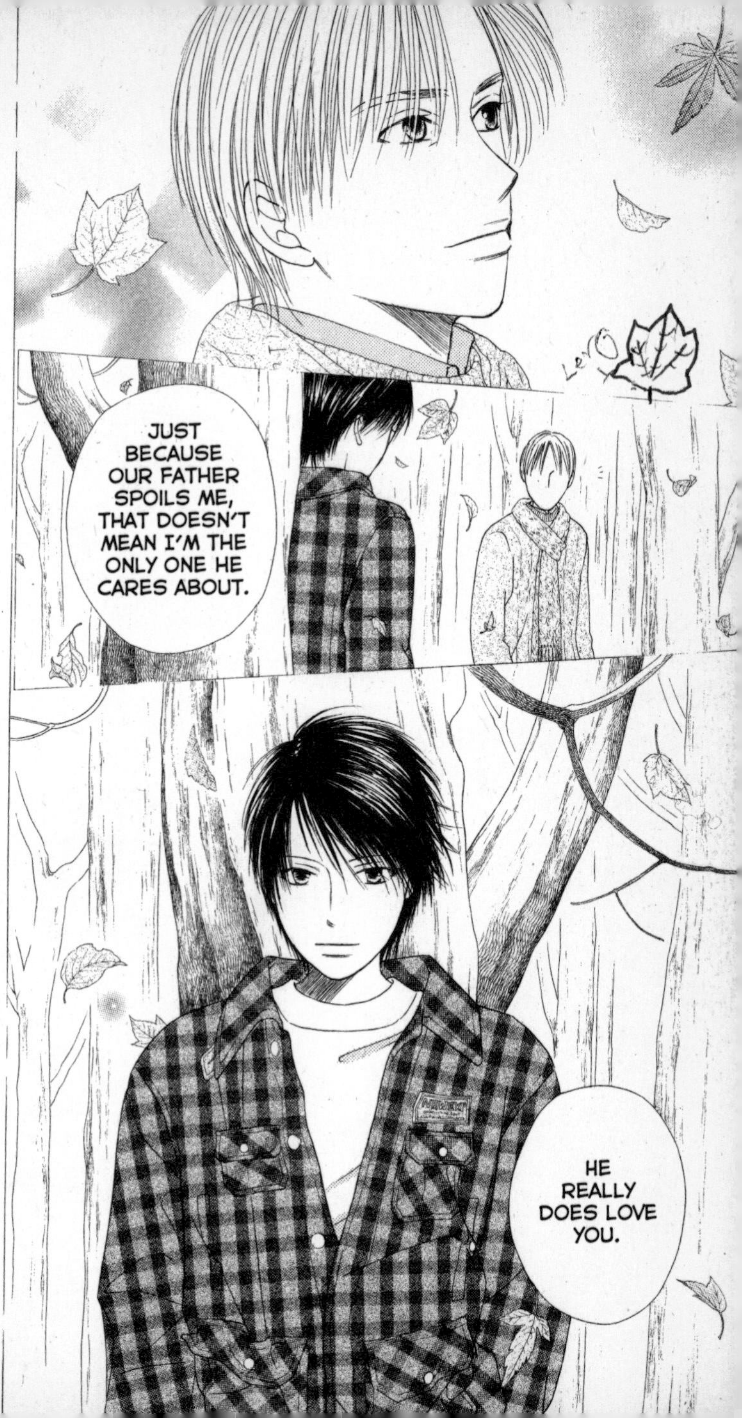
JUST BECAUSE OUR FATHER SPOILS ME, THAT DOESN'T MEAN I'M THE ONLY ONE HE CARES ABOUT.
HE REALLY DOES LOVE YOU.

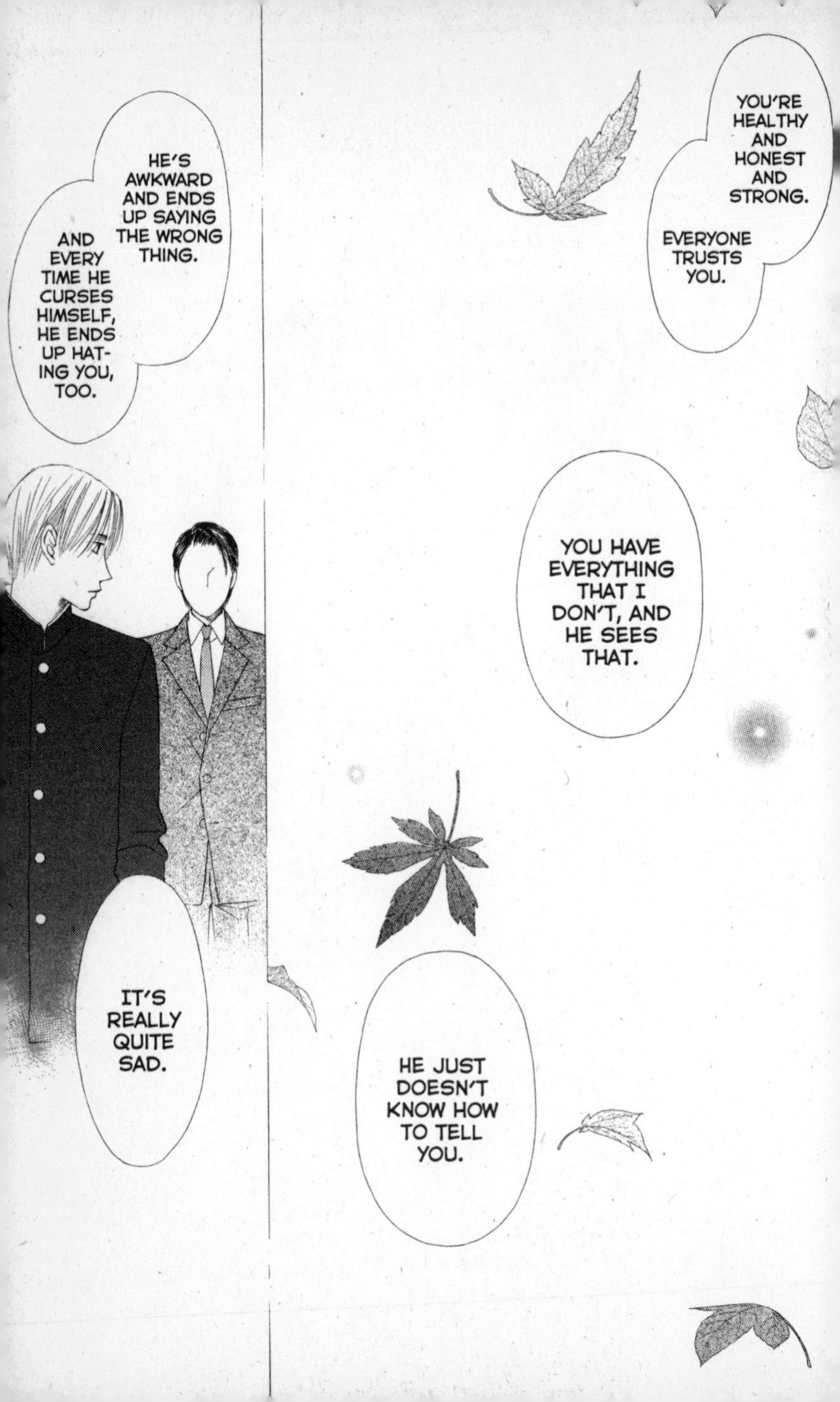
YOU'RE HEALTHY AND HONEST AND STRONG.
EVERYONE TRUSTS YOU.
YOU HAVE EVERYTHING THAT I DON'T, AND HE SEES THAT.
HE JUST DOESN'T KNOW HOW TO TELL YOU.
HE'S AWKWARD AND ENDS UP SAYING THE WRONG THING.
AND EVERY TIME HE CURSES HIMSELF, HE ENDS UP HATING YOU, TOO.
IT'S REALLY QUITE SAD.

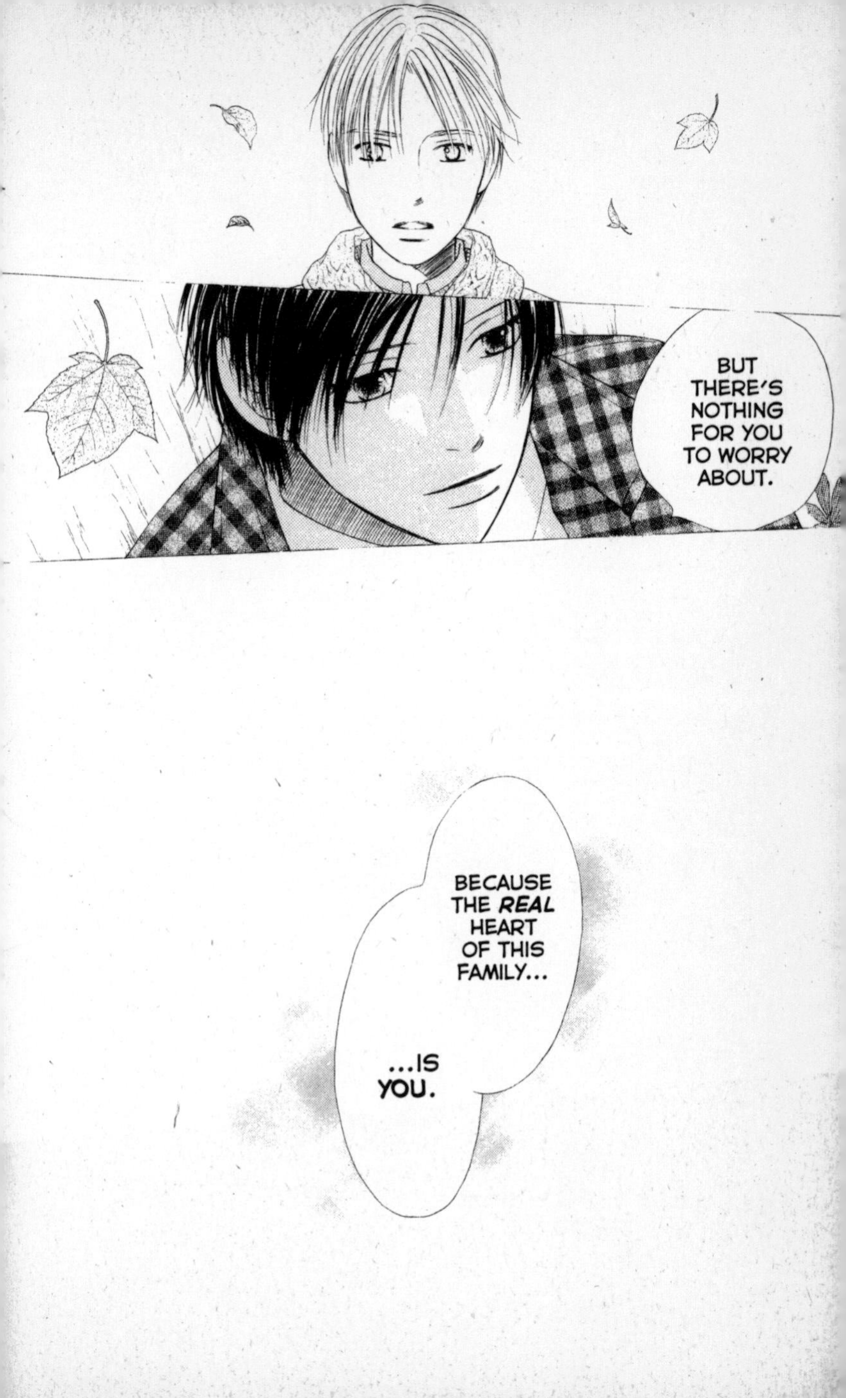
BUT THERE'S NOTHING FOR YOU TO WORRY ABOUT.
BECAUSE THE *REAL* HEART OF THIS FAMILY...
...IS YOU.

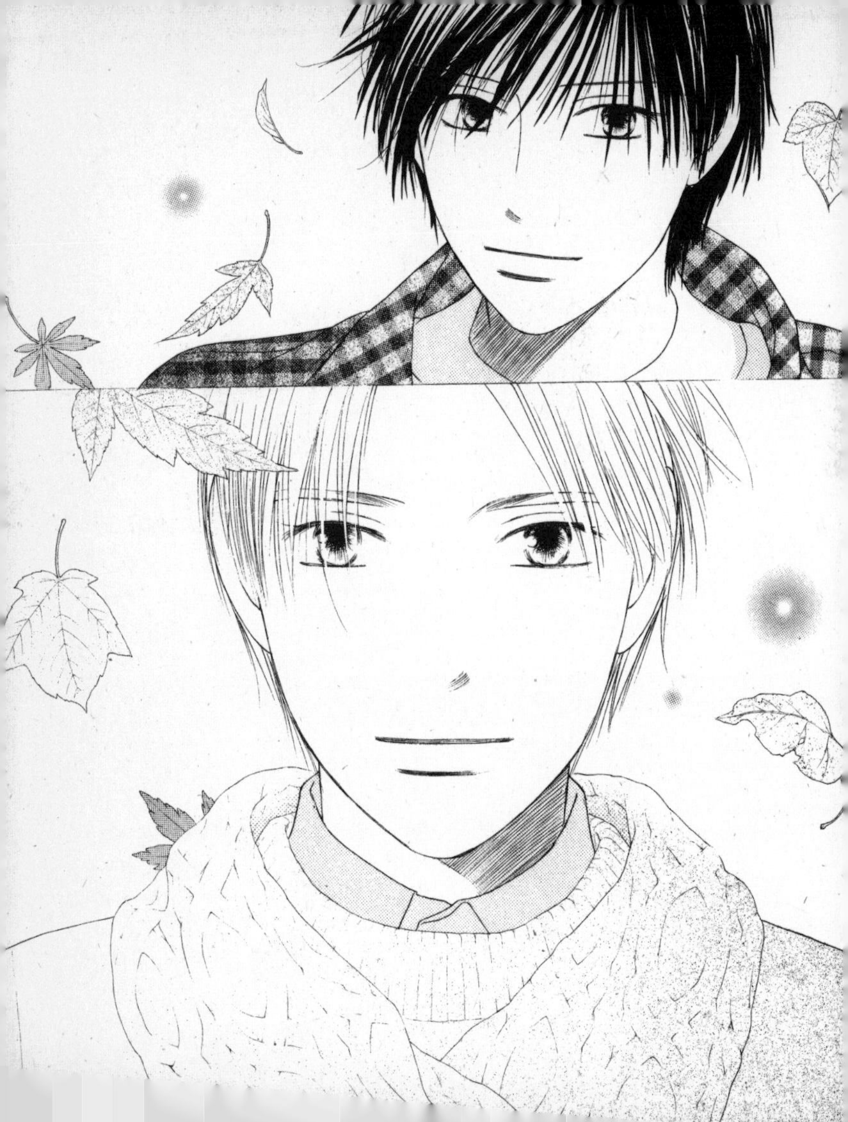

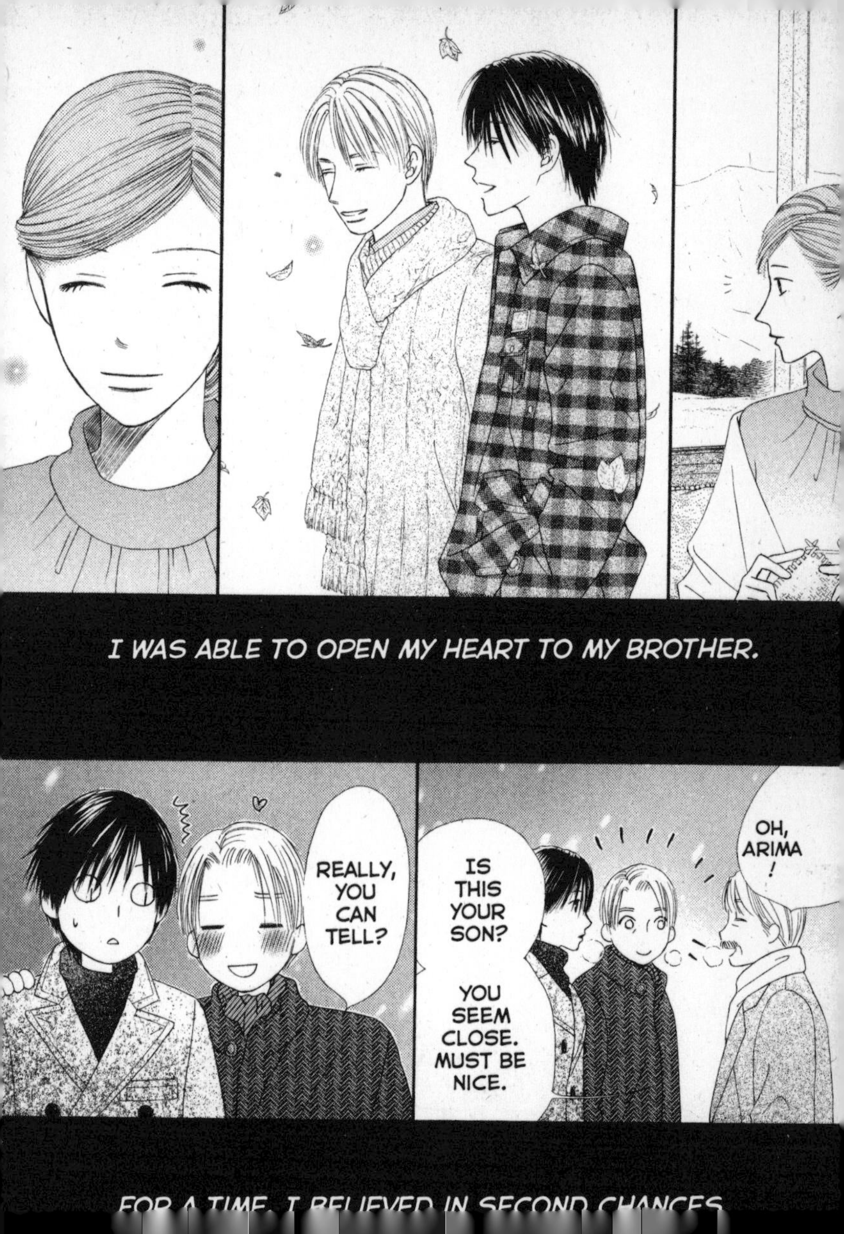
I WAS ABLE TO OPEN MY HEART TO MY BROTHER.
OH, ARIMA!
IS THIS YOUR SON?
YOU SEEM CLOSE. MUST BE NICE.
REALLY, YOU CAN TELL?
FOR A TIME, I BELIEVED IN SECOND CHANCES.

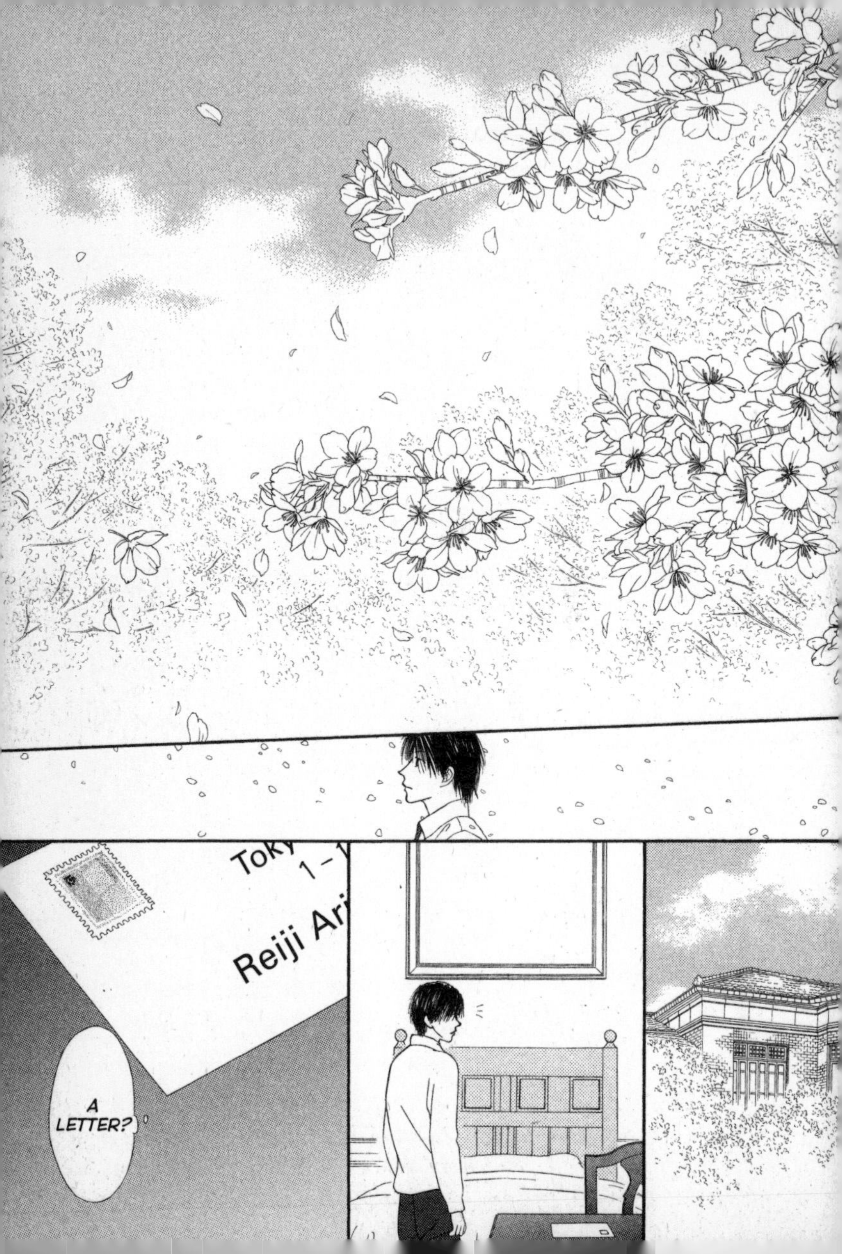
Toky
1 – 1
Reiji Ari
A LETTER?

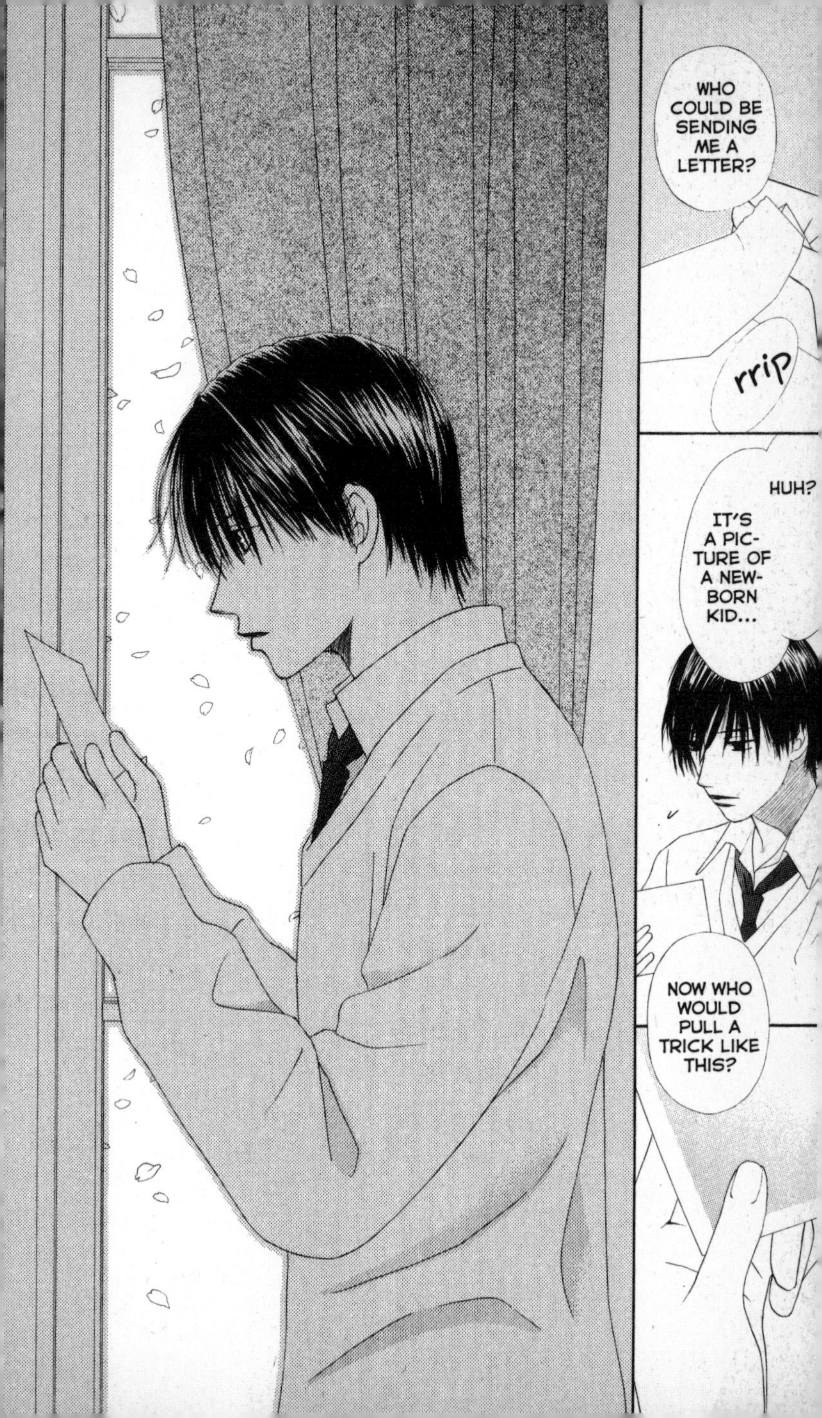
WHO COULD BE SENDING ME A LETTER?
rrip
HUH?
IT'S A PIC-TURE OF A NEW-BORN KID...
NOW WHO WOULD PULL A TRICK LIKE THIS?

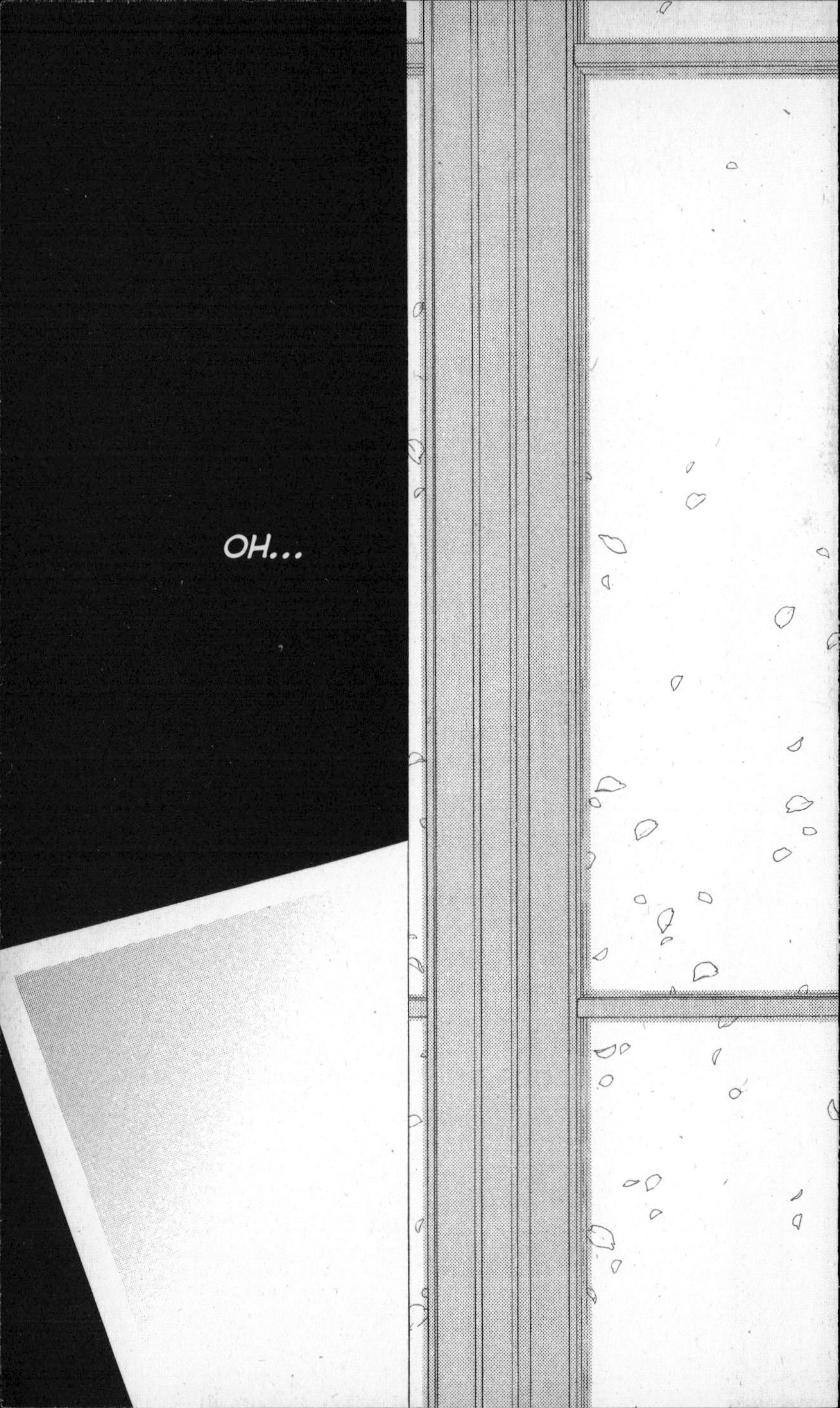
OH...

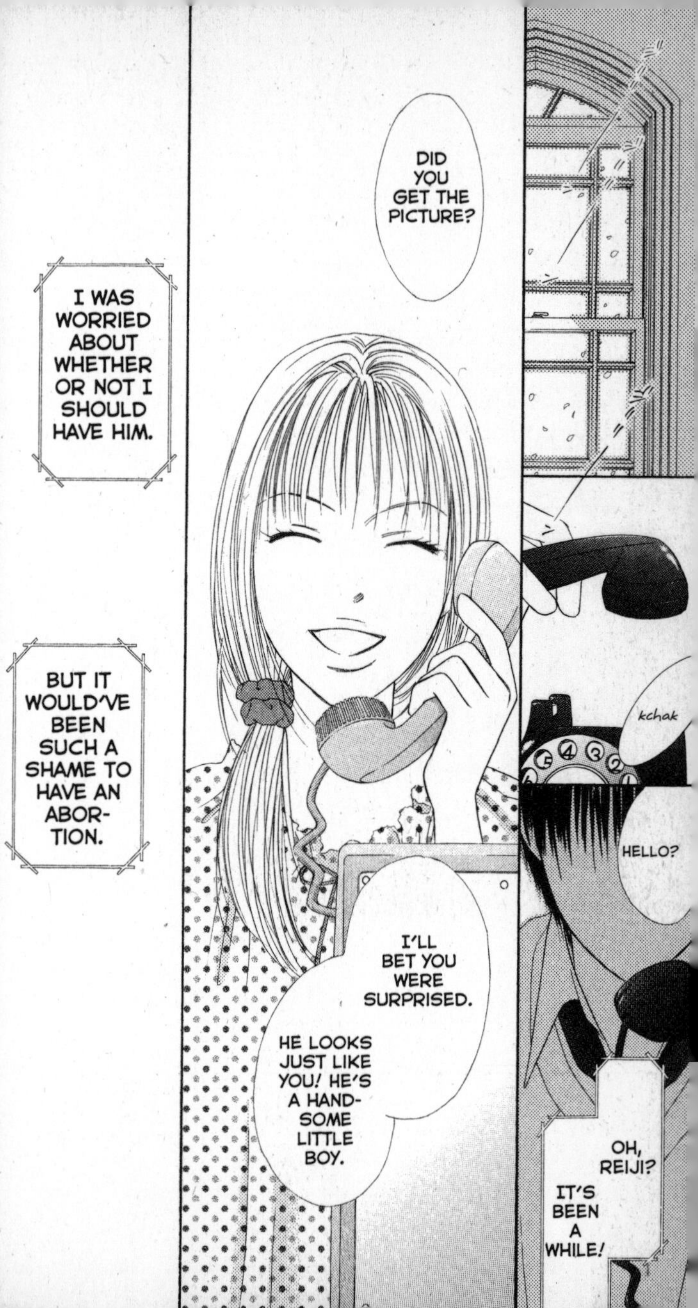
kchak
HELLO?
OH, REIJI?
IT'S BEEN A WHILE!
DID YOU GET THE PICTURE?
I'LL BET YOU WERE SURPRISED.
HE LOOKS JUST LIKE YOU! HE'S A HAND-SOME LITTLE BOY.
I WAS WORRIED ABOUT WHETHER OR NOT I SHOULD HAVE HIM.
BUT IT WOULD'VE BEEN SUCH A SHAME TO HAVE AN ABOR-TION.

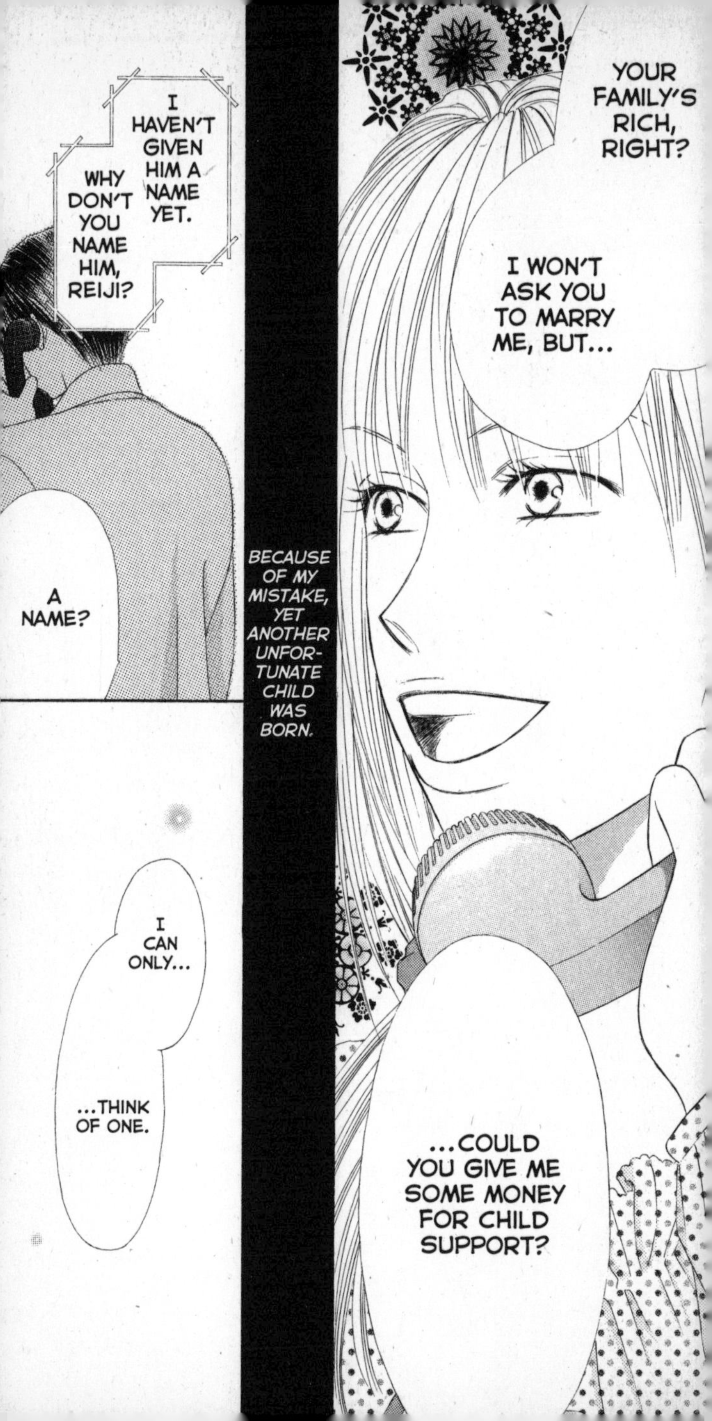
YOUR FAMILY'S RICH, RIGHT?
I WON'T ASK YOU TO MARRY ME, BUT...
...COULD YOU GIVE ME SOME MONEY FOR CHILD SUPPORT?
BECAUSE OF MY MISTAKE, YET ANOTHER UNFORTUNATE CHILD WAS BORN.
I HAVEN'T GIVEN HIM A NAME YET.
WHY DON'T YOU NAME HIM, REIJI?
A NAME?
I CAN ONLY...
...THINK OF ONE.

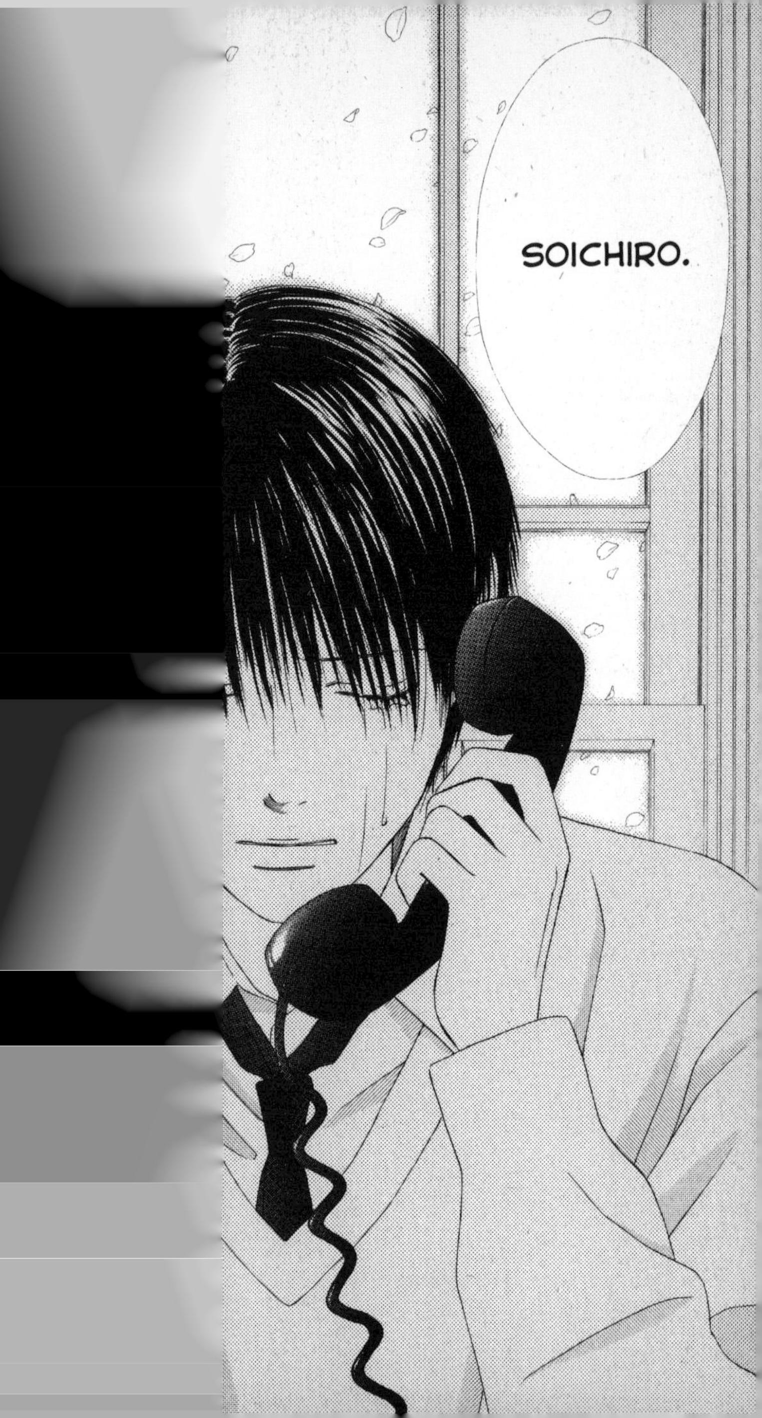
SOICHIRO.

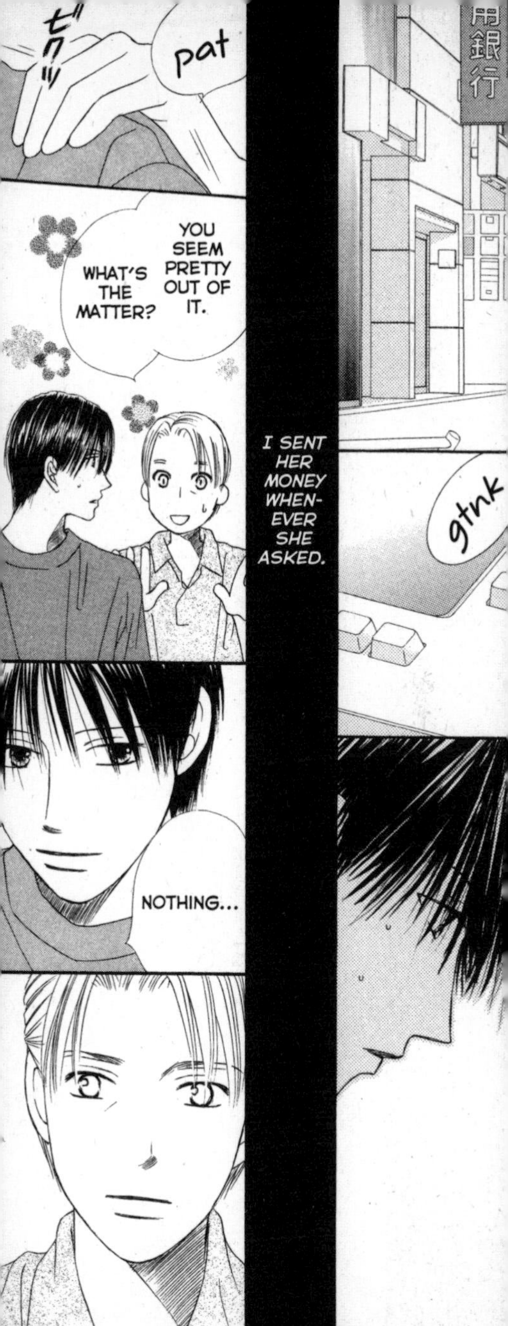
銀行
gtnk
I SENT HER MONEY WHEN-EVER SHE ASKED.
ビクッ
pat
YOU SEEM PRETTY OUT OF IT.
WHAT'S THE MATTER?
NOTHING...

...I WAS AFRAID OF HOW HIS FEELINGS TOWARD ME WOULD CHANGE IF I DID.
WHAT KIND OF LIFE DO YOU EXPECT US TO HAVE WITH THIS PATHETIC MONEY?
Waaaah!
IT'S NOT ENOUGH! SEND MORE!
Waaaah!
RYOKO DEMANDED MORE AND MORE MONEY. AND I WAS EXHAUSTED.
HAT WENT
I AND ON.
HEN ONE
DAY, I
ALIZED...
AND BESIDES, WHY SHOULD MY LIFE BE RUINED BECAUSE OF ONE NIGHT WITH A WOMAN I COULDN'T STAND, AND A CHILD I DIDN'T WANT?
I SENT YOU PLENTY! I'M JUST A STUDENT-- THAT'S ALL I CAN SEND YOU!
MAYBE...
...I'LL GO TO YOUR DADDY...
Waaaah!

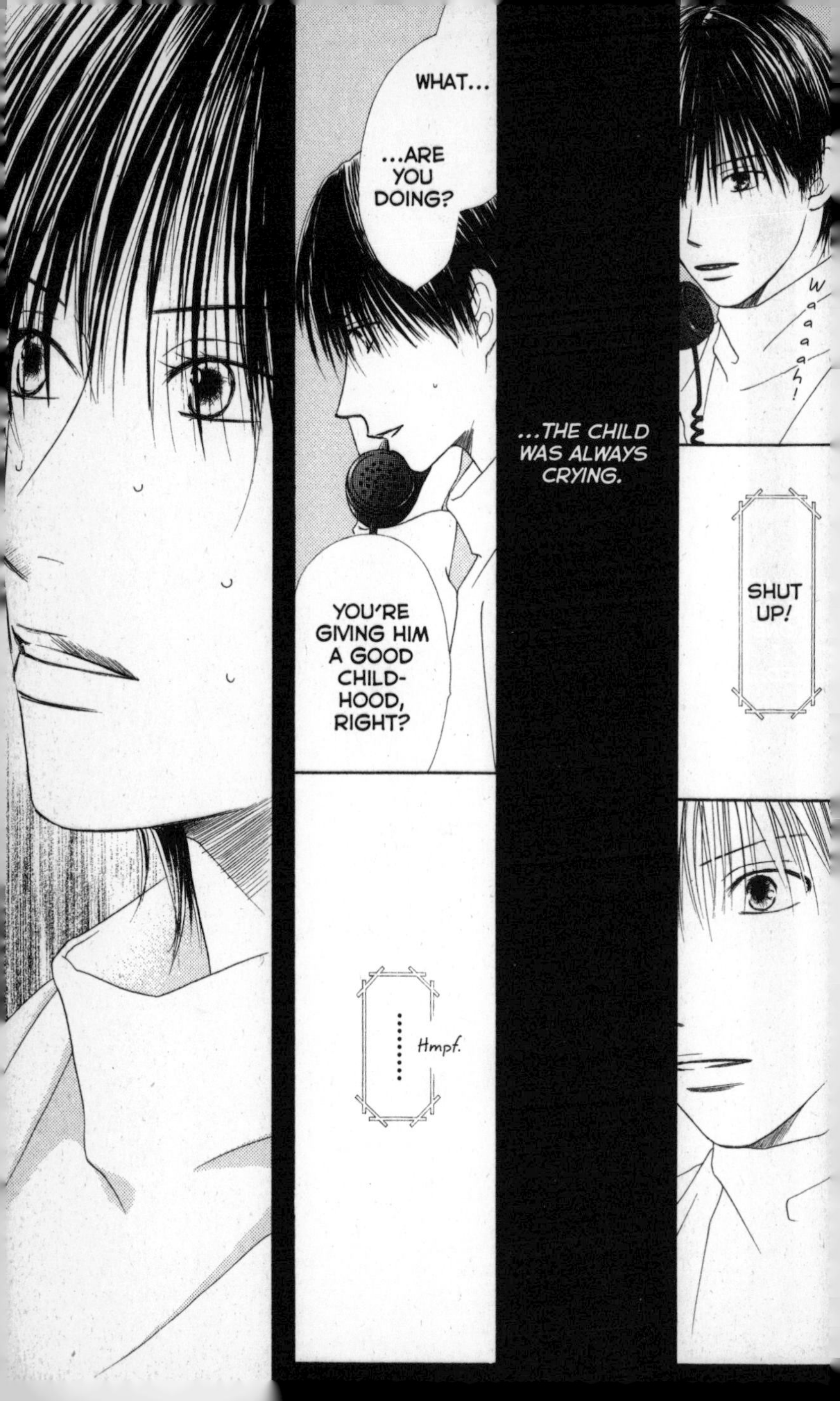
Waaaah!
SHUT UP!
...THE CHILD WAS ALWAYS CRYING.
WHAT...
...ARE YOU DOING?
YOU'RE GIVING HIM A GOOD CHILD-HOOD, RIGHT?
....
Hmpf.

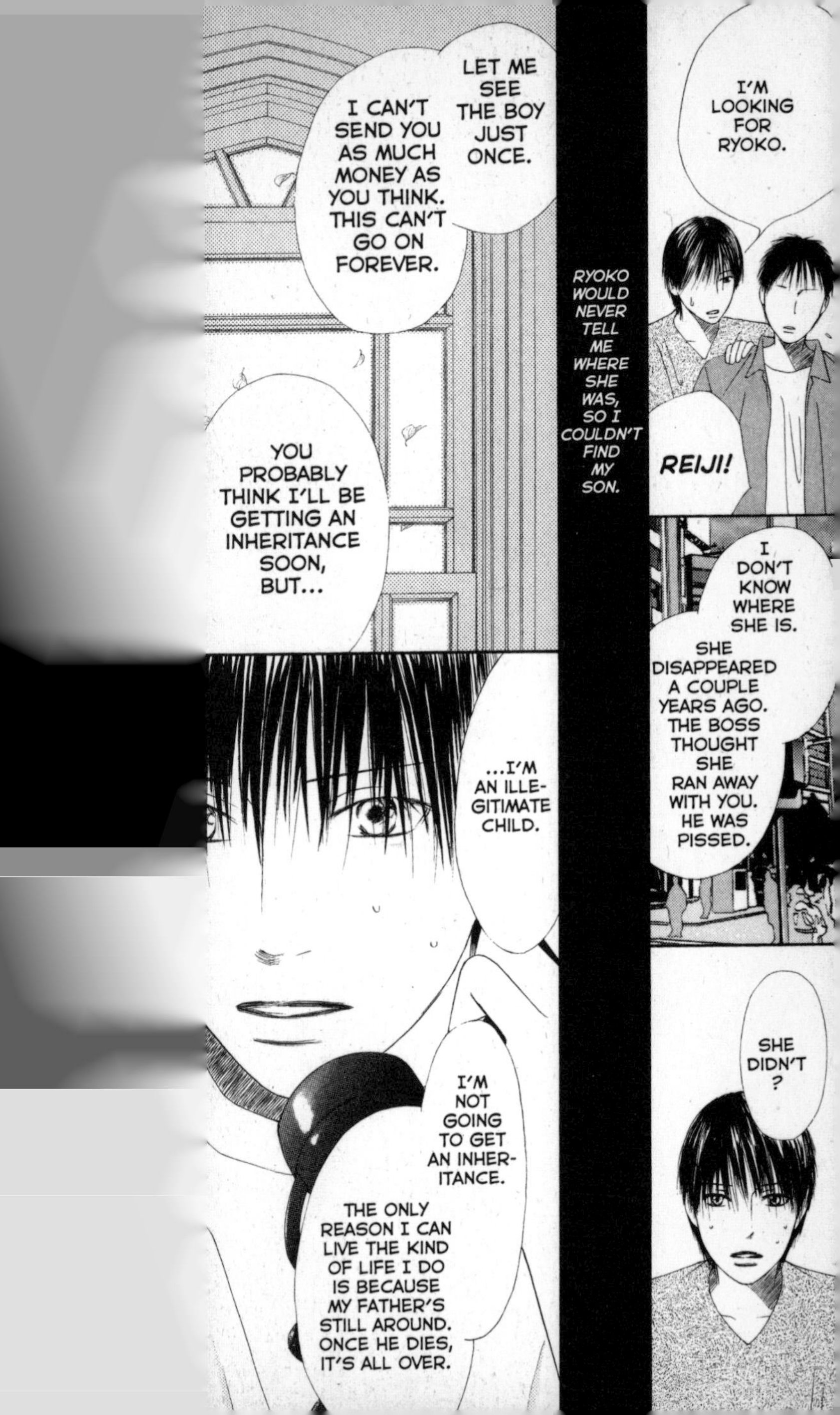
I'M LOOKING FOR RYOKO.
REIJI!
I DON'T KNOW WHERE SHE IS.
SHE DISAPPEARED A COUPLE YEARS AGO. THE BOSS THOUGHT SHE RAN AWAY WITH YOU. HE WAS PISSED.
SHE DIDN'T?
RYOKO WOULD NEVER TELL ME WHERE SHE WAS, SO I COULDN'T FIND MY SON.
LET ME SEE THE BOY JUST ONCE.
I CAN'T SEND YOU AS MUCH MONEY AS YOU THINK. THIS CAN'T GO ON FOREVER.
YOU PROBABLY THINK I'LL BE GETTING AN INHERITANCE SOON, BUT...
...I'M AN ILLE-GITIMATE CHILD.
I'M NOT GOING TO GET AN INHER-ITANCE.
THE ONLY REASON I CAN LIVE THE KIND OF LIFE I DO IS BECAUSE MY FATHER'S STILL AROUND. ONCE HE DIES, IT'S ALL OVER.

SOON, SHE LOST INTEREST IN ME, STOPPED CALLING AND NEVER HAD ANYTHING TO DO WITH ME AGAIN.

I FINALLY HIRED A DETECTIVE AGENCY TO FIND HER. I WAS 20 YEARS OLD.

huff
huff
huff

IT WAS A SNOWY WINTER'S NIGHT.

3

Cloth

I'm into cotton, hemp and gauze cloth now.

I love how organic cotton T-shirts don't cling to you even in summer, and how long hemp skirts gently shape themselves to your body. I'm just so into cloth! And I adore how as you wear something and keep washing it over and over, the feeling of the material changes.

There are so many different materials in this world that I really like.

Since I work at home though, I have a lot of clothes for wearing around the house.

Stuffed

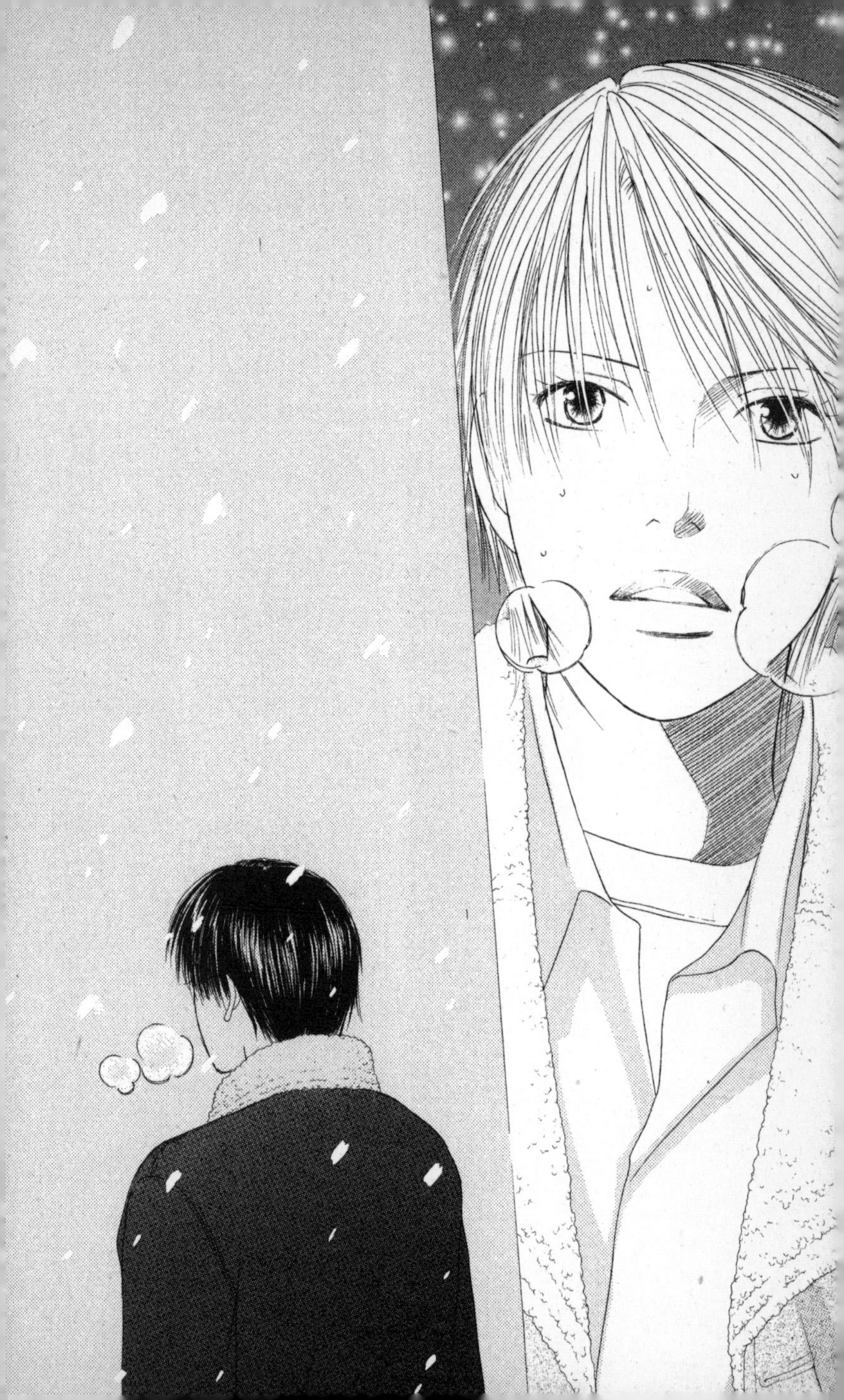

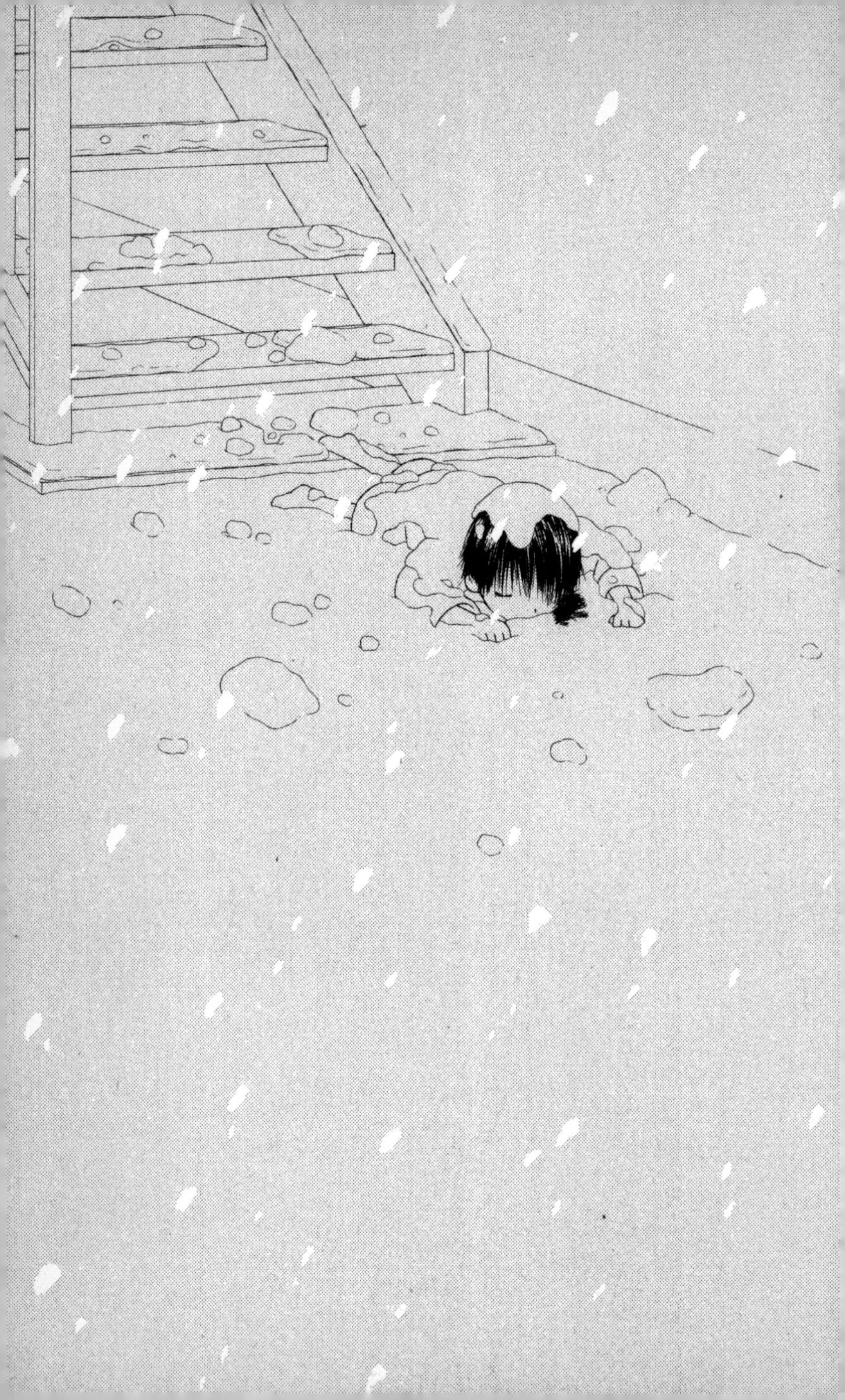

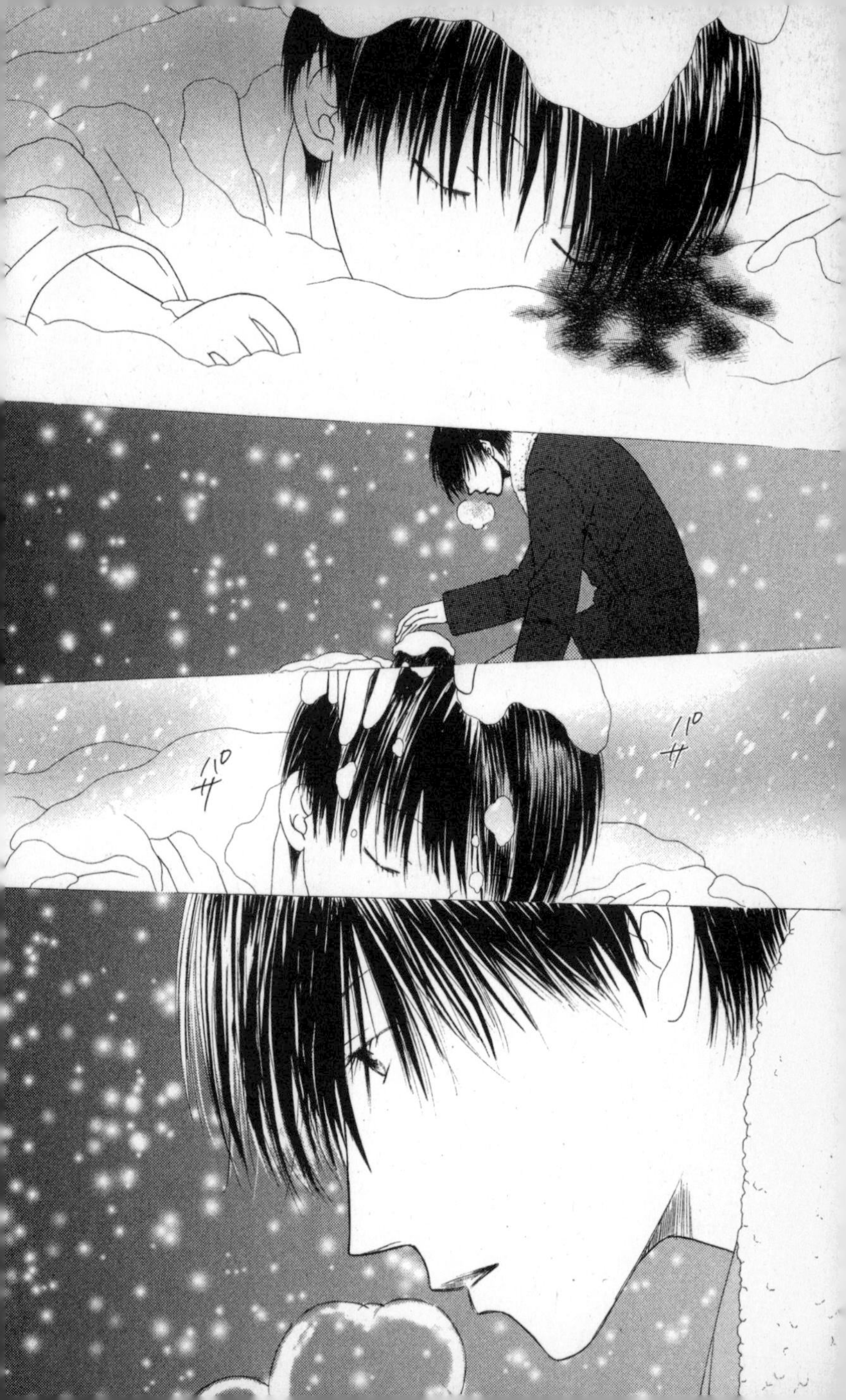
パサ
パサ

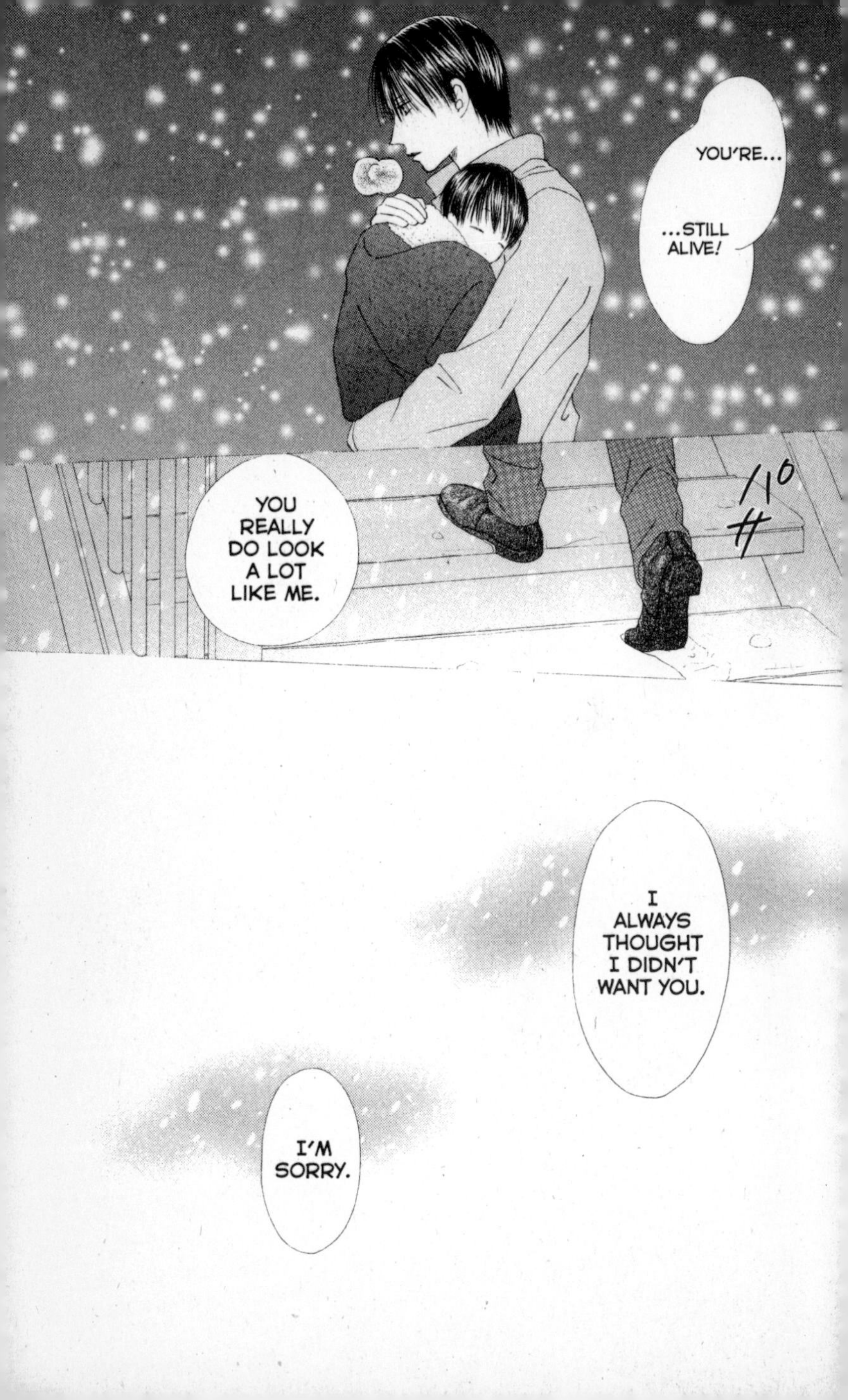
YOU'RE...
...STILL ALIVE!
YOU REALLY DO LOOK A LOT LIKE ME.
I ALWAYS THOUGHT I DIDN'T WANT YOU.
I'M SORRY.

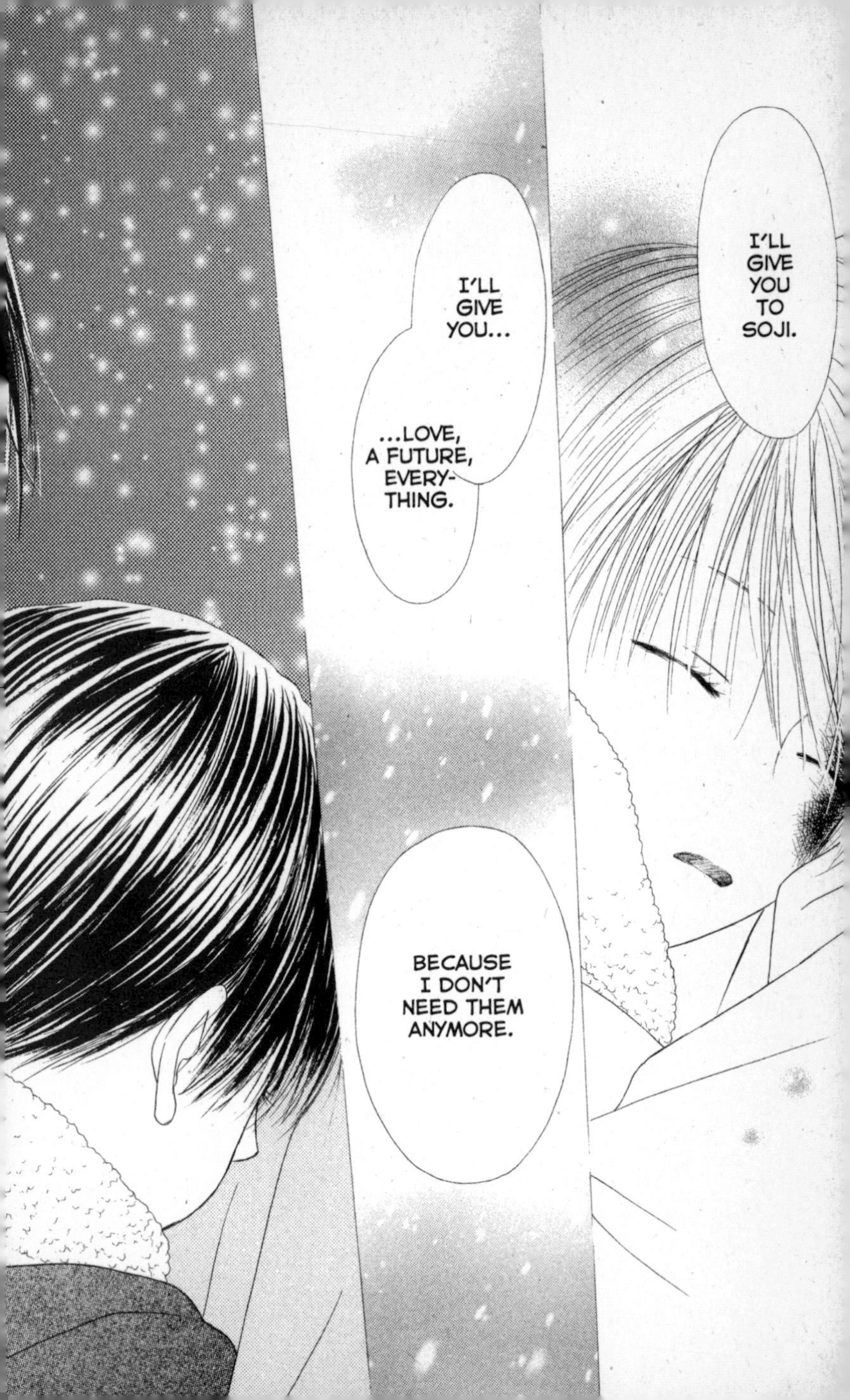
I'LL GIVE YOU TO SOJI.
I'LL GIVE YOU...
...LOVE, A FUTURE, EVERY-THING.
BECAUSE I DON'T NEED THEM ANYMORE.

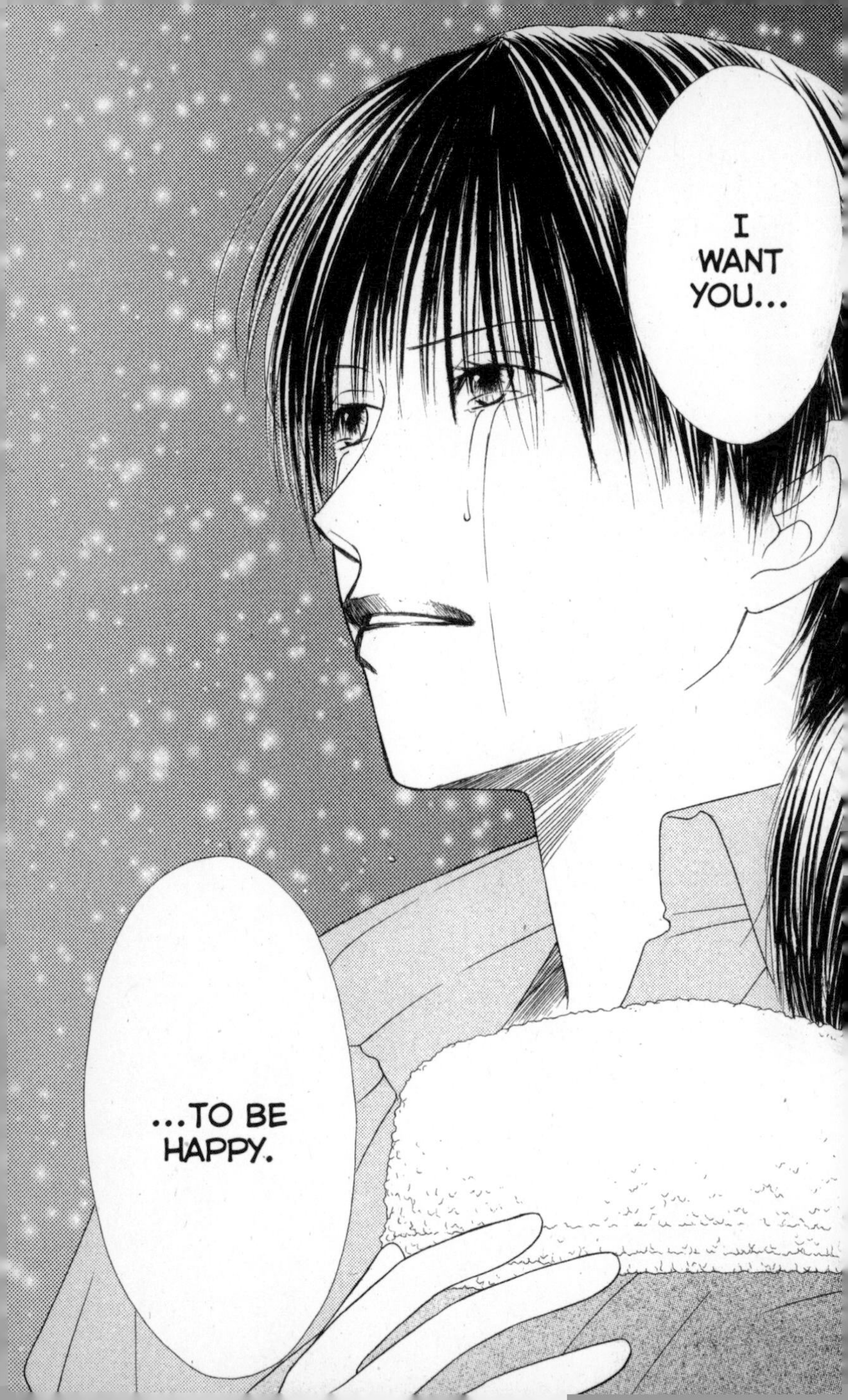
I WANT YOU...
...TO BE HAPPY.

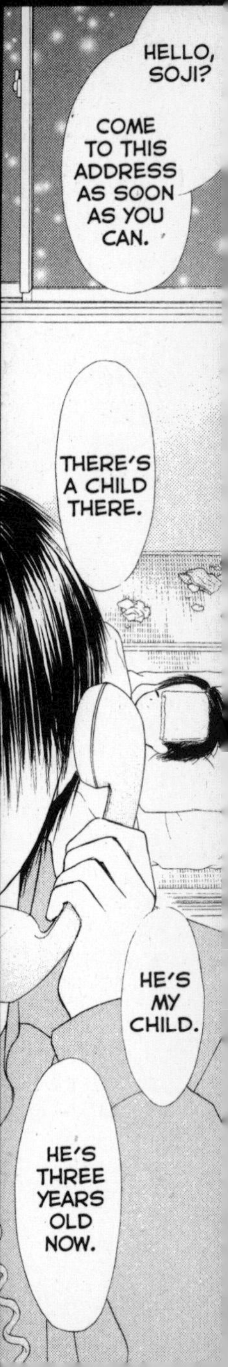
HELLO, SOJI?
COME TO THIS ADDRESS AS SOON AS YOU CAN.
THERE'S A CHILD THERE.
HE'S MY CHILD.
HE'S THREE YEARS OLD NOW.
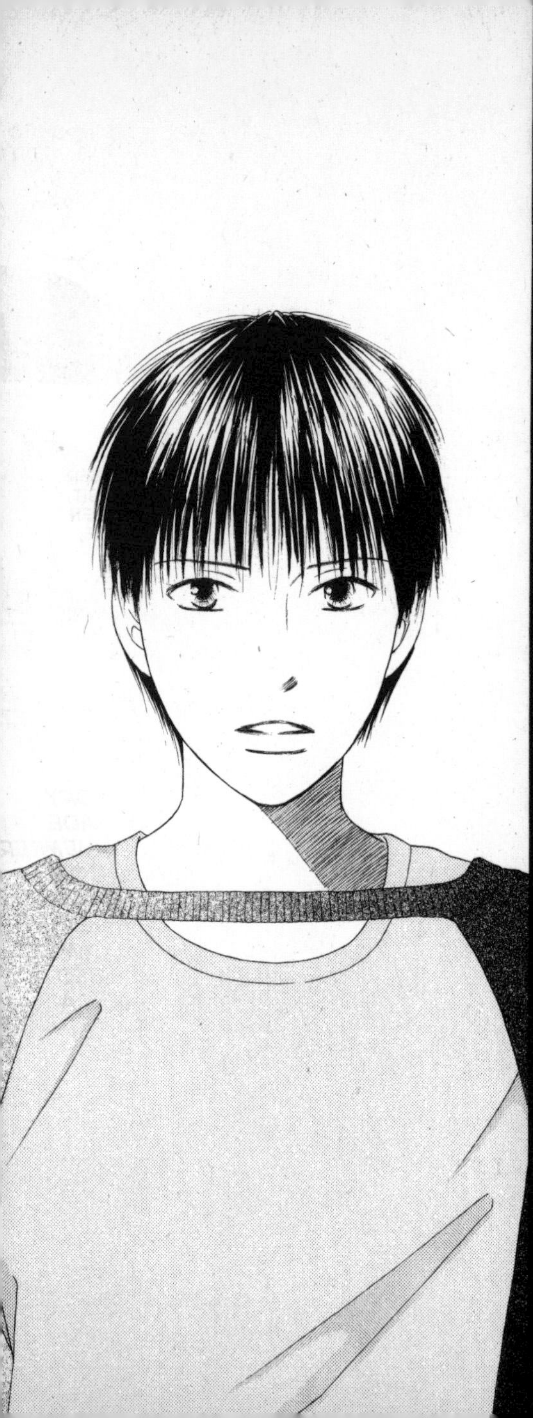

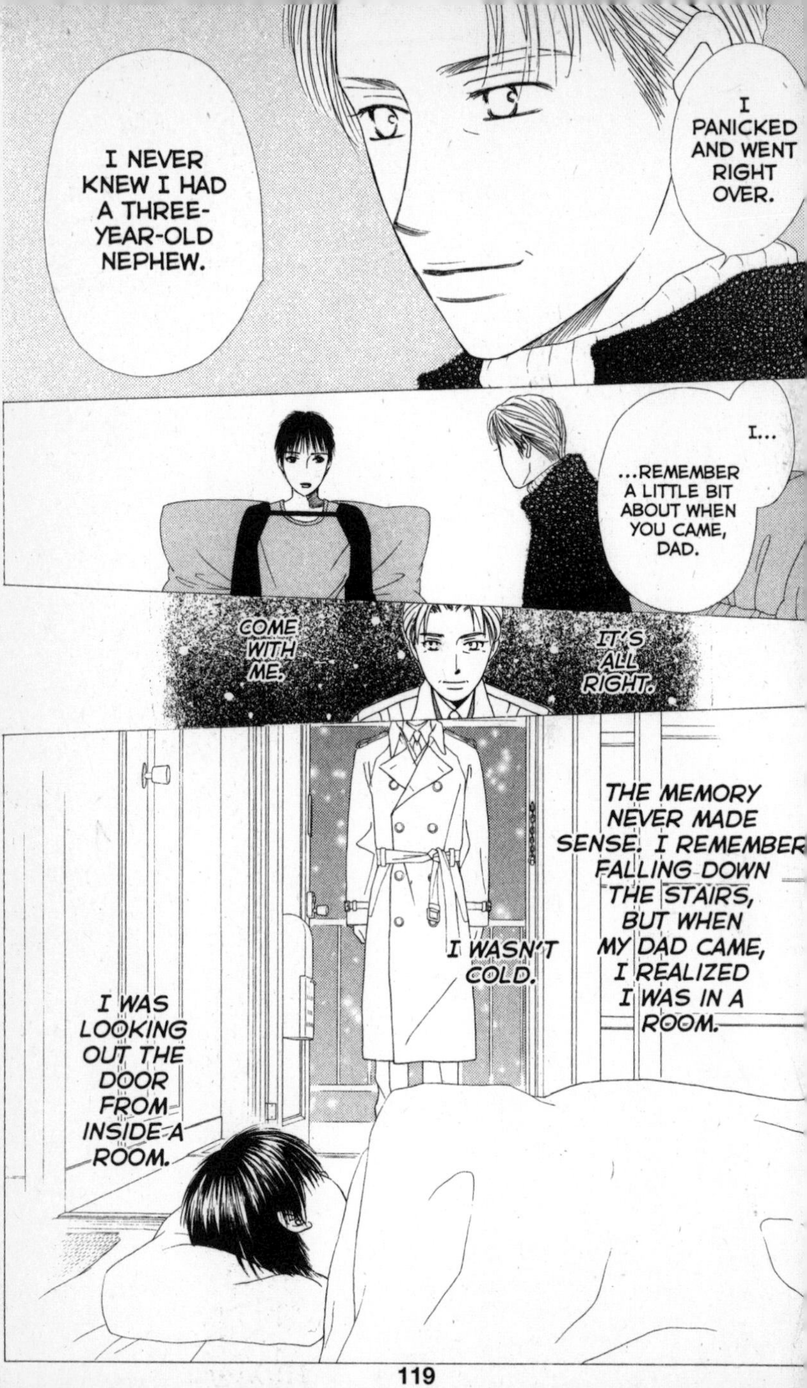
I PANICKED AND WENT RIGHT OVER.
I NEVER KNEW I HAD A THREE-YEAR-OLD NEPHEW.
I...
...REMEMBER A LITTLE BIT ABOUT WHEN YOU CAME, DAD.
IT'S ALL RIGHT.
COME WITH ME.
THE MEMORY NEVER MADE SENSE. I REMEMBER FALLING DOWN THE STAIRS, BUT WHEN MY DAD CAME, I REALIZED I WAS IN A ROOM.
I WASN'T COLD.
I WAS LOOKING OUT THE DOOR FROM INSIDE A ROOM.

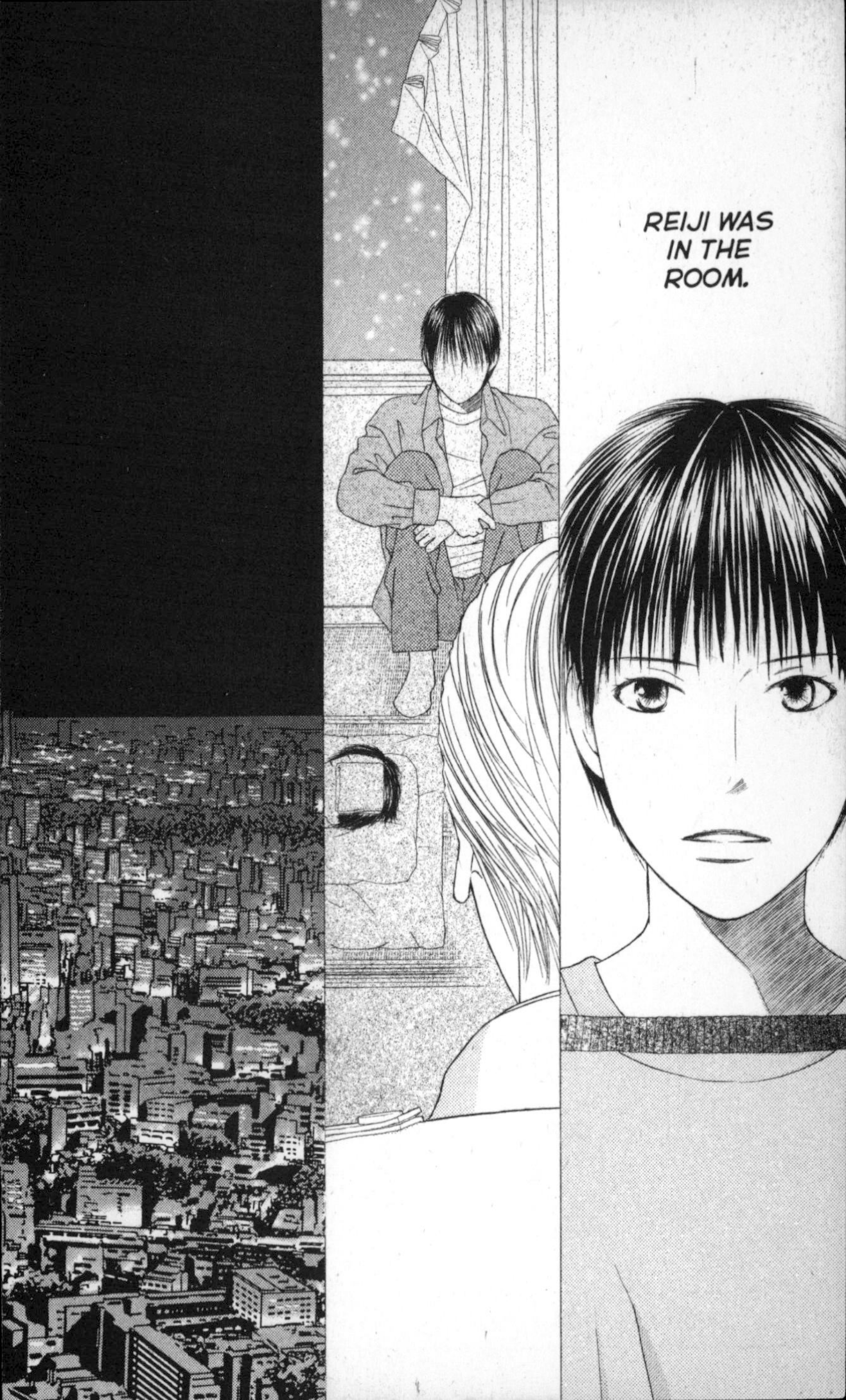
REIJI WAS IN THE ROOM.

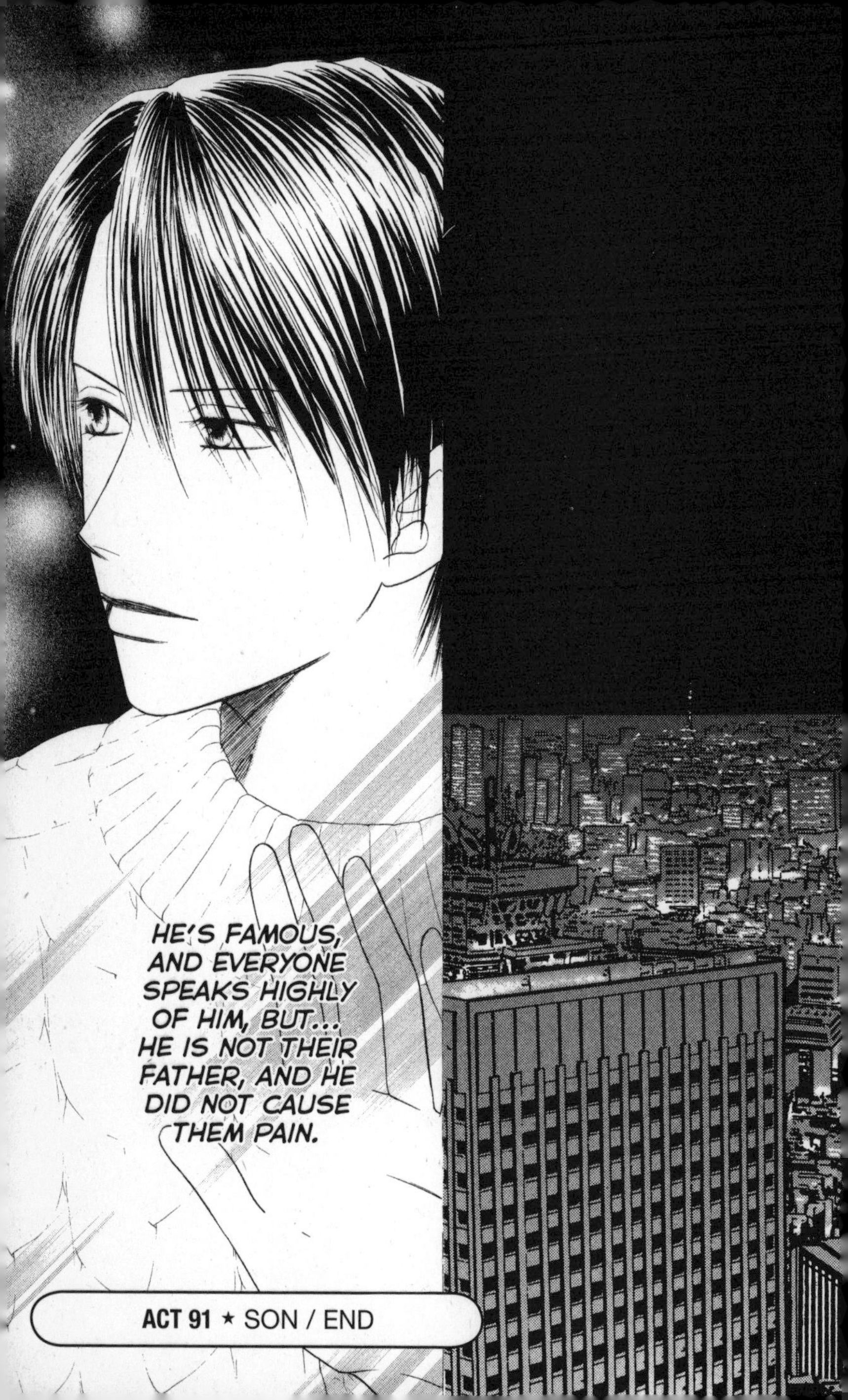
HE'S FAMOUS, AND EVERYONE SPEAKS HIGHLY OF HIM, BUT... HE IS NOT THEIR FATHER, AND HE DID NOT CAUSE THEM PAIN.
ACT 91 ★ SON / END

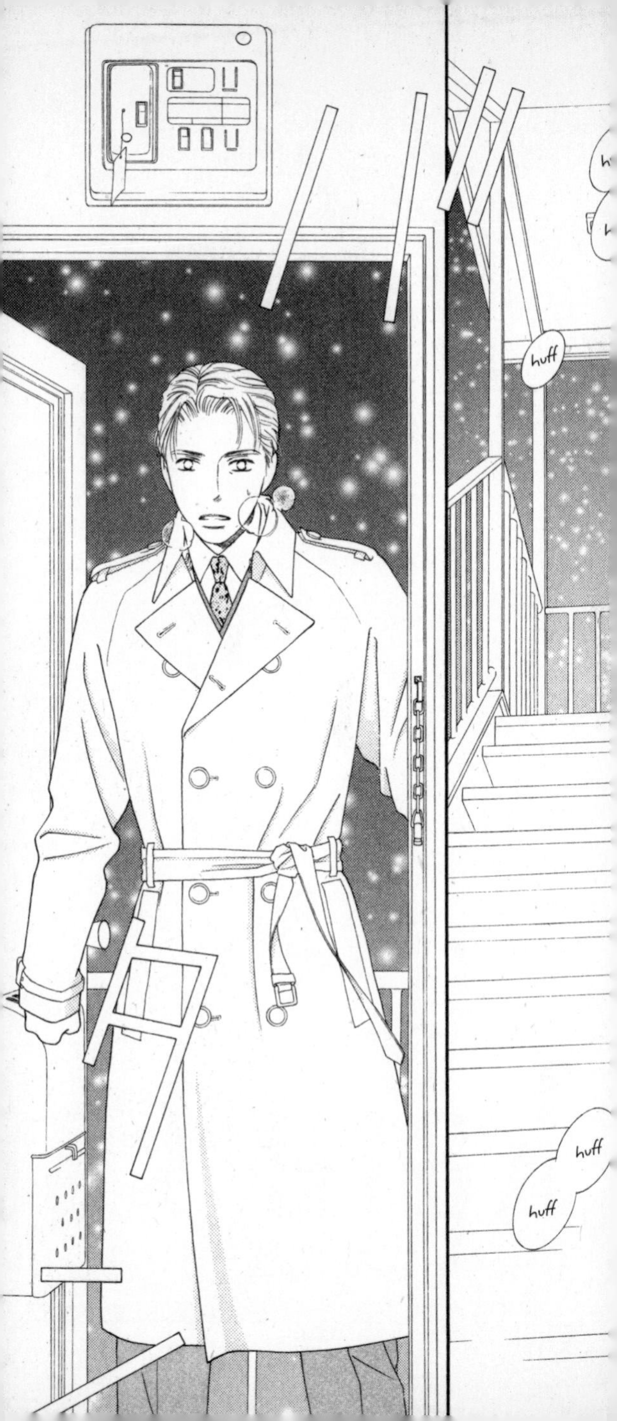
huff
huff
huff

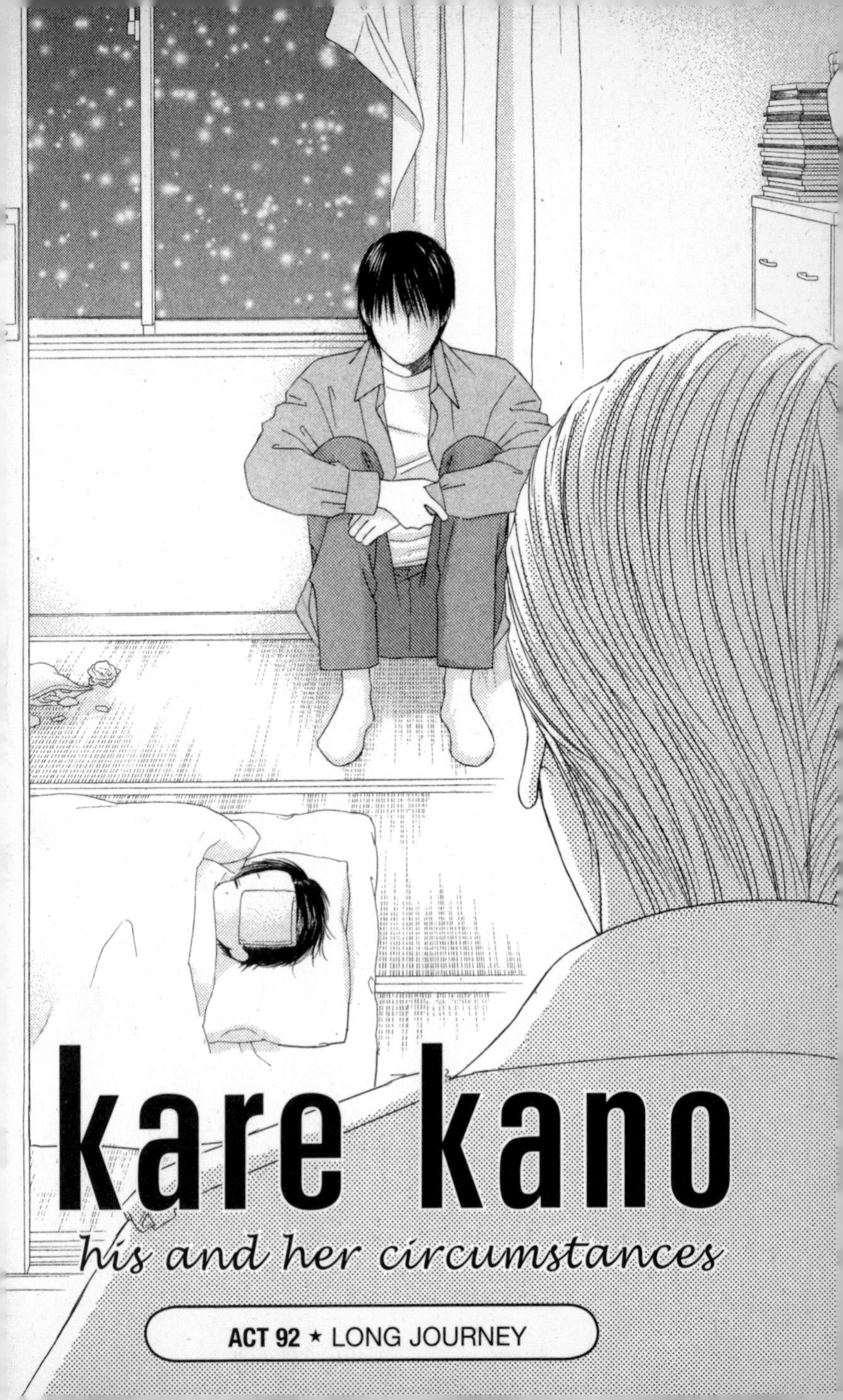
kare kano
his and her circumstances
ACT 92 ★ LONG JOURNEY

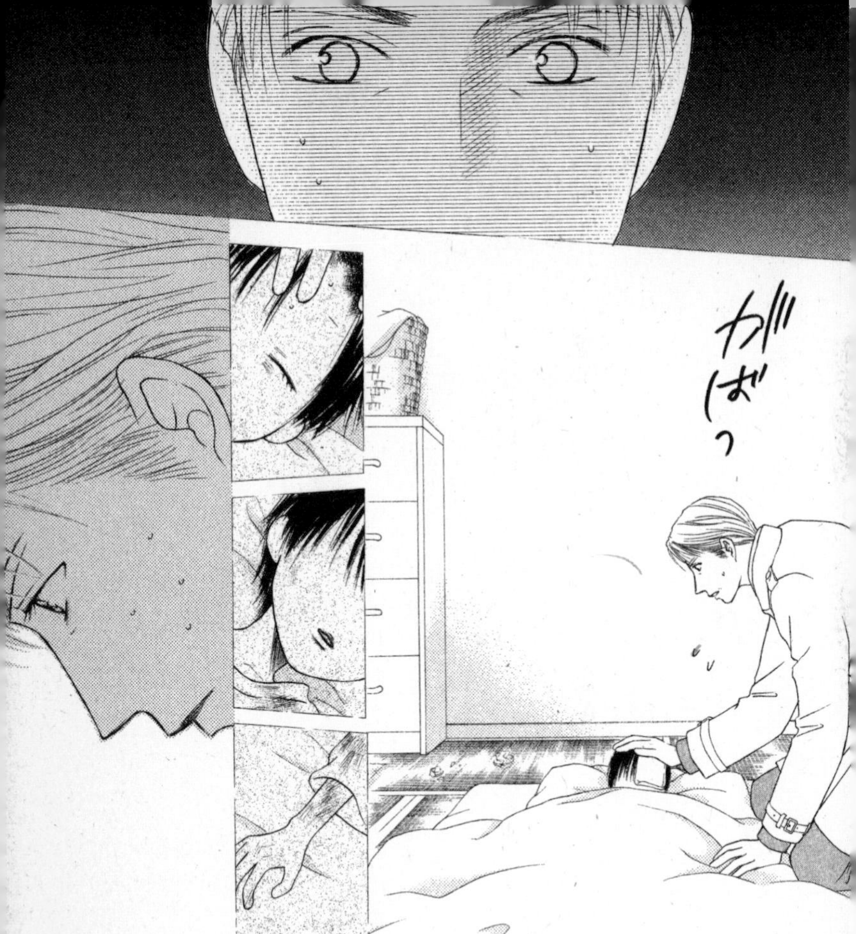
がばっ

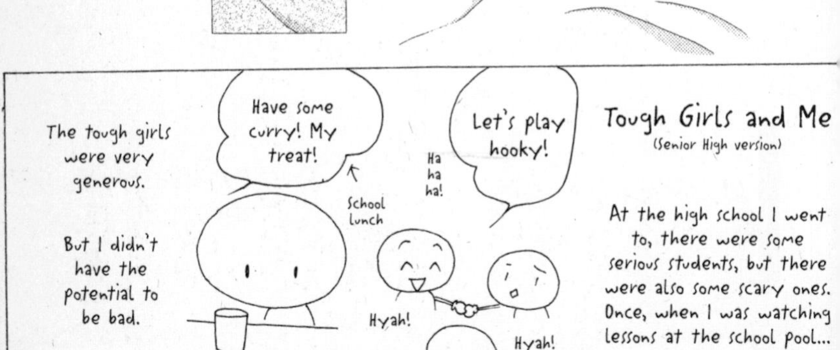
Tough Girls and Me
(Senior High version)
At the high school I went to, there were some serious students, but there were also some scary ones. Once, when I was watching lessons at the school pool...
Let's play hooky!
Ha ha ha!
Hyah!
Hyah!
Have some curry! My treat!
School lunch
The tough girls were very generous.
But I didn't have the potential to be bad.
She treated me to juice, too.

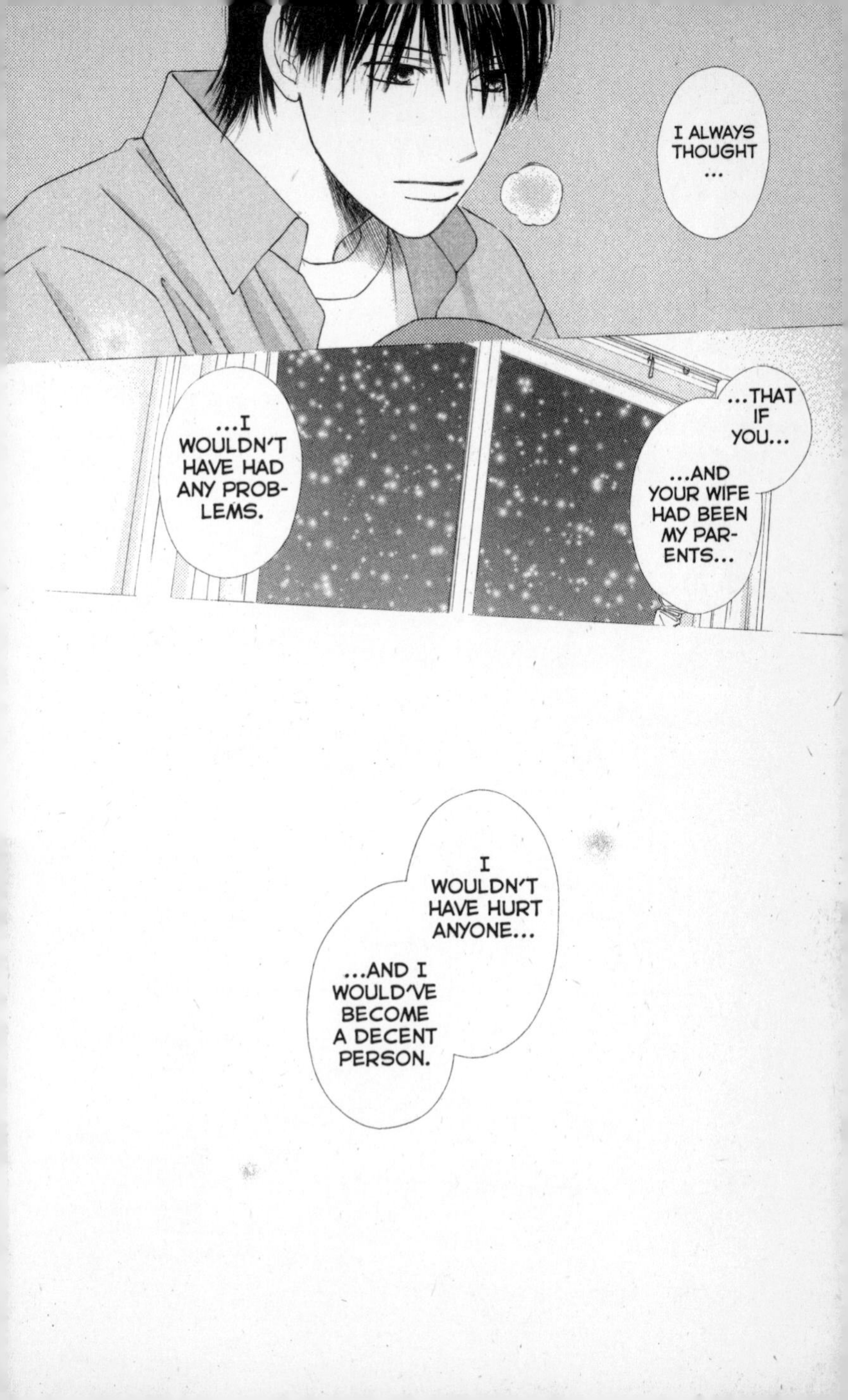
I ALWAYS THOUGHT ...
...THAT IF YOU...
...AND YOUR WIFE HAD BEEN MY PAR-ENTS...
...I WOULDN'T HAVE HAD ANY PROB-LEMS.
I WOULDN'T HAVE HURT ANYONE...
...AND I WOULD'VE BECOME A DECENT PERSON.

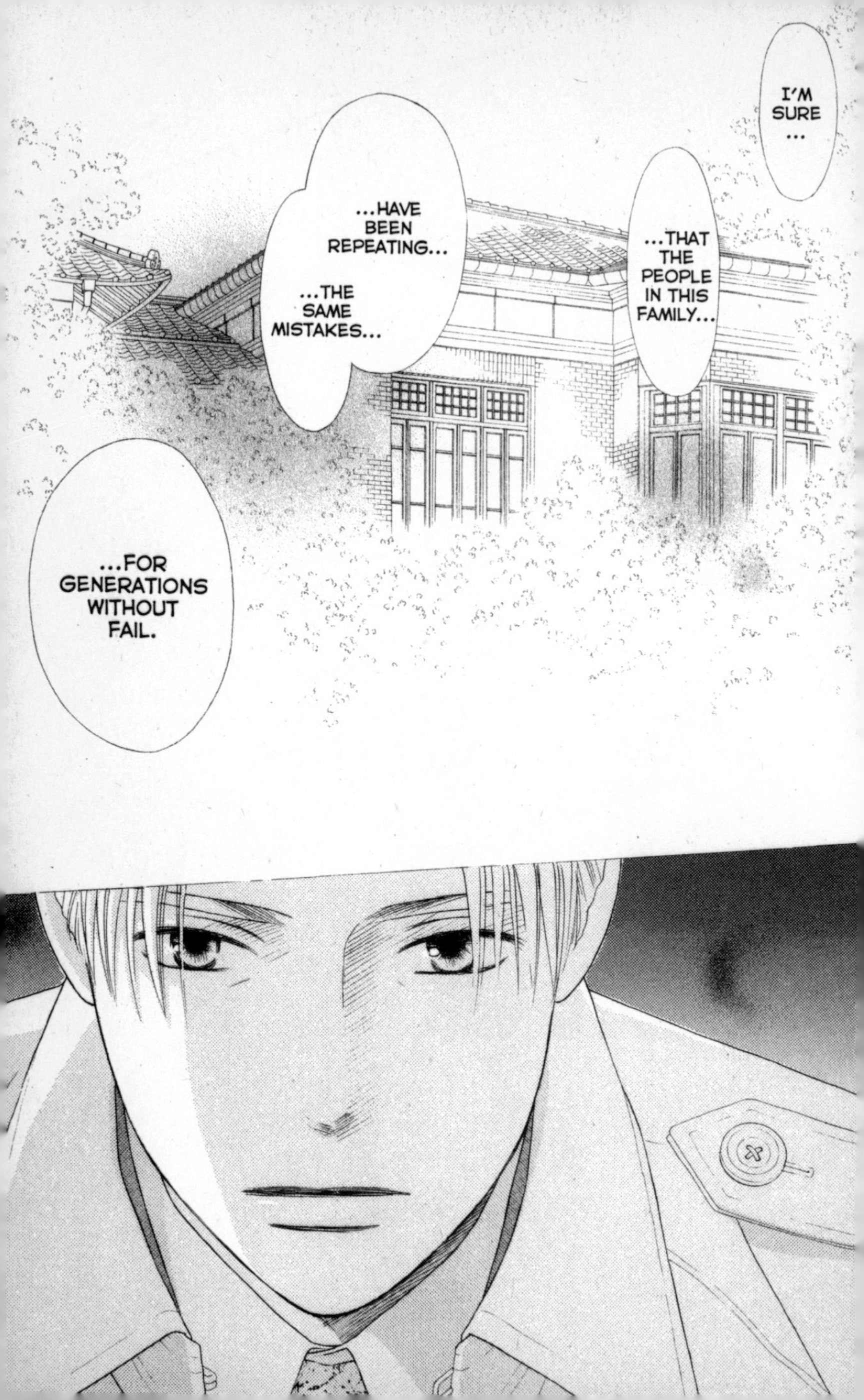
I'M SURE ...
...THAT THE PEOPLE IN THIS FAMILY...
...HAVE BEEN REPEATING...
...THE SAME MISTAKES...
...FOR GENERATIONS WITHOUT FAIL.

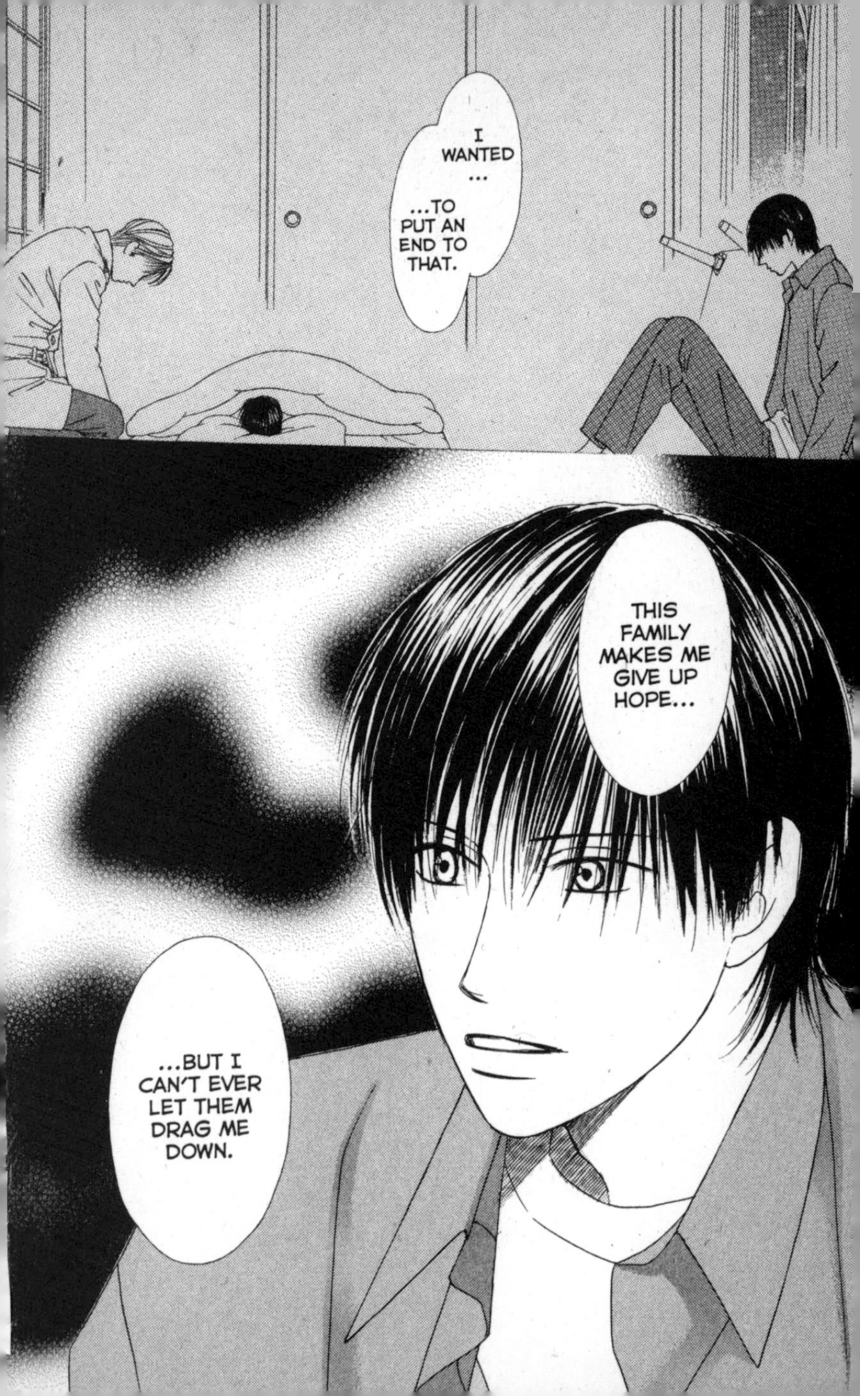
I WANTED ...
...TO PUT AN END TO THAT.
THIS FAMILY MAKES ME GIVE UP HOPE...
...BUT I CAN'T EVER LET THEM DRAG ME DOWN.

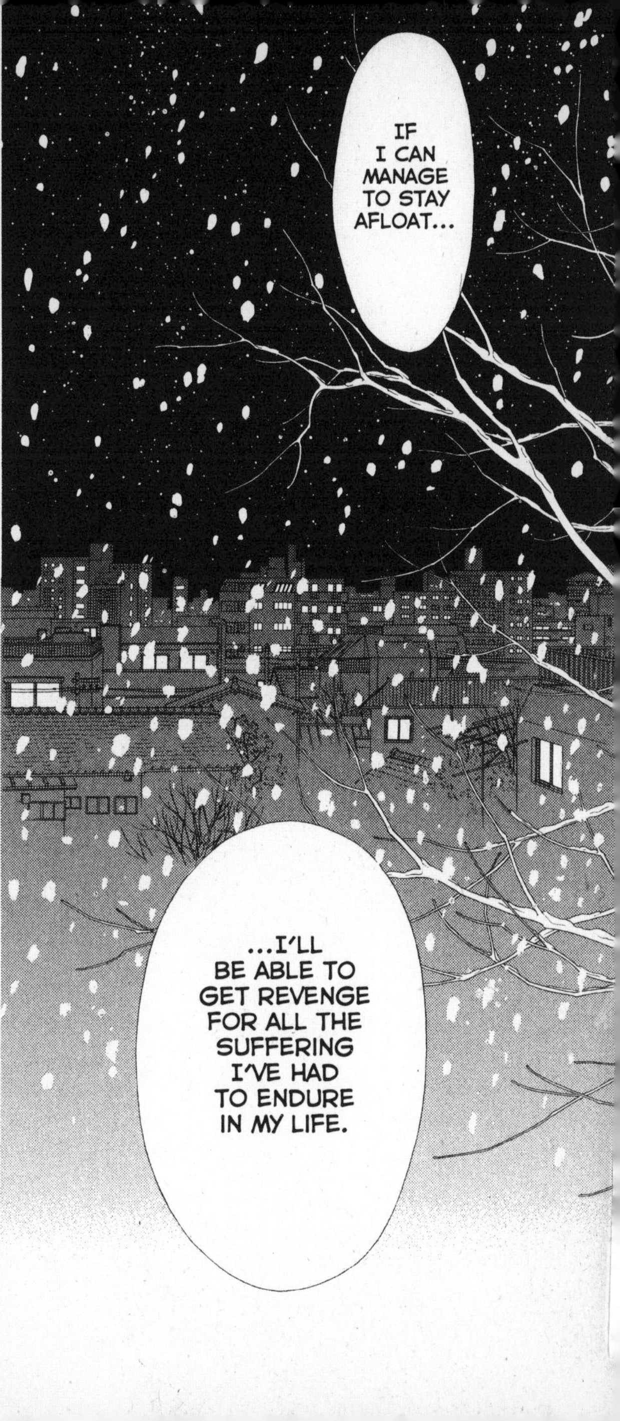
IF I CAN MANAGE TO STAY AFLOAT...
...I'LL BE ABLE TO GET REVENGE FOR ALL THE SUFFERING I'VE HAD TO ENDURE IN MY LIFE.

4

Western-style clothing

If I hadn't drawn Reiji, I probably wouldn't have been interested in this at all.

In order to get the right feel, I went to some stores and I bought an outfit to wear to my editor's wedding ceremony. The top brands feel so comfortable to wear--the cloth feels nice, the colors look great... It was educational.

They might not be widely popular, but beautiful clothes and pretty models sure do look nice.

A white camisole is 90,000 yen?!

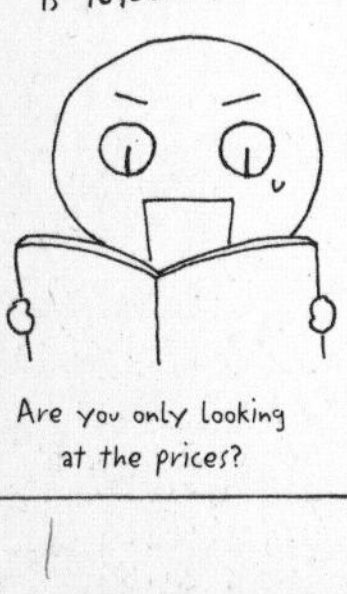

Are you only looking at the prices?

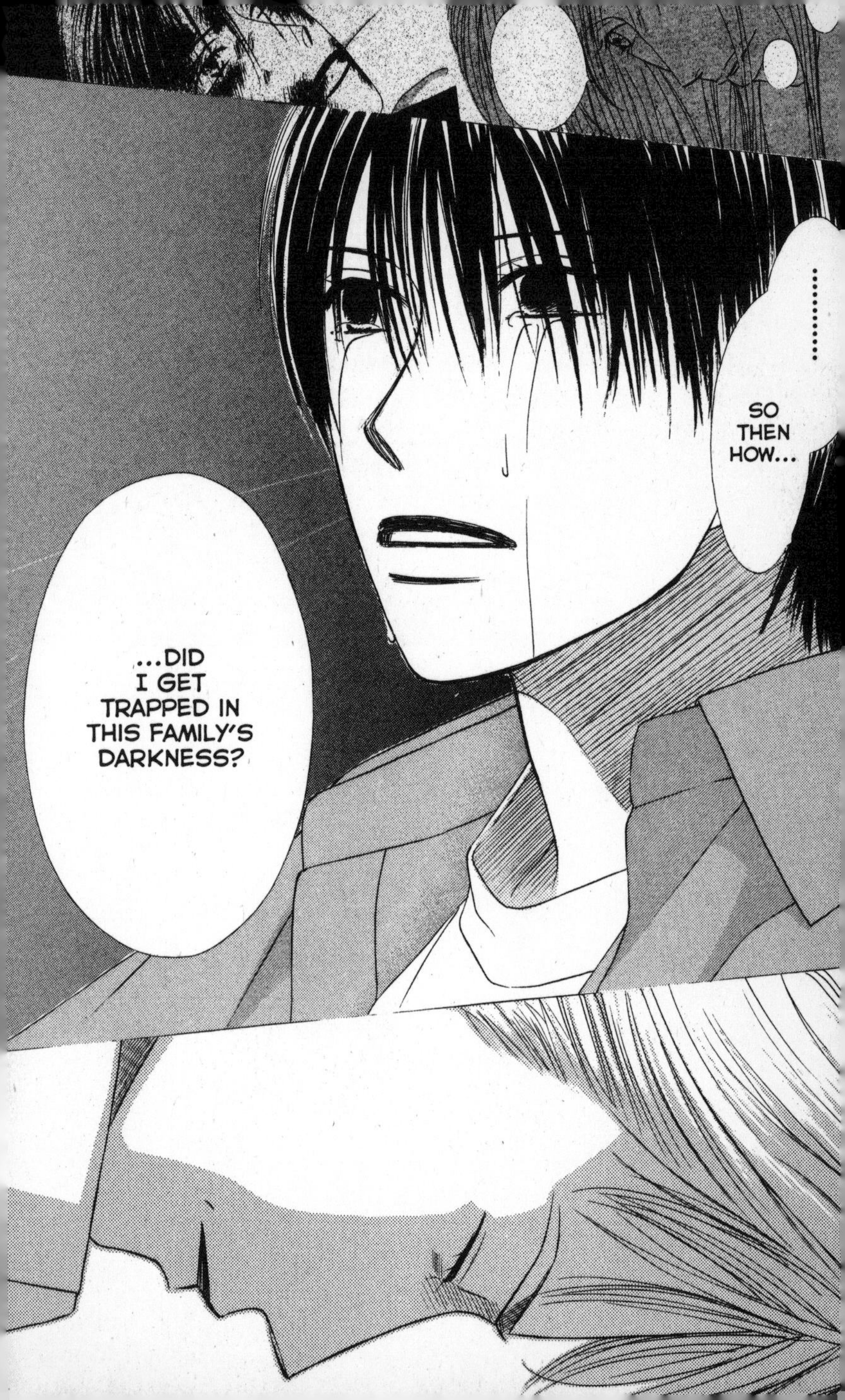
......
SO THEN HOW...
...DID I GET TRAPPED IN THIS FAMILY'S DARKNESS?

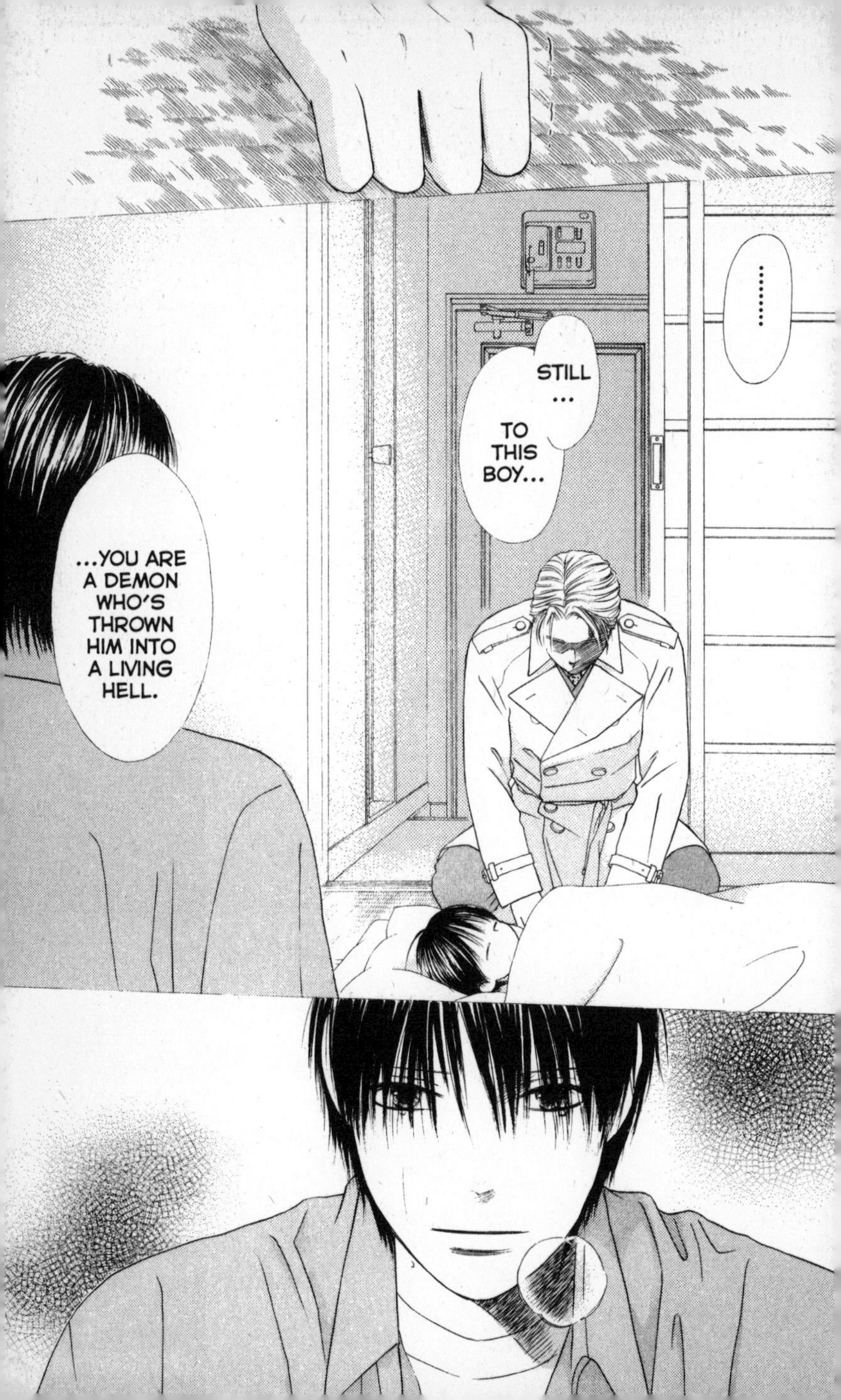
......
STILL ... TO THIS BOY...
...YOU ARE A DEMON WHO'S THROWN HIM INTO A LIVING HELL.

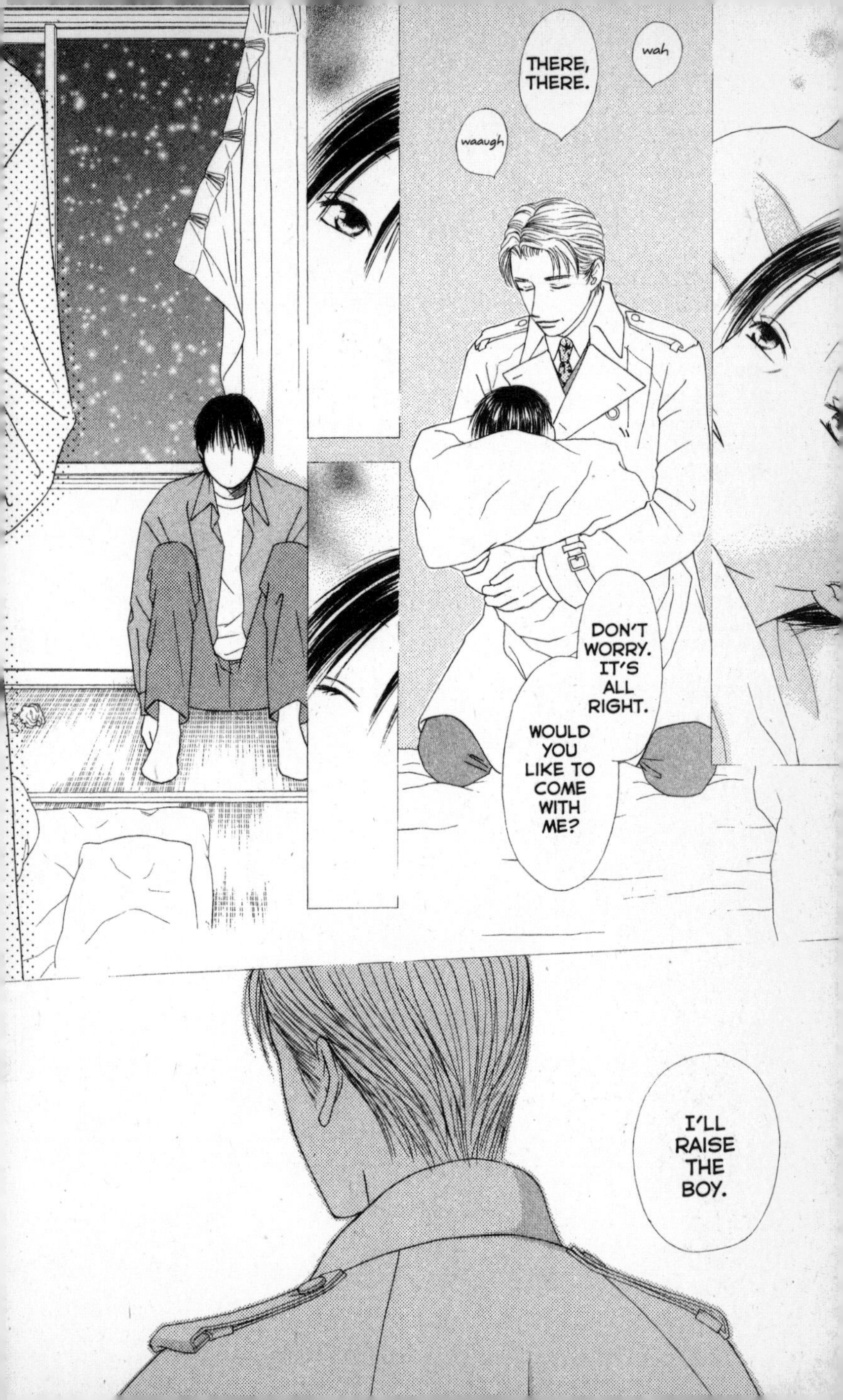
wah
THERE, THERE.
waaugh
DON'T WORRY. IT'S ALL RIGHT.
WOULD YOU LIKE TO COME WITH ME?
I'LL RAISE THE BOY.

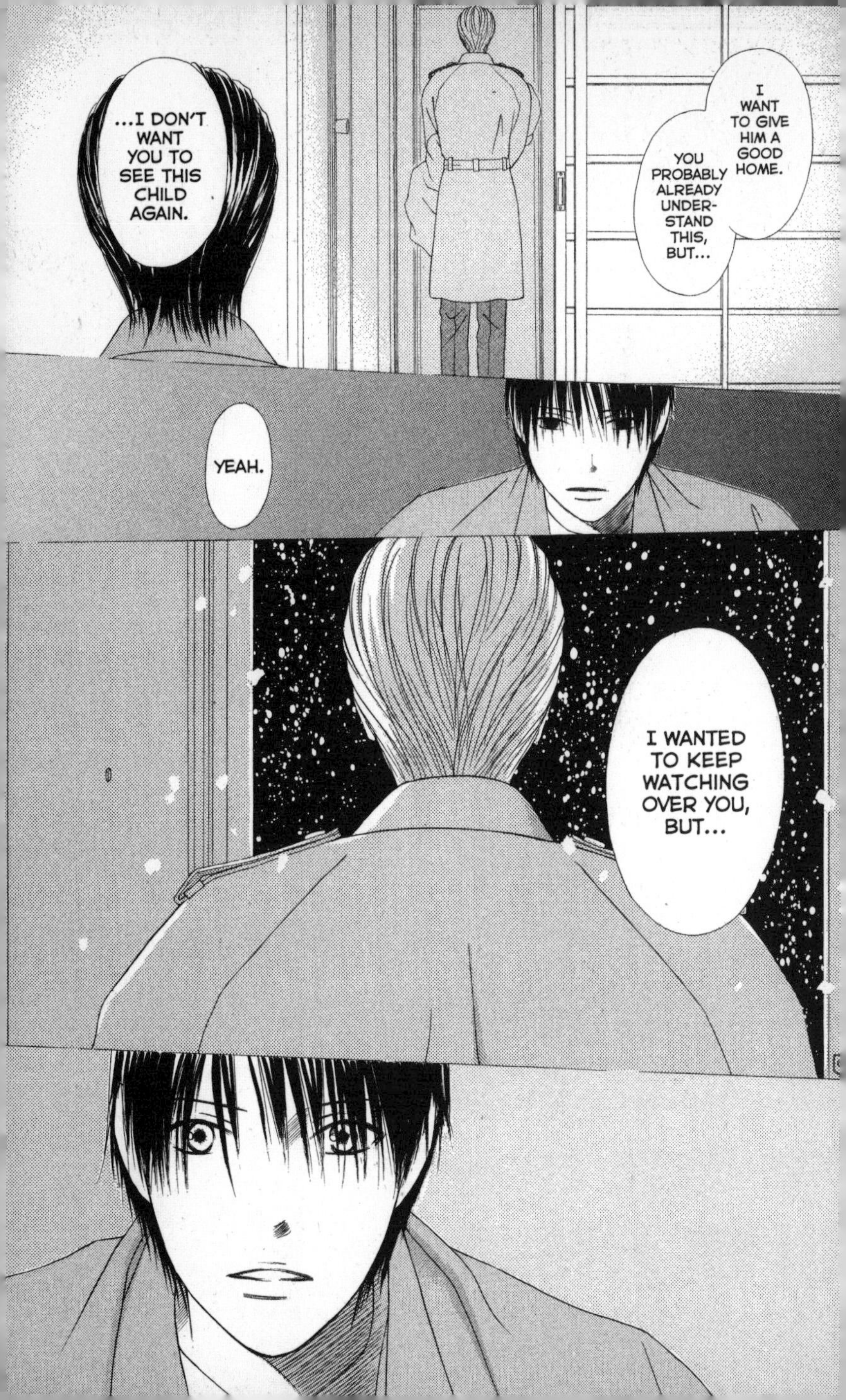
I WANT TO GIVE HIM A GOOD HOME.
YOU PROBABLY ALREADY UNDERSTAND THIS, BUT...
...I DON'T WANT YOU TO SEE THIS CHILD AGAIN.
YEAH.
I WANTED TO KEEP WATCHING OVER YOU, BUT...

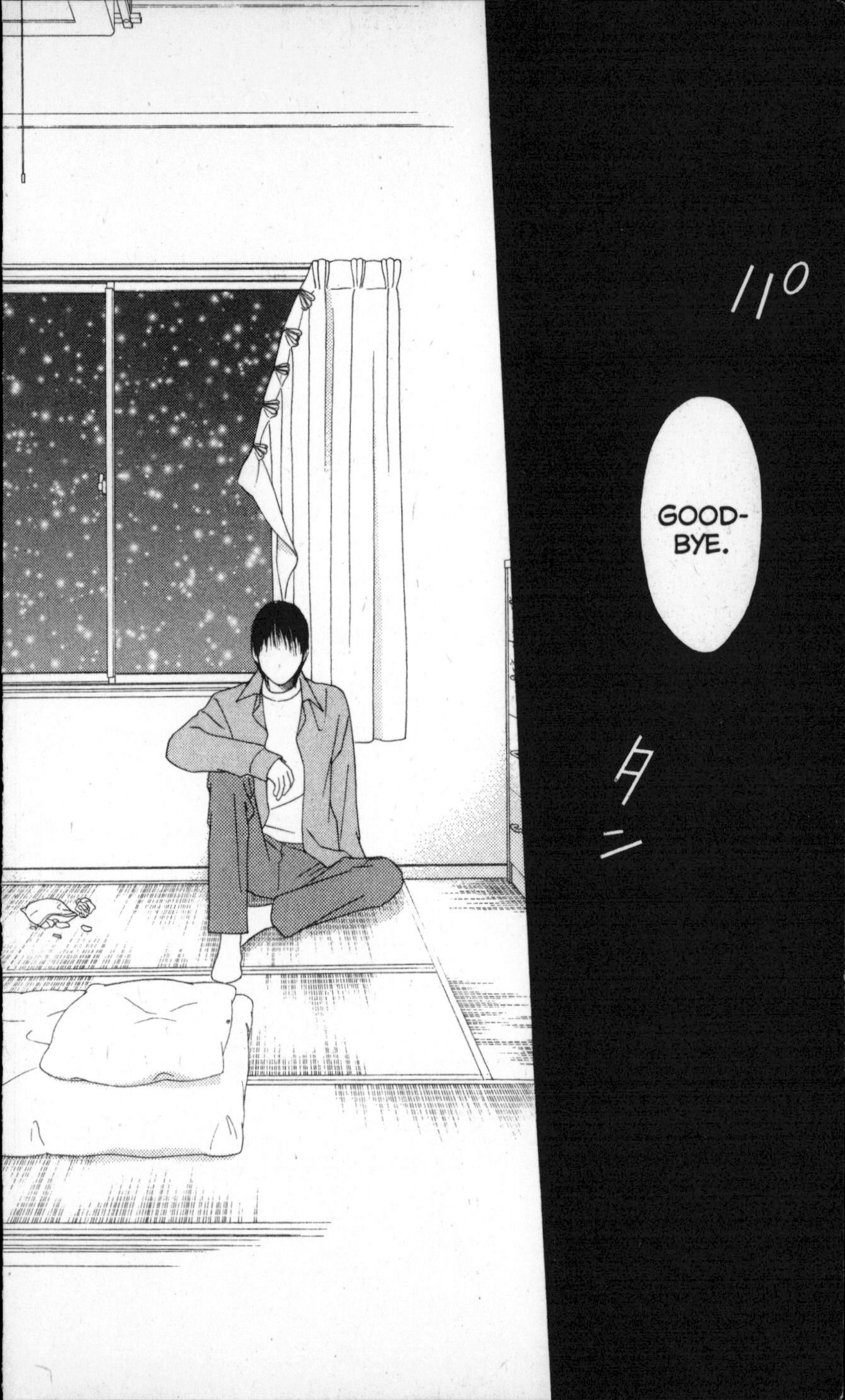
パ
GOOD-BYE.
タン

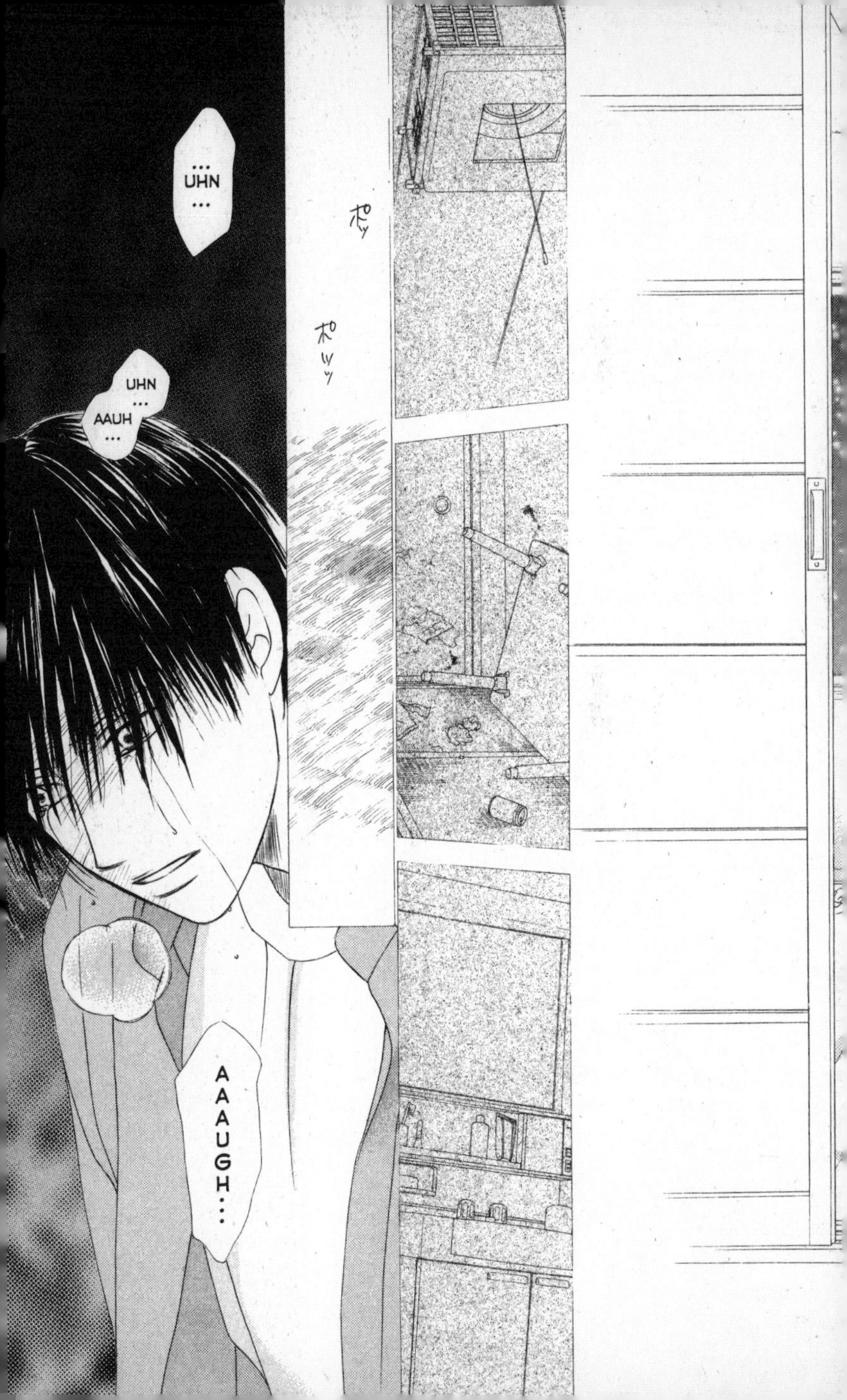
ポッ
ポッッ
...UHN...
UHN... AAUH...
AAAUGH...

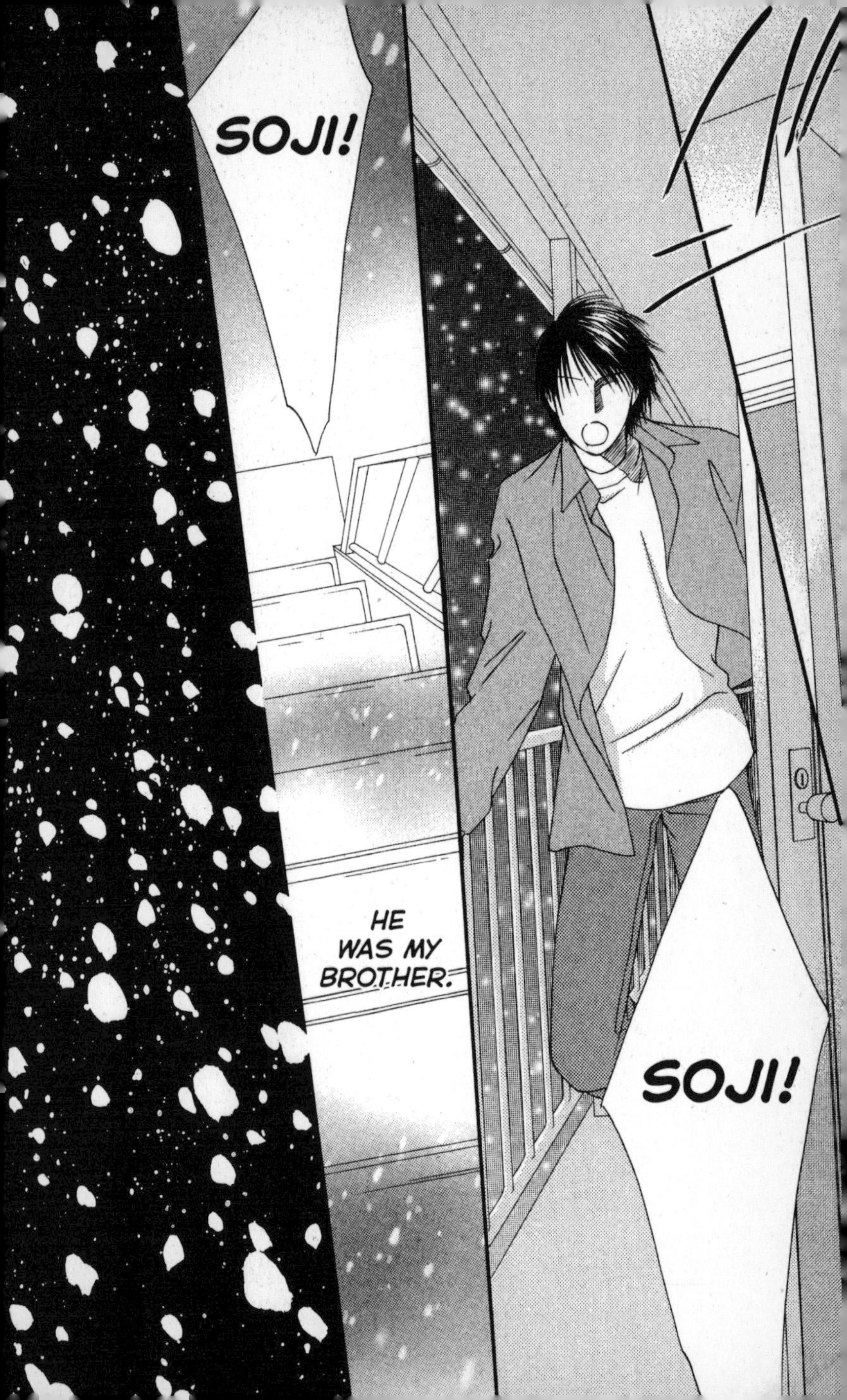
SOJI!
SOJI!
HE WAS MY BROTHER.

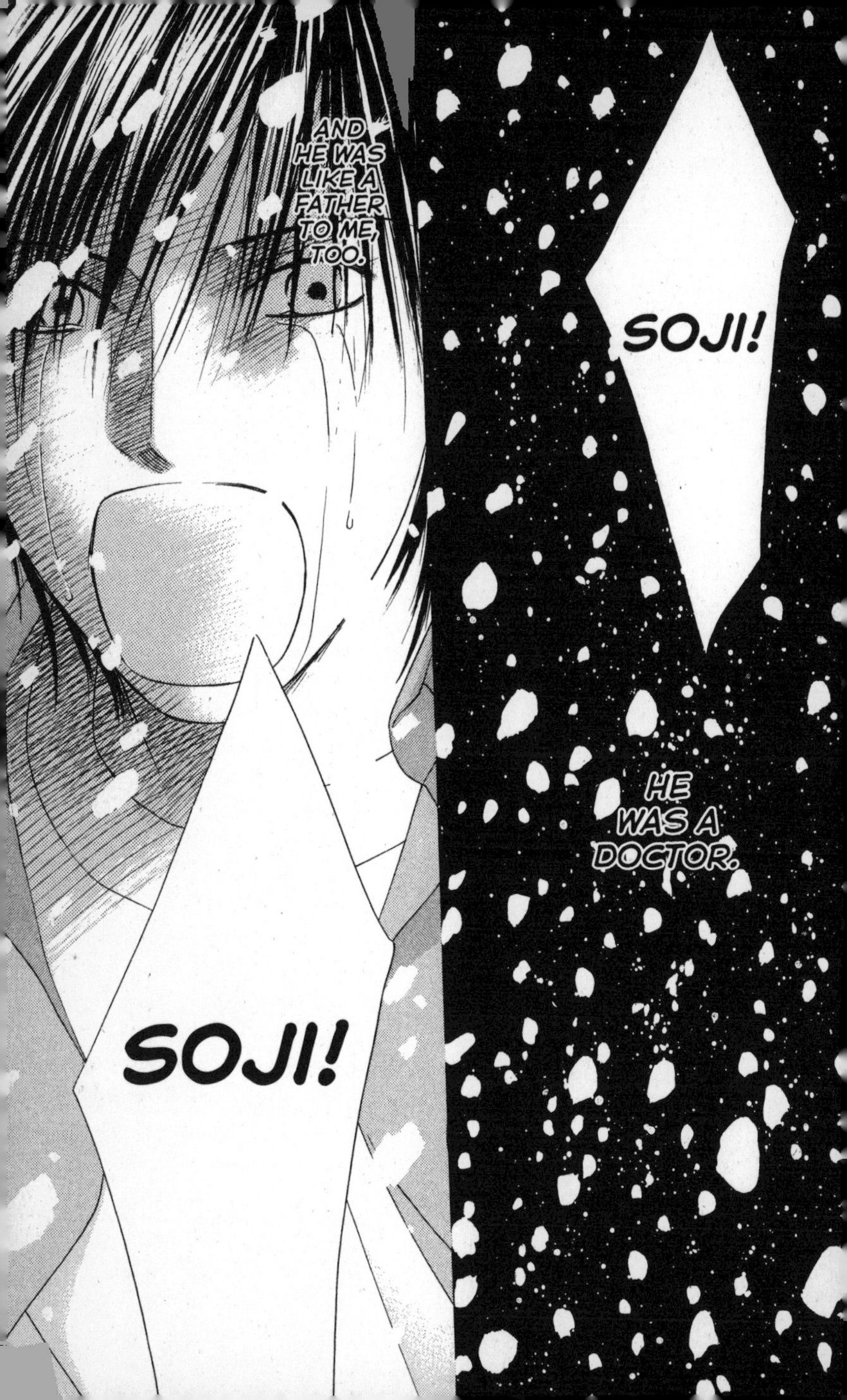
SOJI!
HE WAS A DOCTOR.
AND HE WAS LIKE A FATHER TO ME, TOO.
SOJI!

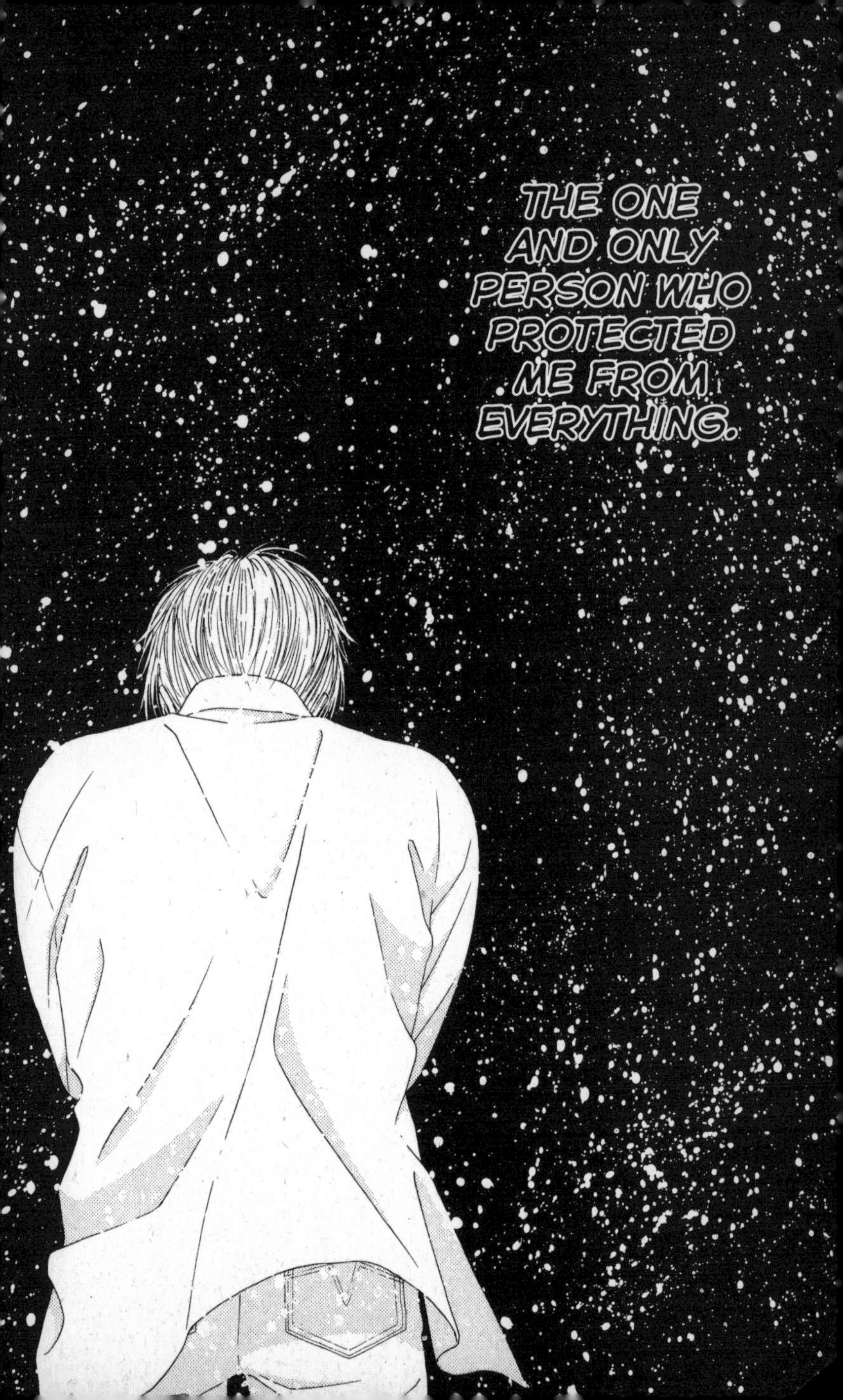
THE ONE AND ONLY PERSON WHO PROTECTED ME FROM EVERYTHING.

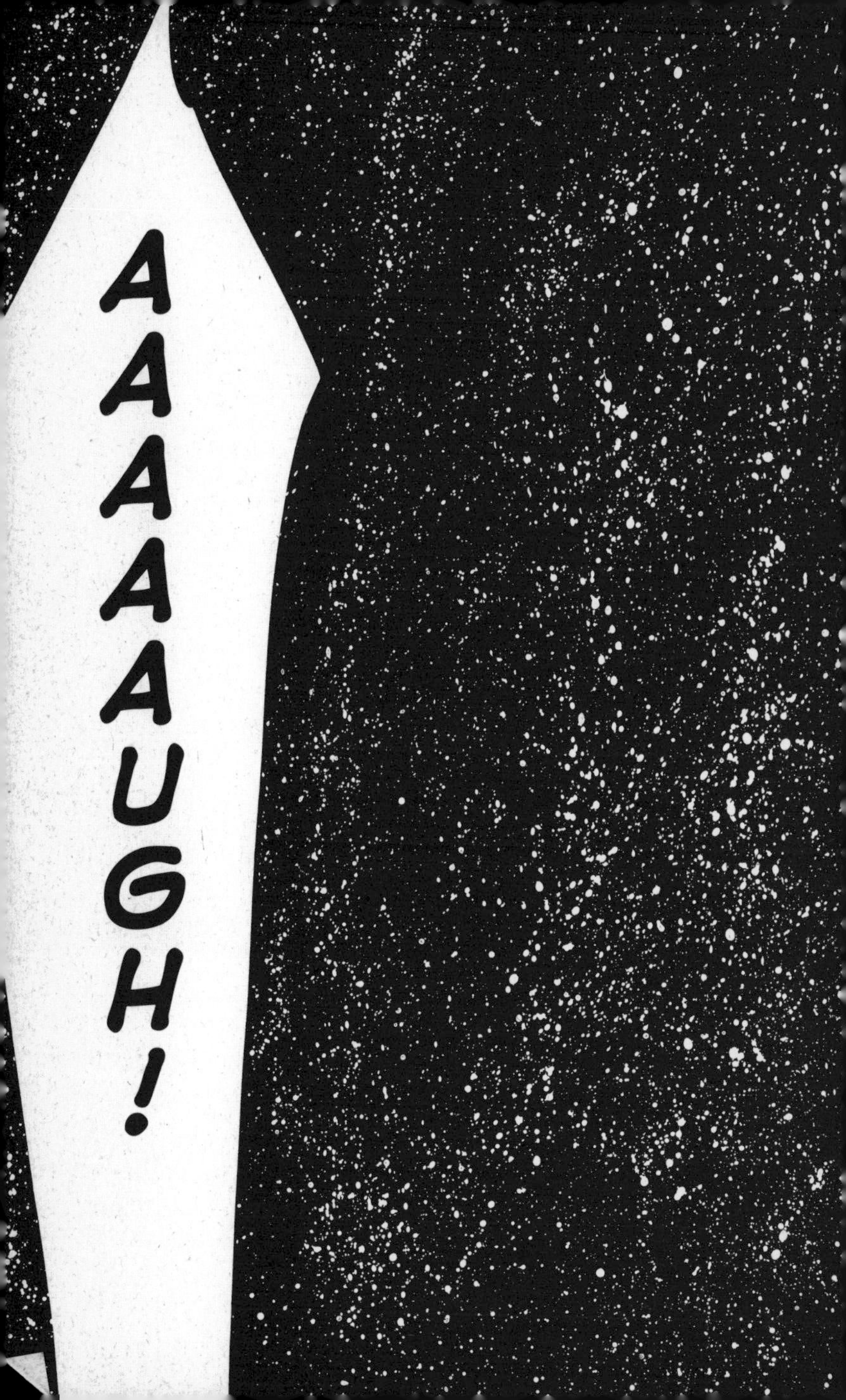
AAAAAAUGH!

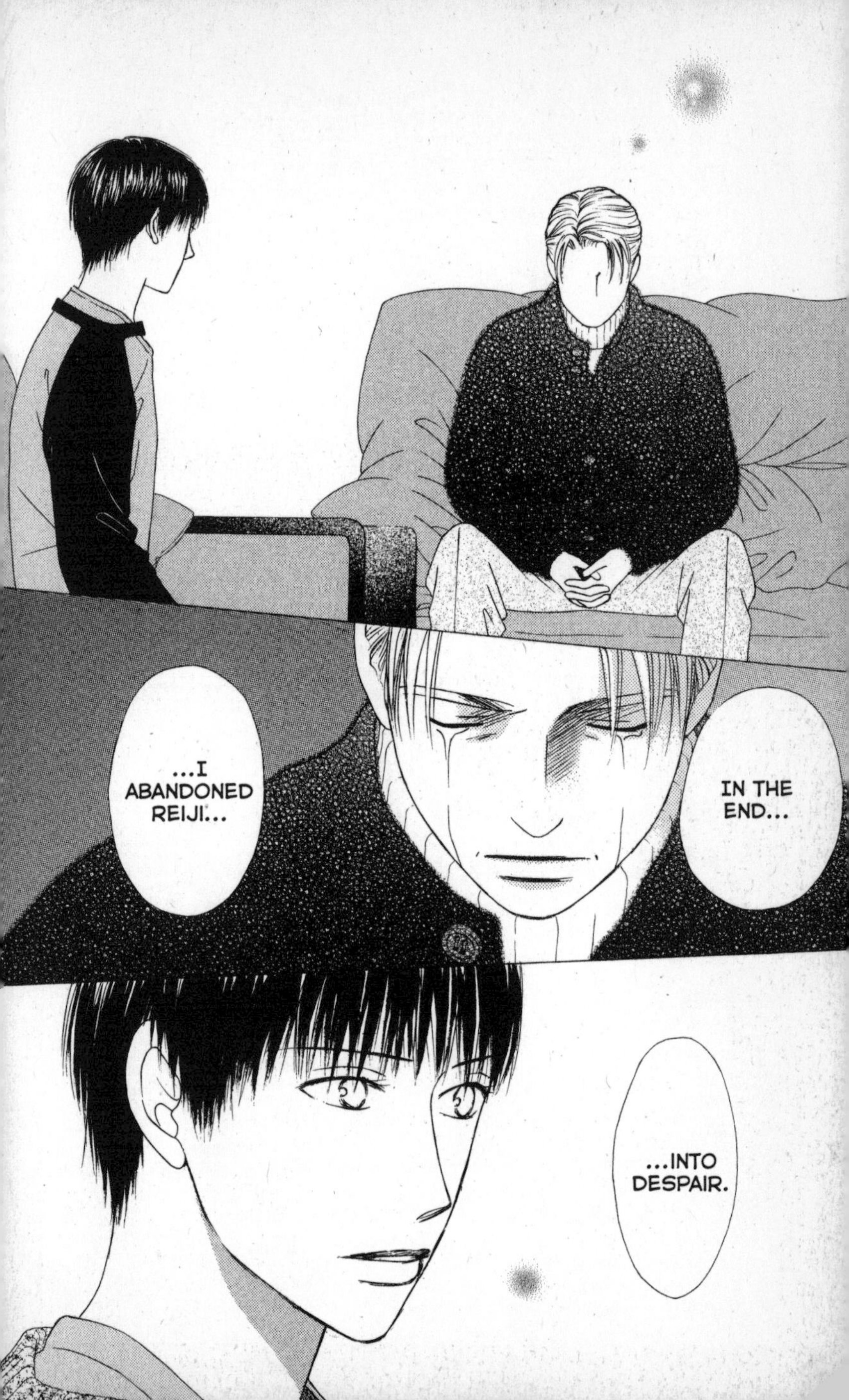
IN THE END...
...I ABANDONED REIJI...
...INTO DESPAIR.

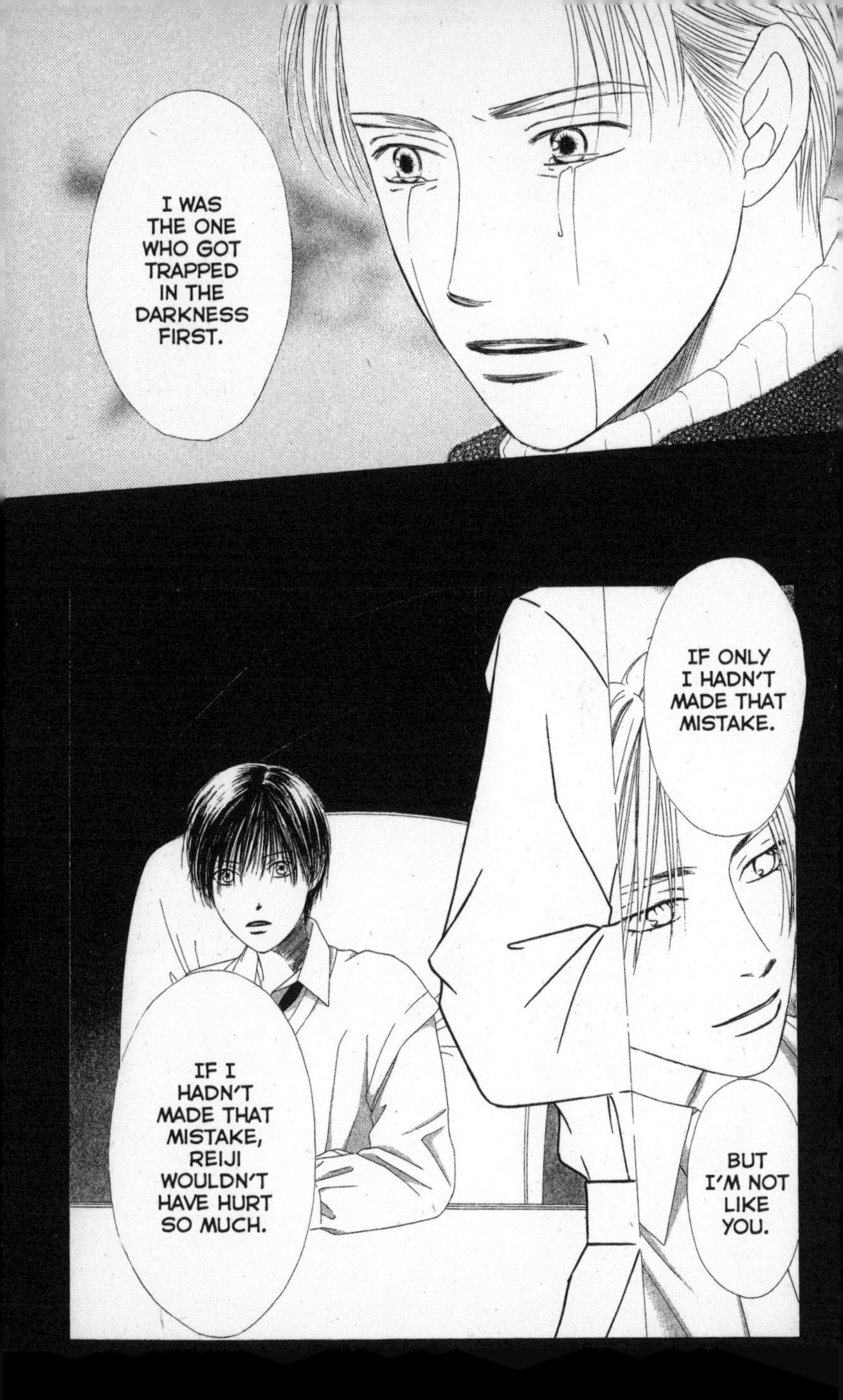
I WAS THE ONE WHO GOT TRAPPED IN THE DARKNESS FIRST.
IF ONLY I HADN'T MADE THAT MISTAKE.
IF I HADN'T MADE THAT MISTAKE, REIJI WOULDN'T HAVE HURT SO MUCH.
BUT I'M NOT LIKE YOU.

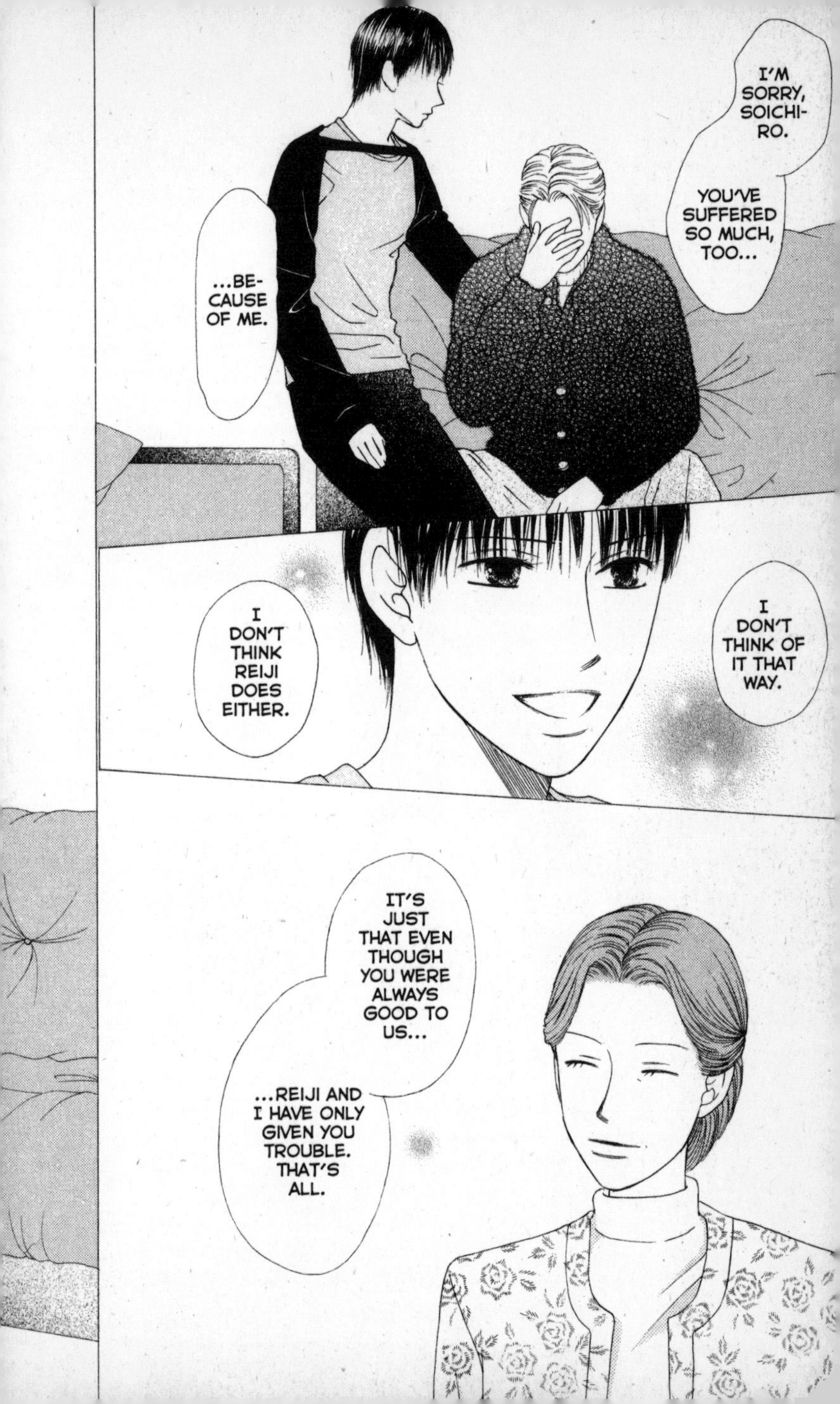

I'M SORRY, SOICHI-RO.
YOU'VE SUFFERED SO MUCH, TOO...
...BE-CAUSE OF ME.
I DON'T THINK OF IT THAT WAY.
I DON'T THINK REIJI DOES EITHER.
IT'S JUST THAT EVEN THOUGH YOU WERE ALWAYS GOOD TO US...
...REIJI AND I HAVE ONLY GIVEN YOU TROUBLE. THAT'S ALL.

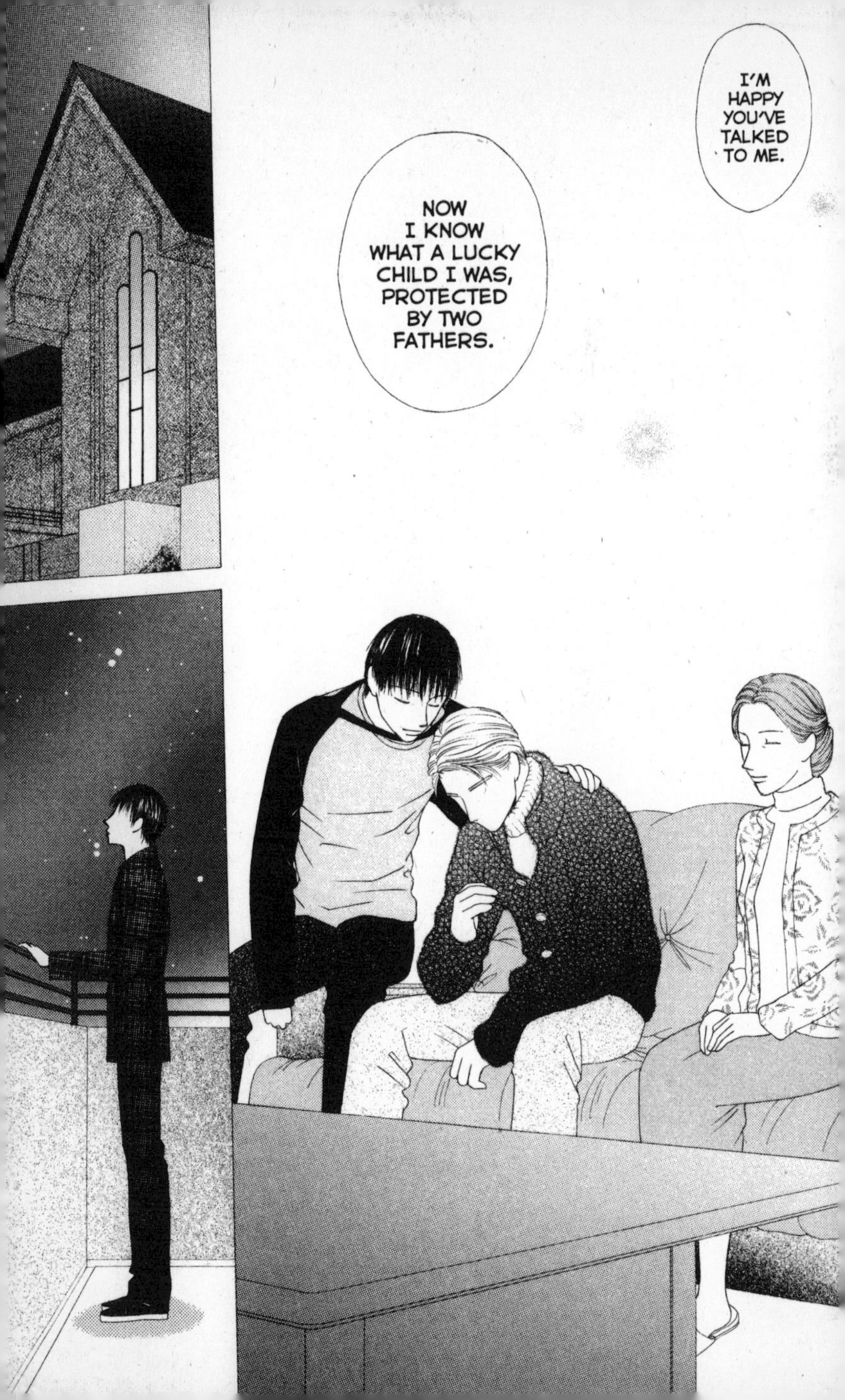
I'M HAPPY YOU'VE TALKED TO ME.
NOW I KNOW WHAT A LUCKY CHILD I WAS, PROTECTED BY TWO FATHERS.

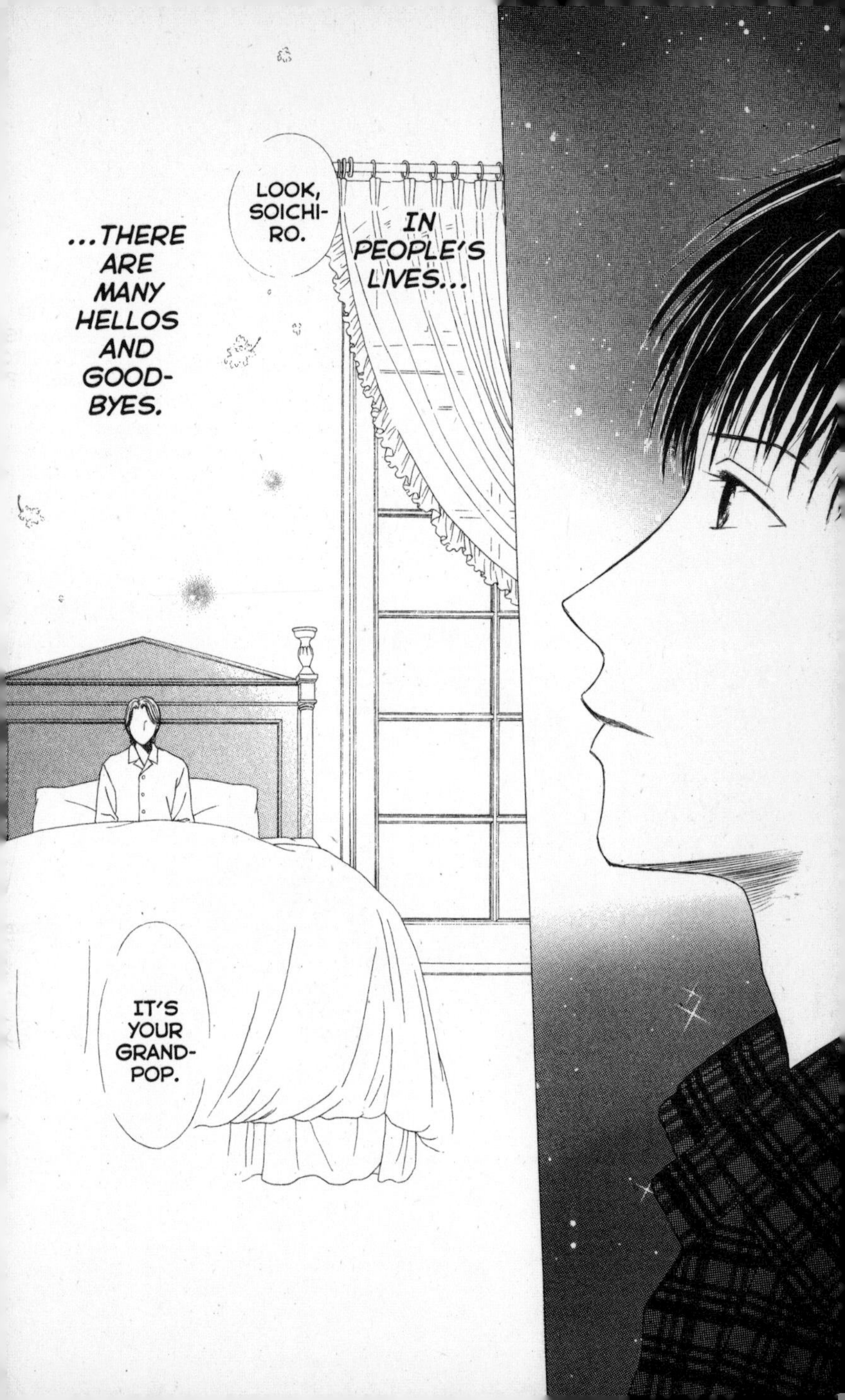
IN PEOPLE'S LIVES...
LOOK, SOICHI-RO.
...THERE ARE MANY HELLOS AND GOOD-BYES.
IT'S YOUR GRAND-POP.

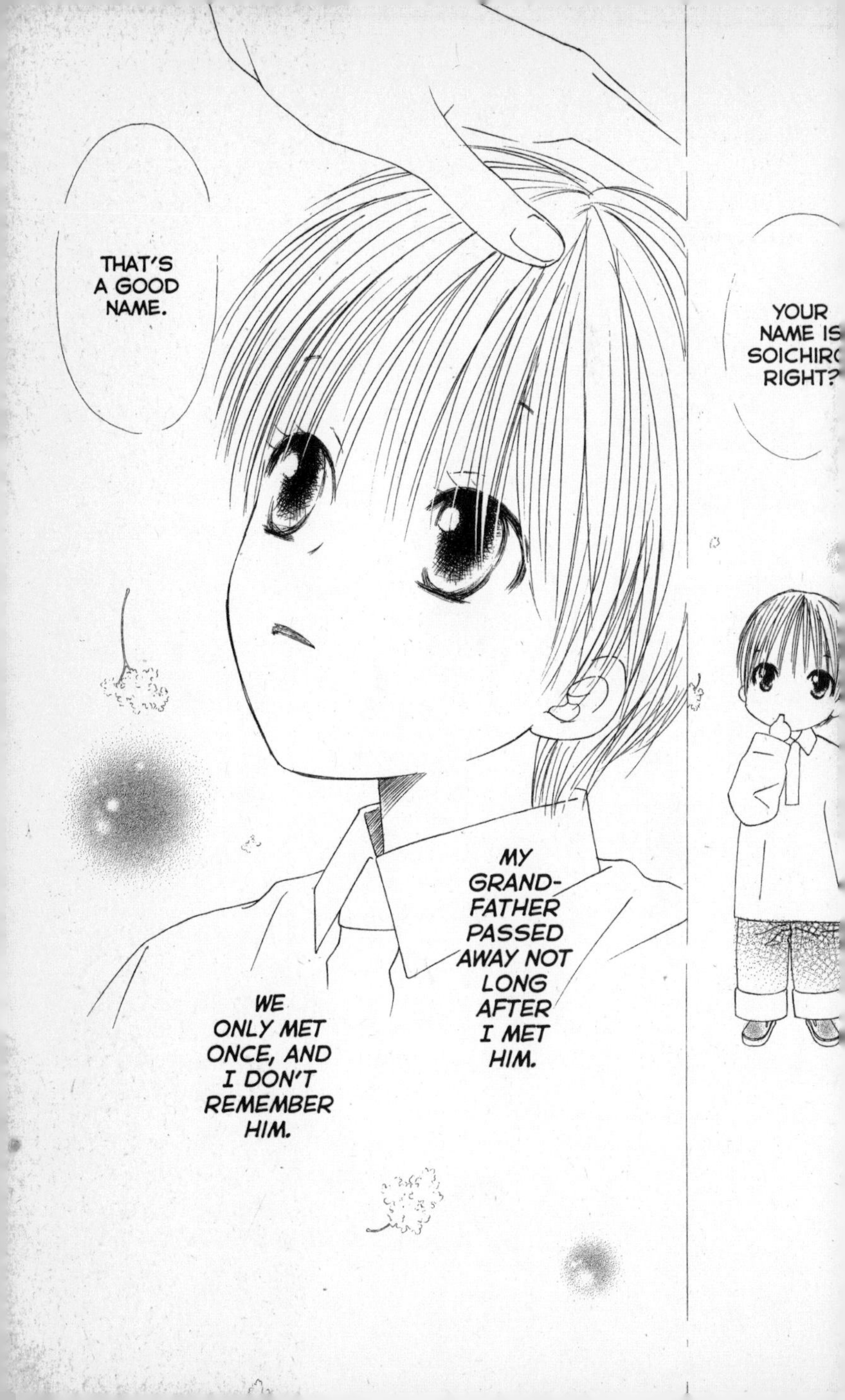
YOUR NAME IS SOICHIR RIGHT?
THAT'S A GOOD NAME.
MY GRAND-FATHER PASSED AWAY NOT LONG AFTER I MET HIM.
WE ONLY MET ONCE, AND I DON'T REMEMBER HIM.

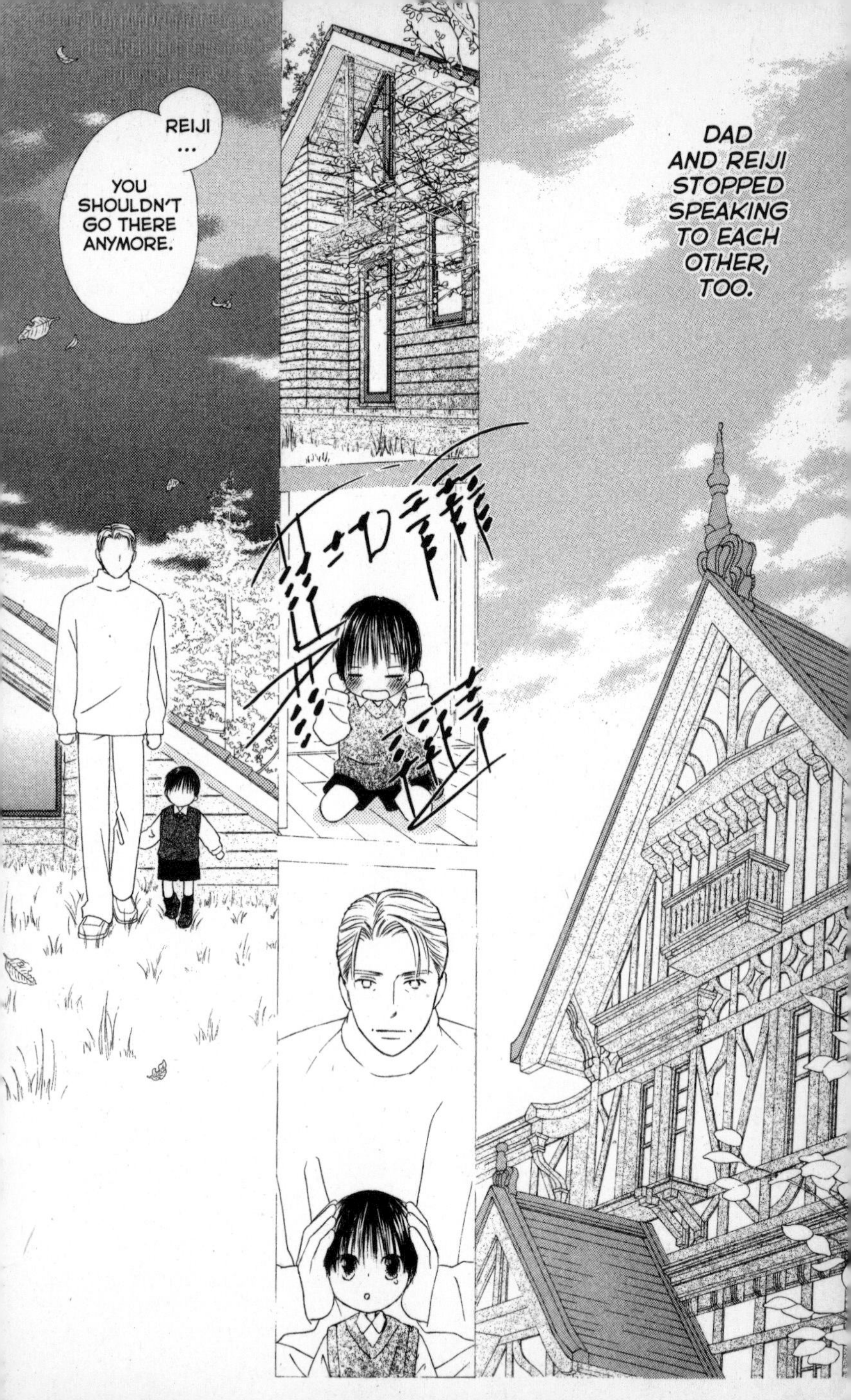
DAD AND REIJI STOPPED SPEAKING TO EACH OTHER, TOO.
REIJI ...
YOU SHOULDN'T GO THERE ANYMORE.

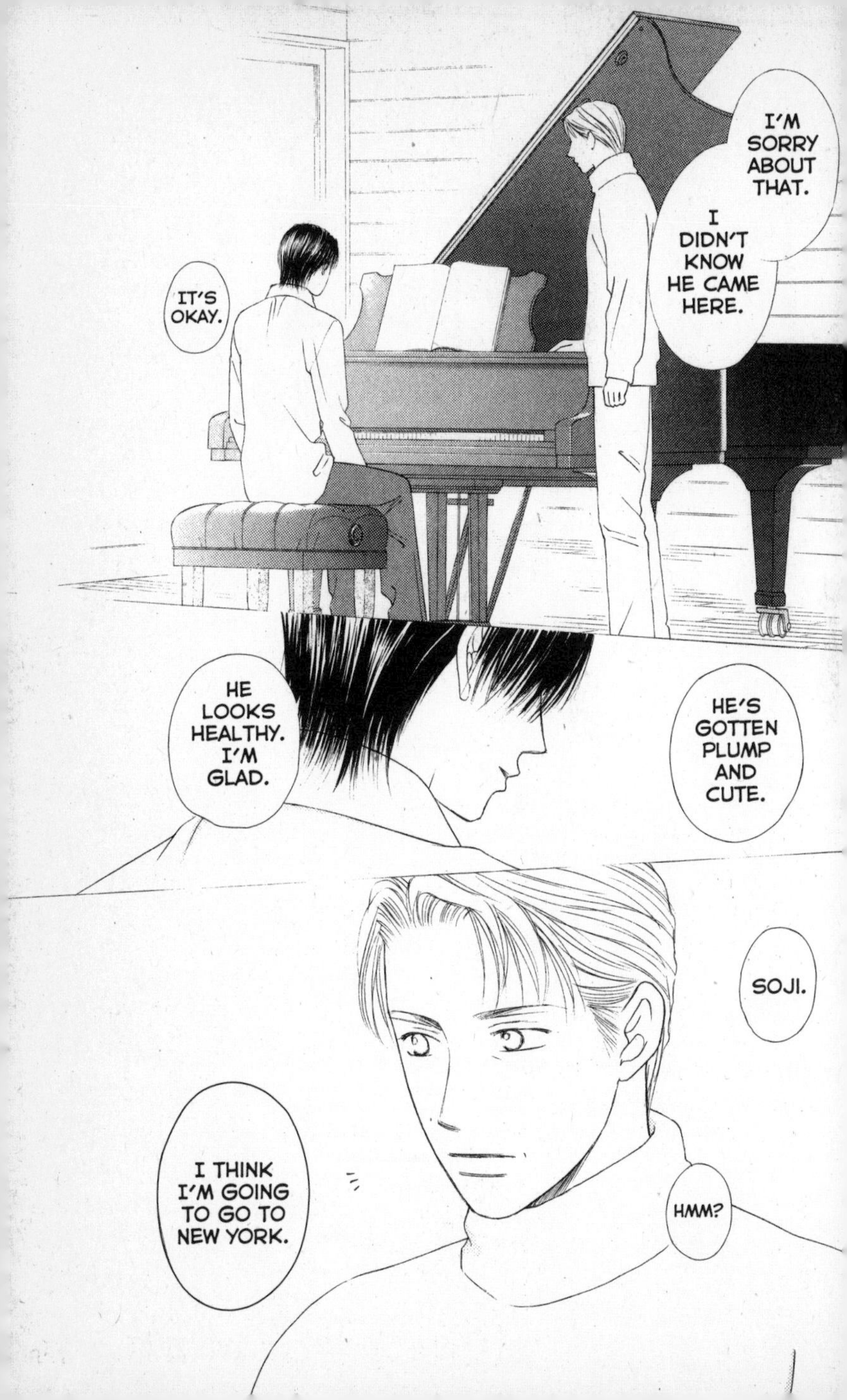
I'M SORRY ABOUT THAT.
I DIDN'T KNOW HE CAME HERE.
IT'S OKAY.
HE'S GOTTEN PLUMP AND CUTE.
HE LOOKS HEALTHY. I'M GLAD.
SOJI.
HMM?
I THINK I'M GOING TO GO TO NEW YORK.

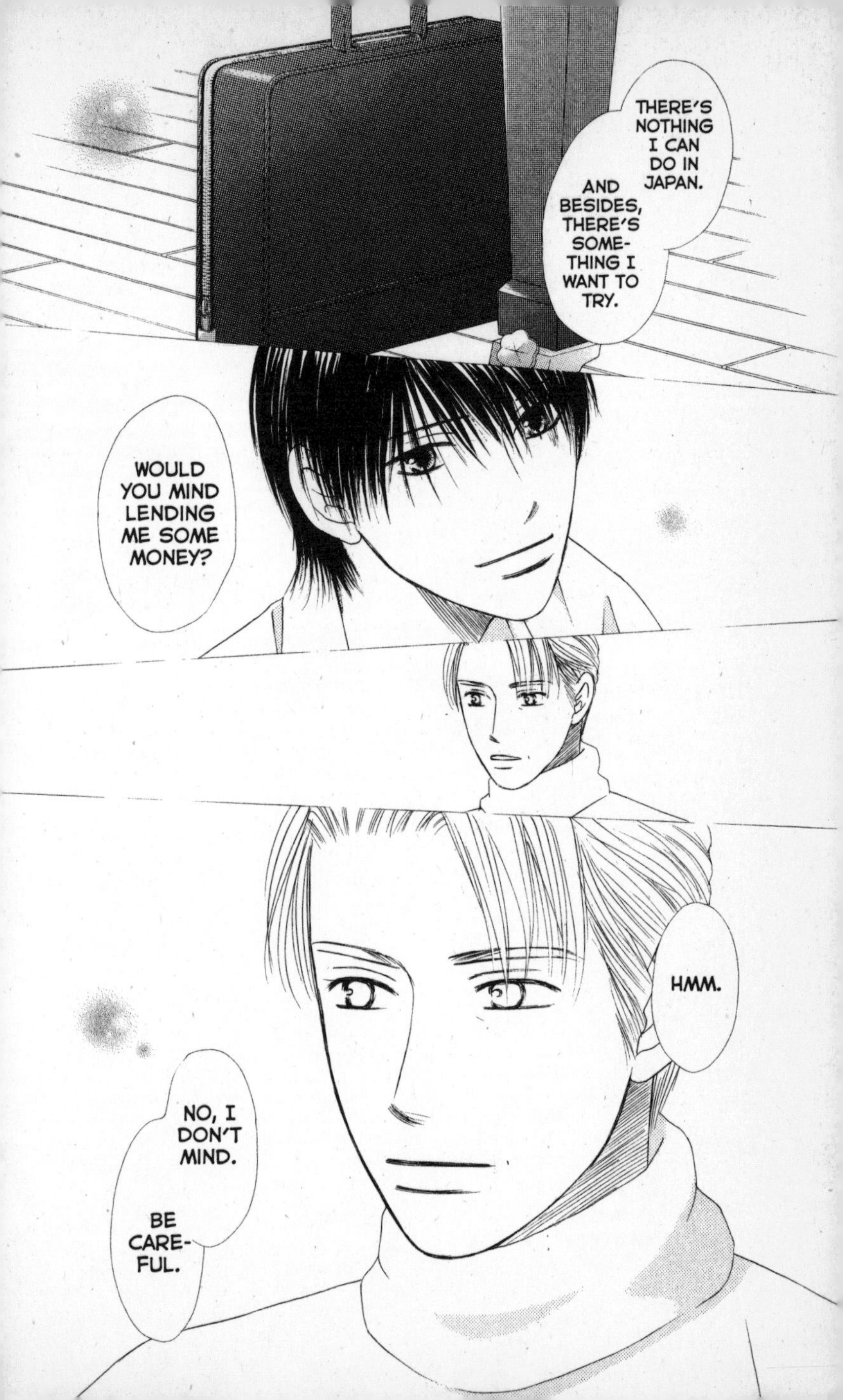
THERE'S NOTHING I CAN DO IN JAPAN.
AND BESIDES, THERE'S SOME-THING I WANT TO TRY.
WOULD YOU MIND LENDING ME SOME MONEY?
HMM.
NO, I DON'T MIND.
BE CARE-FUL.

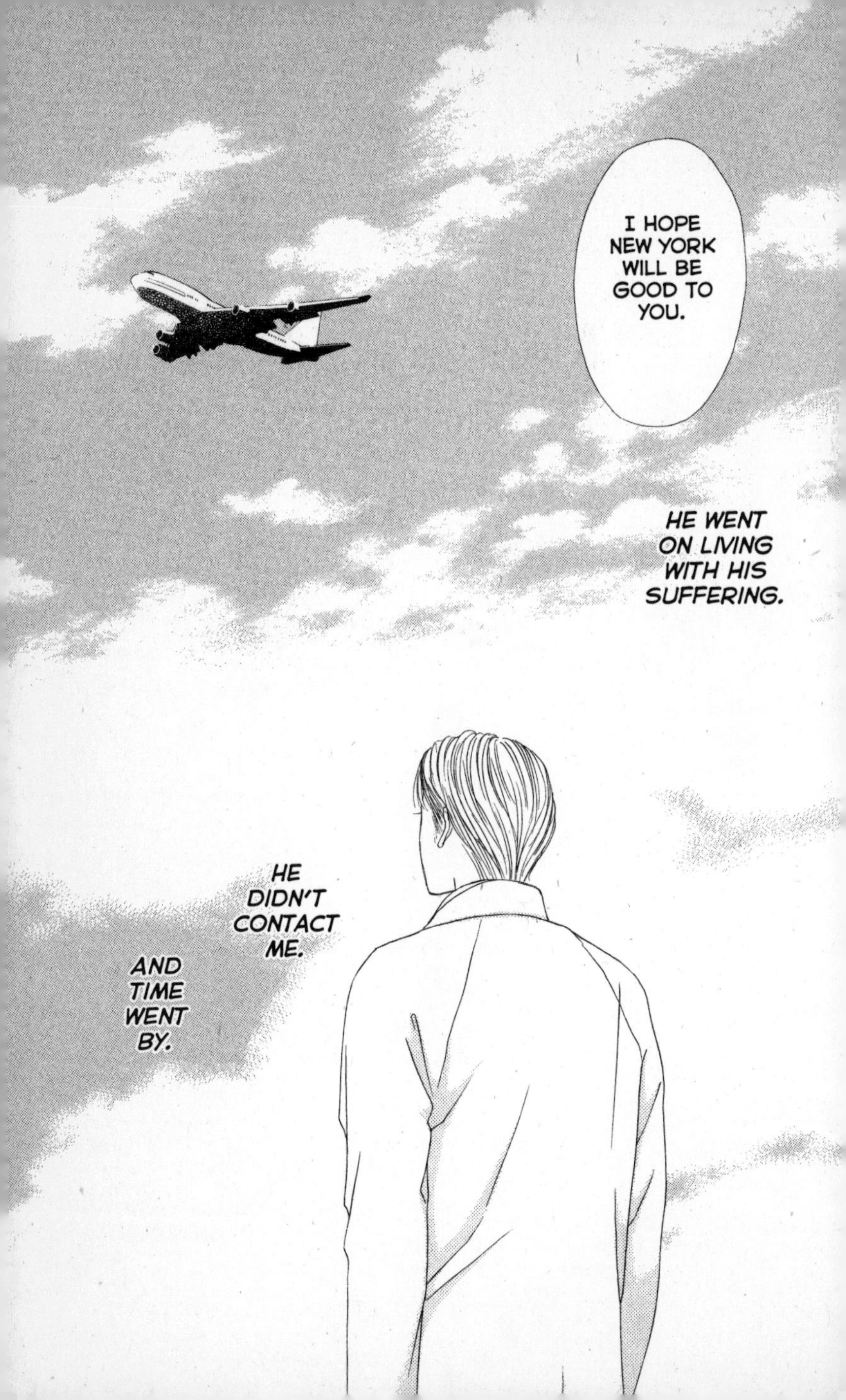
I HOPE NEW YORK WILL BE GOOD TO YOU.
HE WENT ON LIVING WITH HIS SUFFERING.
HE DIDN'T CONTACT ME.
AND TIME WENT BY.

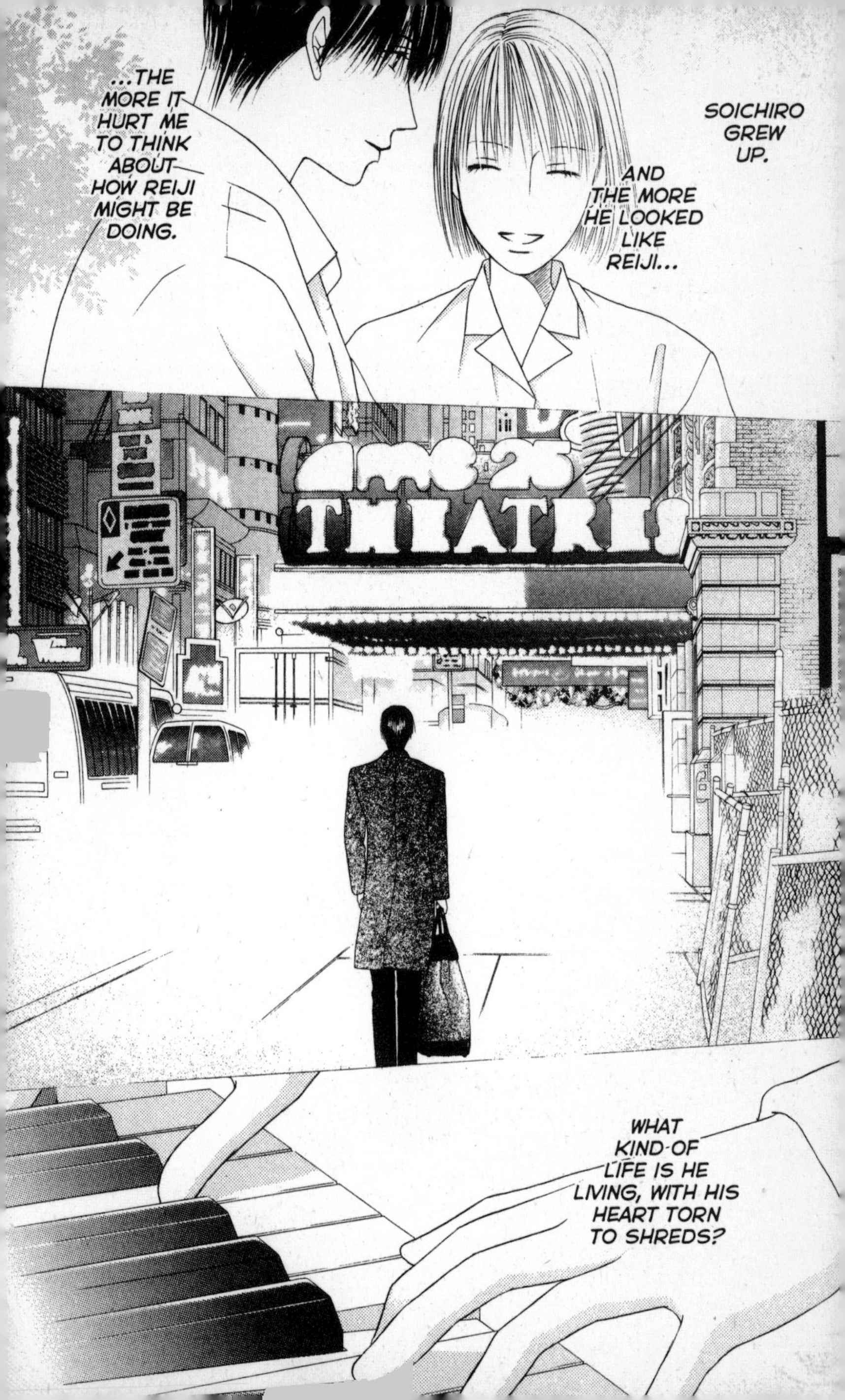
SOICHIRO GREW UP.
AND THE MORE HE LOOKED LIKE REIJI...
...THE MORE IT HURT ME TO THINK ABOUT HOW REIJI MIGHT BE DOING.
WHAT KIND OF LIFE IS HE LIVING, WITH HIS HEART TORN TO SHREDS?

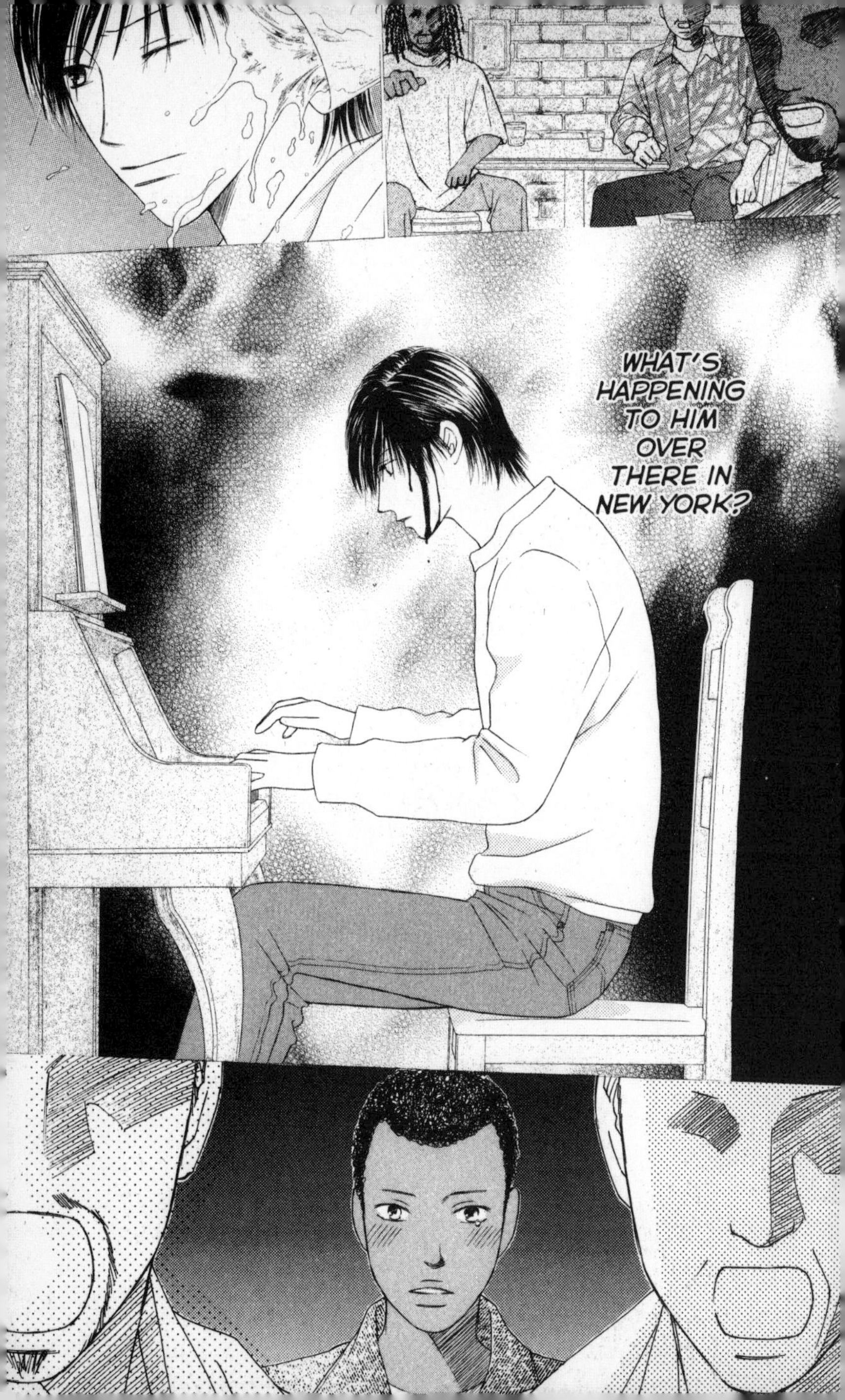
WHAT'S HAPPENING TO HIM OVER THERE IN NEW YORK?

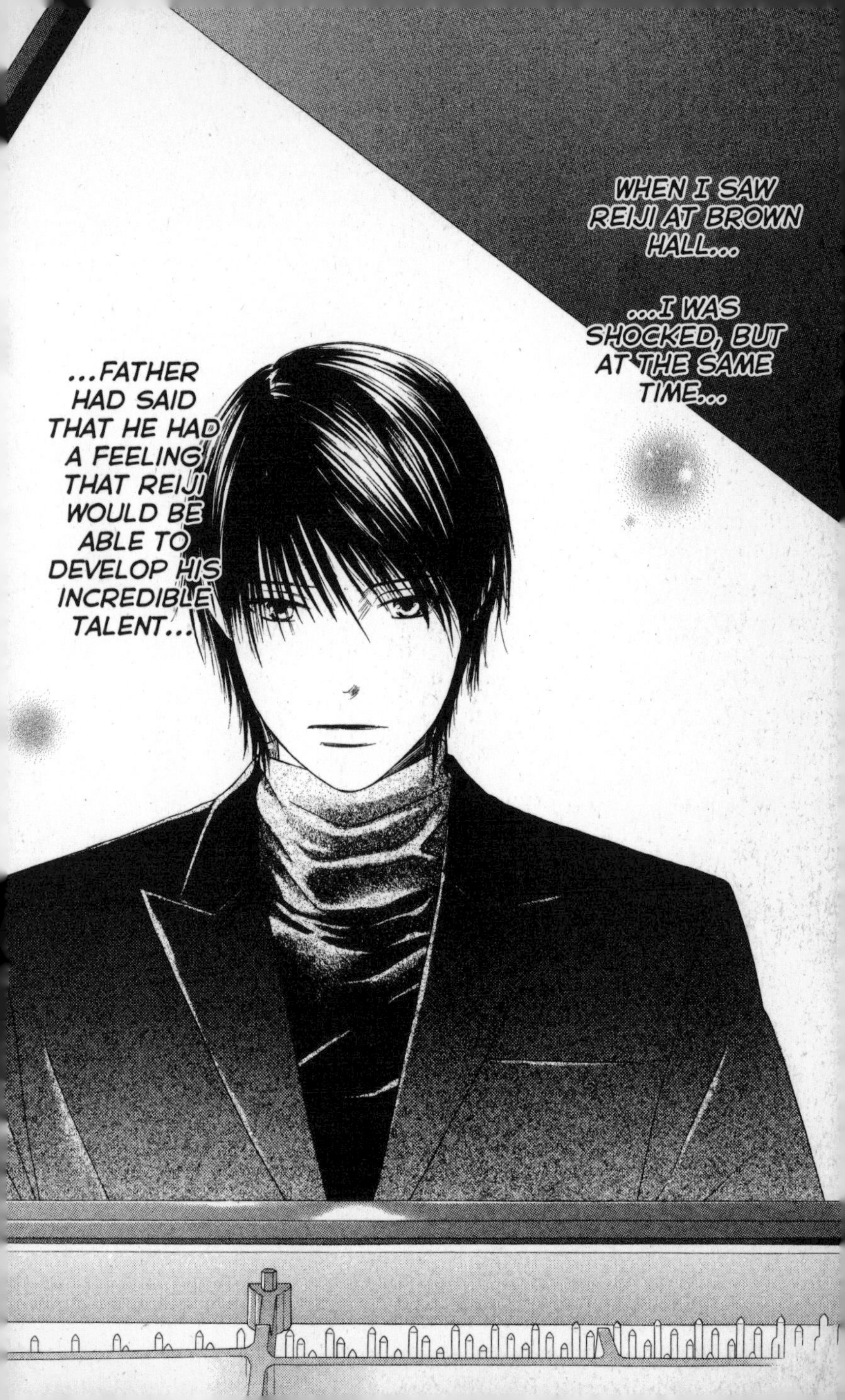
WHEN I SAW REIJI AT BROWN HALL...
...I WAS SHOCKED, BUT AT THE SAME TIME...
...FATHER HAD SAID THAT HE HAD A FEELING THAT REIJI WOULD BE ABLE TO DEVELOP HIS INCREDIBLE TALENT...

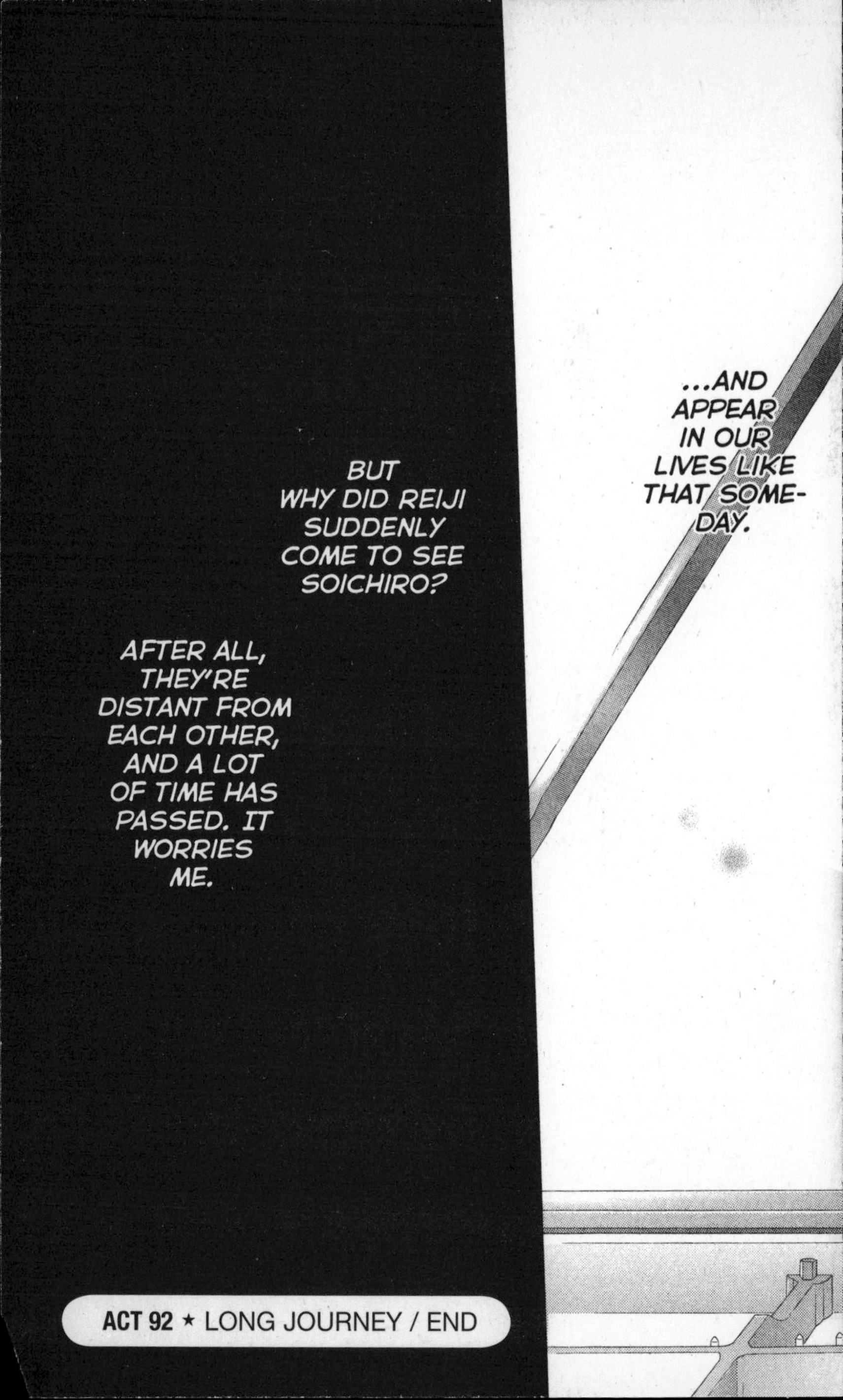
...AND APPEAR IN OUR LIVES LIKE THAT SOME-DAY.
BUT WHY DID REIJI SUDDENLY COME TO SEE SOICHIRO?
AFTER ALL, THEY'RE DISTANT FROM EACH OTHER, AND A LOT OF TIME HAS PASSED. IT WORRIES ME.

ACT 92 ★ LONG JOURNEY / END

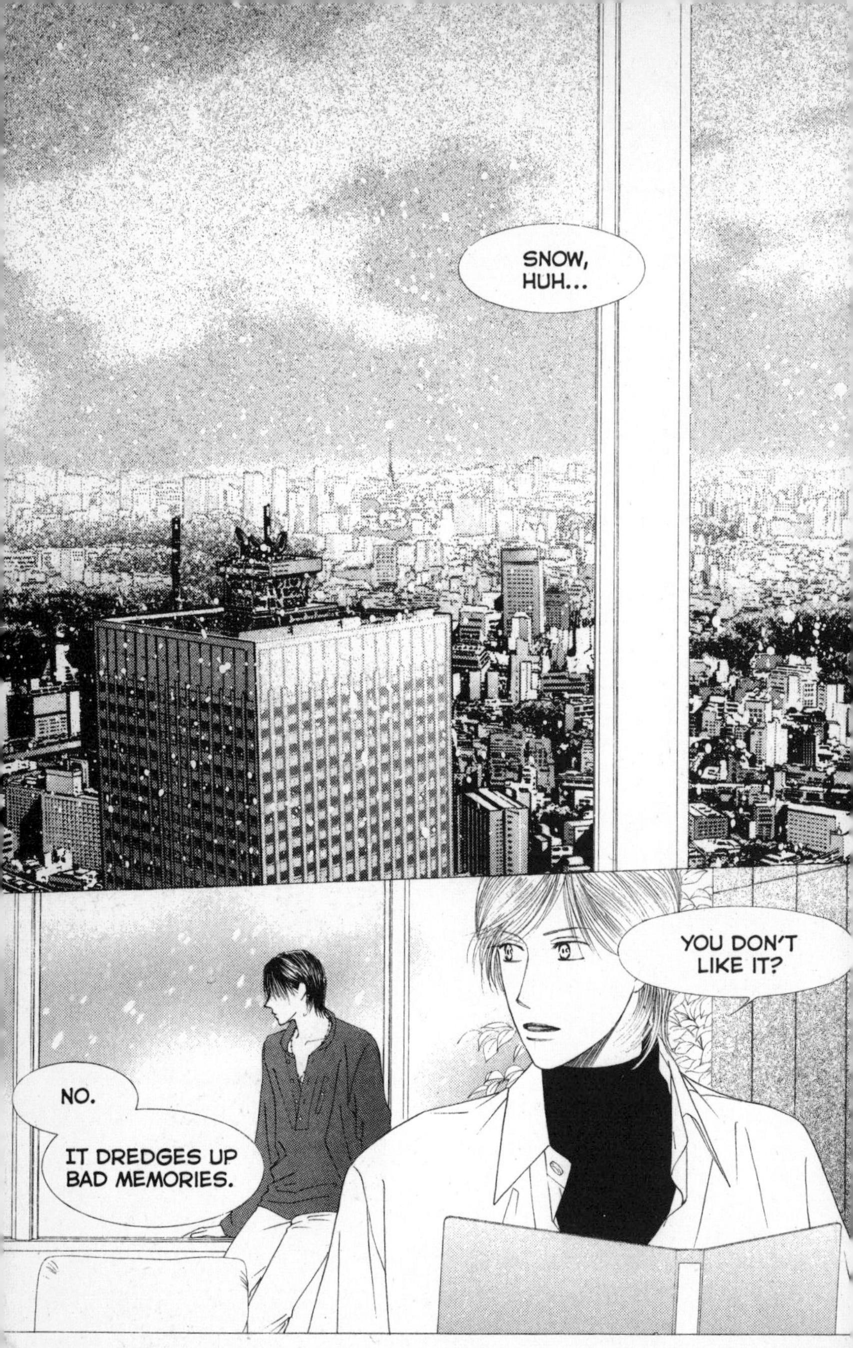
SNOW, HUH...
YOU DON'T LIKE IT?
NO.
IT DREDGES UP BAD MEMORIES.

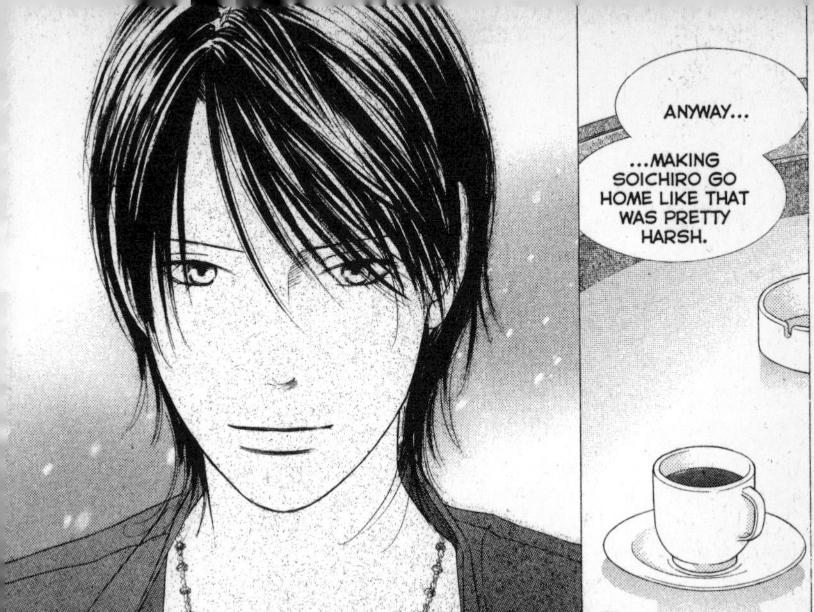
ANYWAY...
...MAKING SOICHIRO GO HOME LIKE THAT WAS PRETTY HARSH.
EVERYONE WILL BE SORRY THEY COULDN'T SAY GOODBYE.

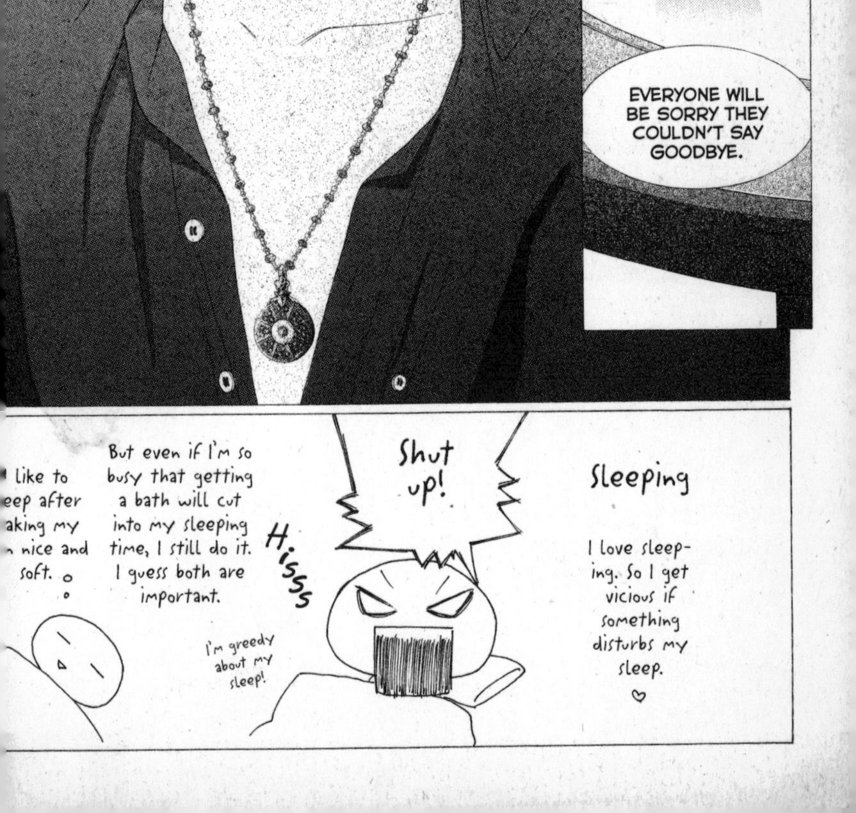
Sleeping
I love sleeping. So I get vicious if something disturbs my sleep. ♡
Shut up!
Hisss
I'm greedy about my sleep!
But even if I'm so busy that getting a bath will cut into my sleeping time, I still do it. I guess both are important.
like to eep after aking my nice and soft.

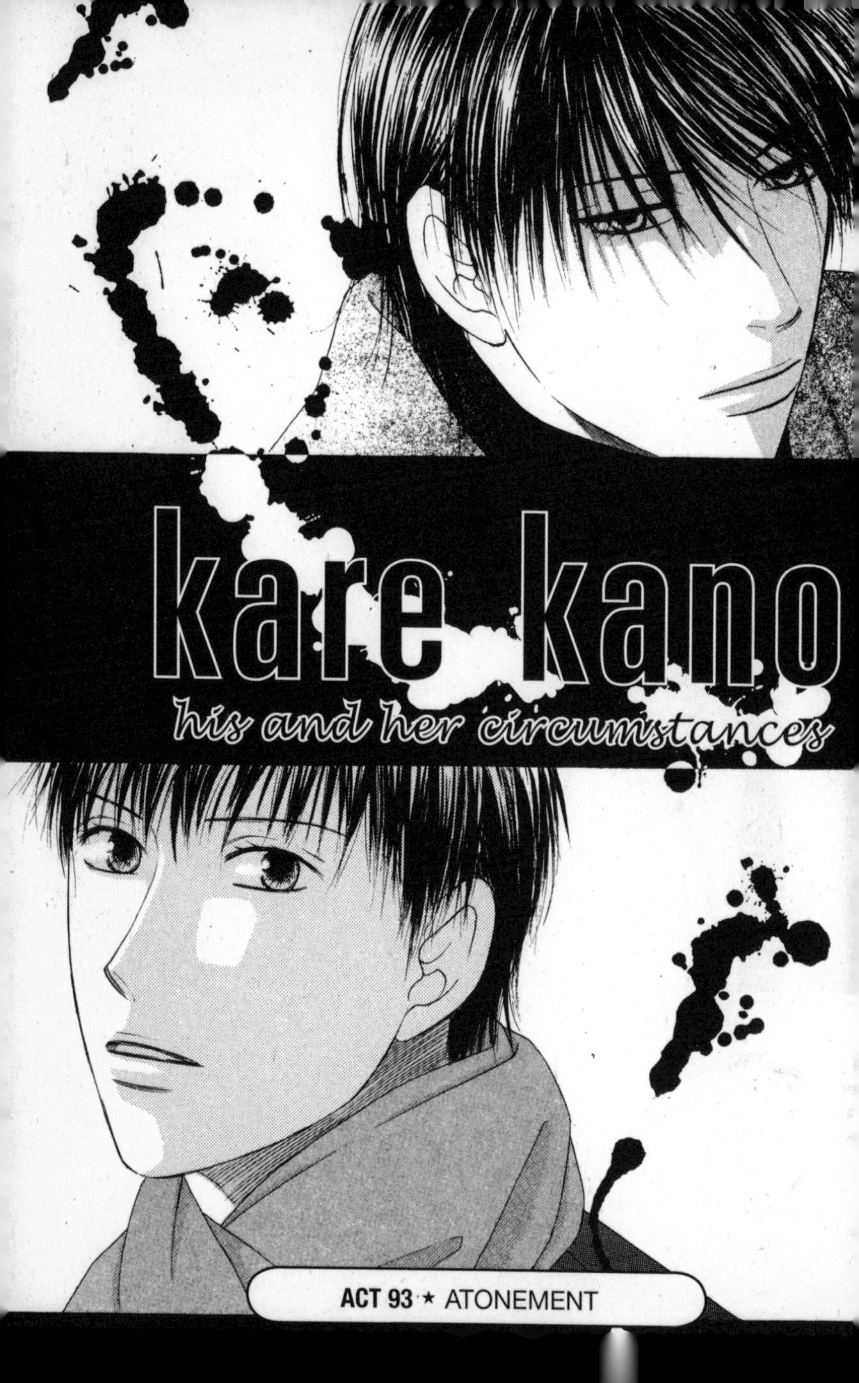
kare kano
his and her circumstances
ACT 93 ★ ATONEMENT

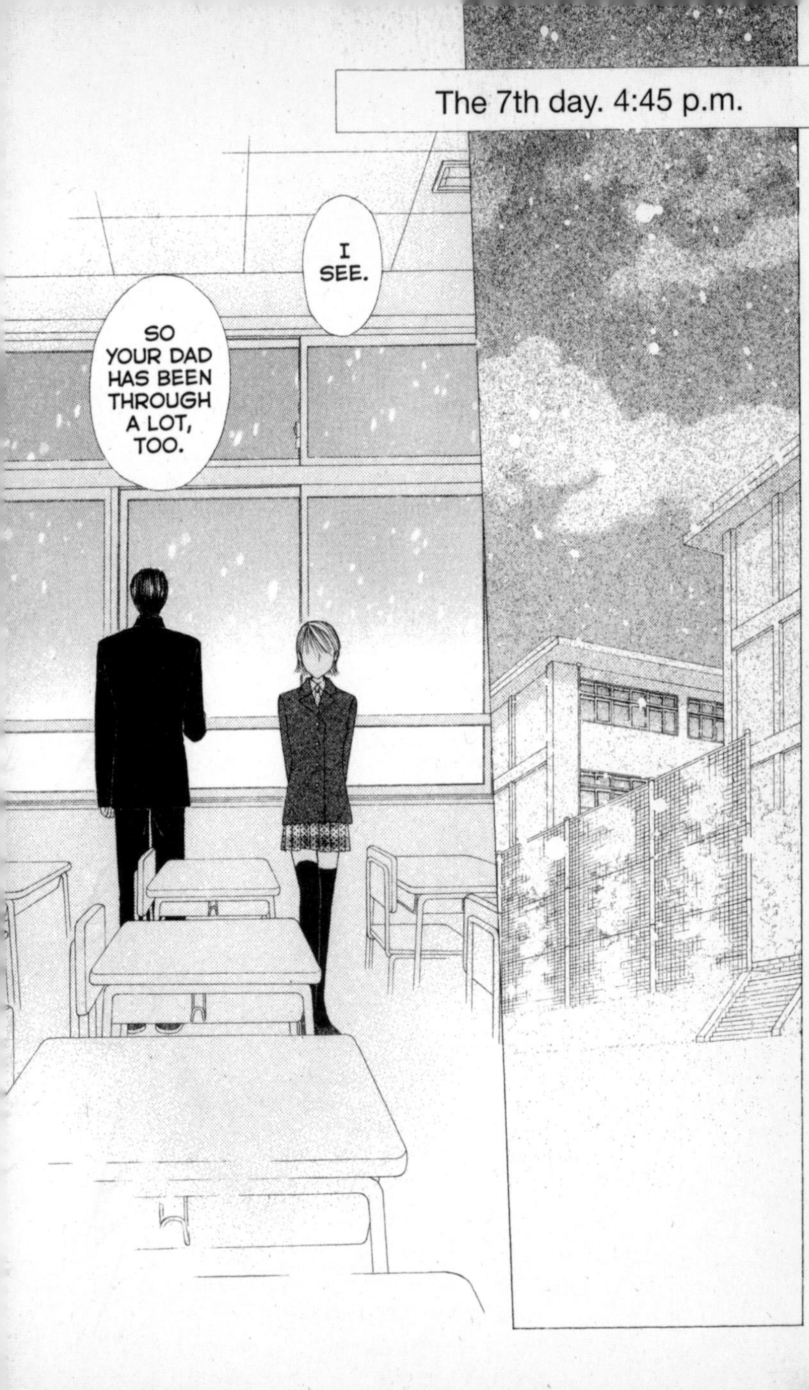
The 7th day. 4:45 p.m.
I SEE.
SO YOUR DAD HAS BEEN THROUGH A LOT, TOO.

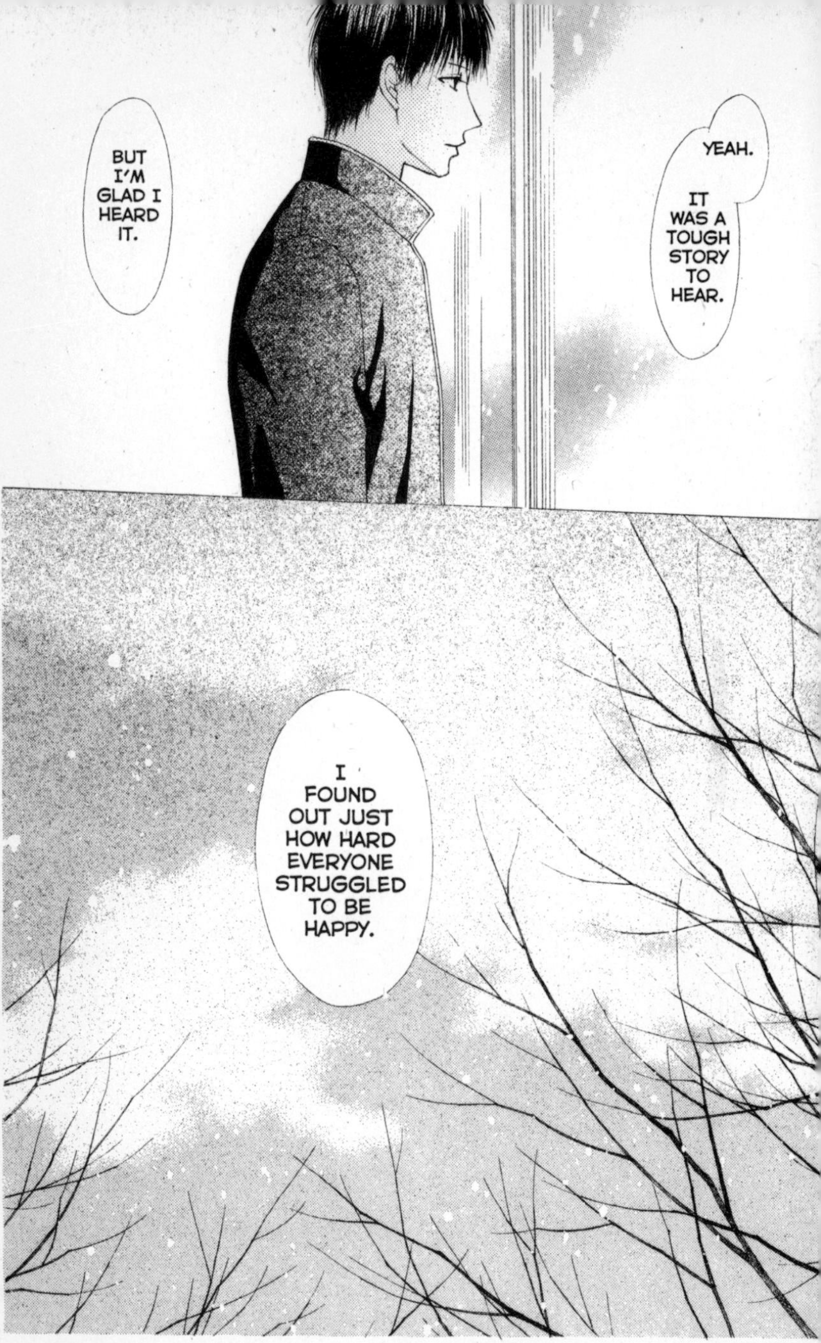
YEAH.
IT WAS A TOUGH STORY TO HEAR.
BUT I'M GLAD I HEARD IT.
I FOUND OUT JUST HOW HARD EVERYONE STRUGGLED TO BE HAPPY.

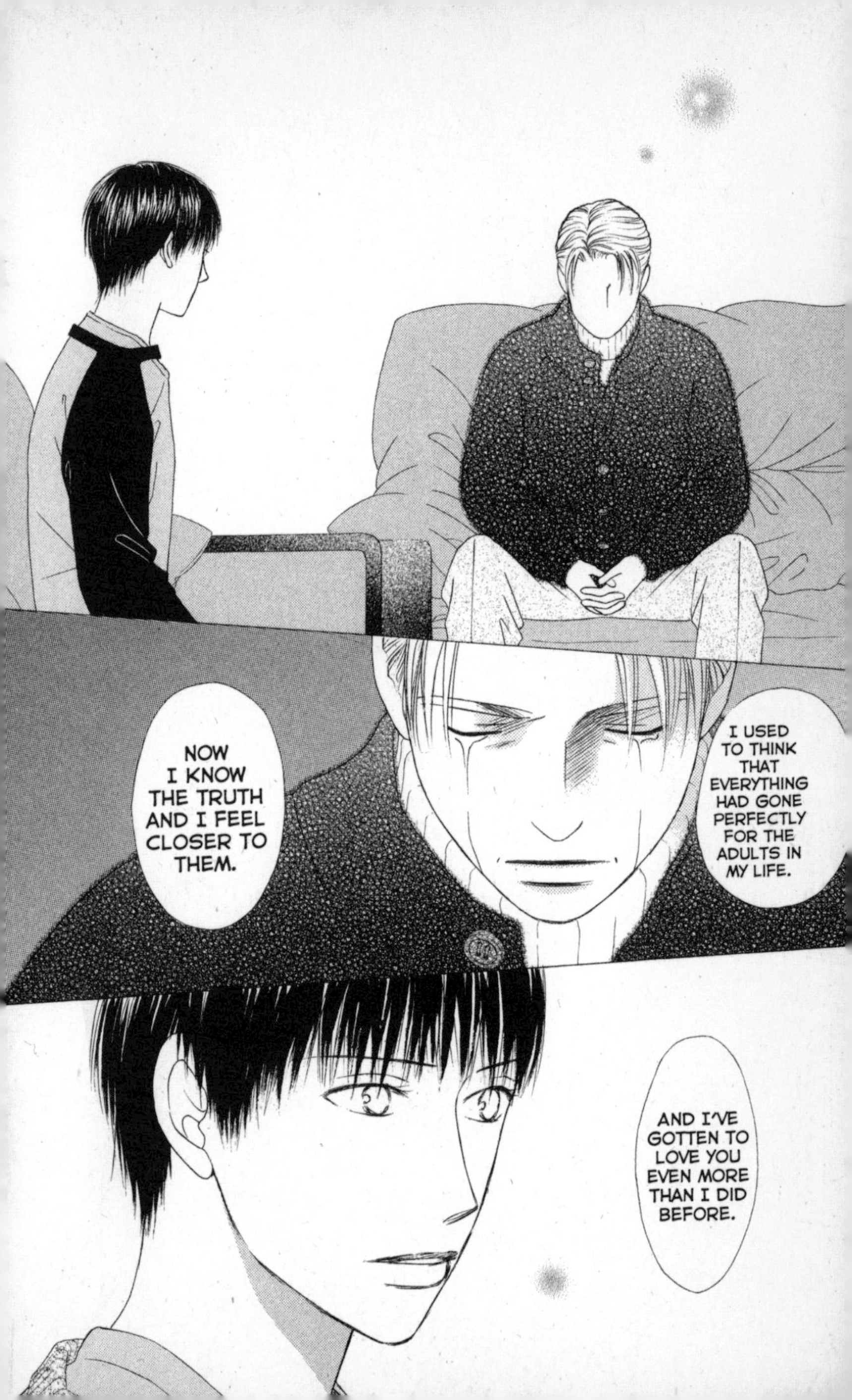
I USED TO THINK THAT EVERYTHING HAD GONE PERFECTLY FOR THE ADULTS IN MY LIFE.
NOW I KNOW THE TRUTH AND I FEEL CLOSER TO THEM.
AND I'VE GOTTEN TO LOVE YOU EVEN MORE THAN I DID BEFORE.

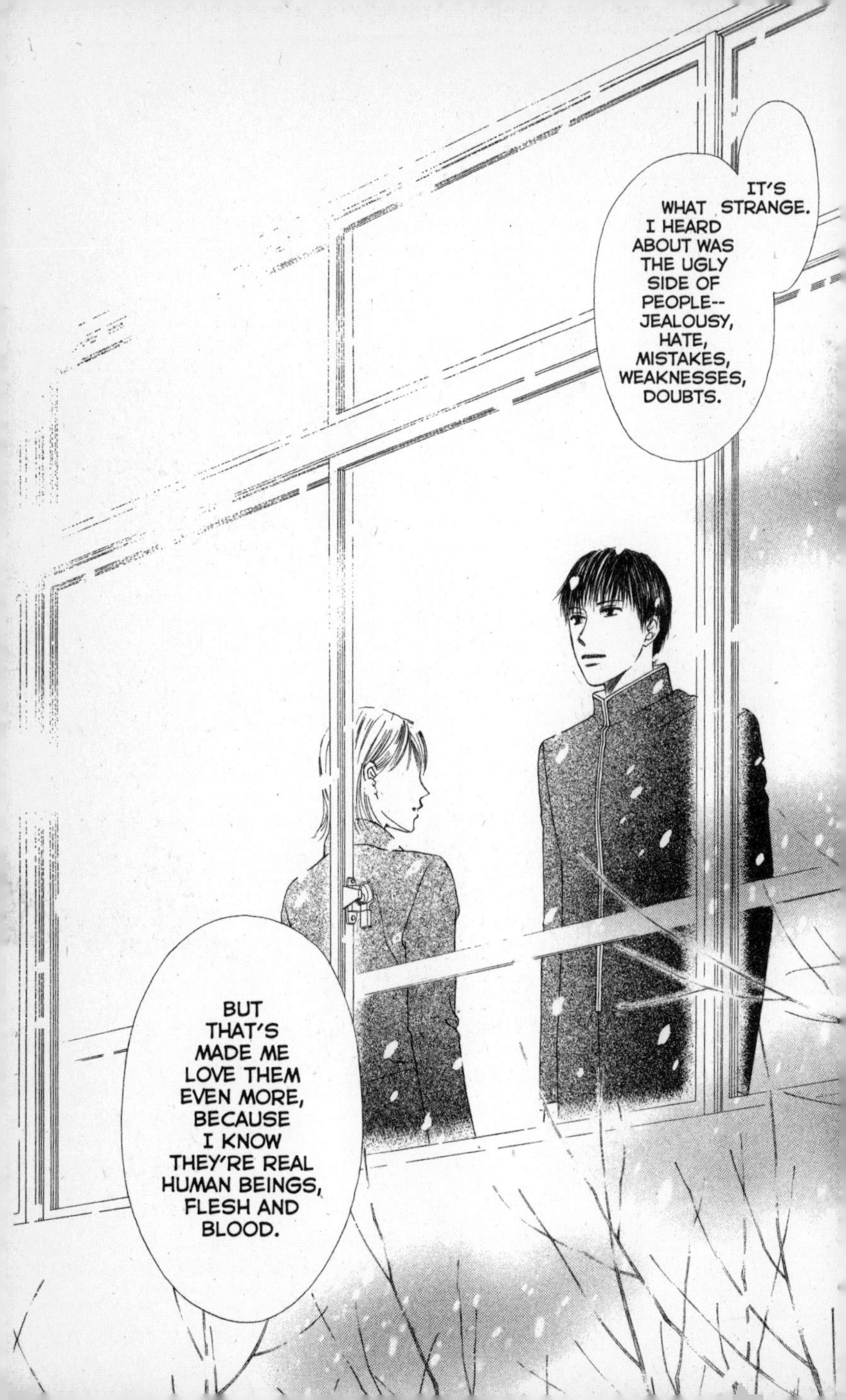
IT'S STRANGE. WHAT I HEARD ABOUT WAS THE UGLY SIDE OF PEOPLE--JEALOUSY, HATE, MISTAKES, WEAKNESSES, DOUBTS.
BUT THAT'S MADE ME LOVE THEM EVEN MORE, BECAUSE I KNOW THEY'RE REAL HUMAN BEINGS, FLESH AND BLOOD.

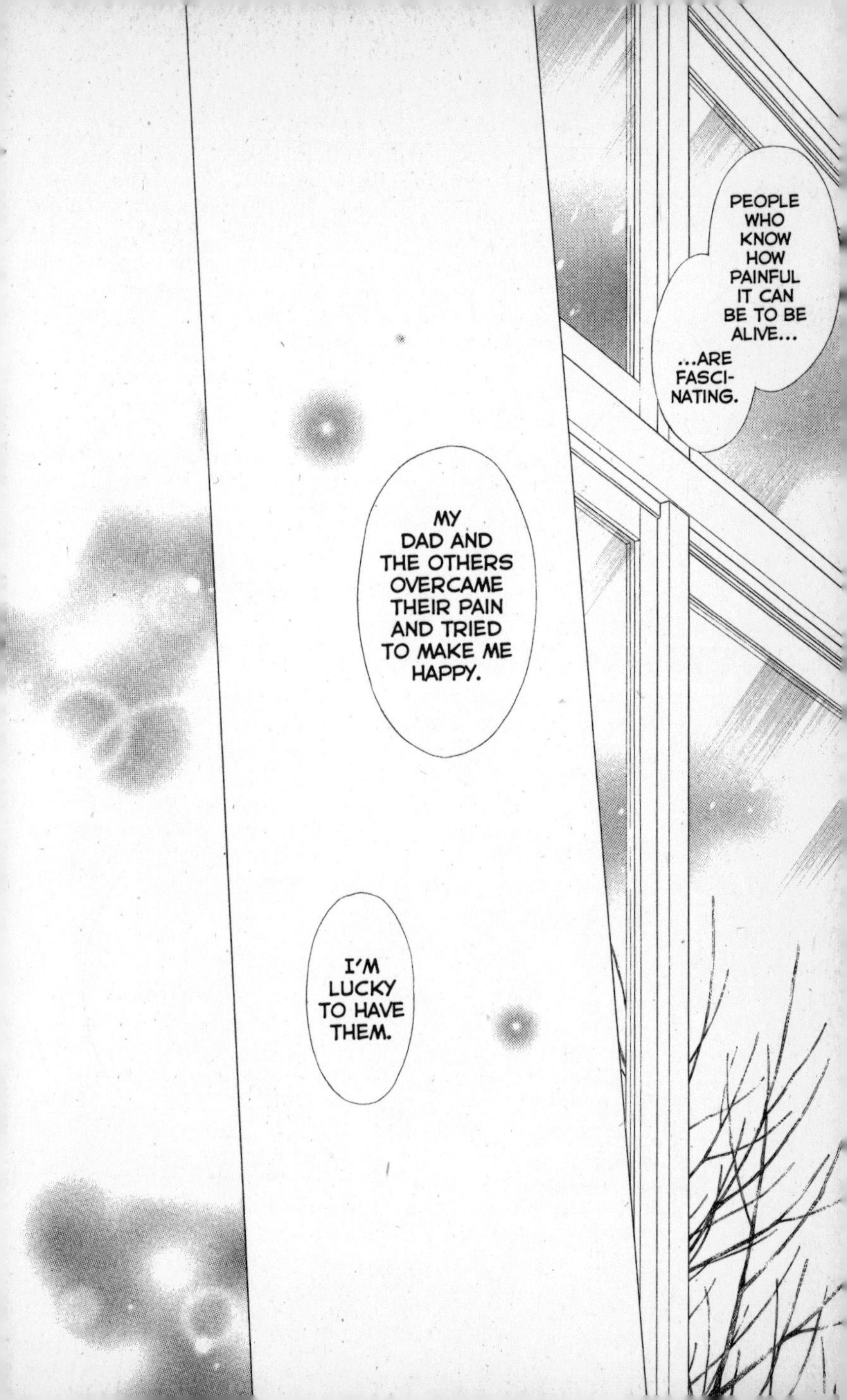
PEOPLE WHO KNOW HOW PAINFUL IT CAN BE TO BE ALIVE...
...ARE FASCI- NATING.
MY DAD AND THE OTHERS OVERCAME THEIR PAIN AND TRIED TO MAKE ME HAPPY.
I'M LUCKY TO HAVE THEM.

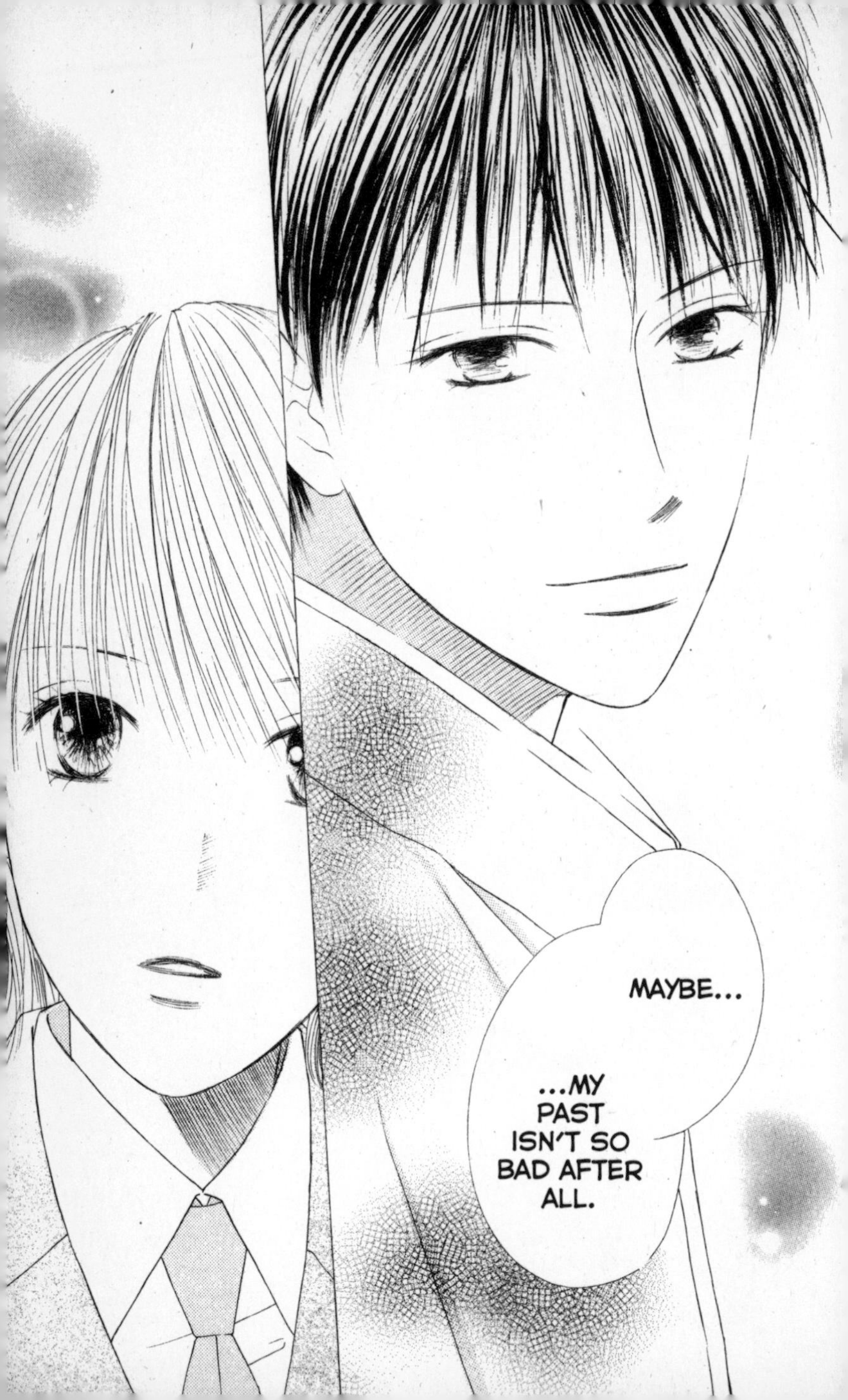
MAYBE...
...MY PAST ISN'T SO BAD AFTER ALL.

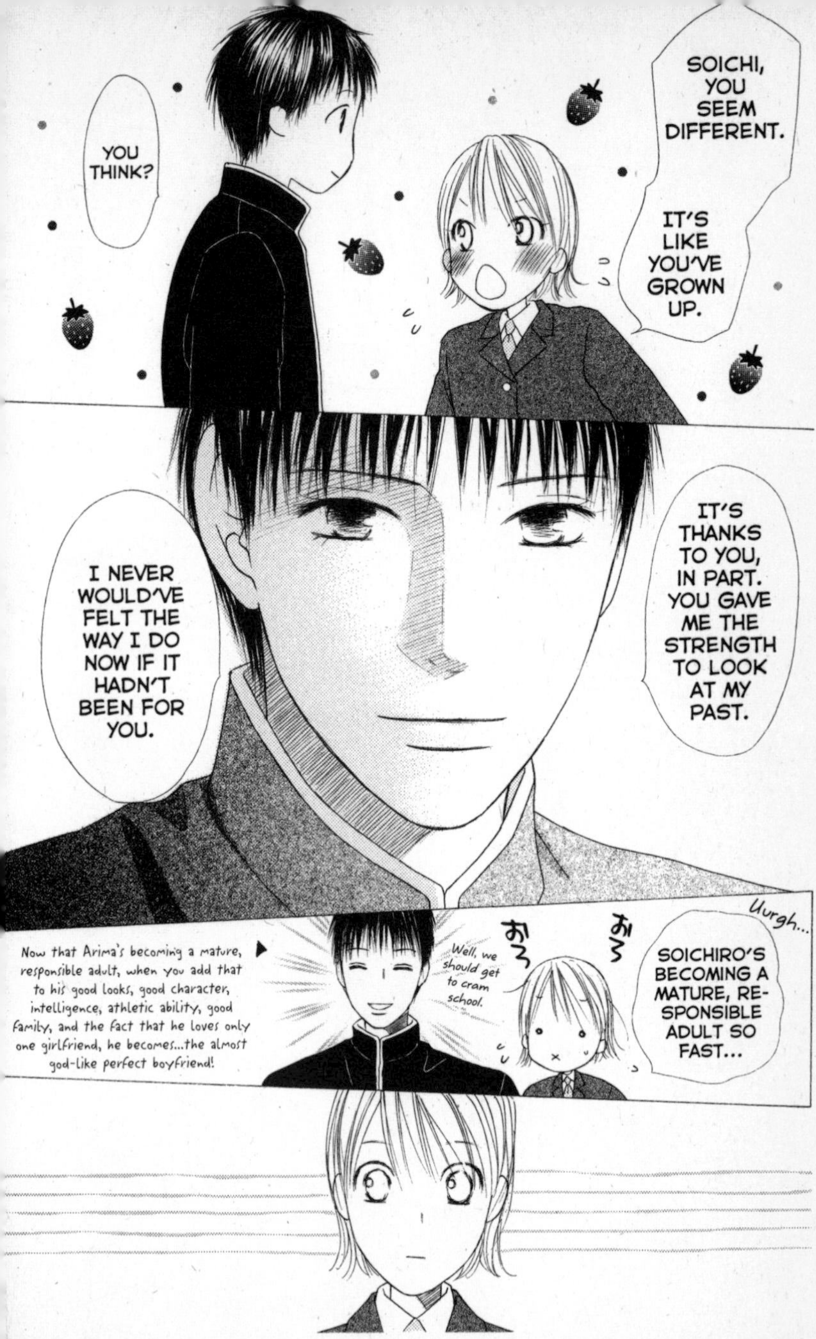
SOICHI, YOU SEEM DIFFERENT.
IT'S LIKE YOU'VE GROWN UP.
YOU THINK?
IT'S THANKS TO YOU, IN PART. YOU GAVE ME THE STRENGTH TO LOOK AT MY PAST.
I NEVER WOULD'VE FELT THE WAY I DO NOW IF IT HADN'T BEEN FOR YOU.
Uurgh...
SOICHIRO'S BECOMING A MATURE, RE-SPONSIBLE ADULT SO FAST...
おろ
おろ
Well, we should get to cram school.
Now that Arima's becoming a mature, responsible adult, when you add that to his good looks, good character, intelligence, athletic ability, good family, and the fact that he loves only one girlfriend, he becomes...the almost god-like perfect boyfriend!

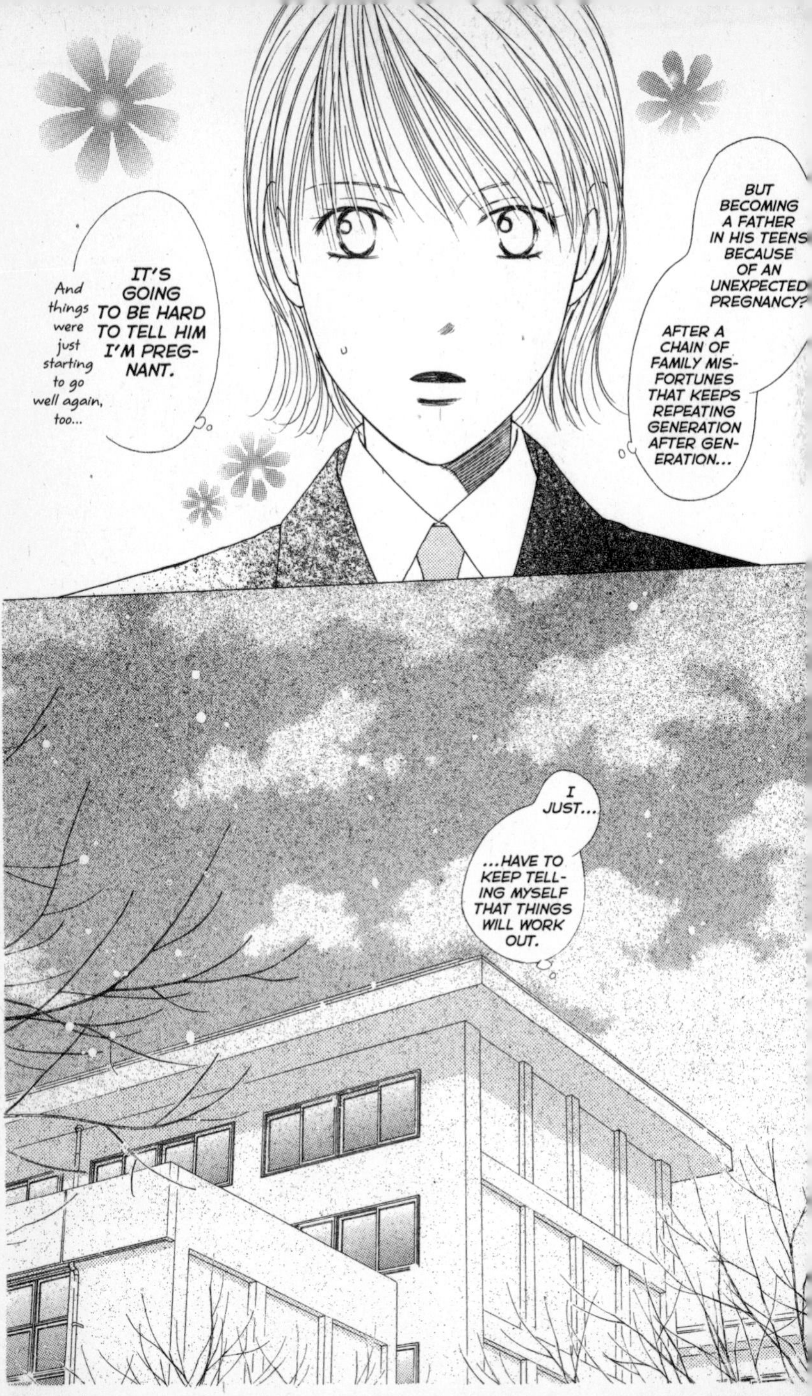
BUT BECOMING A FATHER IN HIS TEENS BECAUSE OF AN UNEXPECTED PREGNANCY?
AFTER A CHAIN OF FAMILY MIS-FORTUNES THAT KEEPS REPEATING GENERATION AFTER GEN-ERATION...
IT'S GOING TO BE HARD TO TELL HIM I'M PREG-NANT.
And things were just starting to go well again, too...
I JUST...
...HAVE TO KEEP TELL-ING MYSELF THAT THINGS WILL WORK OUT.

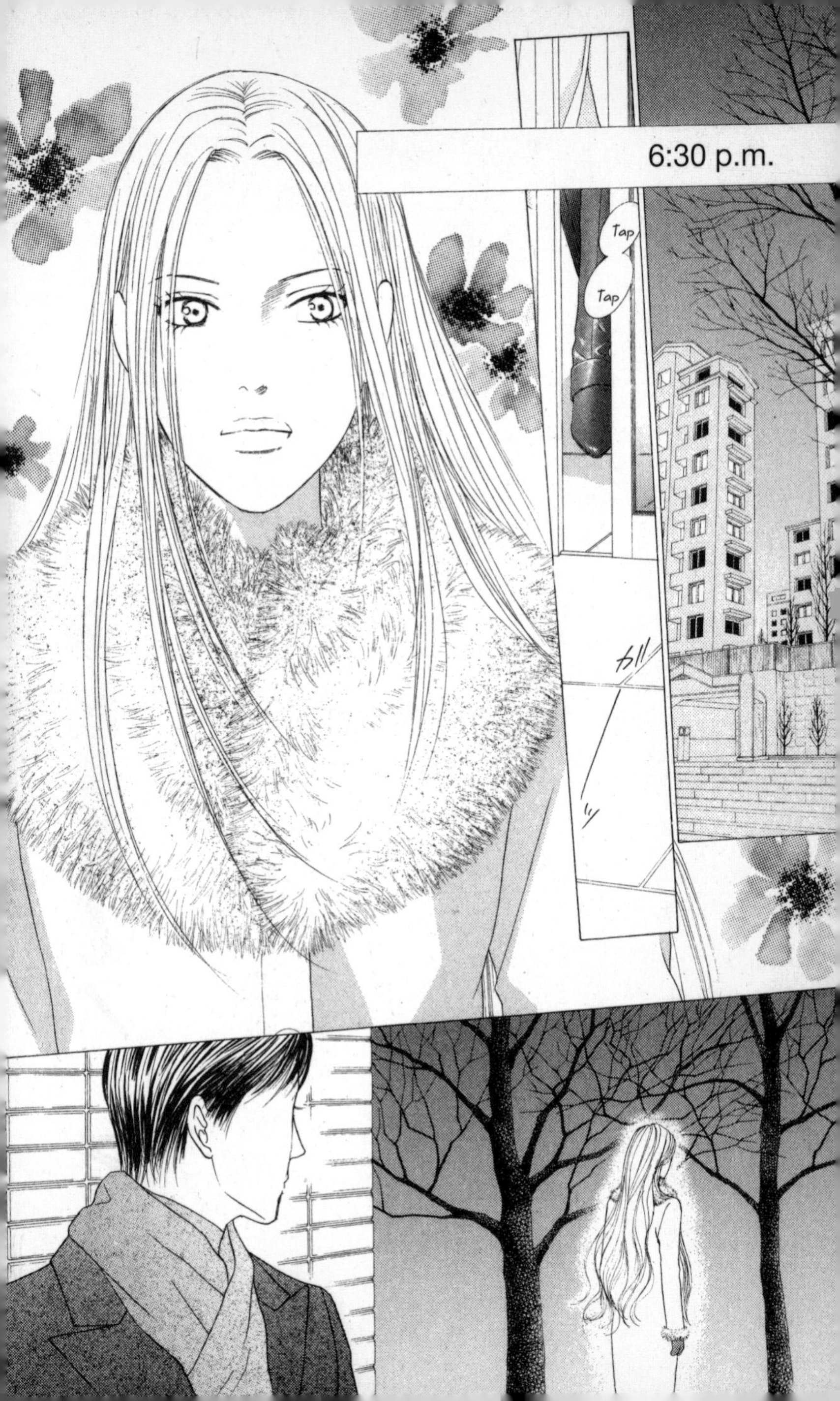
6:30 p.m.
Tap
Tap

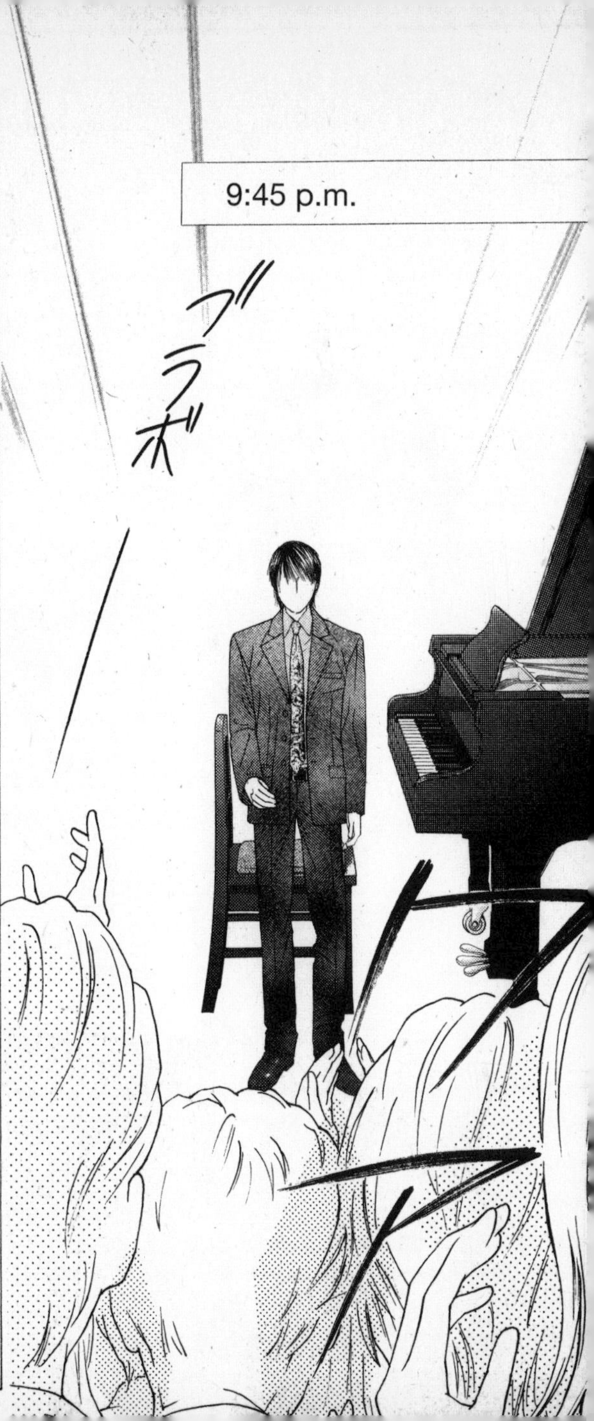
9:45 p.m.
ブラボー

5

This is my last chat space.

Starting with the next volume, Yukino will make her comeback as a main character.

There isn't much bonus material in this volume. But you can look forward to more in the next volume!

Send letters to:

5900 Wilshire Blvd
Suite 2000
Los Angeles, CA 90036

Carol Fox
Editor

感謝

Masami Tsuda

Thanks

S. Taneoka

N. Shimizu
R. Ogawa
Y. Etou
R. Takahashi

The therapists at the massage parlor

AND K. U

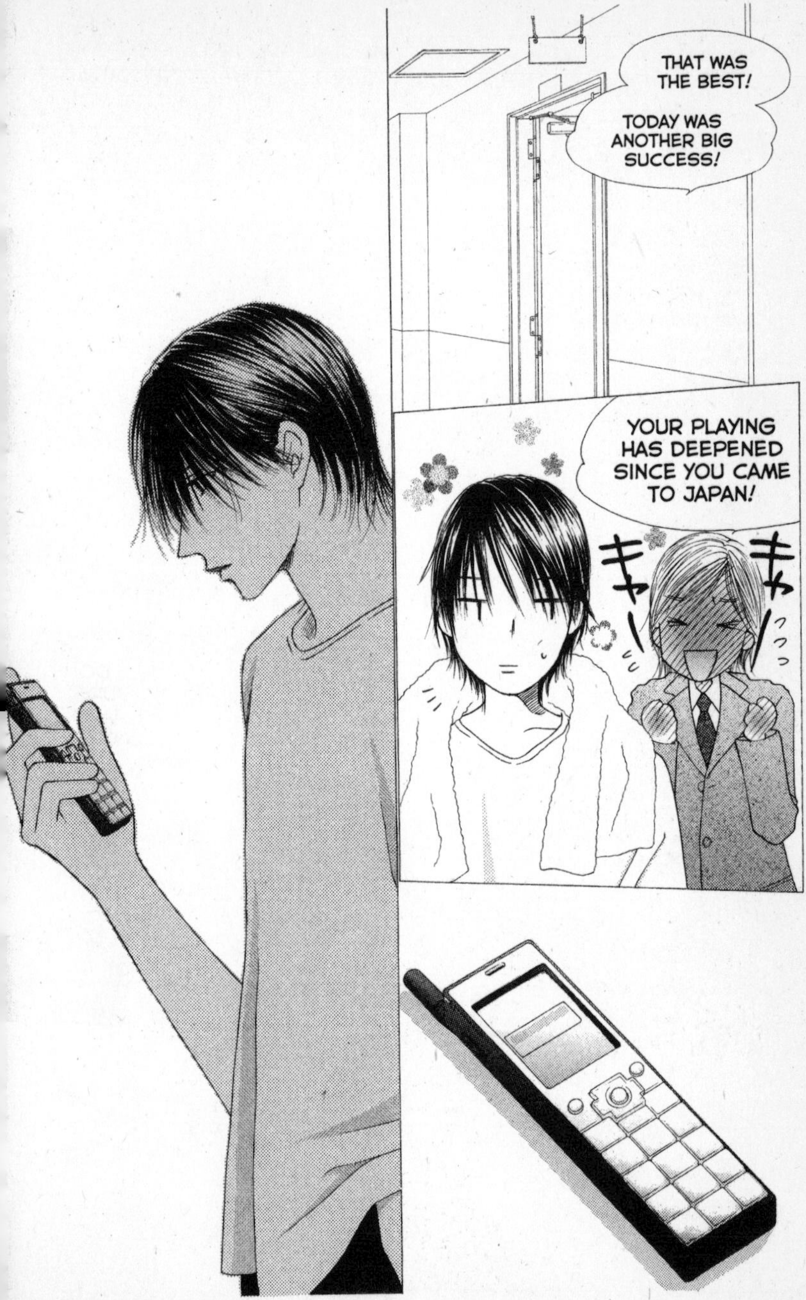
THAT WAS THE BEST!
TODAY WAS ANOTHER BIG SUCCESS!
YOUR PLAYING HAS DEEPENED SINCE YOU CAME TO JAPAN!
キャー
キャー

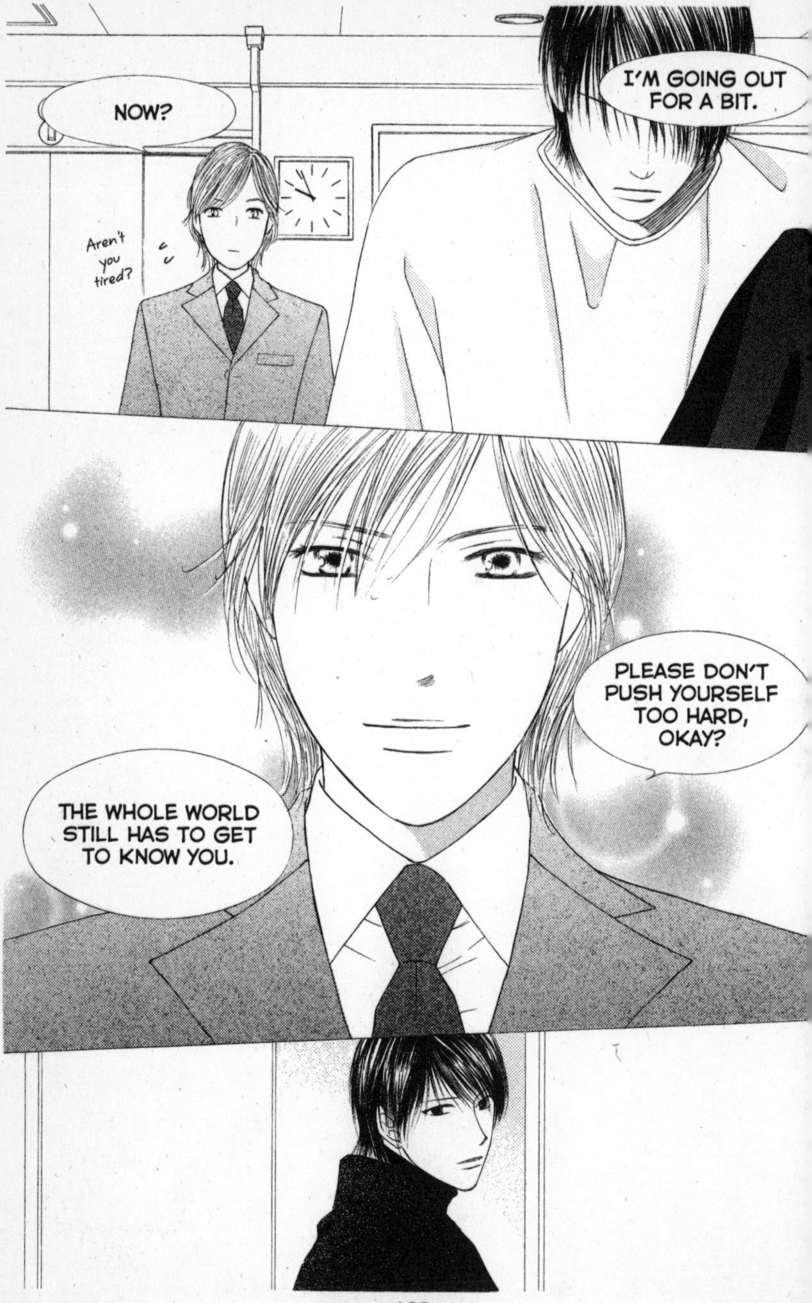
I'M GOING OUT FOR A BIT.
NOW?
Aren't you tired?
PLEASE DON'T PUSH YOURSELF TOO HARD, OKAY?
THE WHOLE WORLD STILL HAS TO GET TO KNOW YOU.

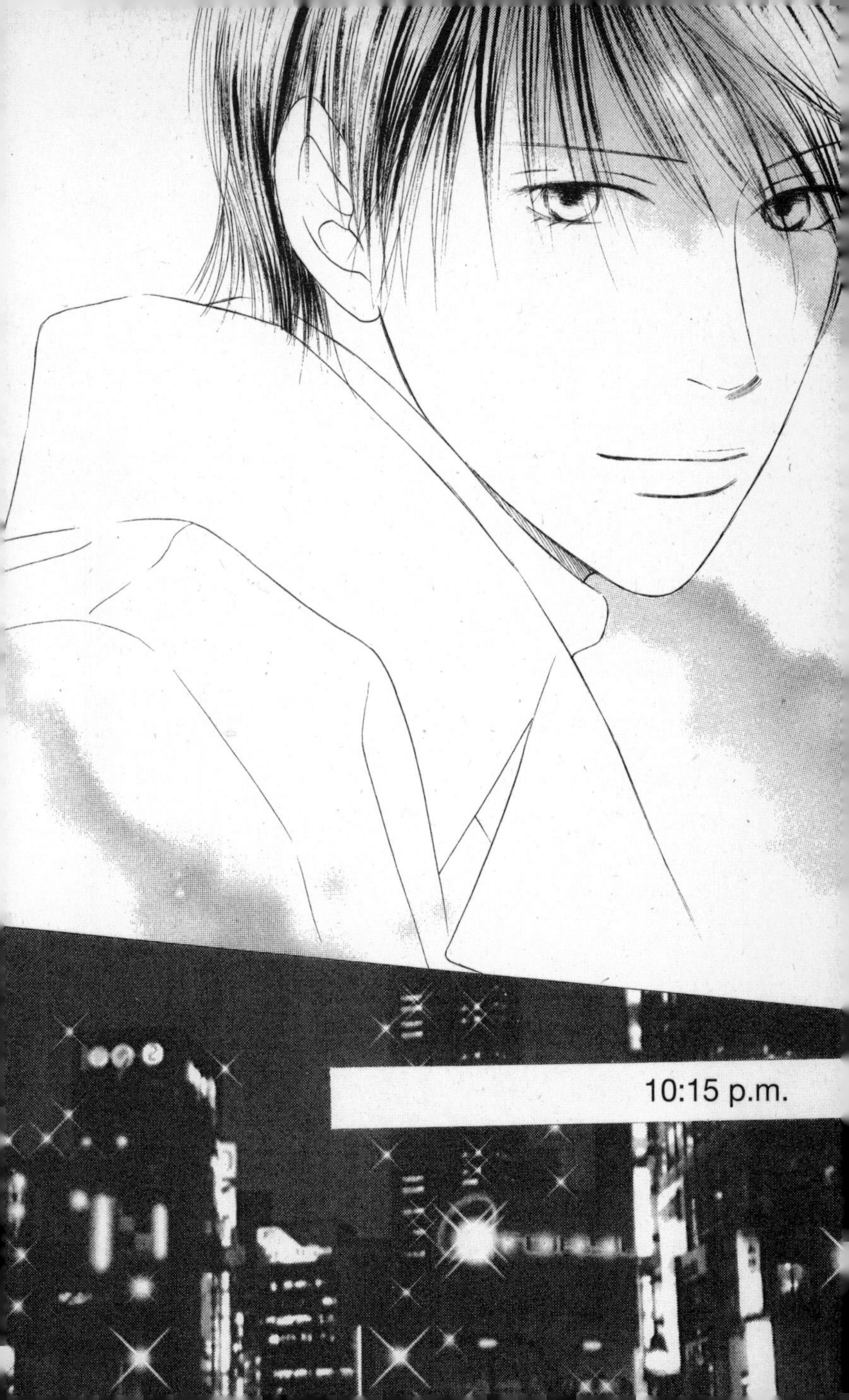
10:15 p.m.

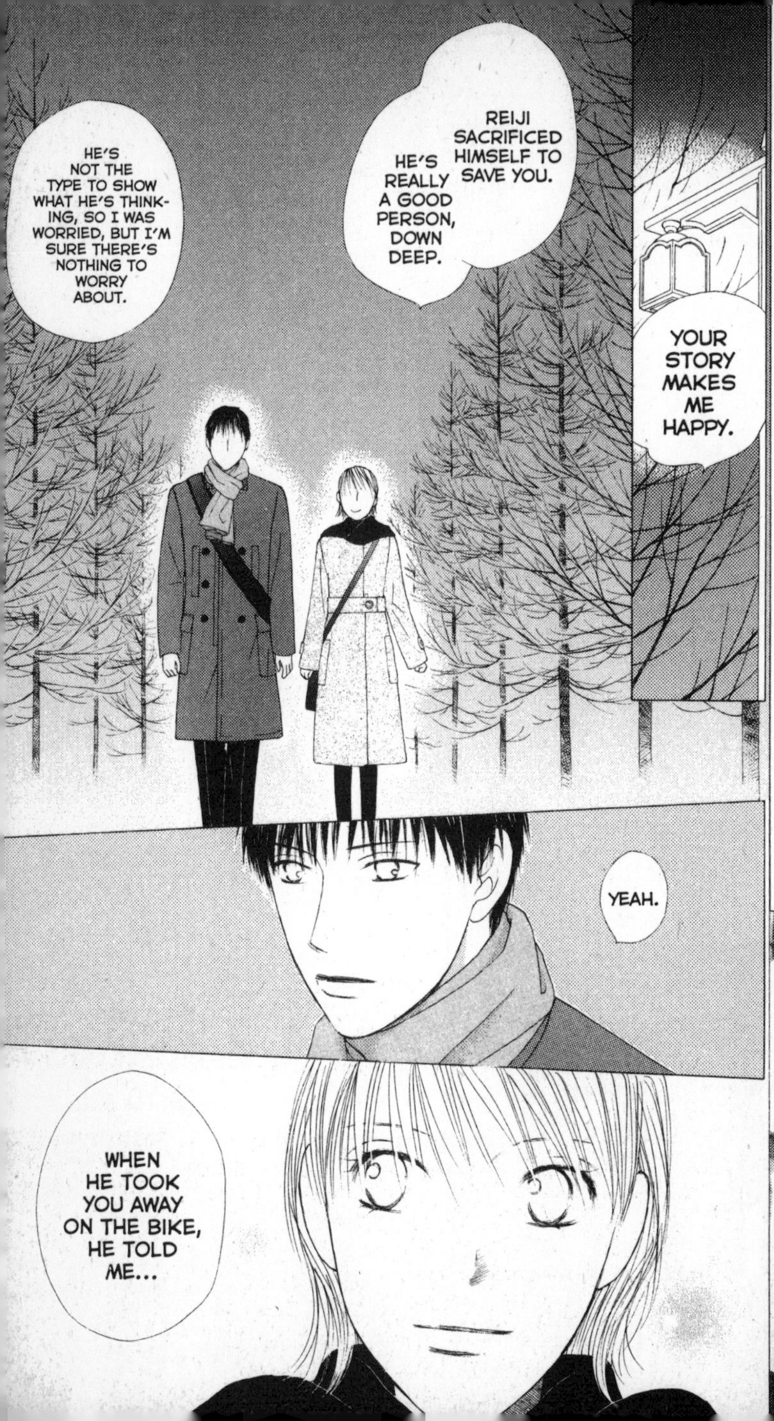
YOUR STORY MAKES ME HAPPY.
REIJI SACRIFICED HIMSELF TO SAVE YOU.
HE'S REALLY A GOOD PERSON, DOWN DEEP.
HE'S NOT THE TYPE TO SHOW WHAT HE'S THINK-ING, SO I WAS WORRIED, BUT I'M SURE THERE'S NOTHING TO WORRY ABOUT.
YEAH.
WHEN HE TOOK YOU AWAY ON THE BIKE, HE TOLD ME...

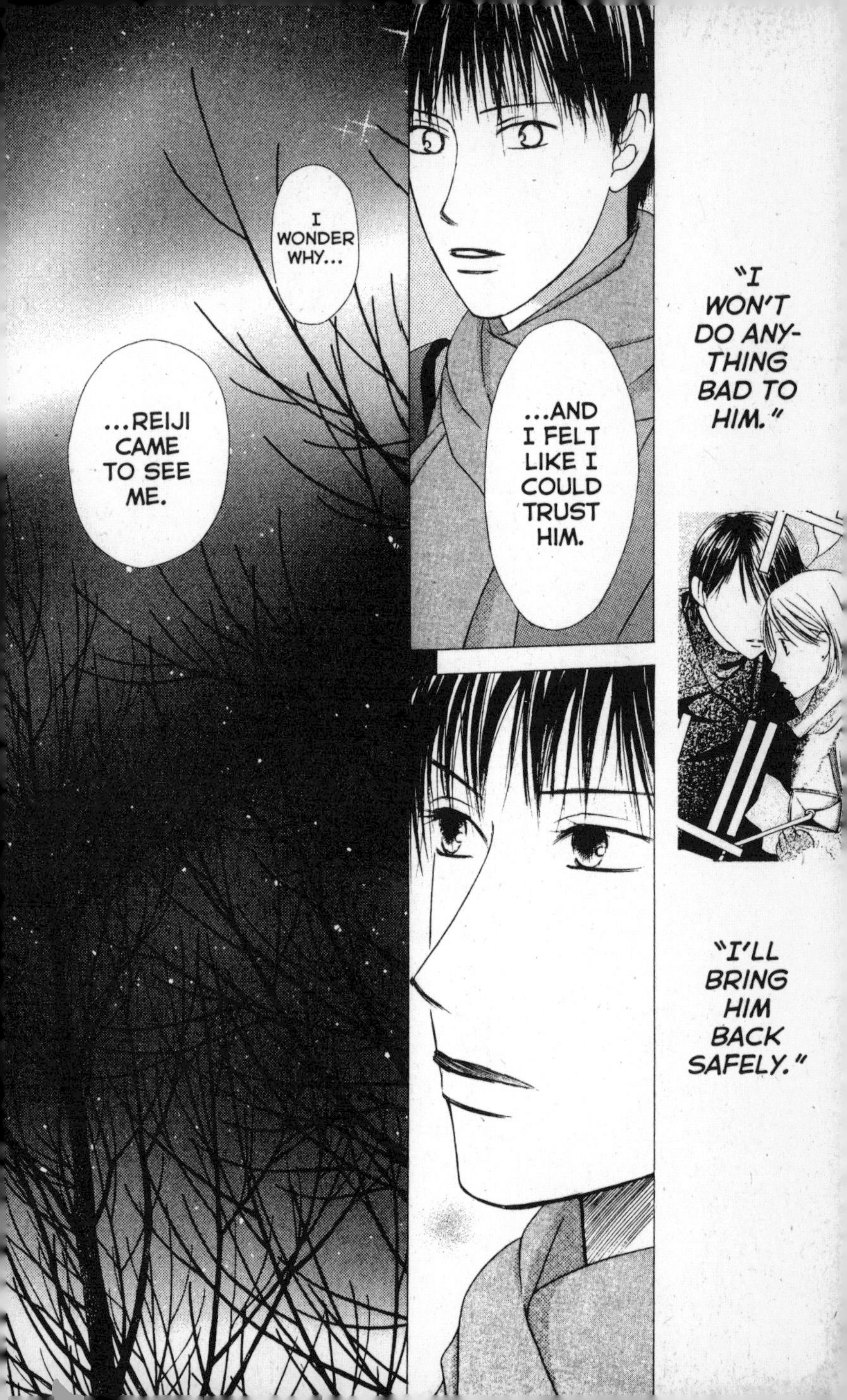
"I WON'T DO ANY-THING BAD TO HIM."
"I'LL BRING HIM BACK SAFELY."
I WONDER WHY...
...REIJI CAME TO SEE ME.
...AND I FELT LIKE I COULD TRUST HIM.

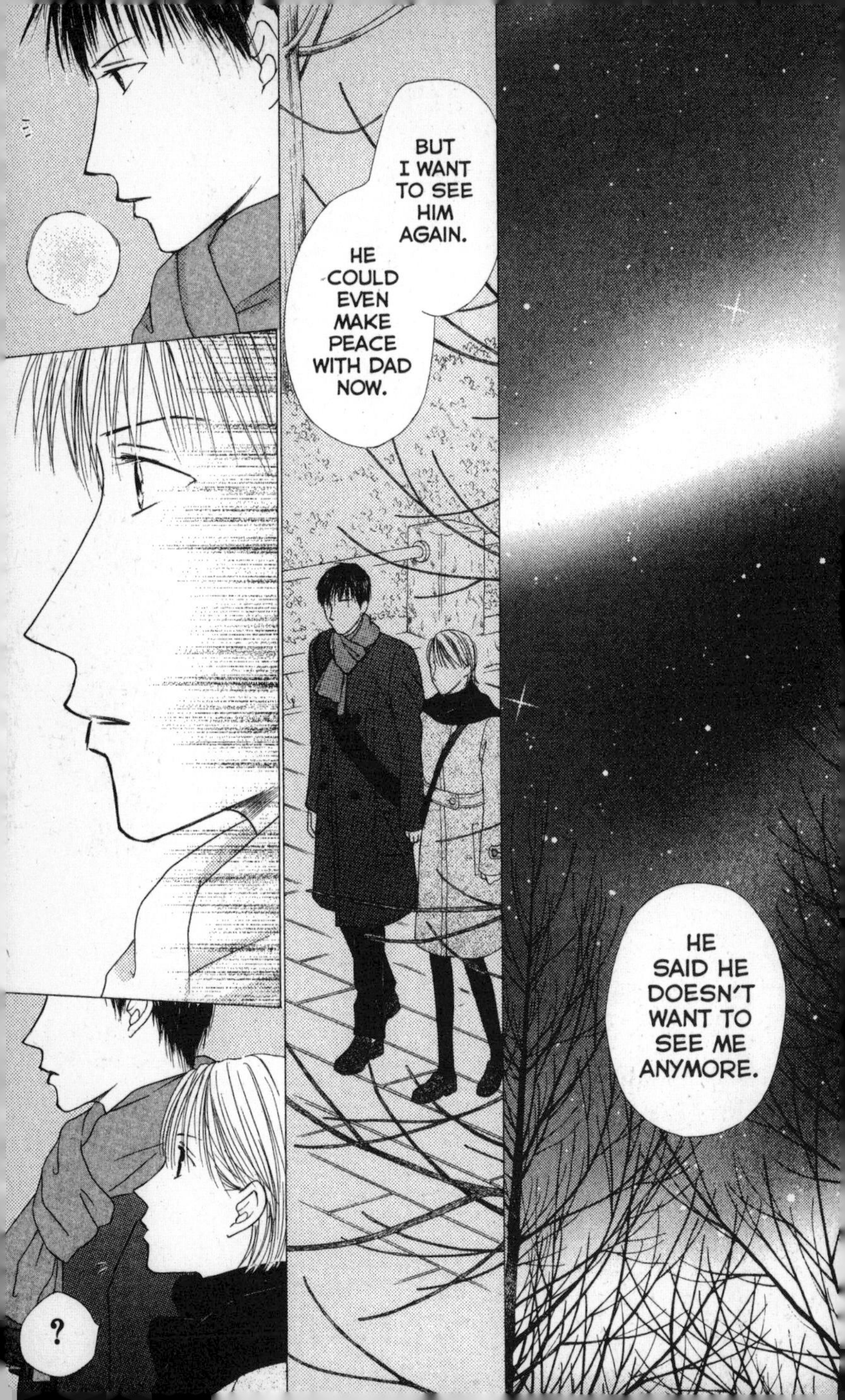
HE SAID HE DOESN'T WANT TO SEE ME ANYMORE.
BUT I WANT TO SEE HIM AGAIN.
HE COULD EVEN MAKE PEACE WITH DAD NOW.
?

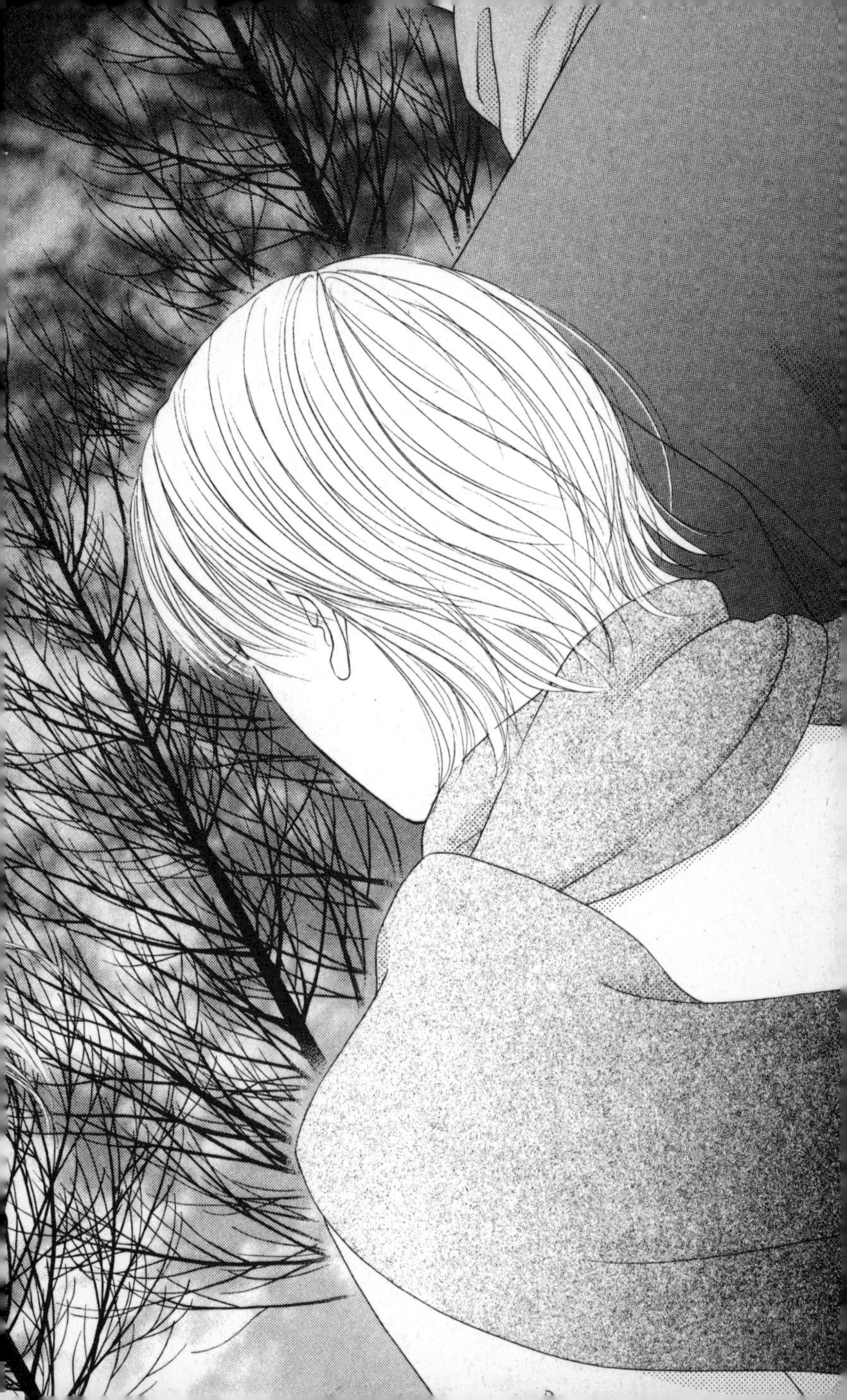

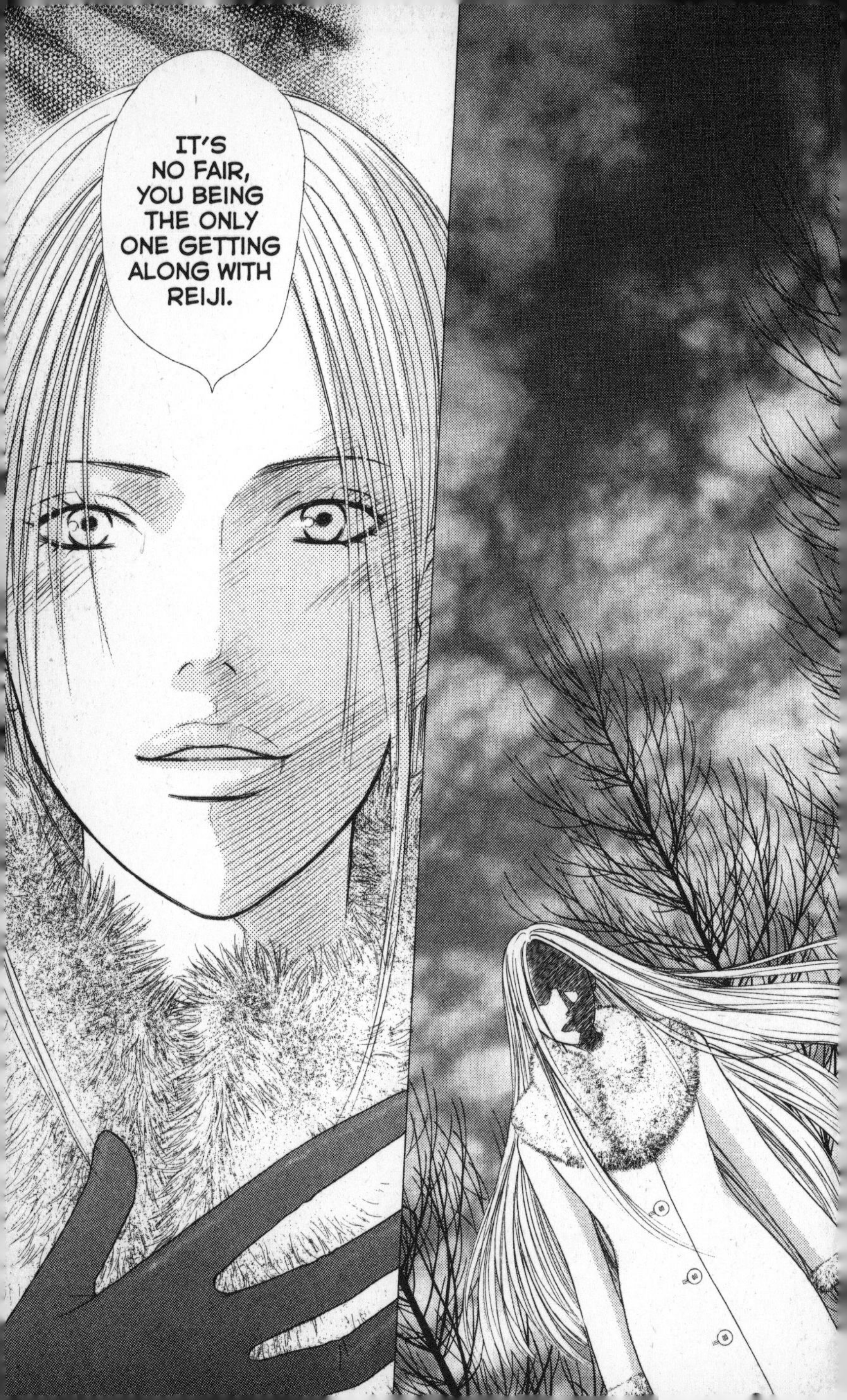
IT'S NO FAIR, YOU BEING THE ONLY ONE GETTING ALONG WITH REIJI.

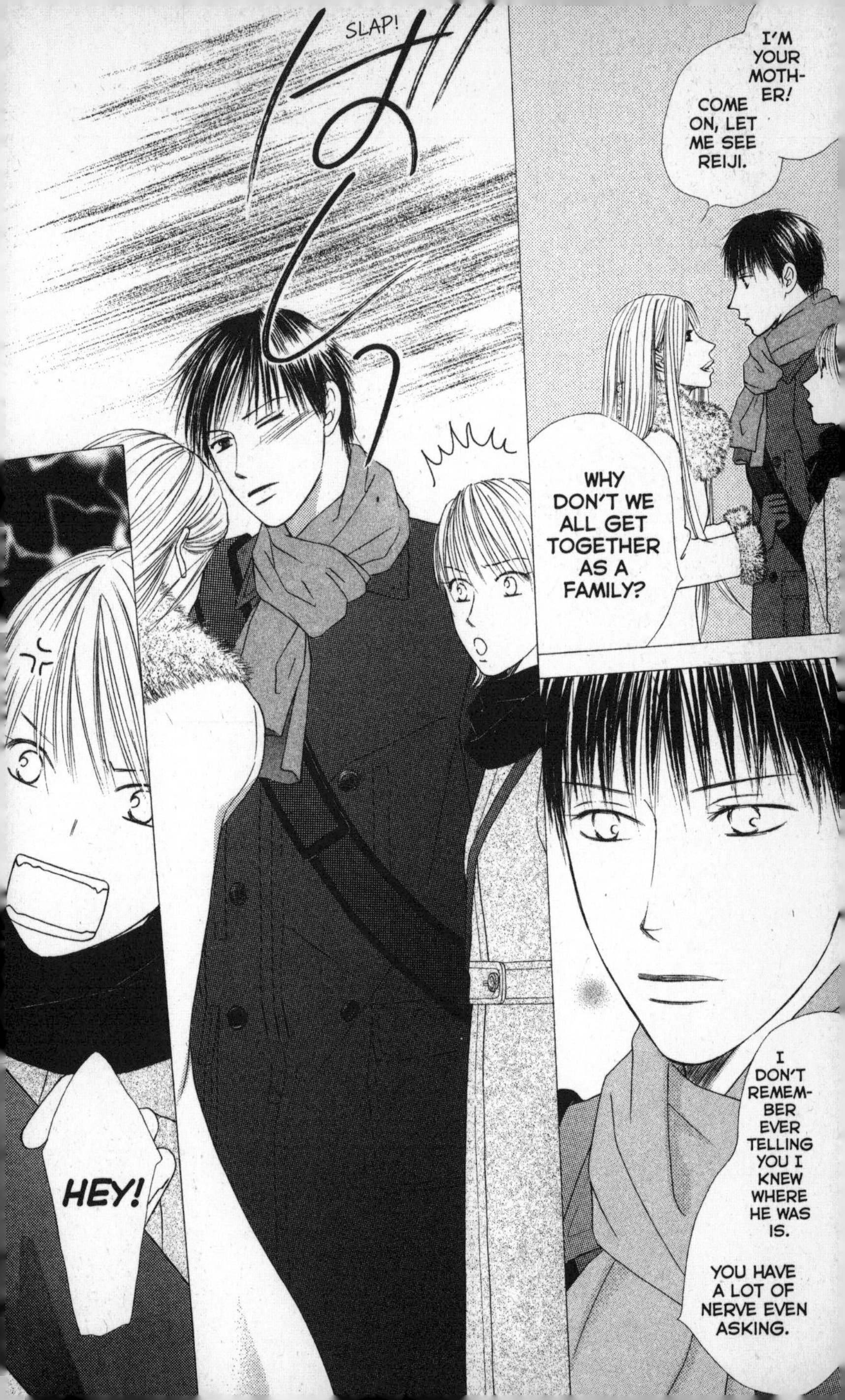
I'M YOUR MOTHER!
COME ON, LET ME SEE REIJI.
WHY DON'T WE ALL GET TOGETHER AS A FAMILY?
I DON'T REMEMBER EVER TELLING YOU I KNEW WHERE HE WAS IS.
YOU HAVE A LOT OF NERVE EVEN ASKING.
SLAP!
HEY!

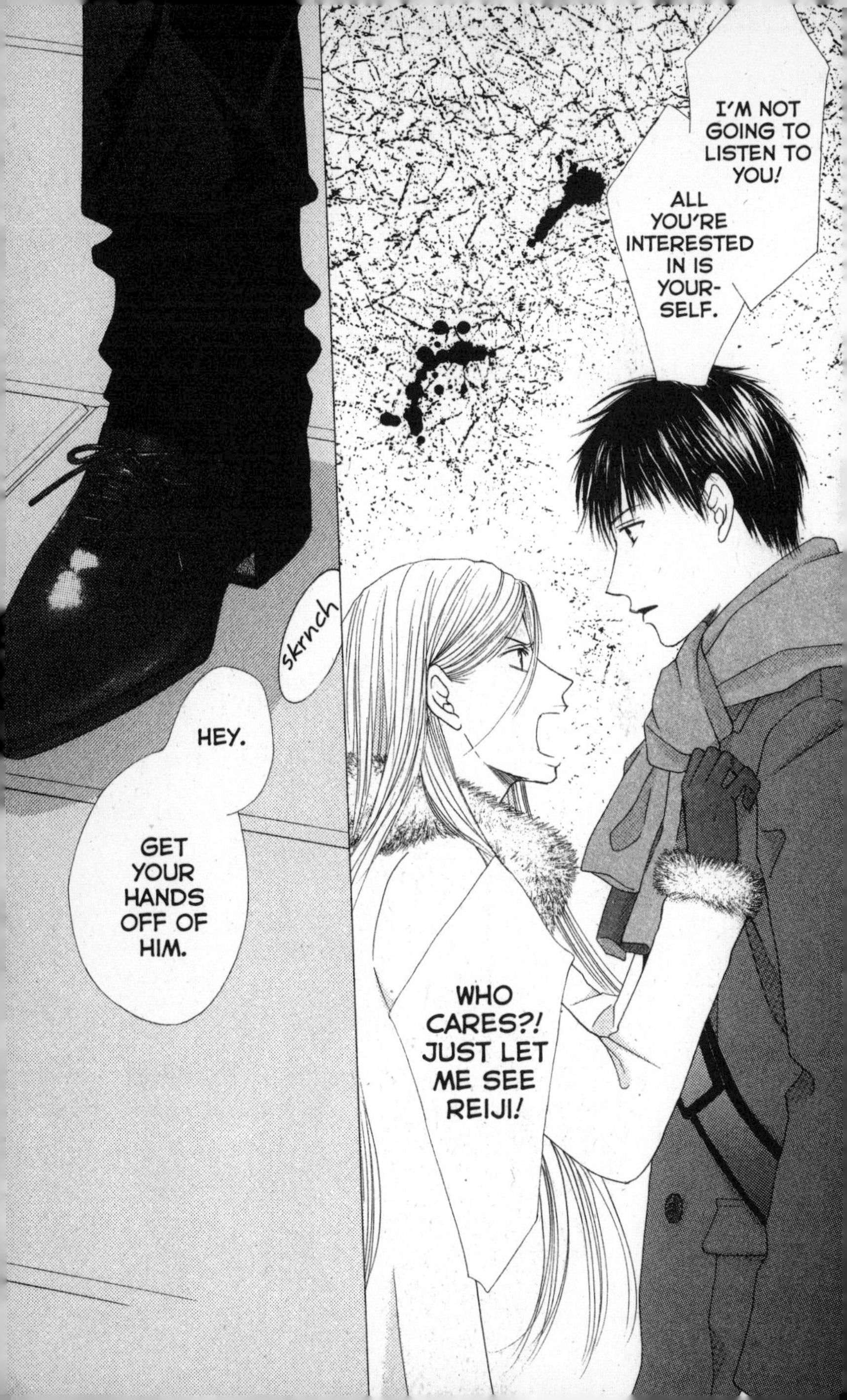
I'M NOT GOING TO LISTEN TO YOU!
ALL YOU'RE INTERESTED IN IS YOUR-SELF.
WHO CARES?! JUST LET ME SEE REIJI!
skrnch
HEY.
GET YOUR HANDS OFF OF HIM.

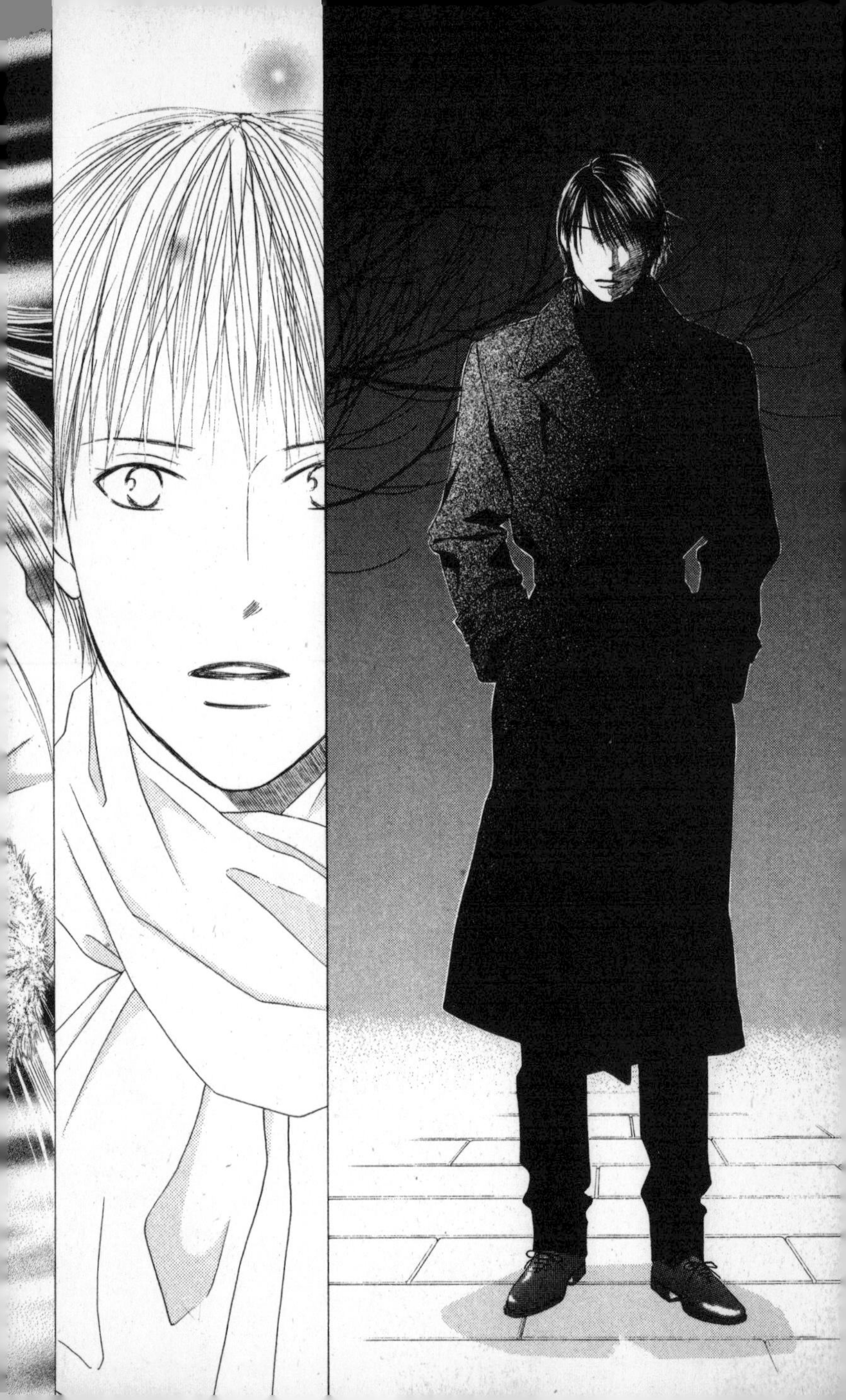

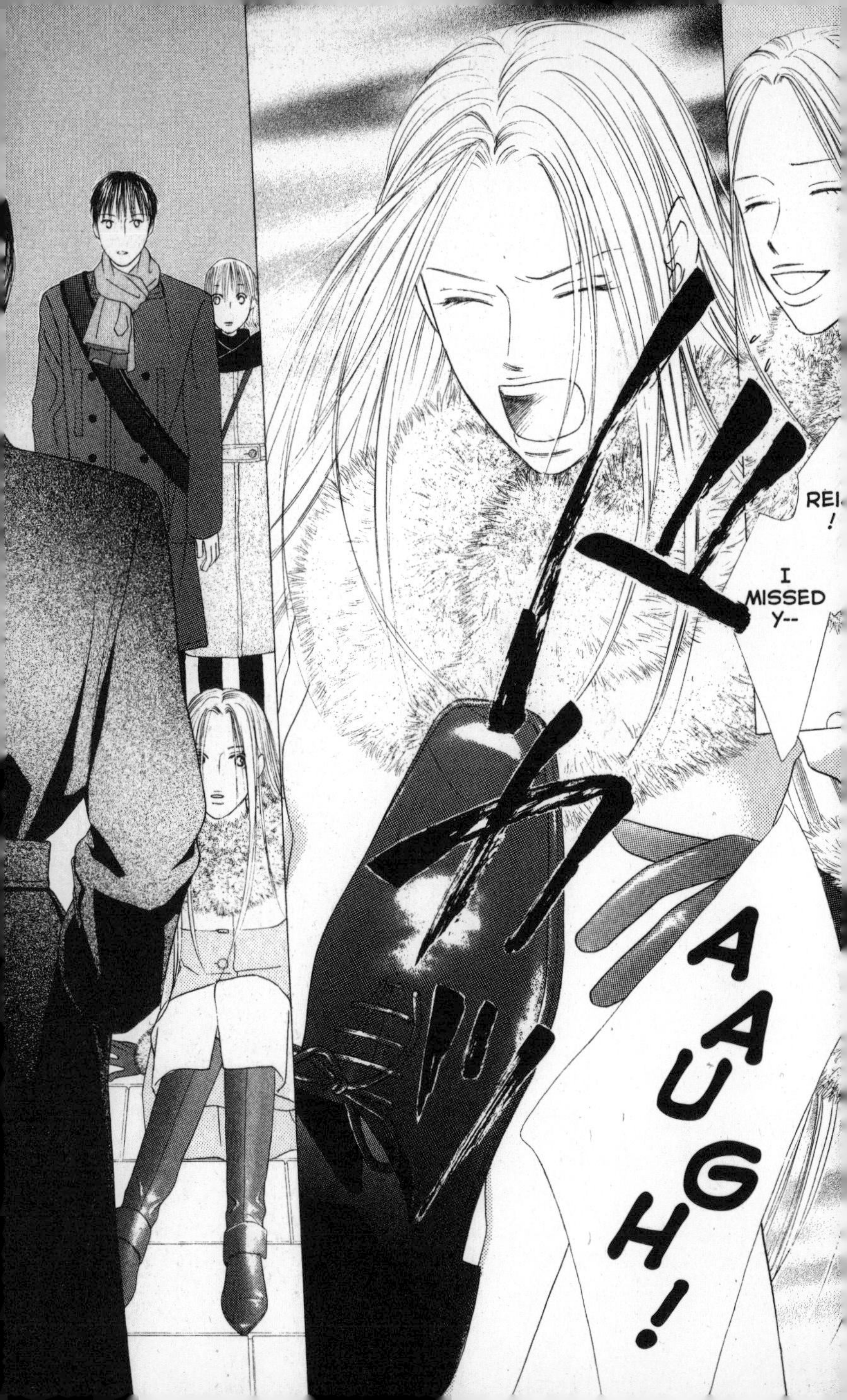
REI-!
I MISSED Y--
AAAUGH!

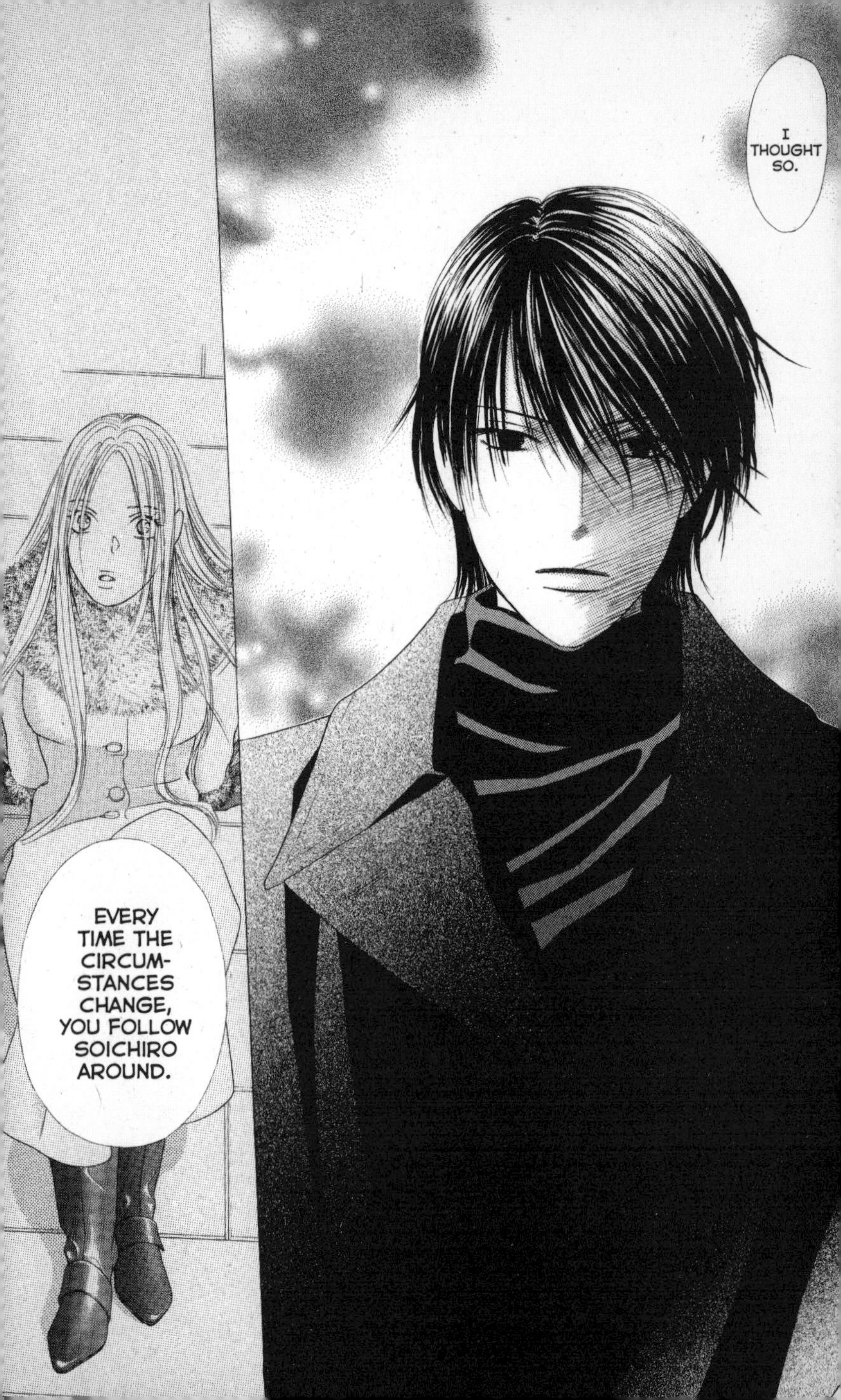
I THOUGHT SO.
EVERY TIME THE CIRCUM-STANCES CHANGE, YOU FOLLOW SOICHIRO AROUND.

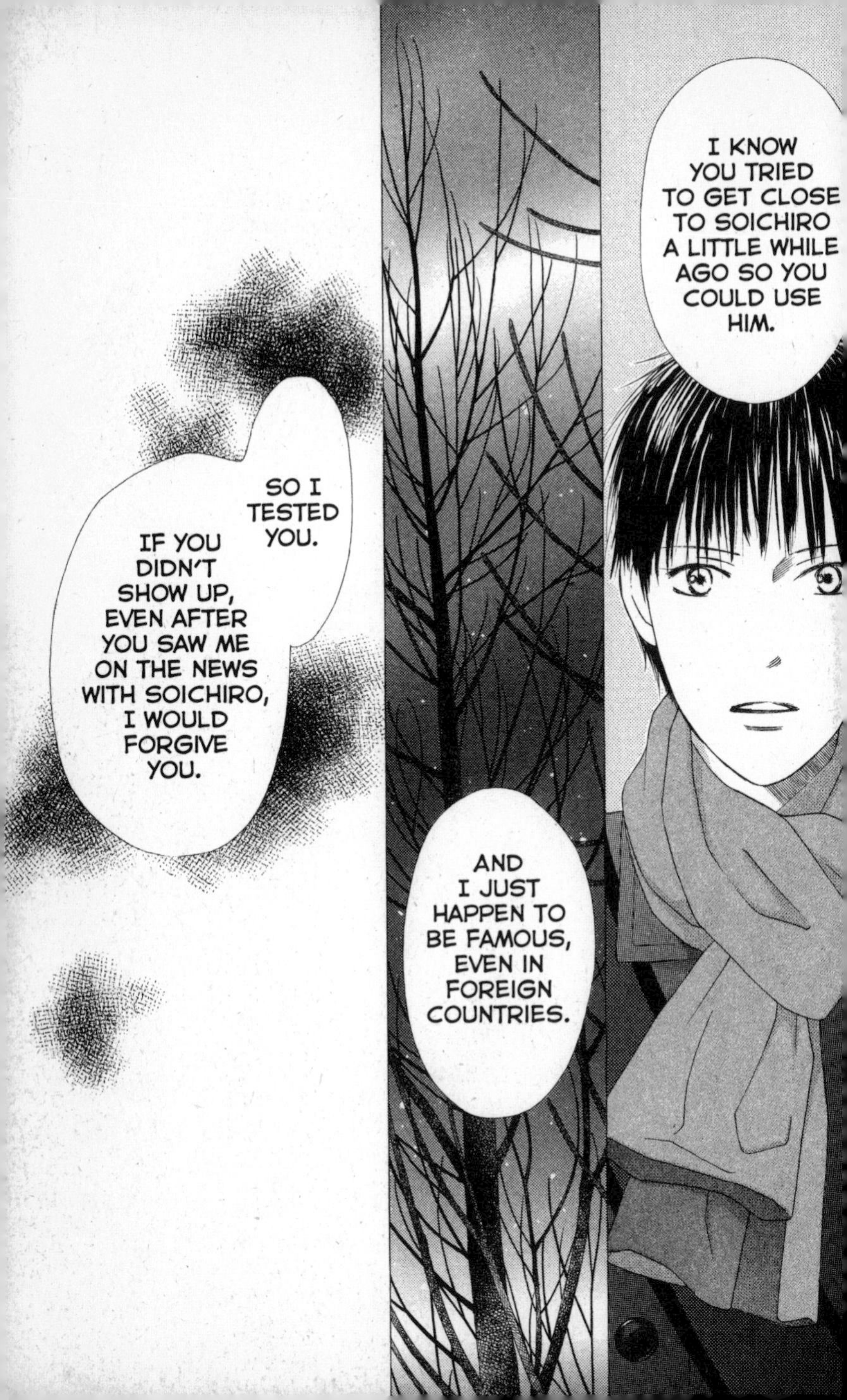
I KNOW YOU TRIED TO GET CLOSE TO SOICHIRO A LITTLE WHILE AGO SO YOU COULD USE HIM.
AND I JUST HAPPEN TO BE FAMOUS, EVEN IN FOREIGN COUNTRIES.
SO I TESTED YOU.
IF YOU DIDN'T SHOW UP, EVEN AFTER YOU SAW ME ON THE NEWS WITH SOICHIRO, I WOULD FORGIVE YOU.

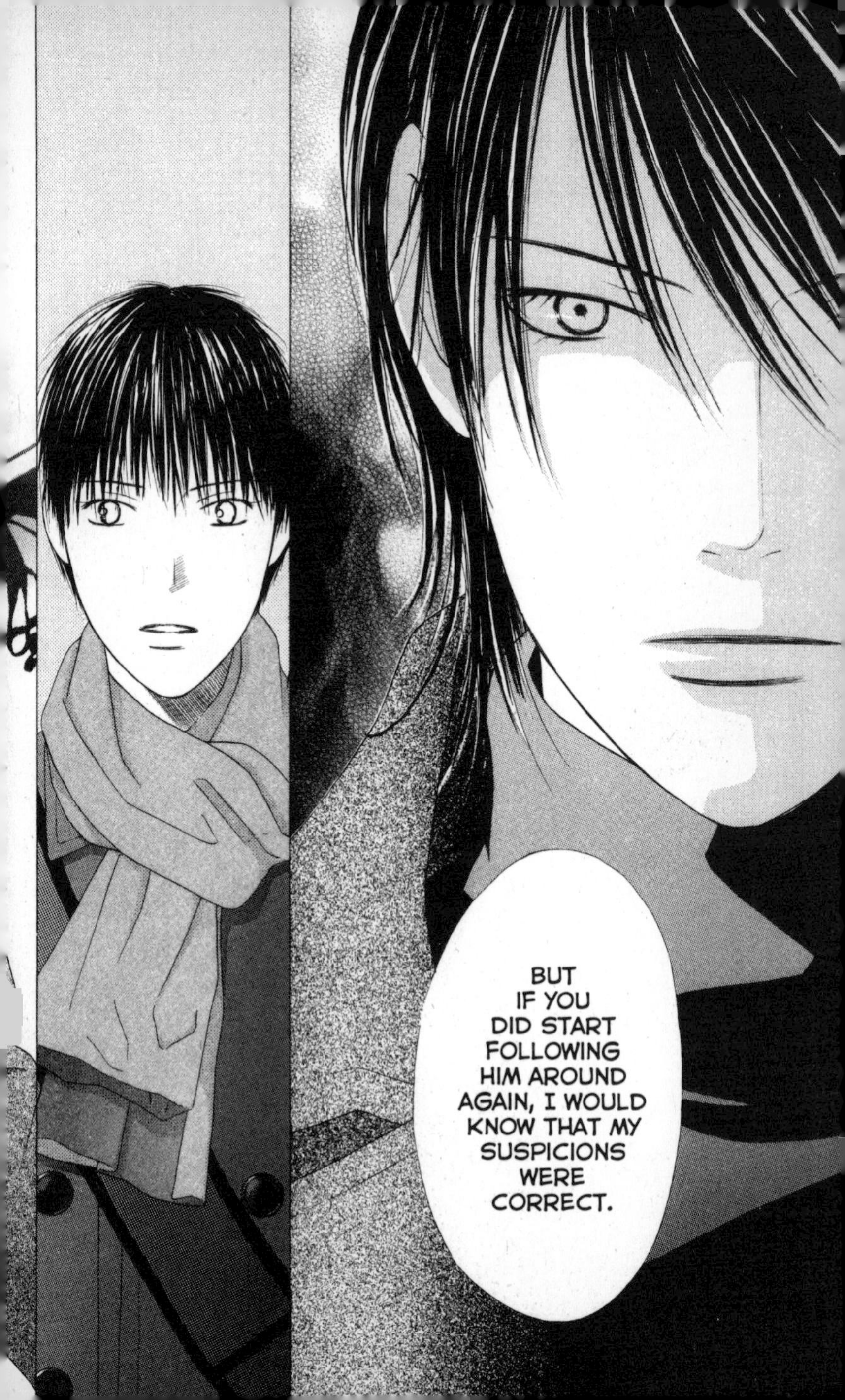
BUT IF YOU DID START FOLLOWING HIM AROUND AGAIN, I WOULD KNOW THAT MY SUSPICIONS WERE CORRECT.

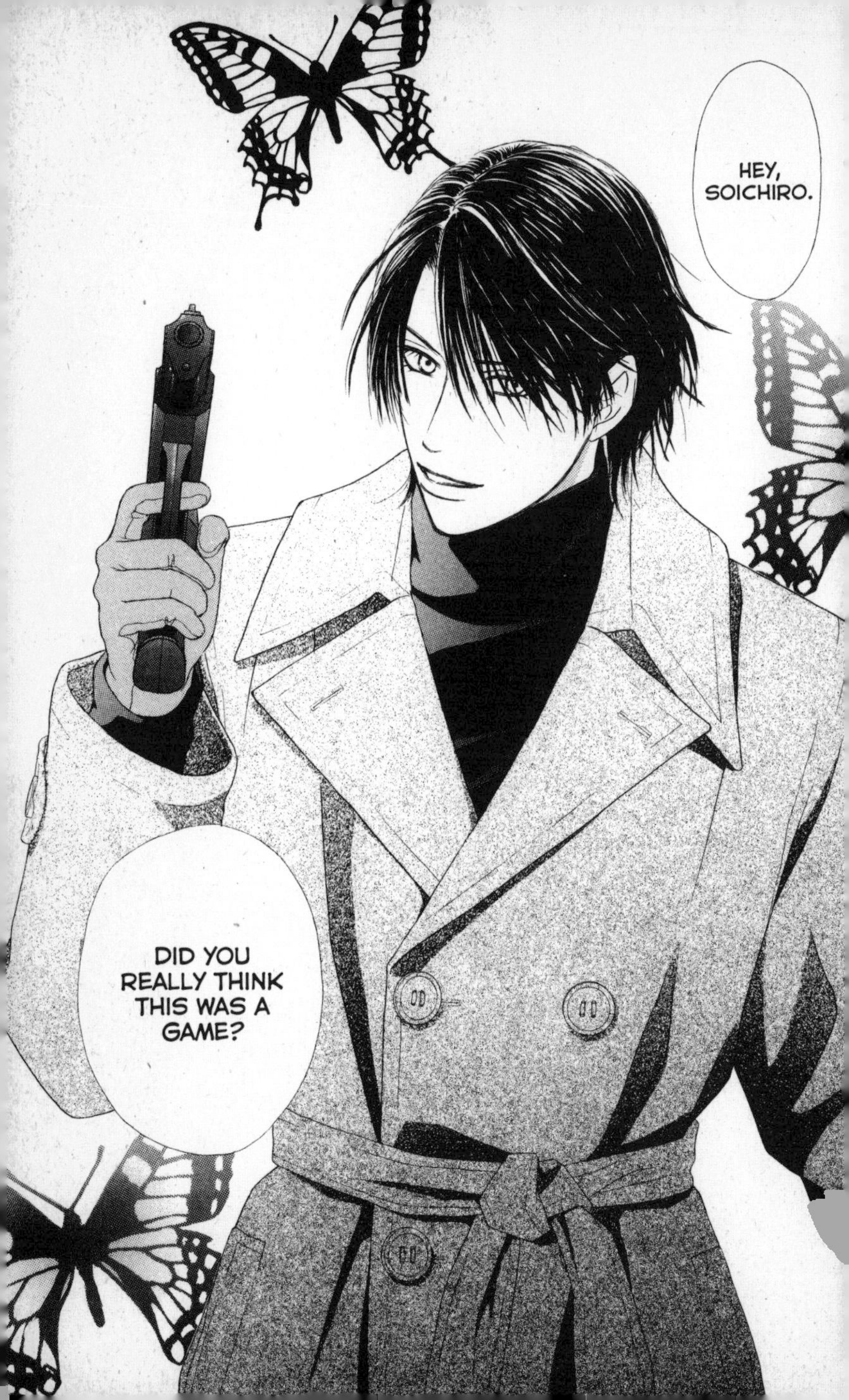
HEY, SOICHIRO.
DID YOU REALLY THINK THIS WAS A GAME?

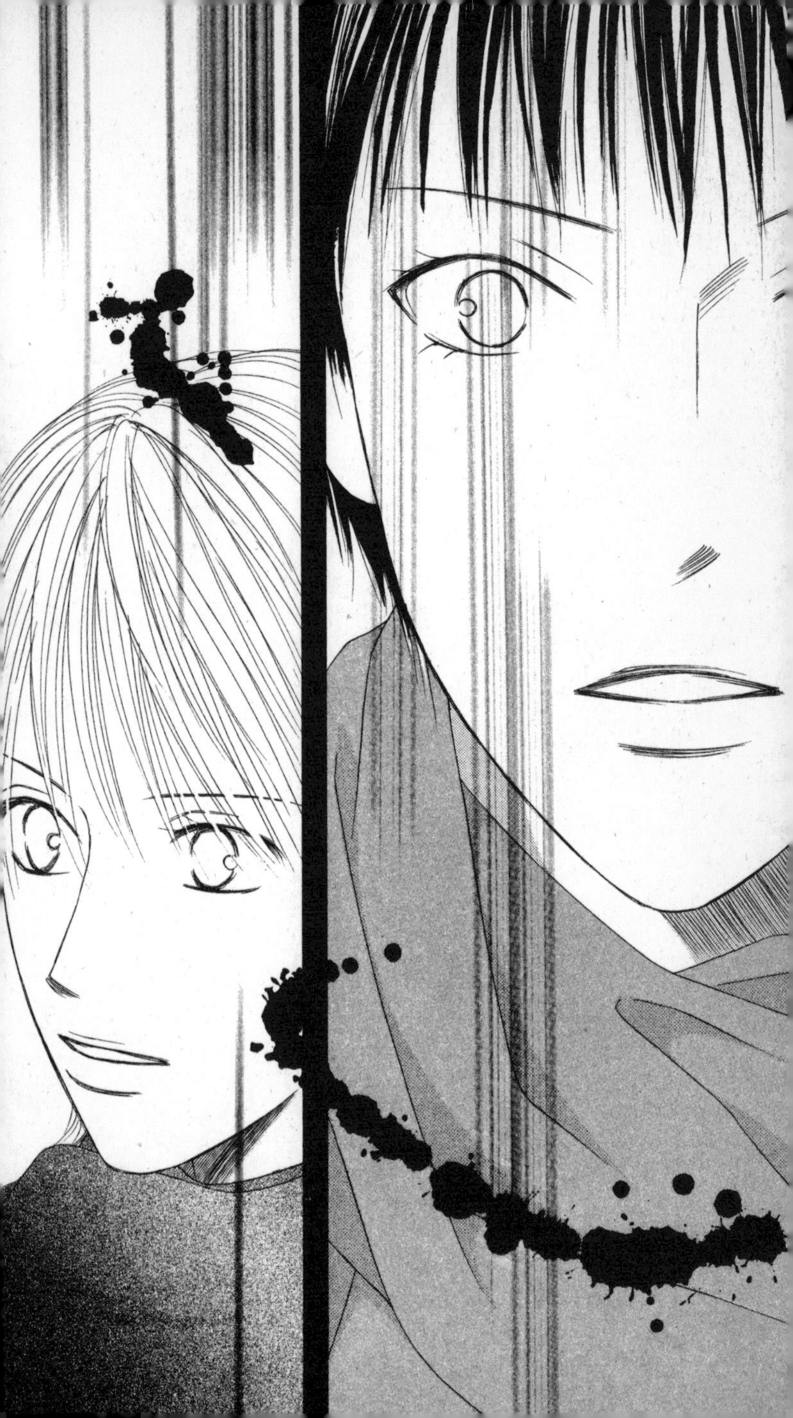

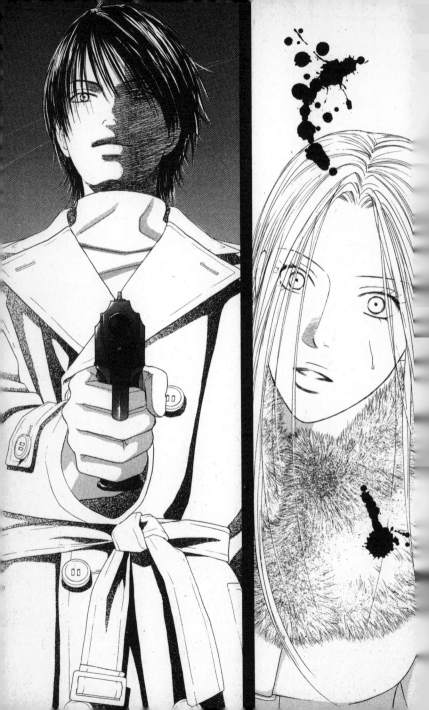

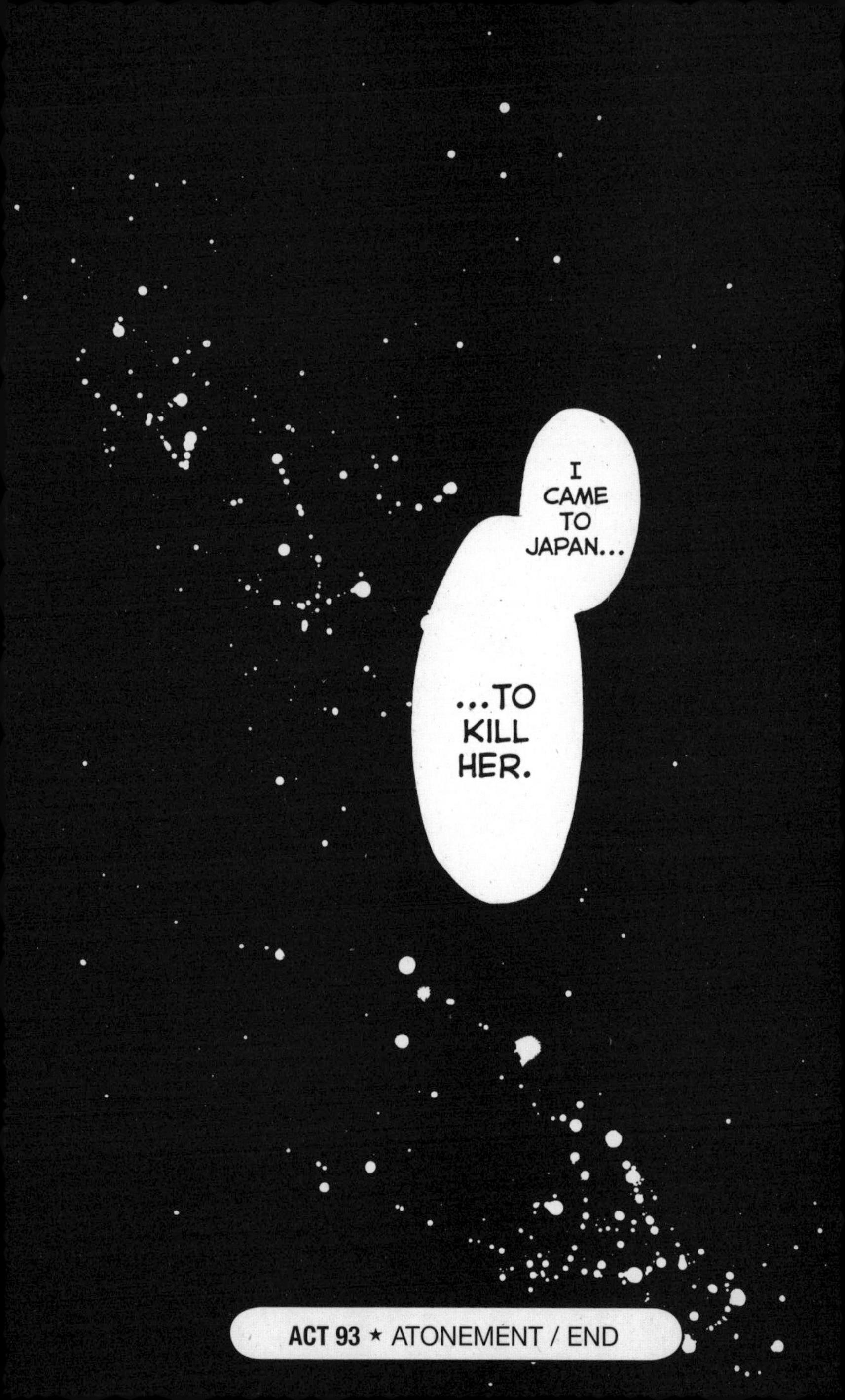
I CAME TO JAPAN...
...TO KILL HER.
ACT 93 ★ ATONEMENT / END

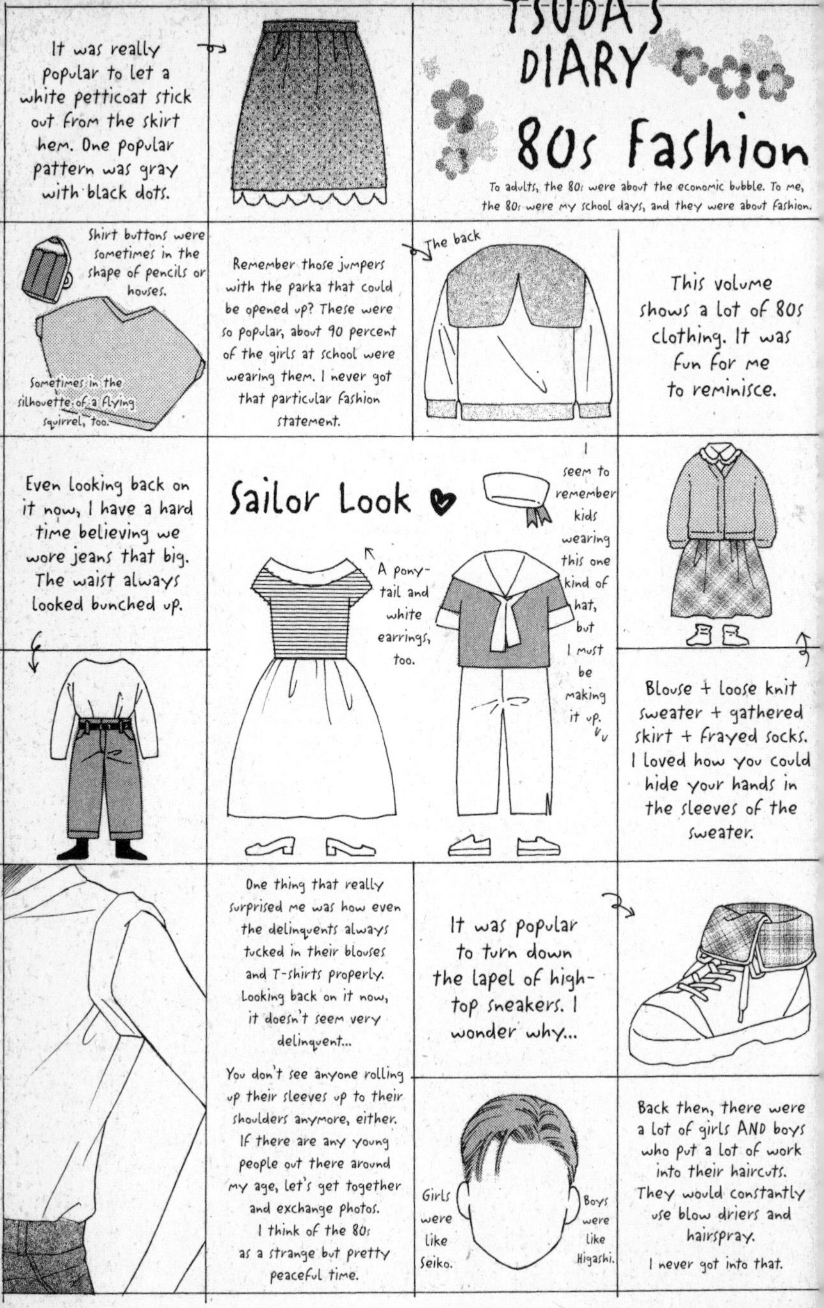
TSUDA'S DIARY
80s Fashion
To adults, the 80s were about the economic bubble. To me, the 80s were my school days, and they were about fashion.
It was really popular to let a white petticoat stick out from the skirt hem. One popular pattern was gray with black dots.
This volume shows a lot of 80s clothing. It was fun for me to reminisce.
The back
Remember those jumpers with the parka that could be opened up? These were so popular, about 90 percent of the girls at school were wearing them. I never got that particular fashion statement.
Shirt buttons were sometimes in the shape of pencils or houses.
Sometimes in the silhouette of a flying squirrel, too.
Blouse + loose knit sweater + gathered skirt + frayed socks. I loved how you could hide your hands in the sleeves of the sweater.
I seem to remember kids wearing this one kind of hat, but I must be making it up.
Sailor Look ♥
A ponytail and white earrings, too.
Even looking back on it now, I have a hard time believing we wore jeans that big. The waist always looked bunched up.
Back then, there were a lot of girls AND boys who put a lot of work into their haircuts. They would constantly use blow driers and hairspray.
I never got into that.
It was popular to turn down the lapel of high-top sneakers. I wonder why...
Boys were like Higashi.
Girls were like Seiko.
One thing that really surprised me was how even the delinquents always tucked in their blouses and T-shirts properly. Looking back on it now, it doesn't seem very delinquent...
You don't see anyone rolling up their sleeves up to their shoulders anymore, either. If there are any young people out there around my age, let's get together and exchange photos. I think of the 80s as a strange but pretty peaceful time.

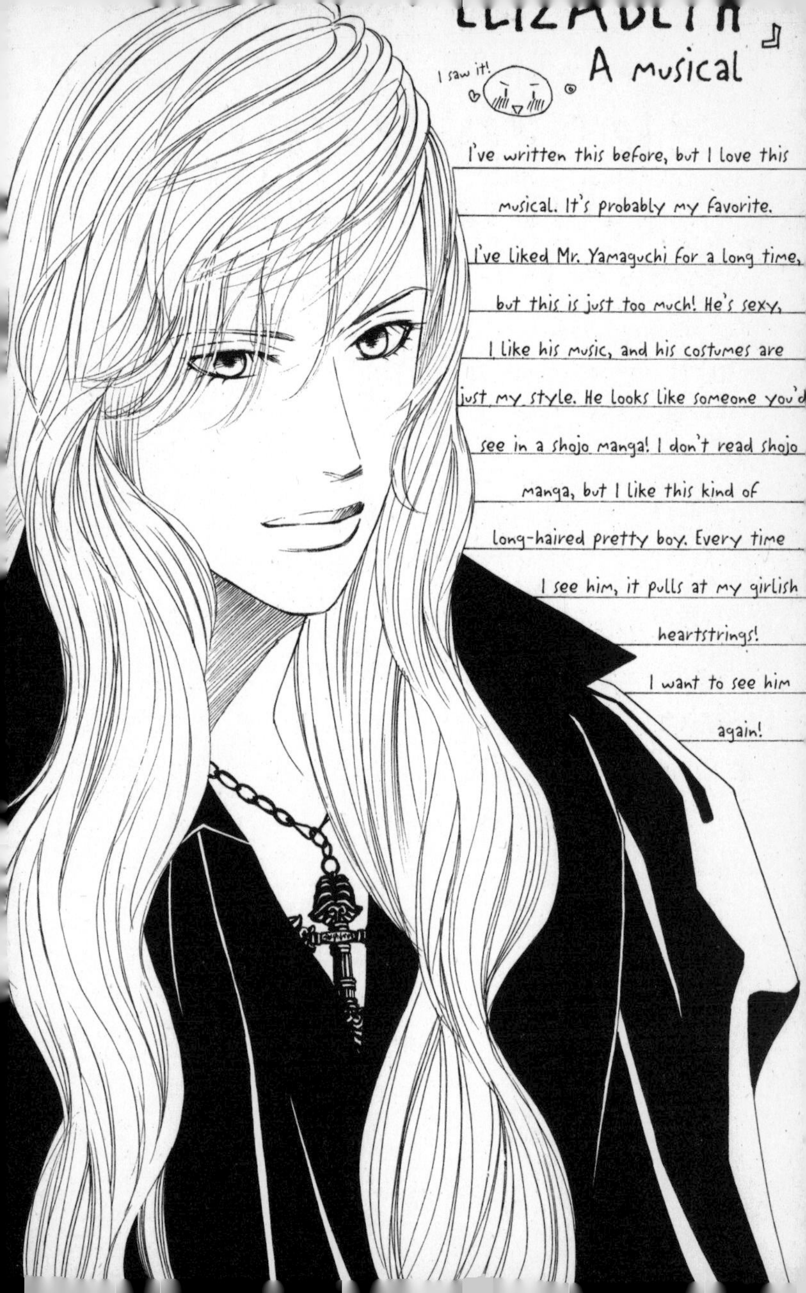

ELIZABETH」 A musical

I saw it!

I've written this before, but I love this musical. It's probably my favorite. I've liked Mr. Yamaguchi for a long time, but this is just too much! He's sexy, I like his music, and his costumes are just my style. He looks like someone you'd see in a shojo manga! I don't read shojo manga, but I like this kind of long-haired pretty boy. Every time I see him, it pulls at my girlish heartstrings!

I want to see him again!

coming soon

kare kano

his and her circumstances

volume twenty

Reiji didn't come back to Japan to catch up with Soichiro...he came for revenge. Can Soichiro ever reconcile with the father he has only just learned to love? And what will this tragic event mean for his future with Yukino?

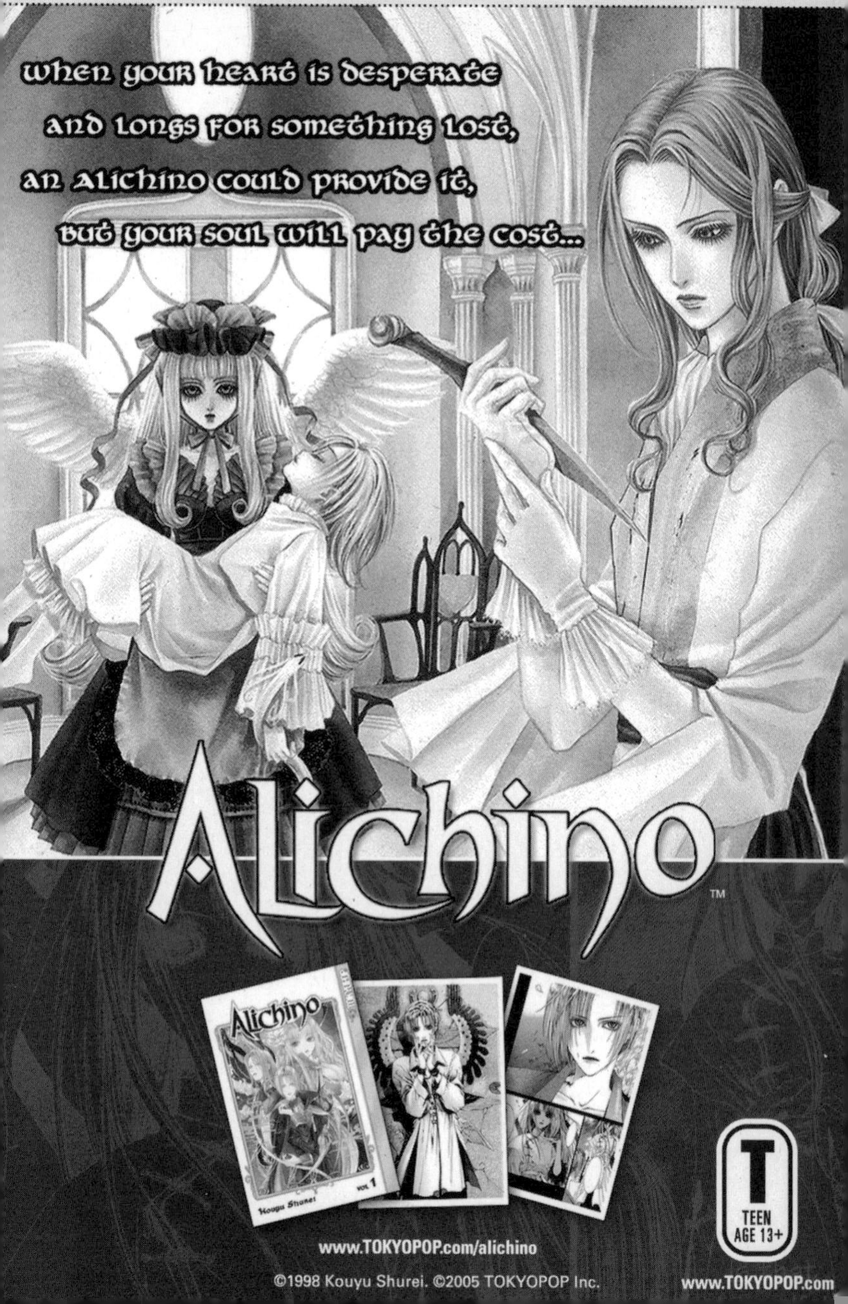
when your heart is desperate
and longs for something lost,
an alichino could provide it,
but your soul will pay the cost...
Alichino™
Alichino
Kouyu Shurei
vol 1
T
TEEN
AGE 13+
www.TOKYOPOP.com/alichino
©1998 Kouyu Shurei. ©2005 TOKYOPOP Inc.
www.TOKYOPOP.com

TOKYOPOP® SHOP

WWW.TOKYOPOP.COM/SHOP

Check out all the sizzling hot merchandise and your favorite manga at the shop!

HOT NEWS!

Check out the TOKYOPOP SHOP! The world's best collection of manga in English is now available online in one place!

BIZENGHAST POSTER

Bizenghast

PRINCESS AI POSTCARDS

Princess Ai

I Luv Halloween Glow-in-the-Dark STICKERS!
I LUV HALLOWEEN

I LUV HALLOWEEN BUTTONS & STICKERS

WWW.TOKYOPOP.COM/SHOP

- LOOK FOR SPECIAL OFFERS
- PRE-ORDER UPCOMING RELEASES
- COMPLETE YOUR COLLECTIONS

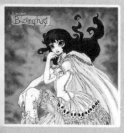

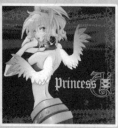

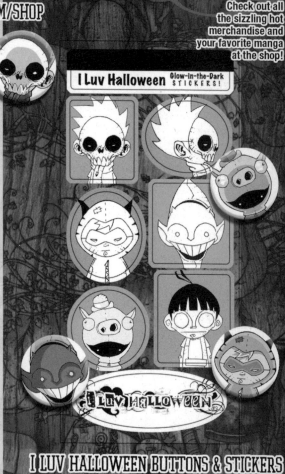

THIS FALL, TOKYOPOP CREATES A FRESH, NEW CHAPTER IN TEEN NOVELS...

For Adventurers...
Witches' Forest:
The Adventures of Duan Surk

By Mishio Fukazawa
Duan Surk is a 16-year-old Level 2 fighter who embarks on the quest of a lifetime—battling mythical creatures and outwitting evil sorceresses, all in an impossible rescue mission in the spooky Witches' Forest!

BASED ON THE FAMOUS
FORTUNE QUEST **WORLD**

For Dreamers...
Magic Moon

By Wolfgang and Heike Hohlbein
Kim enters the engimatic realm of Magic Moon, where he battles unthinkable monsters and fantastical creatures—in order to unravel the secret that keeps his sister locked in a coma.

THE WORLDWIDE BESTSELLING FANTASY
THRILLOGY **ARRIVES IN THE U.S.!**

TOKYOPOP PRESENTS

POP FICTION

For Believers...

Scrapped Princess: A Tale of Destiny

By Ichiro Sakaki

A dark prophecy reveals that the queen will give birth to a daughter who will usher in the Apocalypse. But despite all attempts to destroy the baby, the myth of the "Scrapped Princess" lingers on...

THE INSPIRATION FOR THE HIT ANIME AND MANGA SERIES!

Scrapped
PRINCESS

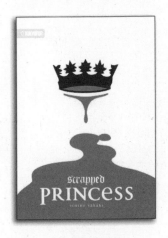

For Thinkers...

Kino no Tabi: Book One of The Beautiful World

By Keiichi Sigsawa

Kino roams the world on the back of Hermes, her unusual motorcycle, in a journey filled with happiness and pain, decadence and violence, and magic and loss.

THE SENSATIONAL BESTSELLER IN JAPAN HAS FINALLY ARRIVED!

TOKYOPOP
The
Beautiful
World
Keiichi
Sigsawa

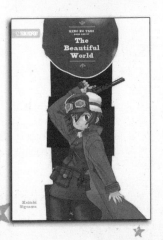

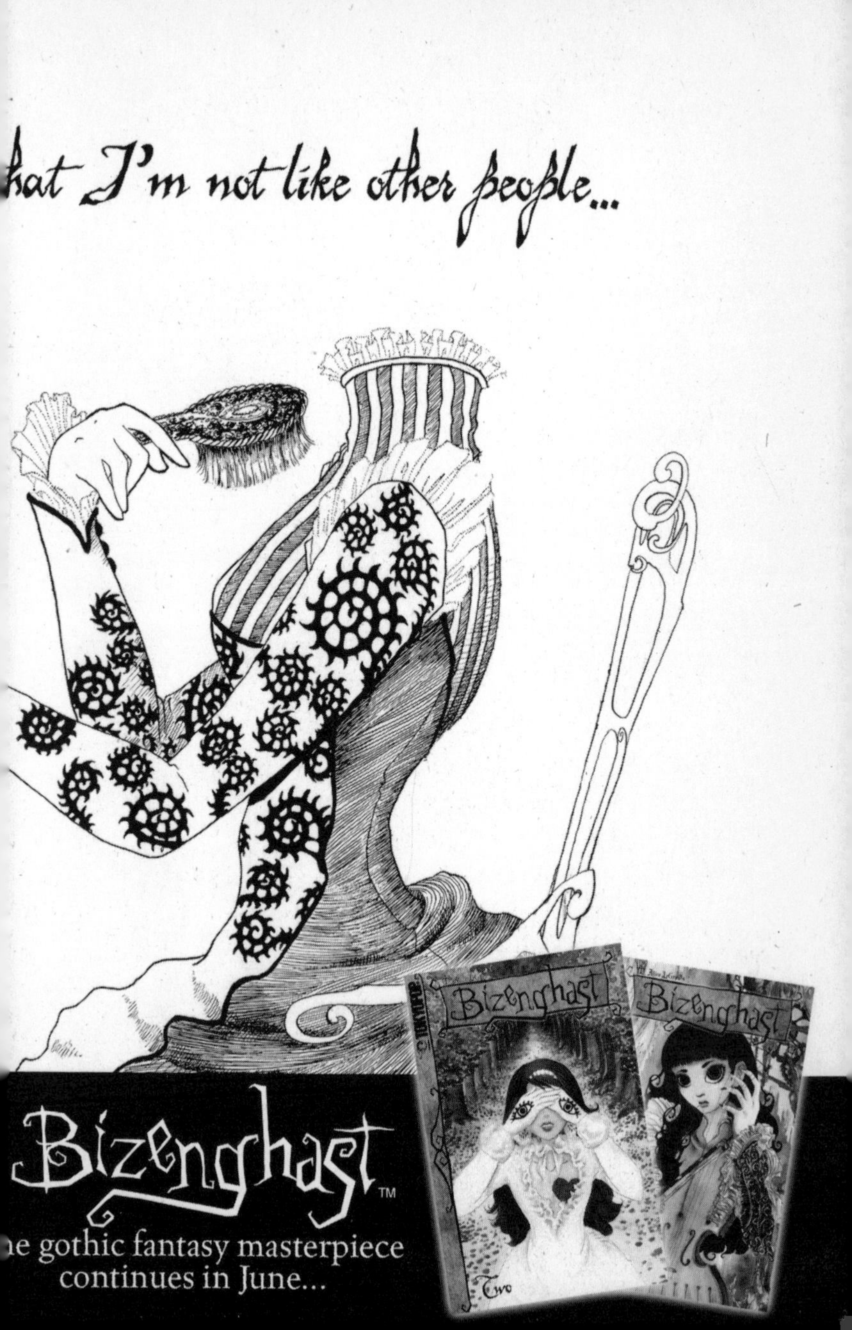
hat I'm not like other people...
Bizenghast™
he gothic fantasy masterpiece
continues in June...
Bizenghast
TOKYOPOP
Two
Bizenghast

BIZENGHAST

Dear Diary,
I'm starting to feel

When a young girl moves to the forgotten town of Bizenghast, she uncovers a terrifying collection of lost souls that leads her to the brink of insanity. One thing becomes painfully clear: The residents of Bizenghast are just dying to come home. ART SUBJECT TO CHANGE © Mary Alice LeGrow and TOKYOPOP Inc.

Ayumu struggles with her studies, and the all-important high school entrance exams are approaching. Fortunately, she has help from her best bud Shii-chan, who is at the top of the class. But when the test results come back, the friends are surprised: Ayumu surpasses Shii-chan's scores and gets into the school of her choice—without Shii-chan! Losing her friend is so painful for Ayumu that she starts cutting herself to ease her sorrow. Finally, Ayumu seeks comfort in a new friend, Manami. But will Manami prove to be the friend that Ayumu truly needs? Or will Ayumu continue down a dark path?

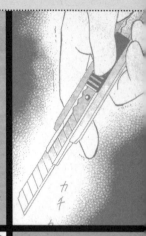

Volume 1

LIFE

Keiko Suenobu

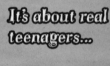

It's about real teenagers...

It's about real high school...

It's about real life.

LIFE
BY KEIKO SUENOBU

Ordinary high school teenagers...
Except that they're not.

© Keiko Suenobu

READ THE ENTIRE FIRST CHAPTER ONLINE FOR FREE:

STOP!

This is the back of the book.
You wouldn't want to spoil a great ending!

This book is printed "manga-style," in the authentic Japanese right-to-left format. Since none of the artwork has been flipped or altered, readers get to experience the story just as the creator intended. You've been asking for it, so TOKYOPOP® delivered: authentic, hot-off-the-press, and far more fun!

DIRECTIONS

If this is your first time reading manga-style, here's a quick guide to help you understand how it works.

It's easy... just start in the top right panel and follow the numbers. Have fun, and look for more 100% authentic manga from TOKYOPOP®!